To,
+ Bob

from

Stephen .

The Order of Things

The Order of Things

Explorations in Scientific Theology

Alister E. McGrath

BLACKWELL PUBLISHING
350 Main Street, Malden, MA 02148-5020, USA
9600 Garsington Road, Oxford OX4 2DQ, UK
550 Swanston Street, Carlton, Victoria 3053, Australia

The right of Alister E. McGrath to be identified as the Author of this Work has been asserted in accordance with the UK Copyright, Designs, and Patents Act 1988.

First published 2006 by Blackwell Publishing Ltd

1 2006

Library of Congress Cataloging-in-Publication Data
McGrath, Alister E., 1953-
   The order of things : explorations in scientific theology / Alister E. McGrath.
      p. cm.
   Includes bibliographical references and index.
   ISBN-13: 978-1-4051-2556-7 (hardcover : alk. paper)
   ISBN-10: 1-4051-2556-X (hardcover : alk. paper)
   ISBN-13: 978-1-4051-2555-0 (pbk. : alk. paper)
   ISBN-10: 1-4051-2555-1 (pbk. : alk. paper) 1. Theology, Doctrinal.
      2. Natural theology. I. Title.
BT75.3.M335 2006
230.01'5—dc22

                                                                2005030631

A catalogue record for this title is available from the British Library.

Set in 10/12 pt Sabon
by SPI Publisher Services, Pondicherry, India
Printed and bound in Singapore
by Fabulous Printers Pte Ltd.

The publisher's policy is to use permanent paper from mills that operate a sustainable forestry policy, and which has been manufactured from pulp processed using acid-free and elementary chlorine-free practices. Furthermore, the publisher ensures that the text paper and cover board used have met acceptable environmental accreditation standards.

For further information on
Blackwell Publishing, visit our website:
www.blackwellpublishing.com

Contents

Preface

This book takes the form of a collection of essays which sets out to continue an exploratory conversation which I began with the three volumes of *A Scientific Theology*, published during the years 2001–3. It assumes that its readers will already be familiar with the basic arguments of *A Scientific Theology*, in that they will not be repeated in this work. The present work aims to develop, explore, and extend – but not to repeat – the themes of those earlier volumes.

The three volumes of the "scientific theology project" – subtitled *Nature*, *Reality*, and *Theory*, respectively – set out an approach to Christian theology which tried to uphold the unique nature of that discipline, while at the same time drawing on the insights of the natural sciences in a process of respectful and principled dialogue.[1] The approach represents a sustained and extended attempt to explore the interface between Christian theology and the natural sciences, on the assumption that this engagement is necessary, proper, legitimate, and productive, offering a lifeline to a philosophically and culturally embattled theology. It allows theology to break free from the intellectual ghettoes of foundationalism and antifoundationalism, and to reclaim and recover its authentic voice.

As that bold statement suggests, a scientific theology is predicated on the assumption that the Enlightenment project has foundered, necessitating the development of new approaches to rationality, or the critical reappropriation or conceptual refurbishment of older ones. It is therefore appropriate to explore the fate of the Enlightenment approach to rationality in a little more detail, before moving on.

---

[1] Alister E. McGrath, *A Scientific Theology* Vol. 1: *Nature*; Vol. 2: *Reality*; Vol. 3: *Theory*. London: Continuum, and Grand Rapids, MI: Eerdmans, 2001–3.

Taking the Enlightenment Seriously

Classic Christian theology was nourished and sustained by a passionate conviction that its vision of reality offered a compelling imaginative resource, fully capable of confronting the spectrum of complexities of human existence and experience without intellectual evasion or misrepresentation. On this view, Christianity offers a rich and viable account of the whole of reality, which theology can articulate and conceptualize. The order of things could be grasped and represented, not totally but adequately, to an extent that is accommodated both to the human capacity to discern and the divine willingness to reveal – neither of which may be determined in advance by human reason, but which are to be determined empirically *a posteriori*. Much contemporary theology, however, seems to find itself tossed about on a restless, raging sea, at one moment thrown up by the swells of foundationalism, and at the next finding itself plummeting into the troughs of relativism. How, we wonder, can reliable knowledge about anything be had, let alone the mystery of God? Must we conclude that, because we can know nothing significant for certain, we are therefore justified in believing what we please?

Rightly, leading representatives of the Enlightenment set out to explore a possible way of securing reliable, universal knowledge, by which the human race could understand its situation and its possibilities. While the Enlightenment can be interpreted in a number of generally critical ways – such as the theologically subversive elevation of human reason over divine revelation, or the philosophically utopian quest for universal truths of reason, liberated from the happenstance and particularity of one's historical situation – there are good reasons for suggesting that it can be understood in much more benign terms, as the quest for reliable knowledge.[2] The abiding and compelling power of this vision is perhaps nowhere set out with as great passion and commitment as in John Locke's celebrated letter to his close friend William Molyneaux, dated January 10, 1697. This letter sets out a devastating critique of those who compare ideas and opinions to "cates" – a sixteenth-century term for "choice pieces of meat," "dainties," or "delicacies" – so that what one believes is merely a matter of personal taste:[3]

---

[2] This view is defended with reference to the scientific enterprise by John M. Ziman, *Reliable Knowledge: An Exploration of the Grounds for Belief in Science.* Cambridge: Cambridge University Press, 1978.

[3] *The Works of John Locke.* 10 vols. London: Thomas Tegg, 1823, Vol. 8, p. 447.

If I could think that discourses and arguments to the understanding were like the several sorts of cates to different palates and stomachs, some nauseous and destructive to one, which are pleasant and restorative to another; I should no more think of books and study, and should think my time better employed at push-pin than in reading or writing. But I am convinced to the contrary: I know there is truth opposite to falsehood, that it may be found if people will, and is worth the seeking, and is not only the most valuable, but the pleasantest thing in the world.

If truth is simply a matter of taste, Locke argues, philosophers might as well retire to the nearest tavern and play push-pin – the popular equivalent of skittles.[4]

The Enlightenment agenda is to be honored and respected. Yet there was found to be a fatal problem, which lay not in the question being put, nor in the honorable intentions that lay behind it. The Enlightenment quest for a universal foundation and criterion of knowledge faltered, stumbled, and finally collapsed under the weight of a massive accumulation of counter-evidence. It simply could not be done; the vision simply could not be achieved. The legacy of the Enlightenment was thus an ideal of rational justification which it has proved impossible to attain in practice.[5] Yet the goal it set out to pursue was fundamentally right, even if its adopted methods could not ultimately sustain that quest. The pursuit of truth can hardly be abandoned because one particular strategy is now recognized to have failed; the point is to find new strategies, or modify existing ones.

Some have sought to evade this rationalist cul-de-sac in alluring, even though ultimately unsuccessful ways. The brave and bold agenda set out by Enlightenment rationalism held that human reason was capable of eliminating and overcoming the limitations of culture, history, and language;[6] in the end, the attempt

---

[4] Jeremy Bentham's comments on push-pin – a simple game in which players push their pins with the object of crossing the pins of their opponents – in his *Rationale of Reward* (1825) are well known: "Prejudice apart, the game of push-pin is of equal value with the arts and sciences of music and poetry. If the game of push-pin furnish more pleasure, it is more valuable than either. Everybody can play at push-pin: poetry and music are relished only by a few." For comment, see Lionel Stevenson, "The Key Poem of the Victorian Age." In *Essays in American and English Literature Presented to Bruce Robert Mcelderry Jr.*, edited by Max F. Schulz, 260–89. Athens: Ohio University Press, 1967, especially p. 261.

[5] This is the thesis of Alasdair MacIntyre, *Whose Justice? Which Rationality?* London: Duckworth, 1988, 6. See further Jennifer A. Herdt, "Alasdair MacIntyre's 'Rationality of Traditions' and Tradition-Transcendental Standards of Justification." *Journal of Religion* 78 (1998): 524–46.

[6] See, for example, Frederick C. Beiser, *The Sovereignty of Reason: The Defense of Rationality in the Early English Enlightenment*. Princeton, NJ: Princeton University Press, 1996.

petered out (although, to the historian, in a very *interesting* way), when confronted with the cold, brutal realization that human reason was not the historical and cultural universality that many believed.[7] The idea of a neutral, detached, objective, transcendent observer of reality has been widely criticized as the "view from nowhere" (Thomas Nagel) or the "God's eye view" (Hilary Putnam).[8] It demands a privileged perspective on reality which ignores both the historical location of the observer and the significance of the contingencies of history.[9]

The pursuit of the "necessary truths of reason" as a foundation on which secure knowledge could be erected proved culturally illuminating, and remains fascinating to intellectual historians, such as myself. But in the end, it failed, straggling home from the intellectual battlefield bruised and wounded, no longer a force to be reckoned with. While some still cling to the wreckage of the Enlightenment project, most have recognized that this intellectual flotsam is little more than a memorial to the past, and have sought to move on.

For a while, it seemed to some that intellectual certainty might be found in the abstract world of mathematics. Gottlob Frege's brilliant attempt to model human knowledge on the certainties of mathematical logic ultimately foundered on the immensely awkward, irritating realization that reality just wasn't like that. Mathematical truth turned out to be just as corrigible and fallible as anything else.[10] In his famous "Incompleteness Theorem," Kurt Gödel showed that within a rigidly logical system – such as that developed by Bertrand Russell and A. N. Whitehead in the case of arithmetic – propositions can be formulated that cannot strictly be demonstrated on the basis of its core axioms. Perhaps more significantly, Gödel demonstrated that any such system is *essentially incomplete*. In other words, given *any* consistent set of arithmetical axioms, there are true mathematical statements that cannot themselves be

---

[7] For some reflections, see Gary Sauer-Thompson and Joseph Wayne Smith, *The Unreasonable Silence of the World: Universal Reason and the Wreck of the Enlightenment Project*. Aldershot: Ashgate, 1997.

[8] Thomas Nagel, *The View from Nowhere*. New York: Oxford University Press, 1986; Hilary Putnam, *Mind, Language, and Reality*. Cambridge: Cambridge University Press, 1975.

[9] Note especially Iris Murdoch's late critique of Sartre on this point: Iris Murdoch, *Metaphysics as a Guide to Morals*. London: Penguin, 1992, 377, 463.

[10] Reuben Hersh, "Some Proposals for Reviving the Philosophy of Mathematics." *Advances in Mathematics* 31 (1979): 31–50. For a more sympathetic approach to both Russell and Frege at this point, see Gideon Makin, *The Metaphysics of Meaning: Russell and Frege on Sense and Denotation*. London: Routledge, 2000.

derived from the set.[11] In other words, there may be statements within that system that *are* true, but cannot be *shown* to be true. Gödel's famous theorem actually consists of two parts: the demonstration of incompleteness of a formal axiomatized system, and the argument that there is no ultimate proof of the consistency of arithmetic. The formalist hope of identifying *truth* with *provability* is thus severely weakened, since in any consistent theory there will always be true but unprovable sentences.[12]

Renewing the Quest for Reliable Knowledge

Recognizing this, many theologians have sought to avoid these epistemological traps by a radical review of existing approaches. The widespread recognition of the failure of foundationalism, in the strict sense of the word, has led to an explosion of interest in retrieving older ways of doing theology, developing new approaches, and occasionally redirecting existing ways of thinking. One of the most intriguing of these is to offer non-foundationalist readings of theologians who might otherwise have been regarded as firmly embedded in a modernist worldview. F. LeRon Shults' fascinating theological repositioning of Wolfhart Pannenberg[13] and Karen Kilby's nuanced rereading of Karl Rahner[14] should both be noted in this respect, not least because they point to the virtue of approaching familiar writers in innovative ways. Kilby's approach has the merit of allowing those who are not persuaded by Rahner's philosophy – especially his problematic notion of *Vorgriff auf esse* – to appropriate at least something of his theology. In a similar vein, Dirk-Martin Grube has argued that Pannenberg and Wilfried Härle are mistaken in their assertion that Karl Barth is a foundationalist.[15] Barth may legitimately be used by those wishing to develop a theological coherentist holism,

---

[11] James Robert Brown, *Philosophy of Mathematics: An Introduction to the World of Proofs and Pictures*. London: Routledge, 1999, 71–8. Theologians might particularly appreciate George Boolos' superb account of the background to Gödel's theorem: George Boolos, "Gödel's Second Incompleteness Theorem Explained in Words of one Syllable." *Mind* 103 (1994), 1–3.

[12] Brown, *Philosophy of Mathematics*, 77.

[13] F. LeRon Shults, *The Postfoundationalist Task of Theology: Wolfhart Pannenberg and the New Theological Rationality*. Grand Rapids, MI: Eerdmans, 1999.

[14] Karen Kilby, *Karl Rahner: Theology and Philosophy*. London: Routledge, 2004.

[15] Dirk-Martin Grube, *Unbegründbarkeit Gottes? Tillichs und Barths Erkenntnistheorien im Horizont der gegenwärtigen Philosophie*. Marburg: Elwert Verlag, 1998, 152–61. For my own views on Barth's relationship to modernity, see Alister E. McGrath, "Karl Barth als Aufklärer? Der Zusammenhang seiner Lehre vom Werke Christi mit der Erwählungslehre." *Kerygma und Dogma* 81 (1984): 383–94.

which eschews any foundationalist assumptions.[16] These creative postmodern rereadings of such theologians have real potential in our current situation.

Others have suggested that the failure of foundationalism and the severe limitations of non-foundationalism point to the need to explore mediating strategies. A wide spectrum of possibilities has been explored as a middle way, avoiding the extremities of the epistemological spectrum. Postliberalism emphasized the importance of linguistic communities and their distinctive languages.[17] Although superficially evading the problems of foundationalism, postliberalism ultimately finds itself justifying its approach through a prior, seemingly somewhat arbitrary, commitment to the language, norms, and beliefs of a specific confessional community. A similar difficulty emerges within the Radical Orthodoxy school, especially John Milbank, whose erudite eschewal of dialogue with the secular world entails an intellectual isolationism which does little to encourage the church's engagement with the world – traditionally held to be an integral part of the church's intellectual, cultural, pastoral, evangelistic, and apologetic agenda.[18] As a result, both these schools risk finding themselves trapped in something of an intellectual ghetto of their own making. This is a protective strategy which sets out to encourage intellectual insulation, yet ends up achieving cultural isolation.

More promisingly, J. Wentzel van Huyssteen has argued for a "postfoundationalist" conception of rationality which avoids the pitfalls of its alternatives.[19] His concept of "postfoundational rationality" is explicitly "traversal" rather than "universal." This useful distinction allows him to insist that the theologian must not be completely determined by a particular tradition, or a specific isolated community. Traversality, as van Huyssteen defines it, has to do with extending beyond cultural or disciplinary boundaries. On this understanding of the concept, postfoundationalism:[20]

---

[16] Grube, *Unbegründbarkeit Gottes?*, 210–20. I should add here that Grube's assertion that it is both possible and necessary to develop a theory of truth without ontology seems highly implausible.

[17] For its classic statement, see George Lindbeck, *The Nature of Doctrine*. Philadelphia: Westminster, 1984. I have criticized this position extensively, and do not propose to repeat these concerns here: see McGrath, *A Scientific Theology 2: Reality*, 39–54.

[18] For my concerns about the approach of John Milbank, see McGrath, *A Scientific Theology 2: Reality*, 102–18.

[19] See especially J. Wentzel van Huyssteen, *The Shaping of Rationality: Toward Interdisciplinarity in Theology and Science*. Grand Rapids, MI: Eerdmans, 1999. His earlier collection of essays also repays study: *Essays in Postfoundationalist Theology*. Grand Rapids, MI: Eerdmans, 1997.

[20] Van Huyssteen, *Essays in Postfoundationalist Theology*, 4.

fully acknowledges contextuality, the epistemically crucial role of interpreted experience, and the way that tradition shapes the epistemic and non-epistemic values that inform our reflection about God ... At the same time, however, a postfoundationalist notion of rationality in theological reflection claims to point creatively beyond the confines of the local community, group, or culture towards a plausible form of interdisciplinary conversation.

A postfoundationalist rationality is thus local and embedded, without entailing its isolation from other attempts to make sense of the world.[21]

On Developing a Scientific Theology

The approach I set out in the scientific theology project, while respecting this discussion and appreciating its importance, suggests that it is ultimately predetermined by philosophical and cultural agendas which may actually have quite little to do with the question of how we encounter and represent the real world. In themselves and of themselves, the natural sciences are neither modern nor postmodern, even though they are patient of both modern and postmodern interpretations. A scientific theology affirms that a realist understanding of the world is possible – *and always has been possible* – without recourse to foundationalism. It offers an approach to engaging with reality which is both internally coherent and firmly grounded in the external world.

The natural sciences do not presuppose or in any sense depend upon foundational beliefs; rather, they propose a method which builds up a body of knowledge through a relentless, cumulative process of interrogation of the natural world, gradually establishing by empirical inquiry a sense of what is secure knowledge and what is not, and of what methods of investigation and representation are most appropriate to any given engagement with the external world. No *a priori* assumptions are made; whatever assumptions seem necessary are initially suggested by our experience of the world, and subsequently validated by the more refined and focused procedures that are devised with a view to verifying or falsifying those hypotheses.[22]

---

[21] There are also important discussions of the concept of postfoundationalism in Kevin J. Vanhoozer, *The Drama of Doctrine: A Canonical-Linguistic Approach to Christian Theology*. Louisville, KY: Westminster John Knox Press, 2005, 265–305; and Nancey C. Murphy, *Beyond Liberalism and Fundamentalism: How Modern and Postmodern Philosophy set the Theological Agenda*. Valley Forge, PA: Trinity Press International, 1996.

[22] For some basic accounts, see Barry Gower, *Scientific Method: An Historical and Philosophical Inquiry*. London: Routledge, 1997.

It does not require a vastly extensive immersion in scientific culture to appreciate the *naïveté* of any suggestion that the natural sciences must be anti-realist or non-realist because they are not foundationalist (whether this is understood to mean a total indifference or a more informed hostility towards the Cartesian notion of foundational beliefs). It may seem self-evidently true to some writers that there is a necessary connection between realism and foundationalism; I have to say, however, that my three years' experience as an active research worker in one of Oxford University's leading scientific laboratories disabused me of any such notion. The working methods and assumptions of the natural sciences are fundamentally independent of such philosophical debates, and proceed without feeling the need to engage with them. This is doubtless an example of the intellectual isolationism that many of us find deplorable, but it has to be said that it does not seem to have adversely affected the explanatory and predictive successes of the natural sciences.

A central theme of a scientific theology is its realism – not simply in terms of its offering a "critical realist" account of reality without recourse to foundational beliefs, but in terms of being totally realistic about the extent to which reality can be known by a human observer. If we are to give a responsible account of reality, we must accept the conditions under which we can investigate it – including the limitations placed upon humanity as observers of reality, the specific nature of the reality under study, and the limitations that this specificity imposes on the manner in which it is to be observed and represented. The manner in which we can interrogate the world is not of our own choosing, but is determined by the object of our investigations. We cannot lay down in advance how the world is to be investigated; rather, we must determine how its various aspects and levels are best to be explored and represented by a sustained engagement with the world. Whatever aspect of reality we are investigating – whether it is the movement of the planets, the social behavior of chimpanzees, the process of human cognition, or the nature of the Christian God – we must acknowledge the epistemological finality of reality itself, and operate under the limiting conditions that this imposes.

This is one of the leading features of a scientific theology – a principled refusal to lay down in advance what knowledge is possible, the conditions under which it may be acquired, the extent of that knowledge, and the criteria by which its adequacy may be determined. *The order of things determines how things are known.* As Thomas F. Torrance (widely regarded as possibly the greatest British systematic theologian of the twentieth century) put it:[23]

---

[23] Thomas F. Torrance, *Preaching Christ Today: The Gospel and Scientific Thinking.* Grand Rapids, MI: Eerdmans, 1994, 45. Torrance refers to this as a "kataphysical" approach to theology.

In any rigorous scientific inquiry you pursue your research in any field in such a way that you seek to let the nature of the field or the nature of the object, as it progressively becomes disclosed through interrogation, control how you know it, how you think about it, how you formulate your knowledge of it, and how you verify that knowledge.

The Enlightenment incorrectly held, in the first place, that a single methodology existed, which could be applied to all disciplines and aspects of reality; and in the second, that this could be uncovered *a priori*, by the activity of the enlightened human reason. The philosophical agenda thus shifted subtly from the Renaissance longing to understand to the Enlightenment longing to control, by a Procrustean imposition of predetermined intellectual categories on reality.

This demand for methodological uniformitarianism, determined in advance by the unfettered exercise of an allegedly universal human reason, was fiercely resisted by three groups of thinkers in the late eighteenth and early nineteenth centuries: those aware of the limits of reason; those demanding the emancipation of individual disciplines from an inappropriately restrictive methodological straitjacket; and those, chiefly in the natural sciences, who held that true knowledge was determined empirically, and thus arose *a posteriori*. The opponents of rationalist hegemony differed among themselves concerning both their motivations for opposing it, and their proposed alternatives.[24] Nevertheless, a common theme can be discerned: the demand to let things be themselves, rather than what the Enlightenment wished to make them. Instead of shoehorning the real world into a preconceived, predetermined mold, that world itself was to be allowed to determine the manner in which it was to be investigated and represented. Or, to put it more succinctly and formally: *ontology is to be allowed to determine epistemology.*[25]

Only when reality is respected for what it is can we hope to understand and represent it; otherwise, we merely reduce it to what is already known, treating

---

[24] See the highly significant differences between three leading critics of the Enlightenment, noted by Isaiah Berlin, *Three Critics of the Enlightenment: Vico, Hamann, Herder.* Princeton, NJ: Princeton University Press, 2000.

[25] Many examples illustrating the importance of this point within the natural sciences could be noted. Perhaps the most obvious is the need for classification of diseases, species, and so forth, in which the need for conceptualities to correspond to the ordering of reality is regarded as fundamental; see, for example, Eleanor Rosch and Barbara B. Lloyd, *Cognition and Categorization.* New York: Laurence Erlbaum, 1978, 27–48. For its importance in recent discussion of biomedical ontology, see Alexa T. McCray, "An Upper-Level Ontology for the Biomedical Domain." *Comparative and Functional Genomics* 4 (2003): 80–4.

the "other" as the "same" – a tendency that has seriously impeded advance in many areas of the natural sciences, including medicine.[26] The critics of the Enlightenment argued that the advance of knowledge was impeded by precisely this failure to respect the integrity of the real world. Instead of approaching it on its own terms, respectful of its distinctive nature and characteristics, modernism preferred to conduct that encounter on terms dictated in advance by the human reason that the Enlightenment believed to be universal across history and culture – but which was in fact subject to social conditioning and construction.[27] The natural sciences, along with others, insisted on the epistemological finality of an encounter with *reality* itself – not derivative, provisional, and often speculative *theories about reality*.

Considerations such as those outlined above led me to develop the distinctive approach to theological method which I have termed "the scientific theology project," distinguished by its use of the working methods and assumptions of the natural sciences as a comparator and helpmate for theology, and especially the insistence that theological reflection is an *a posteriori* discipline, determined by the distinctive nature of the object of its investigation.[28] While claims to universality are to be viewed with caution, there are excellent reasons for suggesting that the natural sciences offer an approach which is most capable of operating across gender, cultural, and historical borders. For this reason alone, it cries out to be considered as a dialogue partner for constructive and critical theological reflection.

Throughout its long history, Christian theology has availed itself of many helpmates and dialogue partners, fully aware of the dangers and opportunities that this entails, but always convinced that the latter outweigh the former. Yes, dialogue partners can easily be allowed to dominate a conversation, diverting it from its chosen topic and preventing the rich, multifaceted engagement with

---

[26] As Rudi Schmidt has pointed out, ontological shortcomings have been of considerable importance in hindering understanding of viral hepatitis: Rudi Schmidt, "History of Viral Hepatitis: A Tale of Dogmas and Misinterpretations." *Journal of Gastroenterology and Hepatology* 16 (2001): 718–22.

[27] This is the point made by Hamann against Kant. For Hamann, Kant appeared to believe that he has constructed a universal philosophical language, whereas in reality his language was shaped by history and culture. See further Gwen G. Dickson, *Johann Georg Hamann's Relational Metacriticism*. New York: De Gruyter, 1995.

[28] For three important landmarks along the road, see Alister E. McGrath, *The Genesis of Doctrine: A Study in the Foundations of Doctrinal Criticism*. Oxford: Blackwell, 1990; *The Foundations of Dialogue in Science and Religion*. Oxford: Blackwell, 1998; *Thomas F. Torrance: An Intellectual Biography*. Edinburgh: T&T Clark, 1999.

complex issues that has characterized the Christian theological tradition at its best. Yet, this risk having been recognized, "rules of engagement" emerged, aiming at stimulating dialogue and encouraging creativity and innovation while still remaining firmly anchored within the great living tradition of theological reflection.

However, this appeal to the natural sciences is neither arbitrary nor opportunistic. It is clear to me that a positive working relationship between Christian theology and the natural sciences is demanded by the Christian understanding of the nature of reality itself – an understanding which is grounded in the doctrine of creation, which demands a unitary approach to knowledge, while being responsive to diversity, including stratification, within that creation. There is thus an ontological imperative for exploring the natural sciences as *ancilla theologiae*.[29]

The decision to use the working methods and assumptions of the natural sciences as the natural dialogue partner for Christian theology thus seems to me to be entirely appropriate. One of the most distinctive themes of Christian theological method down the ages has been its quest for a theological elixir – a universal method, independent of the irritating and restricting specificities of history, geography, and culture, which is capable of being used by all thinking people in all places and at all times. In the first period of serious Christian theological reflection, the *philosophia perennis* of Plato, refracted through many rather different prisms, was held to be the key to a universal theology. As we noted earlier, leading representatives of the Enlightenment believed that it was possible to establish a universal and necessary rational foundation for all human thought, theology included, through the recognition of the sovereignty of reason. Yet both these approaches ultimately ran into the sands, the victims of the relentless and unforgiving tendency of history to expose as particular what was believed to be universal.

The quest for universality might be chastened; it has never, however, been completely abandoned. It has not escaped the notice of philosophers or theologians that the methods and assumptions of the natural sciences seem to many today to represent the closest approximation conceivable to a universal method, capable of transcending ethnic, gender, cultural, and religious barriers. Without in any way making Christian theology dependent on such methods and assumptions, a scientific theology aims to use the common themes of the scientific enterprise – such as how reality may be discerned, represented, and encountered – to illuminate the related (though not identical) challenges faced by theology.[30]

---

[29] See especially the discussion in McGrath, *A Scientific Theology 1: Nature*, 20–5.

[30] In connection with this point, Mark Worthing's careful account of Pannenberg and Rahner makes some useful observations: Mark W. Worthing, *Foundations and Functions of Theology as Universal Science: Theological Method and Apologetic Praxis in Wolfhart Pannenberg and Karl Rahner*. Frankfurt am Main: Peter Lang, 1996.

While *A Scientific Theology* can be read both as a treatise on the relation of Christian theology and the natural sciences and a substantial constructive essay on the recalibration of theological method, it is probably best seen as a defense of the entire theological enterprise itself. I set out the case for insisting that Christian theology be recognized as a distinct legitimate intellectual discipline in its own right, with its own sense of identity and purpose, linked with an appreciation of its own limitations and distinctive emphases within the human quest for wisdom as a whole. The scientific theology advocated in *Nature*, *Reality*, and *Theory* is fundamentally a theological *system* (rather than a loose assemblage of essentially independent ideas), which seamlessly integrates a number of themes to yield a coherent vision of the theological enterprise, and provides a justification of its existence and methods in the face of modern and postmodern criticisms and anxieties.

The method can be applied at both the microtheological and macrotheological levels – in other words, both *analytically* in exploring specific issues within theology (such as developing models of doctrinal development or the emergence of heterodoxy, both of which can be accommodated with ease within the theoretical framework the method affords), and *synthetically* in the development of a "big-picture" systematic theology.

To judge both from my personal correspondence and the review columns of leading theological journals, the scientific theology project has generated immense interest within both the theological and scientific communities, and led to the most extensive review coverage of any of my works thus far in the learned literature and beyond. Many wrote to me asking it if might be possible to present the core ideas of a scientific theology in a more accessible form, and perhaps explaining more about how I came to develop this approach in the first place. It was an entirely reasonable request. In 2004, I published *The Science of God: An Introduction to Scientific Theology*, which was very generously received.

Yet other reviewers and correspondents raised deeper issues. They rightly asked for clarification of some points, and a more extended engagement with some issues which they believed arose from the work. In particular, many asked for at least some indication of how my projected "scientific dogmatics" might relate to the methodology set out in *Nature*, *Reality*, and *Theory*. I would like to take the opportunity to thank my reviewers and correspondents – who I fear are too many to allow me to name them individually – for the obvious care with which they have read these long volumes, and the penetrating questions they posed.[31]

---

[31] I would particularly single out the following reviews for their comprehensive and critical engagement with my approach, as set out in these three volumes: Brad Shipway, "The Theological Application of Bhaskar's Stratified Reality: The Scientific Theology of

I believe firmly in honoring such criticisms, which have rightly probed my thinking at points of importance. This book is my holding response. I hope that it will not seem defensive; if anything, I have found myself to be stimulated and encouraged by my critics, and am delighted to be able to explore some of the themes of my work in greater detail. Rather than respond to criticisms on a point by point basis, this work consists of a series of essays, focusing on some of the more pressing questions raised by these many requests for further clarification, explanation, and expansion.

One point needs to be made immediately. The scientific theology project is driven and directed by a methodology. This has certain obvious advantages, most notably those of conceptual coherence and intellectual robustness. One major disadvantage must, however, be conceded. As some of my correspondents correctly pointed out, *methodologically directed theologies are necessarily limited by that methodology.* The method may establish a framework; it cannot flesh out its every aspect. The method proposed for a scientific theology creates a robust skeleton; it cannot, however, create nor situate all the muscles, sinews, and internal organs that go to make up the Christian vision of reality in its totality. Those must be added either by an extension of the original methodology, or by the application of ancillary approaches.

Readers with a good knowledge of historical theology will immediately appreciate the point at issue, which is particularly evident in the writings of most theologians who combine academic and pastoral ministries. For example, F. D. E. Schleiermacher's sermons show a much greater cultural and intellectual breadth and vitality, not to mention a judicious pastoral application, than his method-driven *Glaubenslehre*. Yet both sermons and systematic theology

---

A. E. McGrath." *Journal of Critical Realism* 3 (2004): 191–203; Benjamin Myers, "Alister McGrath's Scientific Theology." *Reformed Theological Review* 64 (2005): 15–34; Elmer Colyer, "Alister E. McGrath, a Scientific Theology, Volume 1: Nature." *Pro Ecclesia* 12 (2003): 226–31; Colyer, "Alister E. McGrath, a Scientific Theology, Volume 2: Reality." *Pro Ecclesia* 12 (2003): 492–7; Colyer, "Alister E. McGrath, a Scientific Theology, Volume 3: Theory." *Pro Ecclesia* 13 (2004): 244–40. For a landmark evaluation from a Catholic perspective, including criticism of my views on the limited capacities of human reason, see James F. Keating, "The Natural Sciences as an *Ancilla Theologiae Nova*: Alister E. McGrath's *A Scientific Theology*." *The Thomist* 69 (2005): 127–52. An important assessment of my approach up to 1999 can be found in Ross H. McKenzie, "Foundations of the Dialogue between the Physical Sciences and Theology." *Perspectives on Science and Christian Faith* 56 (2004): 242–54. This review is especially significant on account of McKenzie's status as one of the world's leading theoretical physicists.

are the work of the same theological mind[32] – in one context, liberated from the limitations of his method, and in the other, given intellectual depth by the coherence of that same method. Any theologian with a vision for the importance of method will experience a similar tension.

I do not myself regard this as a major difficulty, given my specific agenda in developing this approach. The theological situation today primarily demands the construction of a skeleton, without which any resulting theology lacks structure or stability. Yet however important this may be, it cannot by itself lead to the construction of the full richness of the Christian theological heritage. In this collection of essays, readers will note my concern both to consolidate and transcend the specific theological method I set out in the three volumes of *A Scientific Theology*. However, they will notice that in some of my other theological writings I develop ideas in somewhat different manners, and often to a greater depth. This is not an inconsistency; it reflects a recognition of the limits of any theological method, and a conscious decision to work around them.

If I can put it simply, a rigorous dogmatic method both *stimulates* and *limits* theological reflection. It stimulates it, by providing a substantial, reliable framework on which a systematic theology may be constructed. Yet it also limits such reflection, by imposing restrictions which are determined by the specifics of the method itself, not by the Christian tradition in general. The task that I have set myself in writing a future *Scientific Dogmatics* is the application of the core method in such a way that its underpinning and illumination of central theological themes will be evident, even if the exposition of such themes ultimately transcends the method. The method establishes the framework; what is placed on that framework is partly determined by that method, and partly by ancillary methods that are required to supplement it. In this present volume, I concern myself only with exploring the shape of the dogmatic skeleton that shapes and supports this future scientific dogmatics.

Introducing the Essays

And so we turn to the essays gathered together in this volume. In what follows, I shall offer a brief introduction to each, so that readers are alerted in advance to points of importance or interest.

---

[32] See the useful analysis of Richard R. Niebuhr, "Schleiermacher on Language and Feeling." *Theology Today* 17 (1960): 150–67.

The first essay needs a little explanation, in that it is an article about me, rather than by me. Many have written to me asking if it might be possible to have a brief, basic summary of the intellectual elements and pathways constituting the "scientific theology" project. While appreciating the relative brevity of my introductory volume *The Science of God*, these correspondents have not unreasonably pointed out that even this compressed account of my ideas might seem to some to be unduly demanding. While it is true that it takes rather less time to read a single work of 75,000 words than three volumes amounting to 400,000 words, many pleaded for something rather more digestible and manageable – if possible, an order of magnitude shorter, 7,500 rather than 75,000 words.

The point is well taken. The first essay in this collection represents exactly such a brief introduction, written from an appreciative yet critical perspective by Dr. Benjamin Myers of the University of Queensland, Australia.[33] Myers does a superb job of contextualizing the "scientific theology" project, summarizing its key themes, and making some important criticisms – all in less than one-tenth of the wordage of my own introduction. In view of its reliability, concision, clarity, and critical acumen, readers wanting a brief introduction to my ideas can do no better than begin by reading Dr. Myers' review. It sets the context admirably for my nine essays that follow it.

As these nine essays assume that readers are already familiar with the basic arguments of the "scientific theology" project, Dr. Myers' review will help newcomers to orientate themselves to those basic themes. However, I must emphasize once more that the present collection of essays does not aim to repeat the arguments of the three original volumes of *A Scientific Theology*. They are set out and defended in those volumes, and those basic lines of reasoning are not replicated here. The essays collected in this volume are chiefly concerned with further development and exploration of those themes, although I have included three items which will help readers gain a sense of the historical development of the arguments of those earlier volumes.

The second essay engages the question of whether the very idea of a "scientific theology" is intellectual nonsense – a contradiction in terms. A large number of my correspondents, while enjoying the high degree of intellectual robustness of my approach, wondered how it would stand up against the criticisms directed against religion in general, and theology in particular, by Richard Dawkins, Oxford University's Professor of the Public Understanding

---

[33] Benjamin Myers, "Alister McGrath's Scientific Theology." *Reformed Theological Review* 64 (2005): 15–34. Dr. Myers has made some minor editorial changes to the original article to adapt it for publication in this format.

of Science. Dawkins is one of the world's most prolific and intellectually engaging atheist writers, who is totally opposed to any relationship between the natural sciences and Christian theology. Having recently written a reasonably comprehensive critique of Dawkins' views on religion,[34] I had little hesitation in deciding to produce such a response.

This essay thus attempts to clear the ground for the more detailed exploration of the themes of my approach, by asking whether the kinds of criticism that Dawkins directs against Christian theology in general can be sustained. Dawkins is an important dialogue partner, even if his criticisms of Christian theology are often somewhat predictable, formulaic, and misdirected. However, his challenge to theology to demonstrate its intellectual credentials and relevance is not unfair, even if some might object to the somewhat strident tone in which that challenge is framed. At its heart, Dawkins' critique of theology can be seen as a legitimate, if unduly dogmatic, demand to know by what standards theological statements are to be adjudicated, tempered by a deep-seated suspicion on his part that they are without a secure foundation or a meaningful criterion of truth. This essay aims to offer at least a preliminary evaluation of this critique.

The next two essays deal with aspects of the critically important discipline of natural theology. Readers of A Scientific Theology, particularly the first and second volumes, will be aware of the importance that I attach to the reform and renewal of natural theology, while expressing concerns about existing approaches, especially those to emerge during the heyday of English rationalism. Each of these two essays was written for quite different purposes, and addresses different themes relating to natural theology. Their common theme is that God is able to address humanity in and through the natural order, raising the question of how we are to *discern* such revelatory actions, patterns, events, and structures in the first place.

The third essay in this collection is primarily of historical interest. It takes the form of a sermon preached before the University of Oxford on Sunday 4, November 2001 at the University Church of St. Mary the Virgin. This "university sermon" lays the groundwork for an assessment of the significance of natural theology, especially in relation to Christian apologetics and spirituality. The sermon opens by citing Joseph Addison's famous "Ode," appended to a major essay entitled "On the impressions of divine power and wisdom in the Universe." This hymn was sung earlier in the service during which

---

[34] Alister E. McGrath, *Dawkins' God: Genes, Memes and the Meaning of Life.* Oxford: Blackwell, 2004.

the sermon was preached, and forms an admirable introduction to its themes. This "Ode" takes the form of an extended meditation on Psalm 19.1–4, which I here cite in the language of the King James Version, familiar to Addison:

> The heavens declare the glory of God; and the firmament sheweth his handy-work.
> Day unto day uttereth speech, and night unto night sheweth knowledge.
> There is no speech nor language, where their voice is not heard.
> Their line is gone out through all the earth, and their words to the end of the world.

In this "Ode" Addison develops the idea of the celestial bodies bearing witness to the power and providence of the one who created them. It seemed an ideal prelude to the topic of my sermon on that occasion, and allowed me to begin to explore issues relating to transcendence and transignification in a reasonably accessible way.

The fourth essay sets out in detail my concerns about the impact of the Enlightenment on natural theology, which I develop with particular reference to classic English approaches to natural theology. As a participant in a number of events held in the late spring of 2005 to celebrate the bicentenary of the death of William Paley (1743–1805), I found myself reflecting on the severe difficulties faced by the specific understanding of natural theology with which he is associated. This essay includes elements of two major addresses on this topic I delivered around this time: a lecture on natural theology delivered at the Villa Serbelloni, Bellagio, Lake Como, on Saturday April 24, and the Paley Memorial Sermon, preached at Carlisle Cathedral on Sunday May 23, 2005. The essay represents a critique of Paley's general approach, and sets out the case both for the intellectual renewal and conceptual repositioning of natural theology in the future.

The essay can be seen both as an affirmation of the intellectual excellence of the English tradition of natural theology, and as a plea for its renewal and redirection. The programmatic renewal of the category of natural theology extends far beyond the natural sciences, and offers the possibility of interdisciplinary connectivity on a significant scale. In particular, it emphasizes that natural theology is an imaginative, as much as a rational, undertaking. Natural theology is an obvious point of convergence for theology, the natural sciences, philosophy, aesthetics, literature, and art, holding out the possibility of reconnecting disciplines that have long since ceased to talk to each other. This essay, while developing some themes of the "scientific theology" project, also lays the ground for a major work I hope to write in the next year, setting out a new vision for natural theology, suggesting that the discipline can and should be renewed.

The fifth essay deals with the all-important concept of stratification, which is an essential component of the critical realism that underpins my theological method. In the second volume of *A Scientific Theology*, I develop the notion of stratification with reference to the works of Roy Bhaskar. In this essay, I note the earlier use of the concept during the 1920s and 1930s by writers such as Nicolai Hartmann, and consider how the growing interest in the phenomenon of "emergence" within the natural sciences relates to this notion. As will be clear from internal references, the essay was written primarily with a German-speaking readership in mind, addressing issues of particular importance within the German-language Protestant theological tradition. Nevertheless, these issues are important to a wider constituency, and I have therefore included it in this collection.

Perhaps the most significant aspect of a stratified approach to reality, whether in the sciences or humanities, is that it poses a fatal challenge to the reductionist tendencies of our age. The importance of the concept of stratification for theological method is explored in this essay through an extended engagement with the intellectual project of Heinrich Scholz. Scholz is not well known in the English-speaking theological world, although his influence on German-language theology and philosophy was considerable, particularly during the 1920s. Most significantly for our purposes, Scholz argued for a *mathesis universalis*, a universalization of intellectual methods along the lines suggested by Leibniz. This essay examines this approach, so characteristic of the Enlightenment, and asks what can be learned from its failure, and how the concept of stratification allows this weakness to be overcome.

The two essays which follow deal with the important theological issue of the development of doctrine, raising the question of whether the natural sciences offer theology any plausible evolutionary models which might illuminate this complex process, in whole or in part. In the third volume of *A Scientific Theology* I proposed that the evolution of scientific theories offered a helpful model for doctrinal development, and put forward a model based on Otto von Neurath's image of a boat at sea as a non-foundational analogue to this complex process.[35] That process of model-building is still under way, and will, I hope, lead to a major future monograph on the development of doctrine. However, many of my correspondents asked for further reflection on how the natural sciences might help us understand the phenomenon of doctrinal development. I am therefore offering two interim responses to these inquiries.

The sixth essay represents a substantial and long overdue evaluation of whether biological evolutionary models possess any validity or heuristic utility

---

[35] McGrath, *A Scientific Theology 3: Theory*, 213–21.

for the development of Christian theology. It is an extremely important, contentious topic, which has long demanded detailed, extensive discussion. Many works of academic and popular theology have begun to use language and schemata which are derived from the neo-Darwinian paradigm, particularly in relation to the development of doctrine and the emergence of church structures. The essay raises significant doubts about the legitimacy of using such biological analogues, while at the same time noting some of the fascinating issues that they raise – above all, the question of whether there exist "islands of stability" within an ongoing evolutionary process.

This substantial, groundbreaking essay evaluates the biological analogies at the theologian's disposal, and arrives at what I believe to be a realistic assessment of their merits and weaknesses. This analysis raises some highly important questions, two of which may be singled out as illustrative of the capacity of biological analogues to evoke serious theological reflection. Is the Chalcedonian Definition of the person of Christ to be seen as an "island of stability," a region of theological convergence in which the guiding forces of the evolutionary process overwhelm the contingencies of history? And, equally important, is Chalcedon's use of specific metaphysical categories to be seen as an evolutionary "spandrel" (to use Stephen Jay Gould's classical evolutionary analogy)? If so, what are the implications for Christological reflection today? This essay opens up new paradigms for understanding and evaluating doctrinal development, which it is hoped will prove illuminating and helpful to the theological task. Like any groundbreaking essay, it will prove to be controversial. However, it is a controversy which I believe has the potential to cast light, rather than create heat, and I make no apologies for getting this overdue discussion under way.

The seventh essay examines the way in which the Swiss developmental psychologist Jean Piaget's empirically derived idea of "assimilation" offers a helpful framework for understanding some aspects of the development of doctrine, noting particularly how it illuminates some significant patterns of change observed during the patristic period. The reason for exploring Piaget's ideas at this point will be obvious: if we are able to achieve at least something of an understanding of how the developing human mind naturally shapes its conceptual frameworks, we will be in a better position to understand what F. D. E. Schleiermacher encourages us to think of as the "natural heresies of Christianity," which arise partially through assimilation of the gospel to existing religious or cultural categories.

The history of doctrine is open to being read from this perspective, and the results are highly instructive – especially when Piaget's related concepts of "accommodation" and "equilibration" are brought into play. While Piaget's conceptual analytical framework may not necessarily enable us to identify which doctrinal developments are to be deemed legitimate and which improper, they certainly alert us to some of the mechanisms by which illegitimate development takes place. It may also be pointed out that Piaget's analysis allows us to appreciate that such assimilation may often be *natural*, rather than degenerate or malevolent, perhaps allowing a degree of theological realism to be injected into the often heated debate over the origins and significance of heresy.

The next two essays take a very different form. In the conclusion to the final volume of *A Scientific Theology*, I mentioned my habit of producing "working papers in scientific theology" as part of the research leading up to the writing of these volumes.[36] I have received a large number of requests to publish at least some of these. Unfortunately, many are not suitable for publication in any form, as they take the form of my running comments on, or annotations of, core texts (particularly from Athanasius, Augustine, Aquinas, Kant, Barth, and Torrance). On rereading them recently, however, some stood out as being more accessible and interesting. Two working papers written in preparation for the "scientific theology" project are included in this collection. I would ask readers to bear in mind that these were written for my own personal purposes, and were not intended to be published. Annotation in these two working papers is sparse, as my main concern was to establish lines of argument for myself, rather than to document and justify them in detail for others.

The first of these working papers, dealing with the role of ordering in a scientific theology, was drafted back in December 1995. It sets out how the idea of "the order of things" can act as a theological *Leitmotif*, establishing an important dialogue with the natural sciences on the one hand, while laying a viable foundation for Christian dogmatics on the other. For example, I note how a theology of atonement could easily be developed using the themes of disruption and restoration of divine order.

This working paper played an important role in persuading me to develop the "scientific theology" project, partly on account of its theological utility. However, it also persuaded me of the possibility of using this approach to enter into dialogue with other disciplines, as well as exploring its apologetic potential. Although I do not address this in the original paper, recent work on the role of order in ancient Assyrian and Egyptian religion suggests that the theme may be of major importance to the wisdom traditions of the Ancient Near East,[37] thus

---

[36] McGrath, *A Scientific Theology 3: Theory*, 295 n.2.

[37] I have in mind works such as Jan Assmann, Bernd Janowski, and Michael Welker, eds., *Gerechtigkeit: Richten und Retten in der abendländischen Tradition und ihren altorientalischen Ursprüngen*. Munich: Fink, 1998; Stefan M. Maul, "Der assyrische König: Hüter der Weltordnung." In *Priests and Officials in the Ancient Near East*, edited by Kazuko Watanabe, 201–14. Heidelberg: Universitätsverlag C. Winter, 1999; Jan Assmann, *Ma'at: Gerechtigkeit und Unsterblichkeit im alten Ägypten*. Munich: C. H. Beck, 2001.

opening the way to a retrieval of some form of natural theology (a topic touched on earlier in this collection) grounded in the ancient wisdom traditions. Again, to be considered as a specifically *Christian* undertaking, such a natural theology would have to be repositioned within a Christian dogmatics, rather than seen as an independent, autonomous entity.

The second of these working papers is of fundamental importance to transitioning from the methodology I set out in *A Scientific Theology* to its application in a future "scientific dogmatics." Written in August 1996, it explores how an iterative theological method can be developed. Theology is not constituted by a single, linear trajectory of analysis, but by multiple iterations involving feedback and development. The fundamental point is that insights gained through the first application of a theological method can be reflected back, and used in its second application. The method, which is based on iterative mathematical procedures I used with great success in carrying out research into molecular biophysics at Oxford in the late 1970s,[38] allows the application of this theological method to be visualized as ascending a spiral staircase through a constant circling of the object under consideration, feeding back derived insights into each cycle of the exploratory process. The method will be applied in the "scientific dogmatics" that is currently under construction.

The tenth and final essay deals with the question of the appropriate starting place for a scientific dogmatics. Although this question is briefly touched on in the previous essay, which deals with the characteristics of an iterative theological method, this concluding essay argues in some detail that the proper starting point for a scientific dogmatics is the actuality of the church as an embodied tradition, characterized by its own distinctive rationality. This essay began its life as a working paper back in 1997, but has been revised, expanded, and annotated as the process of development has proceeded, reaching its final form in December 2004. It aims to show why a systematic theology ought to begin from the empirical encounter with the church as a visible social reality, and addresses a number of difficulties that confront such an approach – particularly the question of whether empiricism can really be said to engage with social, rather than natural, entities. It goes without saying that I particu-

---

[38] The iterative procedure I used was the "method of moments," developed to help analyze complex fluorescence decay spectra of molecular probes used to investigate the viscosity of biological membranes and their synthetic analogues. For the approach, see I. Isenberg and R. D. Dyson, "Analysis of Exponential Curves by a Method of Moments, with Special Attention to Sedimentation Equilibrium and Fluorescence Decay." *Biochemistry* 10 (1971): 3233–41; "The Analysis of Fluorescence Decay by a Method of Moments." *Biophysical Journal* 9 (1969): 1337–50.

larly welcome assessment and criticism of this final essay, in that this will allow me to write the proposed "scientific dogmatics" with a heightened awareness of potential difficulties and limitations.

It remains for me to thank those who have made this collection of essays possible. I must begin by thanking many students and academic colleagues at Oxford University who have stimulated me, corrected me, challenged me, and invariably *encouraged* me as I have explored the question of how theology might be undertaken scientifically. I particularly wish to thank Marilyn McCord Adams, Denis Alexander, John Barrow, John Hedley Brooke, Francis Collins, Ross McKenzie, Alvin Plantinga, John Roche, and John Webster for their advice, assistance, criticism, and encouragement. My greatest debt is to Joanna Collicutt McGrath, who has contributed much to my thinking, not least by pointing out its shortcomings and suggesting constructive alternatives. All remaining errors of fact or judgment are, of course, entirely mine.

I also wish to acknowledge the kindness of others who have helped in other ways. In particular, I would like to thank the editors of *Reformed Theological Review* for so readily agreeing to reproducing Dr. Benjamin Myers' review of the three volumes of *A Scientific Theology* in this collection. The John Templeton Foundation, which has been instrumental in encouraging academic dialogue between science and religion, most generously supported the research underlying this work. And finally, I thank Rebecca Harkin of Blackwell Publishing for her support and encouragement as this volume was being assembled.

Alister E. McGrath
Oxford, September 2005

CHAPTER I

Alister McGrath's Scientific Theology

A review article by Dr. Benjamin Myers,
University of Queensland

Alister McGrath's recent work, *A Scientific Theology*,[1] aims to offer a uniquely comprehensive exploration of the methodological relation between Christian theology and the natural sciences, and to effect a systematic integration of scientific and theological thought-forms. McGrath is well equipped to have undertaken so ambitious a task. He earned an Oxford doctorate in 1977 for work in molecular biophysics, and, stimulated by Karl Barth's *Church Dogmatics* and by a desire to engage Christian thought with natural science, he went on to study and then teach theology at Oxford. McGrath quickly distinguished himself as a leading authority on historical theology and as a remarkably prolific evangelical writer. Not until 1996 – some twenty years after first conceiving of such a project – did McGrath feel adequately prepared to begin developing a thoroughgoing engagement between science and theology. This engagement has already produced several books: first an account of the methodological foundations of dialogue between theology and science;[2] then an

---

[1] A. E. McGrath, *A Scientific Theology*, 3 vols. Edinburgh: T&T Clark, 2001–3. The three volumes are respectively subtitled *Nature* (2001), *Reality* (2002), and *Theory* (2003). McGrath has also published a single-volume abridgement of this work: *The Science of God: An Introduction to Scientific Theology*. London: T&T Clark, 2004.

[2] A. E. McGrath, *The Foundations of Dialogue in Science and Religion*. Oxford: Blackwell, 1998.

introductory textbook on the relation between science and Christian faith;[3] and then a study of the great Scottish "theological scientist," T. F. Torrance.[4] More recently, McGrath has explored the ecological implications of a Christian view of creation,[5] and he has developed an important critique of the thought of Richard Dawkins.[6] But his most important and most systematic theological engagement with the natural sciences is set out in the major three-volume work, *A Scientific Theology*.

Important influences on McGrath's *Scientific Theology* include Barth's doctrine of revelation, Roy Bhaskar's critical realism, George Lindbeck's cultural-linguistic view of doctrine,[7] and McGrath's own firsthand experience of scientific experimentation. But towering over the whole scientific theology project is the influence of T. F. Torrance, a thinker whom McGrath describes as "the greatest British theologian of the twentieth century" and as his "role model" in producing the *Scientific Theology*.[8] Through a penetrating analysis of the scientific character of theological knowledge, Torrance has sought to relate theological and scientific ways of thinking and so both to deepen theological objectivity and to nurture mutually fruitful dialogue between the two disciplines.[9] In the judgment of one commentator, Torrance's theological science offers "the most highly developed version of realism" available in modern theology.[10] Several of McGrath's most important insights into the nature of scientific theology are already apparent in his 1999 study of Torrance; and McGrath describes his *Scientific Theology* as a

---

[3] A. E. McGrath, *Science and Religion: An Introduction*. Oxford: Blackwell, 1999.

[4] A. E. McGrath, *Thomas F. Torrance: An Intellectual Biography*. Edinburgh: T&T Clark, 1999.

[5] A. E. McGrath, *The Re-Enchantment of Nature: Science, Religion and the Human Sense of Wonder*. London: Hodder & Stoughton, 2002.

[6] A. E. McGrath, *Dawkins' God: Genes, Memes, and the Meaning of Life*. Oxford: Blackwell, 2004.

[7] Lindbeck's influence is primarily negative: McGrath seeks to offer a powerful alternative to Lindbeck's social constructivism.

[8] A. E. McGrath, "Contributors: An Appreciation and Response," in *Alister E. McGrath and Evangelical Theology: A Dynamic Engagement*, ed. S. W. Chung. Carlisle: Paternoster, 2003, 341. The first volume of the *Scientific Theology* is dedicated to Torrance.

[9] See especially T. F. Torrance, *Theological Science*. Oxford: Oxford University Press, 1969.

[10] D. W. Hardy, "Thomas F. Torrance," in *The Modern Theologians: An Introduction to Christian Theology in the Twentieth Century*, ed. D. F. Ford, Oxford: Blackwell, 1989, 86.

sustained attempt "to develop and extend Torrance's vision of theological science."[11]

The *Scientific Theology* is a large and formidably detailed work, seeking at once to engage critically with natural science, philosophy, and theology; to present a sophisticated contemporary theological method; and to defend the legitimacy of theology as a distinctive discipline in its own right. It is impossible here even to summarize McGrath's argument as it develops on all these levels. It is likewise impossible to convey the sheer breadth of McGrath's engagement with science – as one professional physicist remarks with admiration, McGrath "has engaged on a reading programme of massive proportions," having read "everything of relevance in the history of science, in contemporary science . . . , in the history of the philosophy of science," and in other fields.[12] The present essay, then, will aim only to discuss McGrath's *Scientific Theology* as a work of theological method, and thus to offer an introduction to McGrath's sophisticated theological proposal and to his acute and distinctive vision of Christian theology as a whole.

Method

A *Scientific Theology* is not a study of the content of theology or of any particular body of scientific findings. Rather, it is concerned with the *methodological* parallels between theology and the natural sciences. A theology which is grounded in any particular scientific findings will inevitably become outdated as scientific knowledge develops,[13] whereas a theology that is related to science methodologically may be of lasting value. McGrath is interested, then, in relating the methods and working assumptions of the natural sciences to the methodology of theological reflection.[14]

But McGrath does not want only to observe the parallels between the two disciplines. He believes that science should serve "a supportive and illuminative role" in contemporary theology, while also opening up apologetic

---

[11] McGrath, *Scientific Theology*, 1:76.

[12] J. J. Roche, "The Scientific Theology Project of Alister E. McGrath," in Chung, *Alister E. McGrath and Evangelical Theology*, 34.

[13] McGrath, *Scientific Theology*, 1:48; cf. 2:165–6. A notable example of the strict subordination of theology to cosmological findings is F. J. Tipler, *The Physics of Immortality: Modern Cosmology, God and the Resurrection of the Dead*. New York: Doubleday, 1994. On the flux of scientific understanding, see L. Sklar, *Theory and Truth: Philosophical Critique without Foundational Science*. Oxford: Oxford University Press, 2000.

[14] McGrath, *Scientific Theology*, 1:50.

possibilities.[15] The natural sciences today can therefore play "precisely the role that Platonism offered our patristic, and Aristotelianism our medieval forebears" – that is, the role of a handmaid of theology (ancilla theologiae).[16] McGrath argues, however, that this appropriation of science is not arbitrary or merely pragmatic, for the Christian view of created reality in fact demands a positive engagement with the natural sciences.[17] He insists, further, that the integrity of theology must be maintained by allowing science to function only "in a ministerial, rather than magisterial, capacity,"[18] and he advocates a direct engagement between the two disciplines, not an engagement mediated by any shared philosophy.[19] McGrath is thus concerned to integrate theology and science without compromising the content of the "great tradition" of classical Christian orthodoxy.[20]

Nature

The first volume, Nature, seeks to develop a viable approach to natural theology through a probing analysis of the concept of "nature." McGrath

---

[15] Ibid, 1:7.

[16] Ibid. McGrath acknowledges that Barth's warning against the systematic use of philosophy in theology "demands to be taken with the utmost seriousness" (2:200). But he believes he is respecting this warning by refusing to grant any worldview a foundational role: "rather than committing itself to any particular worldview, Christian theology should use or appropriate as many worldviews and forms of language as are appropriate to explicate the truth of God's Word without allowing itself to enter into a relation of dependence on them" (2:201).

[17] Ibid, 1:20–5.

[18] Ibid, 1:10; cf. 2:118. Overstatements of the role of science are unfortunately not uncommon among theologians. See, for example, the historical observation of H. Schwarz, Creation. Grand Rapids: Eerdmans, 2002, 110: "Either theology aligns itself with science or it simply dies of atrophy." On the contrary, the fact that theology is a distinctive discipline with its own object and methods means that its engagement with science (or with any discipline) can only be an exercise of theological freedom and integrity. A slavish engagement with science has always already ceased to be a theological engagement.

[19] Here McGrath is above all concerned to emancipate scientific-theological discourse from reliance on process thought (as, for example, in the writings of Barbour). Process theology is, McGrath argues, both scientifically and theologically implausible.

[20] On McGrath's understanding of the "great tradition," which parallels C. S. Lewis' notion of "mere Christianity," see A. E. McGrath, "Engaging the Great Tradition: Evangelical Theology and the Role of Tradition." In Evangelical Futures: A Conversation on Theological Method, edited by John G. Stackhouse, 139–58. Grand Rapids, MI: Baker, 2000.

demonstrates that, historically, "nature" has always been a socially constructed concept rather than an objective entity. Since the concept of nature is always the product of some specific worldview,[21] it will be a "meaningless" concept in contemporary discussion unless it is given some explicit ontological foundation.[22] Any attempt to base a philosophy or theology on nature must therefore first ground nature itself in a prior ontology; after all, "how can we construct a philosophy based on nature, when nature has already been constructed by our philosophical ideas?"[23] According to McGrath, the doctrine of creation offers such an ontology, allowing Christian theology to reclaim nature as a useful intellectual concept. Instead of starting with nature as such, the Christian approach is to see nature as God's creation, which entails viewing it "through the prism of revelation."[24]

The entire *Scientific Theology* is thus theologically grounded in the Christian doctrine of creation.[25] McGrath discusses the portrayal of creation in the Genesis narratives, the prophetic tradition, and the wisdom tradition,[26] emphasizing the motif that "the Lord creates by defeating or ordering an already existent chaotic entity."[27] This Old Testament creation-theology, McGrath argues, should be read through the hermeneutic grid of the New Testament's christological and trinitarian view of creation, in which Christ is regarded as both the agent and the goal of creation.[28] Exploring the historical development of the doctrine of creation, McGrath further notes the importance of *creatio ex nihilo* as an affirmation of the freedom of God and of "the ontological dependence of the cosmos upon its creator."[29] And engaging with

---

[21] McGrath, *Scientific Theology*, 1:121.

[22] Ibid, 1:87.

[23] Ibid, 1:133.

[24] Ibid, 1:137.

[25] For McGrath's full account of the doctrine of creation, see ibid, 1:135–91.

[26] Ibid, 1:144–55. McGrath notes that the habit of theologically "privileging" the Genesis accounts because of their mere location within the biblical canon is unjustified, and that a theology of creation must be informed by the "various understandings of creation found in the Old Testament" (1:144).

[27] Ibid, 1:148.

[28] Ibid, 1:158–9.

[29] Ibid, 1:166. This point is also significant in material engagements of science with the doctrine of creation; for, rightly understood, the traditional *ex nihilo* would retain its meaning even if it should turn out that the universe has no absolute beginning. Cf. I. G. Barbour, *Religion in an Age of Science*. San Francisco: Harper & Row, 199, 145; and M. W. Worthing, *God, Creation, and Contemporary Physics*. Minneapolis, MN: Fortress, 1996, 73–110.

Thomas Aquinas, Calvin, Barth, and Torrance, McGrath argues that, according to the doctrine of creation, "the same divine rationality ... which the natural sciences discern within the created order is to be identified within the *logos* incarnate, Jesus Christ."[30] This single divine rationality is thus both "embedded in creation" and "embodied in Christ."[31]

McGrath takes up and develops this insight in an exploration of the scientific implications of the doctrine of creation. Most importantly, the doctrine of creation implies that there is a fundamental correspondence between divine rationality, human rationality, and the intrinsic structures of the created order.[32] The rationality of the world and of the human mind allows the orderly patterns within nature to be identified and conceptually represented, while the fact that God is himself reflected in creation explains the beauty of scientific theories.[33] McGrath thus shows that the doctrine of creation is basic to a scientific theology, since it provides the grounds of both theological and scientific engagements with reality. In short, by employing the doctrine of creation as "a Kantian net" thrown over our experience of the world, we will find "a strong degree of resonance between this doctrine and this world of experience," that is, between theology and science.[34]

Thus on the basis of the doctrine of creation, McGrath thus proceeds to set out a positive approach to natural theology.[35] In contrast to the modern notion of natural theology,[36] McGrath affirms that nature, autonomously considered, cannot serve as a foundation for theological reflection – or, indeed, for any kind of reflection, since "nature" is itself always a constructed concept.[37] Rather, a responsible natural theology must take as its starting point "the

---

[30] McGrath, *Scientific Theology*, 1:188.

[31] Ibid.

[32] Ibid, 1:196–218. On theological grounds, McGrath thus defends a Platonic theory of mathematics: see ibid, 1:209–14; 2:170–6.

[33] Ibid, 1:232–40.

[34] Ibid, 1:240.

[35] In a review of this volume in *Theology Today* 59: 2 (2002), 312–16, W. Pannenberg criticizes McGrath for speaking of "natural theology" instead of a "theology of nature." But the fact that McGrath so carefully defines and elucidates his own usage of "natural theology" makes the choice of terms relatively unimportant.

[36] As a typically modern understanding of natural theology, McGrath cites the definition of W. P. Alston, *Perceiving God: The Epistemology of Religious Experience.* Ithaca, NY: Cornell University Press, 1991, 289: natural theology is "the enterprise of providing support for religious beliefs by starting from premises that neither are [religious] nor presuppose any religious beliefs."

[37] McGrath, *Scientific Theology*, 1:257.

specifically Christian understanding of creation as a trinitarian event, and the concept of the creation of humanity in the *imago Dei*.[38] Responding to the criticism that natural theology is an erroneous attempt to prove the existence of God,[39] McGrath argues that pre-Enlightenment natural theology made no such attempt,[40] and that "it is perfectly possible to frame a natural theology in such a manner that it does not involve ... an intention to prove God's existence."[41] Indeed, natural theology is better understood as "a demonstration, from the standpoint of faith, of the consonance between that faith and the structures of the world."[42] Instead of trying to prove the existence of God, natural theology in fact presupposes God's existence,[43] so that revelation provides an interpretive framework through which nature can be understood.[44] Natural theology is therefore legitimate "within the scope of a revealed knowledge of God"; its foundational insight is derived from revelation.[45] Undertaken in this way, natural theology may seek to demonstrate the plausibility of an already existing belief in God,[46] so that as a whole it both presupposes and reinforces basic Christian theological positions.[47] This approach to natural theology, McGrath argues, is compatible both with the biblical concept of revelation[48] and with Barth's denunciation of any autonomously construed natural theology.[49]

---

[38] Ibid, 1:249.

[39] The criticism is of course common, but McGrath engages in detail with the objections of Barth and A. Plantinga: see ibid, 1:264–86.

[40] Here McGrath differs from T. F. Torrance, *God and Rationality*. Edinburgh: T&T Clark, 1997, 133, who criticizes medieval natural theology for being "abstracted on its own as an antecedent science" which as such "supplied the general frame of reference in which 'revealed theology' was interpreted." Criticisms of this kind tend especially to have Thomas Aquinas in view; but on Thomas' natural theology as grounded in a doctrine of God as creator, see F. Kerr, *After Aquinas: Versions of Thomism*. Oxford: Blackwell, 2002, 35–72.

[41] McGrath, *Scientific Theology*, 1:266.

[42] Ibid, 1:267; cf. McGrath, *Science and Religion*, 128.

[43] McGrath, *Scientific Theology*, 1:267.

[44] Ibid, 1:294.

[45] Ibid, 1:295. Cf. J. Polkinghorne, *Science and Christian Belief: Theological Reflections of a Bottom-Up Thinker*. London: SPCK, 1994, 3: natural theology is "an integral part of the whole theological quest for understanding and by no means an isolable or merely preliminary sub-department of it."

[46] McGrath, *Scientific Theology*, 1:267.

[47] Ibid, 2:73.

[48] Ibid, 1:257–63. Cf. J. Barr, *Biblical Faith and Natural Theology*. Oxford: Clarendon Press, 1993.

[49] McGrath, *Scientific Theology*, 1:267–86. Here McGrath follows Torrance's influential interpretation of Barth: T. F. Torrance, "The Problem of Natural Theology in the Thought of Karl Barth," *Religious Studies* 6 (1970): 121–35.

On the basis of a natural theology in which nature is "construed in a trinitarian manner as the creation of the self-revealing God,"[50] McGrath thus speaks of the capacity of the created order to disclose God.[51] With Wolfhart Pannenberg, he argues that such a natural theology offers "a comprehensive means by which theology may address the world and engage in a productive dialogue concerning the legitimation and consequences of belief systems,"[52] so that theological discourse is liberated "from any self-imposed imprisonment within an intellectual ghetto."[53] A scientific theology is, in other words, a *public* theology, and therefore a theology with significant apologetic possibilities.

Reality

Having examined the theological status of nature, in the second volume, subtitled *Reality*, McGrath explores "the epistemological and ontological status of the real world."[54] In polemic against both Enlightenment objectivism on the right and postmodern relativism on the left, McGrath develops an account of theological realism in which there is a complex interplay – rather than any simplistic antithesis – between objectivity and social construction. Throughout this volume, McGrath defends the view that "knowledge arises through a sustained and passionate attempt to engage with a reality that is encountered or made known";[55] and he defines theology as "a principled uncovering of the spiritual structures of reality, and a responsible attempt to represent them in a manner appropriate to their distinctive natures."[56]

---

[50] McGrath, *Scientific Theology*, 1:296.

[51] Ibid, 1:296–8. At this point McGrath raises, but leaves unanswered, the crucial question of whether this capacity is intrinsic to creation (thus an *analogia entis*), or whether it rests solely on the gracious choice of God so to disclose himself (thus an *analogia fidei*). This complex problem is taken up in a different connection in ibid, 3:104–32; see my discussion below.

[52] Ibid, 1:303.

[53] Ibid, 1:304.

[54] Ibid, 2:xi.

[55] Ibid, 2:3–4. On the "passionate" or personal character of knowledge, see M. Polanyi, *Personal Knowledge: Towards a Post-Critical Philosophy*. London: Routledge & Kegan Paul, 1958.

[56] McGrath, *Scientific Theology*, 2:4.

Discussing the collapse of Enlightenment foundationalist epistemology,[57] McGrath argues that the consequences of this collapse are "almost entirely positive" for a scientific theology.[58] On the one hand, scientific thinking today cannot make any foundational assumptions about the world; and on the other hand, we must acknowledge that there is no tradition-independent vantage point from which we can view our beliefs.[59] Such a postfoundationalist approach to knowledge entails a coherentist view of truth, in which "truth" is predicated not simply of isolated elements of a belief-system, but of the belief-system as a whole.[60]

A rejection of foundationalism does not, however, entail a rejection of realism or of a correspondence theory of truth.[61] McGrath develops this point in contrast to the postliberalism of Lindbeck and the Yale School.[62] He affirms with Lindbeck that theology must be undertaken "within the believing tradition,"[63] but against Lindbeck's purely coherentist view of doctrine McGrath argues for a correspondence between doctrinal statements and theological reality: "Christian theology aims to offer a coherent account of a reality to which it ultimately refers."[64] Further, while Lindbeck denies the possibility of any meta-traditional points of contact between different

---

[57] J. W. van Huyssteen, *Essays in Postfoundationalist Theology.* Grand Rapids, MI: Eerdmans, 1997, 226, defines "foundationalism" as "the thesis that our beliefs can be warranted or justified by appealing to some item of knowledge that is self-evident or beyond doubt."

[58] McGrath, *Scientific Theology*, 2:29. Other positive appraisals of the demise of foundationalism include van Huyssteen, *Essays in Postfoundationalist Theology*; and S. J. Grenz, *Renewing the Center: Evangelical Theology in a Post-Theological Era.* Grand Rapids, MI: Baker, 2000, 184–217.

[59] McGrath, *Scientific Theology*, 2:34–5.

[60] Ibid, 2:36. On the importance of holistic belief-systems, cf. Nancey Murphy, "Postmodern Apologetics, or why Theologians *must* pay attention to Science." In *Religion and Science: History, Method, Dialogue*, edited by W. Mark Richardson and Wesley J. Wildman, 104–20. New York: Routledge, 1996.

[61] McGrath, *Scientific Theology*, 2:38.

[62] Ibid, 2:39–54. Cf. G. A. Lindbeck, *The Nature of Doctrine: Religion and Theology in a Postliberal Age.* Philadelphia: Westminster, 1984. For McGrath's earlier engagement with Lindbeck, see A. E. McGrath, *The Genesis of Doctrine: A Study in the Foundation of Doctrinal Criticism.* Oxford: Blackwell, 1990, ch. 2; and *A Passion for Truth: The Intellectual Coherence of Evangelicalism.* Downers Grove, IL: Intervarsity Press, 1996, ch. 3.

[63] McGrath, *Scientific Theology*, 2:41.

[64] Ibid, 2:53–4.

belief-systems, McGrath regards natural theology as a "meta-traditional device" by which the Christian tradition may engage in dialogue with other traditions, since nature itself (although always interpreted in a tradition-specific way) is a publicly accessible reality.[65] Although the "myth of universal rationality" has now expired,[66] so that we are left only with a plurality of rationalities,[67] a Christian natural theology nevertheless provides a means of engagement with other traditions and belief-systems. The Christian doctrine of creation, for example, offers to explain problems which the natural sciences cannot explain, such as the order and uniformity of creation, and the fact that the natural world "has a rationality which human rationality can discern and systematize."[68] In this way, the tradition-specific Christian understanding of creation offers both intra-systemic and extra-systemic insights into reality.[69]

A Christian natural theology therefore allows the Christian tradition to position other disciplines and traditions. The Christian story offers "a coherent organizing logic which accounts for its own existence, as well as that of its rivals," so that although "there is no *grand récit* [metanarrative] which commands universal assent," Christian theology's own *récit* allows it to "evaluate and critique other traditions and narratives."[70] Indeed, Christianity's tradition-specific rationality allows the Christian tradition to explain why other traditions exist, and to offer a compelling account of the intelligibility of the universe and the intelligence of its human interpreter.[71]

According to McGrath, a scientific theology is therefore able to hold together both "intra-systemic coherence" and "extra-systemic correspondence," that is, it can offer a belief-system which is internally consistent and which is grounded in the structures of reality.[72] Theology is in this way able to appropriate the valid insights of both Enlightenment objectivism and postmodern social constructivism, without capitulating to the one-sidedness of either.

Turning to an explicit exploration of realism, McGrath observes that all existing rationalities have in common an attempt to engage with an external

---

[65] Ibid, 2:54.
[66] Ibid, 2:60.
[67] Ibid, 2:63. Here McGrath draws especially on A. MacIntyre, *Whose Justice? Which Rationality?* London: Duckworth, 1988.
[68] McGrath, *Scientific Theology*, 2:75. Cf. McGrath, *The Re-Enchantment of Nature*, 21–2; and A. R. Peacocke, *Science and the Christian Experiment*. Oxford: Oxford University Press, 1971, 132–5.
[69] McGrath, *Scientific Theology*, 2:76.
[70] Ibid, 2:78.
[71] Ibid, 2:86.
[72] Ibid, 2:56.

reality.[73] A basic assumption of both natural science and theology is that there is a reality independent of the human mind, which is intelligible in spite of the "inescapable historicity" of the human subject.[74] This assumption of an intelligible reality is not, however, an *a priori* dogma either in science or in theology, but rather it is the outcome of an engagement with the world, and so is "an *empirical* thesis."[75] McGrath thus critiques postmodern anti-realism, noting that postmodern thinkers have typically failed to reckon seriously with the explanatory successes of the natural sciences.[76] Indeed, the postmodern assertion of the pure social construction of scientific theories constitutes "little more than sociological imperialism,"[77] and rests on a lack of actual scientific knowledge.[78] McGrath argues that postmodern anti-realism has in fact defeated itself, and that although knowledge is socially produced it is not finally reducible to sociological factors.[79]

McGrath therefore advocates a critical realism[80] which neither absolutizes the social location of knowledge, as in postmodern thought, nor denies this social location, as in foundationalist thought.[81] Critical realism recognizes "the active involvement of the knower in the process of knowing";[82] in the words of N. T. Wright, knowledge "is never itself independent of the knower," even though in principle it "concern[s] realities independent of the knower."[83]

---

[73] Ibid, 2:120.

[74] Ibid, 2:122. Cf. J. Polkinghorne, *Belief in God in an Age of Science.* New Haven, CT: Yale University Press, 1998, 109–10.

[75] McGrath, *Scientific Theology,* 2:123–4.

[76] Ibid, 2:178.

[77] Ibid, 2:184.

[78] Ibid, 2:189.

[79] Ibid, 2:192. Although McGrath's critique of postmodern anti-realism is useful, at points it exhibits an insufficient appreciation of poststructuralist insights and a failure to engage seriously with poststructuralist thinkers on their own terms. See especially the comments on Derrida (2:179–80) and the puzzling foundationalist criticism that deconstruction "offers no secure foundation for any intellectual system" (2:165).

[80] For an introduction to contemporary approaches to critical realism, see J. López and G. Potter, eds., *After Postmodernism: An Introduction to Critical Realism.* London: Athlone, 2001.

[81] McGrath, *Scientific Theology,* 2:193.

[82] Ibid, 2:196.

[83] N. T. Wright, *The New Testament and the People of God.* London: SPCK, 1992, 35; cited in McGrath, *Scientific Theology,* 2:196.

McGrath develops the contours of his critical realism in dialogue with the sociological philosopher Roy Bhaskar,[84] who elucidates the "complex interplay of the realm of the socially constructed and the ontologically given."[85] For Bhaskar, "it is the nature of the object that determines the form of its possible science."[86] Ontology determines epistemology. Therefore, each intellectual discipline must, McGrath argues, adopt a methodology which is appropriate to its own specific object.[87] This approach to knowledge clearly "forbids the sociological imperialism which insists upon the reduction of everything to social categories."[88] Further, in contrast to the sharp Kantian division between phenomena and noumena, critical realism affirms that surface appearances are "the experiential, or empirical, aspect of deeper structures ... about which it is possible to gain knowledge."[89]

Moreover, this critical realist approach affirms that reality is stratified,[90] and that different methods must be used for the investigation of the different strata of reality.[91] Especially important here is the insight that the reality of God and the contingent reality of creation are distinct yet related strata of reality, each with its own ontology and hence its own proper method of investigation.

---

[84] See McGrath, *Scientific Theology*, 2:209–26. For McGrath's earlier account of critical realism, before he had appropriated Bhaskar's insights, see *Foundations of Dialogue in Science and Religion*, 140–64.

[85] McGrath, *Scientific Theology*, 2:210.

[86] R. Bhaskar, *The Possibility of Naturalism: A Philosophical Critique of the Contemporary Human Sciences*. London: Routledge, 1998, 3; cited in McGrath, *Scientific Theology*, 2:217.

[87] McGrath, *Scientific Theology*, 2:225. Cf. J. W. van Huyssteen, "Postfoundationalism in Theology and Science: Beyond Conflict and Consonance," in *Rethinking Theology and Science: Six Models for the Current Dialogue*, ed. N. H. Gregersen and J. W. van Huyssteen (Grand Rapids, MI: Eerdmans, 1998), 45: since God is personal, theology and science are "very different kinds of activities, each with its own rules in its own domain, but neither one necessarily less rational than the other."

[88] McGrath, *Scientific Theology*, 2:217.

[89] Ibid, 2:213. Cf. Bhaskar, *The Possibility of Naturalism*, 9–13.

[90] As examples of theological stratification, McGrath cites Barth's doctrine of the threefold form of the Word of God and Torrance's account of the stratification of trinitarian doctrine. Nevertheless, McGrath is less concerned with this kind of "horizontal," epistemological stratification, and more concerned with the "vertical," ontological stratification of reality. Thus he identifies nature (understood as creation), history (viewed as the arena of divine revelation), and experience (interpreted in a theological framework) as three of the basic strata with which Christian theology must engage (2:240–4).

[91] McGrath, *Scientific Theology*, 2:218.

According to McGrath there is a created correspondence between these strata: God's "creative and redemptive being" is "the most fundamental of all strata of reality," and this reality is in turn "rendered in the created order."[92] But McGrath insists that this correlation between divine and creaturely reality is not a self-evident truth; rather, it is a truth that depends on the doctrine of creation, that is, on revelation.

Having developed and defended his theological realism, McGrath proceeds to explicate the main features of a theological encounter with reality. In the first place, theology is "obligated" to respond to reality, and is responsible for its account of reality.[93] Understood from a realist standpoint, theology can never be merely the free exercise of human creativity; on the contrary, it must be "a response to reality," and "a deliberate and principled attempt to give a faithful ... account of the way things are."[94] Because it must respond to reality, theology must also proceed *a posteriori*: "theological reflection paradoxically *begins* with an actual knowledge of God, and in the light of this proceeds to inquire as to how this knowledge might be possible."[95] Further, because its method is *a posteriori*, a scientific theology must also be *critical*; it must constantly test theological theories and hypotheses against the realities they describe.[96] Part of the task of theology is to critique the vocabulary of faith, in order to ensure that terms are "used and understood as they relate to the object of the Christian faith" and not otherwise.[97]

But above all, if we are to respect the integrity of Christian tradition and to respond adequately to theological reality, a scientific theology must be Christocentric.[98] The central themes of Christian theology, such as the doctrines of the Trinity and of salvation, are not derived from *a priori* ideas about God, but are "grounded in *a posteriori* reflection on the biblical witness to Christ."[99] Engaging constructively with Schleiermacher, McGrath argues

---

[92] Ibid, 2:227–8.

[93] Ibid, 2:247.

[94] Ibid, 2:248. McGrath therefore takes issue with D. Cupitt's "tag-along theology," which "takes its cues ... from whatever happen[s] to be interesting or fashionable at the time" (2:250). McGrath's own approach is especially indebted to Barth's theological realism, with its christological concentration on the primacy of actuality over possibility, and to Torrance's realism, with its correlation between creation and incarnation: see ibid, 2:257–68.

[95] Ibid, 2:269; cf. Torrance, *Theological Science*, 9.

[96] McGrath, *Scientific Theology*, 2:277.

[97] Ibid, 2:289–90.

[98] McGrath develops this point with undue hesitancy in the *Scientific Theology*. In his later abridgement, however, he is more forthright about the importance of Christocentricity: see *Science of God*, 168–9.

[99] Ibid, 2:301.

that it is Jesus Christ who constitutes the basic foundation and criterion of Christian theology.[100] The rational ordering of creation is correlated with the incarnation, so that "to study creation is to study the same *logos* that was incarnated in Christ, and which also shaped the contours of human rationality."[101] Thus Jesus Christ, creation, and human reason are interrelated through their fundamental relationship to the divine *logos*.[102] A scientific theology is therefore a theology "grounded and governed, founded and guided, by the logic of the incarnate Word."[103]

Theory

Having addressed the theological status of nature and of reality, McGrath turns in his third and final volume, *Theory*, to the complex problem of the theoretical representation of reality.

Basic to McGrath's conception of the legitimacy of theory is a profound awareness of the *mystery* of Christian faith. The "supreme task of theology" is to keep alive the wonder and mystery of the vision of God. Theory is an attempt to render in words the mysteries of faith.[104] If ever theological theory becomes a substitute for an engagement with the vision of God, or scientific theory a substitute for an engagement with the wonder of nature, then the outcome can only be impoverishment.[105] But instead of detracting from mystery, theoretical representation should serve the crucial role of "allowing a mystery to be *recognized as such*";[106] and our provisional glimpses of mystery impel us to long for the ultimate eschatological disclosure of reality.[107]

---

[100] Ibid, 2:306.

[101] Ibid, 2:309. For this crucial insight, McGrath is indebted to Torrance: cf. T. F. Torrance, *Divine and Contingent Order*. Oxford: Oxford University Press, 1981, 33.

[102] McGrath, *Scientific Theology*, 2:309.

[103] Ibid, 2:313.

[104] Ibid, 3:3.

[105] Ibid, 3:xv.

[106] Ibid, 3:xiii. Cf. E. A. Milne, *Modern Cosmology and the Christian Idea of God*. Oxford: Oxford University Press, 1952, 1: "all true science" is a "rejoicing in the splendid mysteries of the world and universe we live in."

[107] McGrath, *Scientific Theology*, 3:100. McGrath suggests that negative theology can play a significant role in preserving our awareness of the fundamental limitations of theological comprehension, but he does not sufficiently emphasize the fact that "mystery" is predicated of the divine reality itself, not simply of the limits of human thought. Cf. E. Jüngel, *God as the Mystery of the World*, trans. D. L. Guder. Edinburgh: T&T

In this way, both the importance of theory and the primacy of reality are affirmed.[108]

But a major problem remains: how are we to move from observable particularities to universal theories?[109] And how can we ensure that in this movement the particularities of reality are not displaced by theoretical abstractions? The answer, McGrath suggests, lies principally in a rigorously *a posteriori* theological method. General theories must be grounded *a posteriori* in the world of particularities, and must arise through a comprehensive engagement with the whole stratified reality of the world.[110] Properly undertaken, then, theoretical representation leads not to a flight from particularities, but to a deeper engagement with them, in which we continually view each particularity "in its inalienable individuality."[111] Theory therefore aims "to offer a representation of reality, which allows us to engage that reality at a new and deeper level, while in no way obliging us to abandon its impact on our imaginations and emotions."[112]

Having thus defended the legitimacy of theory, McGrath develops his critical realist approach in an exploration of the social functions of Christian doctrine and the role of social construction in the development of doctrine. Formal dogma, he notes, is an inevitable feature of Christian tradition because of the church's social need to define its identity and boundaries;[113] certain doctrines function as demarcators between different ecclesial traditions.[114] The social function of a doctrine "is determined by the contingencies of the social situation faced by the ecclesial communities at a given moment in history," so that when historical circumstances change, a doctrine's social function can also change or even become redundant.[115]

Clark, 1983, 245–61; and the statement of K. Barth, *Church Dogmatics* 2/1. Edinburgh: T&T Clark, 1957, 183: "When we say that God is hidden, we are not speaking of ourselves, but, taught by God's revelation alone, of God."

[108] McGrath, *Scientific Theology*, 3:xv.

[109] See ibid, 3:31: a suspicion of universals is "the natural epistemological attitude of a scientific theology."

[110] Ibid, 3:13.

[111] Ibid, 3:43.

[112] Ibid, 3:36.

[113] Ibid, 3:64.

[114] Ibid, 3:75. As an example of the social function of doctrine, McGrath discusses the New Perspective on Paul. It is, he says, legitimate to suggest that the Pauline doctrine of justification constitutes "a theoretical justification for the separation of Gentile Christian communities from Judaism," but this should not lead to the conclusion that the doctrine "is solely a social epiphenomenon." Although its ecclesial function may be socially constructed, this does not mean that the doctrine is a mere invention or that it lacks broader theoretical significance (3:68–9).

[115] Ibid, 3:75.

This understanding of the changing social function of doctrine is of considerable ecumenical importance. In ecumenical rapprochement, "it is not the truth of certain doctrines that is being denied or marginalized," but instead "a social function of those doctrines, specific to a past age, is declared to be no longer valid."[116] Ecumenical dialogue on the doctrine of justification, for instance, involves the recognition that this particular doctrine is no longer centrally important to the identity of Protestantism, so that the doctrine need no longer function as a marker of social division between Protestantism and other ecclesial communities.[117]

But an understanding of the social function of doctrine need not weaken or relativize theological truth-claims. Although theological theory is socially constructed, it nevertheless represents reality. In exploring the way theoretical statements represent reality, McGrath's basic realist insight remains decisive: "Ontology determines epistemology."[118] Each level of reality may demand not only its own mode of investigation but also a correspondingly distinct mode of representation. Theoretical representation often demands advances in human language; existing language is adopted and reinterpreted in the service of theological representation, and at times new vocabulary is developed in order to represent the discovery of new entities and the uncovering of new structures.[119]

Further, as well as using technical terms and propositions, Christian theology must employ analogies in order to speak responsibly of God. According to McGrath, the possibility of analogical representation is grounded in the doctrine of creation, which affirms "created correspondences between humanity, the world and their divine creator."[120] Against Barth, McGrath defends the analogy of being (*analogia entis*) as articulated by Thomas Aquinas and Erich Przywara. The *analogia entis*, McGrath argues, is "theologically *derivative*, rather than theologically *autonomous*,"[121] for it is grounded in a doctrine of creation. Thus the capacity of the created order to represent God analogically is a revealed rather than a natural insight. But although analogies are *possible* because of creation, the justification of their *actual* use lies not in their intrinsic

---

[116] Ibid.
[117] Ibid, 3:75–6.
[118] Ibid, 3:82.
[119] As McGrath notes (3:86), the most significant example of new vocabulary is Athanasius' recognition that in spite of existing biblical language the term *homoousion* was needed to articulate the church's deepening understanding of the identity of Jesus Christ.
[120] Ibid, 3:108.
[121] Ibid, 3:111.

capacity to represent God but only in their "divine authorization."[122] The analogy of faith (*analogia fidei*) therefore presupposes the analogy of being, but it is only the former, not the latter, which may properly be employed in theological representation.[123] And since the representation of complex realities requires multiple models, theology cannot represent reality by any single analogy, but only by "a network of interlocking images."[124]

McGrath further argues that theology must seek to explain not only reality, but also the past development and present form of the Christian tradition itself. McGrath's analysis of this explanatory task of theology is centered on the idea of revelation, understood from a critical realist perspective which affirms both the Christian tradition's objective encounter with reality and the tradition-specific social construction of theory. Christian theology, McGrath notes, is confronted with various levels of social construction with historical, literary, institutional, and experiential features, which together constitute the developing Christian tradition.[125] These levels of the tradition were all "brought into existence, or given a new depth of meaning, as a result of the original revelatory events which lie behind them."[126] McGrath understands revelation as essentially a past event in history: the proper question is not "What is revelation?" but "What *was* revelation?"[127] Although we do not presently experience revelation, we now encounter its "aftermath," its "indentation in the historical process."[128] We therefore know what revelation is by its

---

[122] Ibid, 3:114. Here McGrath claims to be in agreement with the basic intention of Barth's polemic against the *analogia entis*.

[123] Ibid, 3:125.

[124] Ibid, 3:126. Thus McGrath suggests that at times (e.g., in christology) seemingly contradictory analogies can exist in a relationship of complementarity, not unlike the complementarity of the classical wave and particle models of light in quantum theory (3:126–31). But on the concept of complementarity, see the criticisms of R. H. McKenzie, "Foundations of the Dialogue between the Physical Sciences and Theology," *Perspectives on Science and Christian Faith* 56: 4 (2004), 247.

[125] Ibid, 3:153.

[126] Ibid, 3:146.

[127] Ibid, 3:150–1. McGrath's understanding of revelation and history is partly indebted to A. Richardson, *History, Sacred and Profane*. London: SCM, 1964. For McGrath's engagement with the problem of revelation and history in German-language theology, see A. E. McGrath, *The Making of Modern German Christology, 1750–1990*. Leicester: Apollos, 1994.

[128] McGrath, *Scientific Theology*, 3:151. McGrath borrows the metaphor from K. Barth, *The Epistle to the Romans*, trans. E. C. Hoskyns. Oxford: Oxford University Press, 1933, 29, but he turns it on its head. For while highlighting the historical singularity of revelation, Barth's intention is precisely *not* to restrict revelation to the past.

historical effects – such as scripture, ecclesiastical institutions, and the liturgy – all of which both "point to something decisive having happened" and mediate the significance of this historical "something."[129] Just as cosmology traces the universe back to its initial conditions and biology traces the human species back to its primitive ancestry, so theology must determine the nature of the revelation which first gave rise to the Christian tradition[130] – and this revelation consists, in short, of "the words and deeds of God in history, culminating in the death and resurrection of Jesus Christ."[131]

The past revelation is, moreover, "charged with significance" for the present and the future,[132] and the transmission of revelation is therefore the continual responsibility of the Christian community. Here McGrath draws on Rudolf Bultmann's thesis that "continuity with the identity-giving past" can be maintained in the present through the kerygma, in which the significance of Christ is transmitted both *to* and *through* history.[133] The concept of revelation thus explains the existence and development of the Christian tradition; and in order to exert an ongoing influence on that tradition, revelation must be historically transmitted through the Christian community. But the importance of revelation in shaping tradition does not mean that doctrine develops "organically" or in any simple trajectory of progress.[134] Rather, using "Neurath's ship" as a model,[135] McGrath describes a complex pattern of doctrinal development which involves an ongoing process of the interpretation of the biblical witness and the exploration and reception of different theological models.[136]

Finally, McGrath's *Scientific Theology* closes with a discussion of the role of metaphysics in theological reflection. In response to positivist denials of the possibility of metaphysics and postmodern anti-realist critiques of metaphysics,

---

[129] McGrath, *Scientific Theology*, 3:152–3.

[130] Ibid, 3:151. Here McGrath finds a model in Schleiermacher, who argues back from present religious experience to its historical cause in the person of Jesus of Nazareth: see ibid, 3:162–4.

[131] Ibid, 3:164.

[132] Ibid, 3:176–7.

[133] Ibid, 3:189–90. This is a useful appropriation of Bultmann's thought, but McGrath seems strangely untroubled by the deeper problem which Bultmann sought to address, namely, the question of how the event of revelation becomes *contemporaneous with* (not merely historically "transmitted to") our present historical existence.

[134] Here McGrath critiques J. H. Newman's view of the organic development of doctrine: see ibid, 3:216–17.

[135] Ibid, 3:217–21; cf. 2:34–5.

[136] Ibid, 3:234–5.

McGrath argues that if metaphysical claims are made *a posteriori*, then they may constitute a legitimate aspect of theological reflection.[137] The question of metaphysics is simply: "What must be true or [must] exist that is *unobservable* if what is *observable* is to be explained?"[138] Following Luther and Eberhard Jüngel, McGrath argues that theology should exclude only *a priori* metaphysical commitments. A scientific theology is free to engage in *a posteriori* metaphysical reflections which are "generated and governed by the act of revelation."[139] Such an engagement may lead to a responsible metaphysics which, instead of being determined in advance, is grounded in and determined by reality itself.[140]

Therefore, just as a scientific theology does not presuppose any specific epistemology, so also it does not presuppose any particular metaphysics. For theology is "a response to its distinctive object, whose character cannot be determined in advance of an engagement with that object."[141] For this reason, we can always only keep "an open mind as to what the intellectual consequences of revelation might be."[142]

Conclusion

"As the Princeton ethical philosopher Jeffrey Stout once commented, writing on method is a bit like clearing your throat before beginning a lecture. You can only go on for so long before the audience starts to get a little restless."[143] With this anecdote, McGrath apologizes for the length and detail of his methodological reflections.

But no such apology is needed. With immense learning and considerable sophistication, McGrath's *Scientific Theology* presents a theology of nature, a defense of the objectivity and knowability of the real world, and an account of the theoretical representation of reality. The whole work develops its argument through extensive engagement with the history of theology and the philosophy of science, while its most decisive formulations remain grounded in the witness

---

[137] Ibid, 3:244.
[138] Ibid, 3:274. Thus McGrath criticizes functional rather than ontological approaches to christology for simply deferring the central christological question: "Who must Jesus Christ *be* if he is able to have this impact?" (3:283–4).
[139] Ibid, 3:289.
[140] Ibid, 3:293.
[141] Ibid, 3:294.
[142] Ibid.
[143] Ibid, 3:296.

of scripture. McGrath's passionate concern to integrate scientific and theological methods is balanced and enriched at every point by his concern to maintain the integrity of theology and by his commitment to an evangelical orthodoxy deeply rooted in the ecumenical faith of Christian tradition. What emerges is a uniquely sustained and wide-ranging demonstration of the methodological value of natural science as a dialogue-partner for and aid to theological reflection.

As well as demonstrating the role of natural science as a handmaid of theology (*ancilla theologiae*), McGrath's *Scientific Theology* offers – perhaps most importantly of all – "an apologia for the entire theological enterprise itself."[144] While British theologians have often been insensitive to the need to give an account of Christian theology as a distinctive discipline, McGrath follows the great European tradition of Schleiermacher and Barth in presenting theology as a legitimate intellectual discipline with its own proper object, identity, methods, and limitations.[145] And precisely by accentuating the distinctiveness and integrity of theology, McGrath is able to highlight the sheer freedom of theology to learn from its contemporary intellectual environment and to engage constructively with the natural sciences and other disciplines.

The entire *Scientific Theology* thus defends the possibility of a "coherent systematic theology" which engages deeply with the working methods of the natural sciences.[146] To produce such a systematic theology, provisionally entitled *A Scientific Dogmatics*,[147] is the task McGrath has now set himself, so that this whole project of theological method has in fact become a prolegomenon to a future systematic theology.

McGrath's *Scientific Theology* is one of the most sustained and sophisticated theological engagements with natural science yet produced, and one of the most important works on theological method to have appeared in recent years. Its nuanced critical realist vision of the nature and task of theology will offer a valuable stimulus to theological reflection in the future.

---

[144] Ibid, 3:297.

[145] On theology as a distinctive discipline, see also McGrath, *Thomas F. Torrance*, 205–11.

[146] McGrath, *Scientific Theology*, 3:296.

[147] McGrath, "Contributors: An Appreciation and Response," 342. McGrath predicts a three-volume work of dogmatics after some ten years of research and writing.

CHAPTER 2

Is a "Scientific Theology" Intellectual Nonsense? Engaging with Richard Dawkins

The basic assumption of a scientific theology is that there can be a fundamental synergy between the working methods and assumptions of the natural sciences and Christian theology. This raises a number of questions, by far the most important of which is whether this proposal is fatally flawed from the outset. Is there not such a fundamental divergence – no, more than that, a fundamental *contradiction* – between Christian theology and the natural sciences that such a dialogue is impossible, illicit, and devoid of significance?

That is certainly the view of Richard Dawkins, widely regarded as the most high profile and aggressive advocate of the "science has eliminated God" school of thought in the English-speaking world. In view of the importance of this viewpoint, it is imperative that we consider it in a little more detail, before returning to the themes of this book. As Dawkins is perhaps the most widely read critic of any theological account of reality, it is clearly appropriate to debate him on this critical issue. His profile as a popularizer of the natural sciences is such that I am under both a moral and intellectual obligation to respond to him.

But there is a second aspect of Dawkins' persona which demands a response. He is more than a scientific popularizer; he is a *public intellectual* who has done much to give credence to a series of ideas of fundamental relevance to theology, insofar as it sees itself as having a *public* dimension, beyond the walls of the church. As a scientific theology regards itself as a *public* theology, it is clearly of critical importance to engage with the public perception of severe tensions between science and theology.

For Dawkins, science has swept God from the public arena, and relegated him to the margins of our culture. God hangs on in its intellectual and cultural backwaters (such as university faculties of theology) – but only temporarily. It is simply a matter of time before the relentless advance of science finally drives the last memories of God from the human mind, and the world will be a better place as a result. That, in a nutshell, is the popular perception of the take-home message of the writings of this Oxford scientific popularizer and atheist apologist. In this essay, I want to raise some fundamental concerns about this perception. Although it is my intention to be respectful and fair throughout this essay, I think I must make it clear from the outset that I believe that his conclusions concerning both religion and theology are conceptually unsafe, intellectually premature, and inadequately grounded evidentially.

I first came across Dawkins in 1977, when I read his first major book, *The Selfish Gene*. At that time, I was completing my doctoral research in Oxford University's department of biochemistry, under the genial supervision of Professor Sir George Radda, who went on to become Chief Executive of the Medical Research Council. I was trying to figure out how biological membranes are able to work so successfully, developing new physical methods of studying their behavior. It was a wonderful book, considered as a piece of popular scientific writing. Yet Dawkins' treatment of religion – especially his thoughts on the "god-meme" – was unsatisfying. He offered a few muddled attempts to make sense of the idea of "faith," without establishing a proper analytical and evidential basis for his reflections. I found myself puzzled by this, and made a mental note to pen something in response sometime. Twenty-five years later, I finally got round to penning that "something": *Dawkins' God: Genes, Memes and the Meaning of Life*.[1]

In the meantime, Dawkins went on to produce a series of brilliant and provocative books, each of which I devoured with interest and admiration. Dawkins followed *The Selfish Gene* with *The Extended Phenotype* (1981), *The Blind Watchmaker* (1986), *River out of Eden* (1995), *Climbing Mount Improbable* (1996), *Unweaving the Rainbow* (1998), the collection of essays *A Devil's Chaplain* (2003), and most recently *The Ancestor's Tale* (2004). It was impossible to avoid noticing the marked change in both the tone and focus of his writing. As philosopher Michael Ruse pointed out in a review of *The Devil's Chaplain*, Dawkins' "attention has swung from writing about science for a popular audience to waging an all-out attack on Christianity."[2] The brilliant scientific popularizer became a savage anti-religious polemicist, preaching rather than arguing (or so it seemed to me) his case.[3] Yet I remained puzzled. Let me explain.

---

[1] Alister E. McGrath, *Dawkins' God: Genes, Memes and the Meaning of Life.* Oxford: Blackwell, 2004.

[2] Michael Ruse, "Through a Glass, Darkly." *American Scientist* 91 (2003): 554–6.

[3] Interestingly, his most recent book – *The Ancestor's Tale* – conspicuously lacks the characteristic anti-religious polemic of earlier writings.

Dawkins writes with erudition and sophistication on issues of evolutionary biology, clearly having mastered the intricacies of his field and its vast research literature. Yet when he comes to deal with anything to do with God, we seem to enter into a different world. It is the world of a schoolboy debating society, relying on rather heated, enthusiastic overstatements, spiced up with some striking over-simplifications and more than an occasional misrepresentation (accidental, I can only assume) to make some superficially plausible points – the sort of arguments that once persuaded me that atheism was the only option for a thinking person when I was a schoolboy. But that was then. What about now?

The approach I shall adopt in this essay is simple: I want to challenge the intellectual link between the natural sciences and atheism that saturates Dawkins' writings. Dawkins proceeds from a Darwinian theory of evolution to a confident atheistic worldview, which he preaches with what often seems to be messianic zeal and unassailable certainty. If he is right, then the whole enterprise of scientific theology would be at best a disastrous intellectual error, showing a complete lack of judgment on the part of its author, and at worst a complete academic fraud. But is that link between science and atheism anything like as secure as Dawkins would have us believe? It is not my intention to criticize Dawkins' science; that, after all, is the prerogative of the scientific community. Rather, my aim is to explore the deeply problematic link that Dawkins at times merely presupposes, and at other times explicitly defends, between the scientific method and atheism which, if even partly valid, would subvert the scientific theology project.

Since this essay represents a critical engagement with Dawkins, I think it is important to begin by making clear from the outset that I have respect, even admiration, for him in some areas. First, he is an outstanding communicator. When I first read his book *The Selfish Gene* back in 1977, I realized that it was obviously a marvelous book. I admired Dawkins' wonderful way with words, and his ability to explain crucial – yet often difficult – scientific ideas so clearly. It was popular scientific writing at its best. No surprise, then, that the *New York Times* commented that it was "the sort of popular science writing that makes the reader feel like a genius." And although every Homer nods occasionally, that same eloquence and clarity has generally remained a feature of his writing ever since.

Second, I admire his concern to promote evidence-based argumentation. Throughout his writings, we find the constant demand to justify statements. Assertions must be based on evidence, not prejudice, tradition, or ignorance. It is his belief that people who believe in God do so in the face of the evidence that gives such passion and energy to his atheism. Throughout Dawkins' writings, religious folk are demonized as dishonest, liars, fools, and knaves, incapable of responding honestly to the real world, and preferring to invent a false, pernicious, and delusionary world into which to entice the unwary, the young, and the naive.

Douglas Adams recalled Dawkins once remarking: "I really don't think I'm arrogant, but I do get impatient with people who don't share with me the same humility in front of the facts."[4] Perhaps we may wince at the pomposity, which will remind Christian readers of the legendary self-righteousness of the Pharisees. Yet an important insight lies embedded in that sentence: the need to reason on the basis of evidence. Dawkins challenges theologians to exercise vigilance. Why believe this? In fact, why believe anything? I believe that recognition of this need – and the taking of appropriate action on its basis – is fully incorporated into a scientific theology.

As a first step, it will be helpful to lay out the basic reasons why Dawkins is so critical of religion, and dismissive of theology. In this essay, I propose to consider five areas of Dawkins' criticism of religion and theology, identify the trajectory of his argument, and raise concerns about its evidential foundations. These criticisms are dispersed throughout his writings, and it will be helpful to bring them together to give a coherent view of his concerns, and see how they bear on the scientific theology project.[5] While at times I will draw on some insights from Christian theology – and then mostly to correct Dawkins' misunderstandings – it will be clear that most of the points I shall be making are grounded in the rather different discipline of the history and philosophy of the natural sciences. The five areas we shall explore are the following, which I shall summarize briefly, before offering a fuller exposition and criticism in what follows.

1 For Dawkins, the natural sciences possess the capacity to explain the world, eliminating the need to draw upon other intellectual disciplines, such as theology. The conceptual space for theology has been eliminated by scientific advance.
2 More specifically, Dawkins asserts that the scientific method in general, and Darwinism in particular, has made belief in God redundant or an intellectual impossibility. To accept a Darwinian worldview entails atheism. Although this theme permeates Dawkins' writings, it is explored in particular detail in *The Blind Watchmaker*.
3 Dawkins insists that religious faith is nothing more than "blind trust, in the absence of evidence, even in the teeth of evidence,"[6] which is totally inconsistent with the scientific method.

---

[4] Cited by Robert Fulford, "Richard Dawkins Talks Up Atheism with Messianic Zeal," *National Post*, November 25, 2003.

[5] I omit discussion of Dawkins' core belief that religion is evil, malignant, and violent, a moral judgment that is not strictly germane to the purposes of this essay. Readers looking for a response to this may like to consult my *Dawkins' God*.

[6] Richard Dawkins, *The Selfish Gene*, 2nd edn. Oxford: Oxford University Press, 1989, 198.

4 For Dawkins, the reason that belief in God remains widespread is due to the effectiveness of its means of propagation, not the coherence of its arguments. This effective transmission is due to a propagator which Dawkins variously refers to as a "meme" or a "virus," which infects otherwise healthy and sane minds.

5 Religion presupposes and propagates a miserable, limited, and deficient view of the universe, in contrast to the bold, brilliant, and beautiful vision of the natural sciences.

We shall proceed immediately to consider the first of these points.

The Universal Scope of the Natural Sciences

Dawkins represents one of the most eloquent and outspoken proponents of the universal scope of the scientific method. Science is the only reliable tool that we possess to understand the world. This view, found throughout Dawkins' body of writings, is given particular emphasis in *Unweaving the Rainbow*, which can be regarded as a vigorous defense of the universal scope, conceptual elegance, and aesthetic fecundity of the natural sciences.[7] It is an idea that is by no means specific to Dawkins, who here both reflects and extends a reductive approach to reality, found in earlier writers such as Francis Crick.[8]

Yet it is an approach that simply cannot be sustained.[9] In their sophisticated recent critique of the philosophical shallowness of much contemporary scientific writing, particularly in the neurosciences, Bennett and Hacker make three fundamental points which undermine the naive "science explains everything" outlook.[10] In the first place, there is really no such thing as "explaining the

---

[7] Richard Dawkins, *Unweaving the Rainbow: Science, Delusion and the Appetite for Wonder*. London: Penguin, 1998. An interesting evaluation of this approach may be found in Luke Davidson, "Fragilities of Scientism: Richard Dawkins and the Paranoid Idealization of Science." *Science as Culture* 9 (2000): 167–99.

[8] For a particularly aggressive statement of this approach, see Peter Atkins, "The Limitless Power of Science." In *Nature's Imagination: The Frontiers of Scientific Vision*, edited by John Cornwell, 122–32. Oxford: Oxford University Press, 1995.

[9] The sustained critique of such approaches found in the later writings of Mary Midgley should be noted: Mary Midgley, *Science as Salvation: A Modern Myth and its Meaning*. London: Routledge, 1992; *Science and Poetry*. London: Routledge, 2001; *Evolution as a Religion: Strange Hopes and Stranger Fears*, 2nd edn. London: Routledge, 2002.

[10] M. R. Bennett, and P. M. S. Hacker, *Philosophical Foundations of Neuroscience*. Oxford: Blackwell, 2003, 372–6.

world" – only explaining the *phenomena* which are observed within the world. Secondly, building on this point, scientific theories do not, and do not intend to, describe and explain "everything about the world" – such as its purpose. Law, economics, and sociology can be cited as examples of disciplines which engage with domain-specific phenomena, without in any way having to regard themselves as acolytes of the natural sciences. To use the language of the critical realism that underlines the "scientific theology" project, reality is stratified, and each level demands to be investigated and represented using methods and concepts appropriate to that stratum.

In the third place, there are many questions that, by their very nature, must be recognized to lie beyond the legitimate scope of the scientific method – such as how we are to explain the fall of the Roman Empire, the rise of Protestantism, or the outbreak of World War I. A case in point is the question of whether there is purpose within nature. This is generally ruled out of debate within the natural sciences, especially evolutionary biology. Yet this cannot for one moment be taken to mean that this is an illegitimate question for human beings to ask, or to hope to have answered. It is simply an acknowledgment that, by their proper methods and their legitimate application, the natural sciences are not in a position to comment upon it. The question is not being dismissed as illegitimate or nonsensical; it is simply being declared to lie beyond the scope of the scientific method. Dawkins' vigorous espousal of "universal Darwinism" leads him to suppose that this "theory of everything" can account for such things. However, as I hope to show in subsequent essays in this volume, such hopes are theoretically implausible and have yet to be shown to be plausible through their application to date.

Darwinism and the Impossibility of Theology

So what of the legitimacy of theology itself? Dawkins has an admirably simple answer to this question. The evolutionary process leaves no conceptual space for God, and hence none for any legitimate intellectual discipline called "theology" – unless this is understood to be a rational, scientific explanation of the (for Dawkins) pathological or skewed mental processes that lead certain people to believe in God, when no such God exists. Anything that an earlier generation explained by an appeal to a divine creator can be accommodated within a Darwinian framework. There is no need to believe in God after Darwin. Humanity was once an infant. Now, we have grown up, and discarded infantile explanations. And Darwin is the one who marks that decisive point of transition. Intellectual history is thus divided into two epochs: before Darwin, and after Darwin. As James Watson, the Nobel Prize winner and co-discoverer of the structure of DNA put it: "Charles Darwin will eventually be seen as a far more influential figure in the history of human thought than either Jesus Christ or Mohammed."

To be fair to Dawkins, these historically uninformed views, often elevating Darwin to ludicrous levels, are widespread within evolutionary biological circles. For example, in his introduction to the concept of evolution, Ernst Mayr makes the astonishing statement that Darwin's *Origin of Species* "almost single-handedly effected the secularization of science"[11] without any apparent awareness of its historical absurdity. It is perhaps unfair to single out Mayr in this way, as he merely follows the familiar simplified cultural history found in many earlier popular evolutionary writings, which have long since been discredited by serious historical scholarship. Even a cursory reading of the response to Darwin within British and American intellectual circles shows this to be a particularly wild overstatement, a piece of historical nonsense which is accepted as factual simply by endless uncritical repetition of the original error.[12] The reality is far more complex; if one is to speak of the "secularization" of science, it is necessary to consider many more factors, spread over a period of nearly a century, rather than declaring one man, or one book, as having secured such a sea-change in established patterns of thought.

Following this "Darwin changed everything" line, Dawkins argues that, before Darwin, it was possible to see the world as something designed by God; after Darwin, we can speak only of the "illusion of design." A Darwinian world has no purpose, and we delude ourselves if we think otherwise. If the universe cannot be described as "good," at least it cannot be described as "evil" either.[13]

> In a universe of blind physical forces and genetic replication, some people are going to get hurt, other people are going to get lucky, and you won't find any rhyme or reason in it, nor any justice. The universe we observe had precisely the properties we should expect if there is, at bottom, no design, no purpose, no evil and no good, nothing but blind pitiless indifference.

---

[11] Ernst Mayr, *What Evolution Is*. New York: Basic Books, 2001, 9.

[12] See, for example, the groundbreaking historical analysis of David C. Lindberg and Ronald L. Numbers, *God and Nature: Historical Essays on the Encounter between Christianity and Science*. Berkeley: University of California Press, 1986. No historian of science would give any credence to Mayr's statement. At the sociological level, Steve Bruce's comment should be noted: Steve Bruce, *God Is Dead: Secularization in the West*. Oxford: Blackwell, 2002, 117: "No contemporary sociologist of religion argues that Christianity has been fatally undermined by science ... The greatest damage to religion has been caused, not by competing secular ideas, but by the general relativism that supposes that all ideologies are equally true (and hence equally false.)"

[13] Richard Dawkins, *River out of Eden: A Darwinian View of Life*. London: Phoenix, 1995, 133.

But some insist that there does indeed seem to be a "purpose" to things, and cite the apparent design of things in support. Surely, such critics argue, the intricate structure of the human eye points to something that cannot be explained by natural forces, and which obliges us to invoke a divine creator by way of explanation? How otherwise may we explain the vast and complex structures that we observe in nature?[14]

Dawkins' answer is set out primarily in two works: *The Blind Watchmaker* and *Climbing Mount Improbable*. The fundamental argument common to both is that complex things evolve from simple beginnings, over long periods of time.[15]

> Living things are too improbable and too beautifully "designed" to have come into existence by chance. How, then, did they come into existence? The answer, Darwin's answer, is by gradual, step-by-step transformations from simple beginnings, from primordial entities sufficiently simple to have come into existence by chance. Each successful change in the gradual evolutionary process was simple enough, *relative to its predecessor*, to have arisen by chance. But the whole sequence of cumulative steps constitutes anything but a chance process.

What might seem to be a highly improbable development needs to be set against the backdrop of the huge periods of time envisaged by the evolutionary process. Dawkins explores this point using the image of a metaphorical "Mount Improbable." Seen from one angle, its "towering, vertical cliffs" seem impossible to climb. Yet seen from another angle, the mountain turns out to have "gently inclined grassy meadows, graded steadily and easily towards the distant uplands."[16]

The "illusion of design," Dawkins argues, arises because we intuitively regard structures as being too complex to have arisen by chance. An excellent example is provided by the human eye, cited by some advocates of the divine design and direct special creation of the world as a surefire proof of God's existence. In one of the most detailed and argumentative chapters of *Climbing Mount Improbable*, Dawkins argues that, given enough time, even such a complex organ could have evolved from something much simpler.[17]

---

[14] An excellent study of this issue may be found in Michael Ruse, *Darwin and Design: Does Evolution Have a Purpose?* Cambridge, MA: Harvard University Press, 2003.

[15] Richard Dawkins, *The Blind Watchmaker: Why the Evidence of Evolution Reveals a Universe without Design*. London: Longman, 1986, 43.

[16] Richard Dawkins, *Climbing Mount Improbable*. London: Viking, 1996, 64.

[17] *Climbing Mount Improbable*, 126–79.

It's all standard Darwinism. What's new is the lucidity of the presentation, and the detailed illustration and defense of these ideas through judiciously selected case studies and carefully crafted analogies. In that Dawkins sees Darwinism as a worldview, rather than a biological theory, he has no hesitation in taking his arguments far beyond the bounds of the purely biological. The word "God" is absent from the index of *The Blind Watchmaker* precisely because he is absent from the Darwinian world that Dawkins inhabits and commends.[18]

But Dawkins is not going to leave things there. Some might draw the conclusion that Darwinism encourages agnosticism. Far from it: for Dawkins, Darwin impels us to atheism. And it is here that things begin to get problematic. Dawkins has certainly demonstrated that a purely natural description may be offered of what is currently known of the history and present state of living organisms. But why does this lead to the conclusion that there is no God? At the most general level, it is widely agreed that the scientific method is incapable of adjudicating the God-hypothesis, either positively or negatively. It is a simple matter of fact that the scientific method is incapable of delivering a decisive adjudication of the God question, when operating within its proper limits. Those who believe that it proves or disproves the existence of God press that method beyond its legitimate limits, and thus run the risk of abusing or discrediting it.

In a 1992 critique of an anti-evolutionary work which posited that Darwinism was *necessarily* atheistic,[19] Stephen Jay Gould invoked the memory of Mrs. McInerney, his third grade teacher, who was in the habit of rapping young knuckles when their owners said or did particularly stupid things:

> To say it for all my colleagues and for the umpteenth million time (from college bull sessions to learned treatises): science simply cannot (by its legitimate methods) adjudicate the issue of God's possible superintendence of nature. We neither affirm nor deny it; we simply can't comment on it as scientists. If some of our crowd have made untoward statements claiming that Darwinism disproves God, then I will find Mrs. McInerney and have their knuckles rapped for it (as long as she can equally treat those members of our crowd who have argued that Darwinism must be God's method of action).

Gould rightly insists that science can work only with naturalistic explanations; it can neither affirm nor deny the existence of God. The bottom line for Gould is that Darwinism actually has no bearing on the existence or nature of God.

---

[18] The index, of course, is not exhaustive; see, for example, the brief (and somewhat puzzling) discussion of God found in *The Blind Watchmaker*, 141. But the omission is interesting.

[19] Stephen Jay Gould, "Impeaching a Self-Appointed Judge." *Scientific American* 267, No. 1 (1992): 118–21.

For Gould, it is an observable fact that evolutionary biologists are both atheist and theist – he cites examples such as the humanist agnostic G. G. Simpson and the Russian Orthodox Christian Theodosius Dobzhansky. This leads him to conclude: "Either half my colleagues are enormously stupid, or else the science of Darwinism is fully compatible with conventional religious beliefs – and equally compatible with atheism." If Darwinians choose to dogmatize on matters of religion, they stray beyond the straight and narrow way of the scientific method, and end up in the philosophical badlands. Nature is patient of being read in atheist, theist, and agnostic manners – but demands none of these. Either a conclusion cannot be reached at all on such matters, or it is to be reached on other grounds.

We see here an important point, which is integral to the "scientific theology" project – namely, that nature itself is capable of being interpreted in a variety of ways, all of which can be regarded as legitimated by the natural sciences, and none of which are actually necessitated by them.[20] To use a textual metaphor, "nature" is a book which can be read in a number of ways, none of which is self-evidently or necessarily the "right" reading. The book of nature can be read in Christian, atheist, and agnostic ways. None of these are necessitated by the original material; all can be argued to be consistent with it.

One of the most striking things about Dawkins' atheism is the confidence with which he asserts its inevitability. It is a curious confidence, which seems curiously out of place – perhaps even out of order – to those familiar with the philosophy of science. As Richard Feynman (1918–88), who won the Nobel Prize for physics in 1965 for his work on quantum electrodynamics, often pointed out, scientific knowledge is a body of statements of varying degrees of certainty – some most unsure, some nearly sure, but none absolutely certain.[21] Yet Dawkins seems to deduce atheism from the "book of nature" as if it were a pure matter of logic. Atheism is asserted as if it was the only conclusion possible from a series of axioms.

Dawkins presents Darwinism as an intellectual superhighway to atheism. In reality, the intellectual trajectory mapped out by Dawkins seems to get stuck in a rut at agnosticism. And having stalled, it stays there. There is a substantial logical gap between Darwinism and atheism, which Dawkins seems to prefer to bridge by rhetoric, rather than evidence. If firm conclusions are to be reached, they must be reached on other grounds. And those who earnestly tell us otherwise have some explaining to do.

---

[20] A point I stress in Alister E. McGrath, A Scientific Theology 1: Nature. London: Continuum, 2001, 81–133.

[21] See especially Richard P. Feynman, What Do You Care What Other People Think? London: Unwin Hyman, 1989; The Meaning of It All. London: Penguin, 1999.

Faith and Evidence in Science and Theology

Faith "means blind trust, in the absence of evidence, even in the teeth of evidence."[22] This view, found even as early as 1976, is an expression of one of the "core beliefs" that determine Dawkins' attitude to religion, and has played a decisive role in his critique of both religion and theology. While he has at times intensified this core belief (for example, arguing that faith now qualified "as a kind of mental illness"),[23] at no point does he subject this definition to the careful scrutiny that it so clearly demands. Is this *really* what Christians mean by faith? Where does it come from?

As we noted, Dawkins asserts that faith "means blind trust, in the absence of evidence, even in the teeth of evidence." Yet Dawkins offers no defense of his definition, which bears little relation to any religious (or any other) sense of the word. No evidence is offered that it is representative of religious opinion. No authority is cited in its support. In reality, of course, it is Dawkins' own definition, constructed rhetorically with his own polemical agenda in mind, being represented as if it were characteristic of those he wishes to criticize. Yet it is perhaps one of the most transparent examples of a straw man in modern anti-religious writing.

I have no doubt that Dawkins genuinely seems to believe that religious people hold that faith actually is "blind trust." Yet if he is to conduct a public debate, it is important that he operate within agreed definitions. I have no objection to Dawkins criticizing Christian ideas of faith. But I see no reason to permit him to misrepresent those ideas, or develop polemical definitions of "faith" for cheap point-scoring purposes. The simple fact is that no major Christian writer adopts such a definition. This is a core belief for Dawkins, which determines more or less every aspect of his attitude to religion and religious people. Yet core beliefs often need to be challenged. The concept of faith that Dawkins subjects to ridicule is not a Christian understanding of the idea.

At one point, Dawkins turns away from crass generalizations, and engages a Christian writer on the nature of faith. He singles out the late second-century writer Tertullian (ca. 160–ca. 225) for particularly acerbic comment, on account of two quotations from his writings: "It is certain because it is impossible" and "it is by all means to be believed because it is absurd."[24] Dawkins has little time for such nonsense. "That way madness lies." In his view, Tertullian's approach – as evidenced by these two isolated citations – is

---

[22] *The Selfish Gene*, 198.
[23] *The Selfish Gene*, 330 (this passage added in the second edition).
[24] Richard Dawkins, *A Devil's Chaplain*. London: Weidenfeld & Nicolson, 2003, 139.

just like the White Queen in Lewis Carroll's *Through the Looking-Glass*, who insisted on believing six impossible things before breakfast. As this dismissive account of Tertullian is one of the very few occasions on which Dawkins engages with serious representatives of the Christian theological tradition, I propose to take his comments with seriousness, and see where they take us.

First, we need to be clear that Tertullian never wrote the words "it is by all means to be believed because it is absurd." This misquotation is often attributed to him, especially in the writings of Sir Thomas Browne, who Dawkins also cites at this point. But it is a misattribution, and has been known to be such for some time.[25] So at least we can reasonably assume that Dawkins has not read Tertullian himself, but has taken this citation from an unreliable, if influential, secondary source.

Tertullian did, however, write the words "it is certain because it is impossible."[26] The context, however, makes it clear that he is not for one moment arguing for a "blind faith." In this passage, contrary to what Dawkins thinks, Tertullian is not discussing the relation of faith and reason, or the evidential basis of Christianity. The point being made is that the Christian gospel is profoundly counter-cultural and counter-intuitive in its emphasis on the centrality of the death of Christ on the cross. So why would anyone want to make it up, when it is so obviously implausible, by those standards of wisdom? Tertullian then parodies a passage from Aristotle's *Rhetoric*, which argues that an extraordinary claim may well be true, precisely because it is so out of the ordinary. It was probably meant to be a rhetorical joke, for those who knew their Aristotle.

It has been known since 1916 that Tertullian is creatively engaging with some ideas of Aristotle concerning the plausibility of beliefs in this passage. James Moffat, who first pointed this out, notes the apparent absurdity of Tertullian's words, before stressing that this is a superficial judgment:[27]

> This is one of the most defiant paradoxes in Tertullian, one of the quick, telling sentences in which he does not hesitate to wreck the sense of words in order to make his point. He deliberately exaggerates, in order to call attention to the truth he has to convey. The phrase is often misquoted, and more often it is supposed to crystallize an irrational prejudice in his mind, as if he scorned and spurned the

---

[25] For details, see Robert D. Sider, "Credo Quia Absurdum?" *Classical World* 73 (1978): 417–19.

[26] Tertullian, *de paenitentia* v, 4. "Crucifixus est dei filius; non pudet, quia pudendum est. Et mortuus est dei filius; credibile prorsus est, quia ineptum est. Et sepultus resurrexit; certum est, quia impossibile."

[27] James Moffat, "Tertullian and Aristotle." *Journal of Theological Studies* 17 (1916): 170–1.

intelligence in religion – a supposition which will not survive any first-hand acquaintance with the writings of the African father.

But this is only one of a whole series of arguments for the Christian faith that Tertullian brings forward at this point, and it is grossly inaccurate to determine his entire attitude towards rationality on the basis of a single, isolated phrase.[28] Tertullian's attitude to reason is summed up definitively in the following quotation:[29]

> For reason is a property of God's, since there is nothing which God, the creator of all things, has not foreseen, arranged and determined by reason. Furthermore, there is nothing God does not wish to be investigated and understood by reason.

The bottom line is that there are no limits to what may be "investigated and understood by reason." The same God who created humanity with the capacity to reason expects that reason to be used in the exploration and representation of the world. And that's where the vast majority of Christian theologians stand today, and have stood in the past. Sure, there are exceptions. But Dawkins seems to prefer to treat exceptions as if they were the rule, offering no evidence in support of this highly questionable conclusion.

Faith, Dawkins tells us, "means blind trust, in the absence of evidence, even in the teeth of evidence." This may well be what Dawkins thinks; it is not what Christians think. Let me provide a definition of faith offered by W. H. Griffith-Thomas (1861–1924), a noted Anglican theologian who was one of my predecessors as Principal of Wycliffe Hall, Oxford. The definition of faith that he offers is typical of any Christian writer.[30]

> [Faith] affects the whole of man's nature. It commences with the conviction of the mind based on adequate evidence; it continues in the confidence of the heart or emotions based on conviction, and it is crowned in the consent of the will, by means of which the conviction and confidence are expressed in conduct.

It's a good and reliable definition, synthesizing the core elements of the characteristic Christian understanding of faith, while showing the charac-

---

[28] See especially Robert D. Sider, *Ancient Rhetoric and the Art of Tertullian*. Oxford: Oxford University Press, 1971, 56–9.

[29] Tertullian, *de poenitentia* I, 2. "Quippe res dei ratio quia deus omnium conditor nihil non ratione providit disposuit ordinavit, nihil enim non ratione tractari intellegique voluit."

[30] W. H. Griffith-Thomas, *The Principles of Theology*. London: Longmans, Green, 1930, xviii. Faith thus includes "the certainty of evidence" and the "certainty of adherence"; it is "not blind, but intelligent" (xviii–xix).

teristic preacher's concern to have three sermon points, all beginning with the same letter of the alphabet. For Griffith-Thomas, faith "commences with the conviction of the mind based on adequate evidence." Other Christian writers down the ages could easily be cited in support of this point.[31] In any case, it is actually Dawkins' responsibility to demonstrate that his skewed and nonsensical definition of "faith" is characteristic of Christianity through rigorous evidence-based argument. His spurious appeal to Tertullian hardly inspires confidence at this point.

The highly simplistic model of evidence-based reasoning proposed by Dawkins seems to recognize only two options: 0 percent probability (blind faith) and 100 percent probability (belief caused by overwhelming evidence). Yet the vast majority of scientific information needs to be discussed in terms of the probability of conclusions reached on the basis of the available evidence. Such approaches are widely used in evolutionary biology. For example, Elliott Sober proposed the notion of "modus Darwin" for arguing for common Darwinian ancestry on the basis of present similarities between species.[32] The approach can only work on the basis of probability, leading to probabilistic judgments. There's no problem here. It's an attempt to quantify the reliability of inferences. But I see no recognition on Dawkins' part for the need for probabilistic judgments, or to reach conclusions which are warranted – but not conclusively *proved* – by the evidence.

It is interesting to turn from this rather sloppy analysis of how we reach judgments to a more careful piece of argument by Richard Swinburne, formerly Oxford University's Nolloth Professor of the Philosophy of Religion, who uses probability theory to assess the reliability of a belief in God – or, more specifically, the Christian belief that Jesus Christ is God incarnate.[33] I do not expect Dawkins to agree with Swinburne's theistic conclusion, or his provocative calculation of the highly probable existence of God. But I do expect him to show the same careful attention to detail in assessing the relative probabilities of belief and unbelief, instead of his usual populist swashbuckling rhetorical exaggerations. After all, Dawkins, not Swinburne, is meant to be the scientist.

There is, however, another issue of importance here. Many of a more philosophical inclination will want to ask Dawkins a question at this point:

---

[31] I have in mind such works as Richard Swinburne, *The Coherence of Theism*. Oxford: Clarendon Press, 1977; Nicholas Wolterstorff, *Reason within the Bounds of Religion*. Grand Rapids, MI: Eerdmans, 1984; Alvin Plantinga, *Warranted Christian Belief*. Oxford: Oxford University Press, 2000.

[32] Elliott R. Sober, "Modus Darwin." *Biology and Philosophy* 14 (1999): 253–78.

[33] Richard Swinburne, *The Resurrection of God Incarnate*. Oxford: Clarendon Press, 2003.

given that the natural sciences proceed by inference from observational data, how can he be so sure about atheism? At times, Dawkins speaks with the conviction of a true believer about the certainties of a godless world. It is as if atheism was the secure and inevitable result of a seamless logical argument. But how can he achieve such certainty, when the natural sciences are not deductive in their methods?

This difficulty has puzzled me throughout my reading of Dawkins' works. Inference is, by definition, an uncertain matter, in which one must take enormous trouble not to reach premature conclusions. So how come Dawkins is so sure about this? Others have examined the same evidence, and come to quite different conclusions.

As will be clear from what has been said thus far, Dawkins' insistence that atheism is the only legitimate worldview for a natural scientist is an unsafe and unreliable judgment. Yet my anxiety is not limited to the flawed intellectual case that Dawkins makes for his convictions; I am troubled by the ferocity with which he asserts his atheism. One obvious potential answer is that the grounds of Dawkins' atheism lie elsewhere than his science, so that there is perhaps a strongly emotive aspect to his beliefs at this point. Yet I have not come across anything that forces me to this conclusion. The answer has to lie elsewhere.

I began to find an answer to my question while reading a careful analysis of the distinctive style of reasoning that we find in Dawkins' writings. In an important comparative study, Timothy Shanahan pointed out that Stephen Jay Gould's approach to the question of evolutionary progress was determined by an inductivist approach, based primarily on empirical data.[34] Dawkins, he noted, "proceeded by elaborating the logic of 'adaptationist philosophy' for Darwinian reasoning." This being the case, Dawkins' conclusions are determined by a set of logical premises, which are ultimately – yet indirectly – grounded in the empirical data. "The very nature of a valid deductive argument is such that, given certain premises, a given conclusion follows of logical necessity quite irrespective of whether the premises used are true." In effect, Dawkins uses an essentially inductive approach to defend a Darwinian worldview – yet then extracts from this worldview a set of premises from which secure conclusions may be deduced.

Although Shanahan limits his analysis to exploring how Gould and Dawkins arrive at such antithetically opposed conclusions on the issue of evolutionary progress, his analysis is clearly capable of extension to his religious views. Having inferred that Darwinism is the best explanation of what may be

---

[34] Timothy Shanahan, "Methodological and Contextual Factors in the Dawkins/ Gould Dispute over Evolutionary Progress." *Studies in History and Philosophy of Science* 31 (2001): 127–51.

observed within the world, Dawkins proceeds to transmute a provisional theory into a certain worldview. Atheism is thus presented as the logical conclusion of a series of axiomatic premises, having the certainty of a deduced belief, even though its ultimate basis is actually inferential.

Dawkins presents atheism as the only acceptable outcome of a meaningful engagement with the evidence. Yet he seems unwilling to recognize the complexity of determining the "big picture" on the basis of observation. The process of determining the "best explanation" of a complex set of observations is notoriously complex, not least because of the lack of agreement concerning how to determine which explanation is the best.

The severe deficiencies of Dawkins' simplistic take on scientific explanation are best seen by considering the classic study of philosopher Gilbert Harman, who argued that the process of inductive inference which is so characteristic of the natural sciences could be described as "inference to the best explanation."[35] This process – which is perhaps better described as "abduction to the best explanation" – can be envisaged as the process of "accepting a hypothesis on the grounds that it provides a better explanation of the evidence than is provided by alternative hypotheses."[36] The issue is not decisive proof, but the cumulative weight of evidence leading to the realization that one of a number of competing explanations is to be preferred. The question is not which can be proved decisively (for such levels of proof are often far beyond our reach), but which is the best. Or (to slip back into a more Bayesian mode of thinking) which is the most probable.

Perhaps the best-known scientific work to make use of this device of "abduction to the best explanation" is Charles Darwin's *Origin of Species*. It is not without relevance to Dawkins' demands for conclusive proof that Darwin himself was content to work with this method of engagement, which Darwin regarded as necessitated by the complexity of the observational data, and the absence of any means of confirming his theory decisively. In this work, Darwin set out a substantial array of observational data which can be explained on the basis of natural selection, but which cause some difficulties for the then-prevailing theory of the special creation of individual species.[37] It should be noted that William Whewell developed the notion of "consilience"

---

[35] Gilbert Harman, "The Inference to the Best Explanation." *Philosophical Review* 74 (1965): 88–95. For more recent explorations of this critical theme in the philosophy of science, see especially Peter Lipton, *Inference to the Best Explanation*. London: Routledge, 2004.

[36] Paul R. Thagard, "The Best Explanation: Criteria for Theory Choice." *Journal of Philosophy* 75 (1976): 76–92, quote at 77.

[37] Thagard, "The Best Explanation," 74.

as a measure of the explanatory power of explanations, and that Darwin was influenced considerably by this notion in his thinking.[38]

In view of the importance of Darwin to Dawkins' approach to science, we may pause to consider how Dawkins' great hero deals with the question of evidence that does not conclusively prove anything, even though it may seem to point in certain directions. For Darwin, certain critical observations required to be explained.[39] So what was their best explanation, given that a number of competing explanations might be offered?

1 The forms of certain living creatures seemed to be adapted to their specific needs. William Paley and others had proposed that these creatures were individually designed by God with those needs in mind. Darwin increasingly regarded this as a clumsy explanation.

2 Some species were known to have died out altogether – to have become extinct. This fact had been known before Darwin, and was often explained on the basis of "catastrophe" theories, such as a "universal flood," as suggested by the biblical account of Noah.

3 Darwin's research voyage on the *Beagle* had persuaded him of the uneven geographical distribution of life forms throughout the world. In particular, Darwin was impressed by the peculiarities of island populations.

4 Many creatures possess "rudimentary structures," which have no apparent or predictable function – such as the nipples of male mammals, the rudiments of a pelvis and hind limbs in snakes, and wings on many flightless birds. How might these be explained on the basis of Paley's theory, which stressed the importance of the individual design of species? Why should God design redundancies?

These aspects of the natural order could all be explained on the basis of Paley's theory. *The Origin of Species* sets out why the idea of "natural selection" is the best explanation of how the evolution of species took place. Darwin's task was to develop an explanation which would account for these four observations more satisfactorily than the alternatives which were then available. The driving force behind his reflections was the belief that the morphological and geo-

---

[38] See Michael Ruse, "Darwin's Debt to Philosophy: An Examination of the Influence of the Philosophical Ideas of John F. Herschel and William Whewell on the Development of Charles Darwin's Theory of Evolution." *Studies in the History and Philosophy of Science* 66 (1975): 159–81; Richard R. Yeo, "William Whewell's Philosophy of Knowledge and Its Reception." In *William Whewell: A Composite Portrait*, edited by Menachem Fisch and Simon Schaffer, 175–99. Oxford: Clarendon Press, 1991.

[39] S. A. Kleiner, "Problem Solving and Discovery in the Growth of Darwin's Theories of Evolution." *Synthese* 62 (1981): 119–62, especially 127–9.

graphical phenomena could be convincingly accounted for by a single theory of natural selection.

It is essential to appreciate that Darwin himself was quite clear that his explanation of the biological evidence was not the only one which could be adduced. He did, however, believe that it possessed greater explanatory power than its rivals, such as the doctrine of special creation. "Light has been shown on several facts, which on the theory of special creation are utterly obscure."[40]

Darwin's theory had many weaknesses and loose ends. For example, it required that speciation should take place; yet the evidence for this was conspicuously absent. Nor could he explain how nature "remembered" variations, so that they could be transmitted to future generations. Nevertheless, Darwin was convinced that these were difficulties which could be tolerated on account of the clear explanatory superiority of his approach. Although Darwin did not believe that he had adequately dealt with all the problems which required resolution, and was fully aware that he could not prove his theory in the naive sense found in Dawkins's popular scientific works, he was confident that his explanation was the best available:[41]

> A crowd of difficulties will have occurred to the reader. Some of them are so grave that to this day I can never reflect on them without being staggered; but, to the best of my judgment, the greater number are only apparent, and those that are real are not, I think, fatal to my theory.

Darwin here argues that a "big picture" explanation may be offered and accepted without decisive proof. Indeed, it might be pointed out that the nature of the historical process is such that direct verification is impossible; we are forced to rely on inference. Yet this does not invalidate this approach to scientific explanation. It simply means that the level and reliability of explanation is determined by the subject matter under consideration, not by criteria of certainty laid down in advance. This is one of the fundamental themes of a scientific theology: ontology determines epistemology. The way things are determines how they may be known, and how well they may be known. Dawkins seems to import quite inappropriate criteria of reliability for "big picture" issues.

So what criteria might be proposed to determine which is the "best" explanation? Harman himself comments that "such a judgment will be based on considerations such as which hypothesis is simpler, which is more plausible,

---

[40] Charles Darwin, *The Origin of Species*. Harmondsworth: Penguin, 1968, 230.
[41] Darwin, *The Origin of Species*, 205.

which explains more, which is less *ad hoc*, and so forth."[42] This is not, it must be admitted, especially illuminating. For a start, the criteria set forth here can easily conflict with one another.[43] Expanding a theory so that it is capable of explaining more usually involves the addition of extra hypotheses – which renders the theory less simple. Further, as Nancy Cartwright has stressed, there often seems to be an inverse relationship between the simplicity of a theory and its ability to represent the world.[44] A careful examination of the development of scientific theory makes it very difficult to generalize whether there are universally accepted criteria for determining which of several explanations is "the best." The simple fact of the matter seems to be that "the best explanation" is essentially a pragmatic notion.[45]

Christian apologists argue that the "best explanation" of the world is that it is the handiwork of a creator God. They have tended to adopt positions which can be broadly grouped under two headings: the "God of the gaps" and the "big picture" approach. The first, which one tends to find in more popular writings, argues that science is unable to offer a complete account of the world. There are gaps in our understandings. These explanatory deficits, it is argued, can be remedied by an appeal to God.

Now I have offered a caricature of the approach, mainly because I am so persuaded of its deficiencies that I would not myself defend it. It is intensely vulnerable, mainly because the inexorable advance of the scientific enterprise means that gaps tend to get filled. This approach inevitably entails that God is squeezed into smaller and fewer gaps. William Paley's celebrated *Natural Theology* (1802) is widely regarded as adopting such an approach, and is clearly vulnerable at this point, even though some of his critics pointed out that his approach could be salvaged. James Moore has shown in his massive and definitive account of Christian responses to Darwin that there were many who believed that the obvious deficiencies in Paley's account of

---

[42] Harman, "Inference," 89. A theory could be described as *ad hoc* if it is devised for the specific and limited purpose of explaining known phenomena (sometimes also referred to as "retrodiction"). This is to be contrasted with predictive theories, which generate novel predictions not themselves contained in the known observations.

[43] As pointed out by Gerd Buchdahl, "History of Science and Criteria of Choice." In *Minnesota Studies in the Philosophy of Science*, edited by Roger H. Steuwer, 204–30. Minneapolis: University of Minnesota Press, 1970.

[44] Nancy Cartwright, *How the Laws of Physics Lie*. Oxford: Clarendon Press, 1983.

[45] As suggested by Bas van Fraassen, "The Pragmatics of Explanation." *American Philosophical Quarterly* 14 (1977): 143–50.

biological life – most notably, the notion of "perfect adaptation" – were actually *corrected* by Darwin's notion of natural selection.[46]

More importantly, a series of writers discarded Paley's interest in specific adaptations (to use a Darwinian term unknown to him), and preferred to focus on the fact that evolution appeared to be governed by certain quite definite laws – a clear application to biology of the general approach developed in the Middle Ages by Aquinas. The fact that evolution seemed to proceed on the basis of certain principles was itself an indirect confirmation of the divine superintendence of the process.

Yet there is a second alternative, which I believe to be much more intellectually resilient and interesting. This builds on a point which we find in many twentieth-century writers, such as Albert Einstein and Ludwig Wittgenstein, to name but two. The intelligibility of the universe itself requires explanation. It is not so much the gaps in our understanding of the world, as the very comprehensiveness of that understanding, which requires an explanation. *Explicability itself requires explanation.*

This approach is, in my view, much to be preferred. It avoids the apparently fatal problem of historical erosion: what apparently cannot be explained today, can be explained tomorrow. But my reasons for preferring this option are not ultimately pragmatic: they are rooted in the belief that belief in God is possessed of explanatory vitality. "I believe in Christianity," wrote C. S. Lewis, "as I believe that the Sun has risen, not only because I see it, but because by it I see everything else."[47] In concluding his essay "Is theology poetry?" with these words, Lewis was highlighting one of the many difficulties associated with a scientific worldview: that it was, in effect, obliged to presuppose its conclusions.

The ordering of the world, so fundamental an assumption of the scientific method itself, demands to be explained.[48] For Lewis, the Christian faith offered illumination of the world which permitted it to be seen in a certain way – and by being seen in this way, to open up ways of exploring and examining it which resonated with reality. On this approach, it is not gaps in the human understanding of reality that point to the existence of God; it is the very breadth of the human grasp of that reality, which itself requires explan-

---

[46] James R. Moore, *The Post-Darwinian Controversies: A Study of the Protestant Struggle to Come to Terms with Darwin in Great Britain and America, 1870–1900.* Cambridge: Cambridge University Press, 1979.

[47] C. S. Lewis, "Is Theology Poetry?" In *C. S. Lewis: Essay Collection*, 1–21. London: Collins, 2000, quote at 21.

[48] This point is stressed at several points by the physicist and theologian John Polkinghorne. See especially John Polkinghorne, *The Way the World Is.* London: SPCK, 1983; *Science and Creation: The Search for Understanding.* London: SPCK, 1988.

ation at a deeper level. Maybe nothing can be proved for certain – but that hardly stops us asking what that best explanation might be, and holding fast to it, once we have found it. And is that not really what faith is? The quest for the best – whether in terms of truth, beauty, or conduct?

Theology as a Virus of the Mind?

As we noted in the previous section, Dawkins incorrectly believes that religious faith is "blind trust," which refuses to take account of evidence. Given Dawkins' axiomatic assumption of the correctness of an atheist worldview, an obvious question follows: Why do so many people believe in God, when there is no God to believe in? Dawkins' answer lies in the ability of a "God-meme" – a virus-like cultural replicator, which has the ability to transmit itself from one human mind to another, in a process similar to pathological infection.[49]

> Just as genes propagate themselves in the gene pool by leaping from body to body via sperm or eggs, so memes propagate themselves in the meme pool by leaping from brain to brain by a process which, in the broad sense of the term, can be called imitation.

As examples of what sort of things he has in mind when speaking of cultural imitation or replication, Dawkins points to such things as tunes, ideas, catch-phrases, fashions, aspects of architecture, songs – and believing in God.

The "god-meme" performs particularly well because it has "high survival value, or infective power, in the environment provided by human culture."[50] People do not believe in God because they have given long and careful thought to the matter; they do so because they have been infected by a powerful meme. (This idea would later be developed in terms of the imagery of God as a virus.) In both cases, the intent and outcome is a subversion of the intellectual legitimacy of belief in God. The God-meme or God-virus is just good at infecting people.

Dawkins' many critics would, of course, retort that precisely the same must also be true for an "atheism"-meme. Dawkins does not deal with how atheism spreads on the basis of his memetic approach, presumably on account of his core belief that atheism is scientifically correct, and thus requires no explanation. In fact, it is itself a belief, and thus requires the same explanation as

---

[49] *The Selfish Gene*, 192.
[50] *The Selfish Gene*, 193.

belief in God. Dawkins' model actually requires that both atheism and belief in God should be seen as memetic effects. They are therefore equally valid – or equally invalid, for that matter.

The problem with this approach is immediately obvious. If all ideas are memes, or the effects of memes,[51] Dawkins is left in the decidedly uncomfortable position of having to accept that his own ideas must also be recognized as the effects of memes. Scientific ideas would then become yet another example of memes replicating within the human mind. This would not suit Dawkins' purposes at all, and he excludes the notion in an intriguing manner:[52]

> Scientific ideas, like all memes, are subject to a kind of natural selection, and this might look superficially virus-like. But the selective forces that scrutinize scientific ideas are not arbitrary or capricious. They are exacting, well-honed rules, and they do not favour pointless self-serving behaviour.

This represents a case of special pleading, in which Dawkins makes an unsuccessful attempt to evade the trap of self-referentiality. Anyone familiar with intellectual history will spot the pattern immediately. Everyone's dogma is wrong except mine. My ideas are exempt from the general patterns I identify for other ideas, which allows me to explain them away, leaving my own to dominate the field.

But why on earth is conformity to scientific criteria allowed to determine whether a meme is "good" or "useful"? On any conventional reading of things, a "good" or "useful" meme would be one that promoted harmony, gave someone a sense of belonging, or increased life expectancy. These would seem far more natural and obvious criteria for "good" memes. But on further reflection, the truth dawns on us. There are no "natural" criteria involved at all. We decide whether we like them or not, and then label the memes accordingly. If you like religion, it's a "good" meme; if not, it's "bad." In the end, all that Dawkins does here is to construct an entirely circular argument, reflecting his own subjective system of values.

We shall consider the idea of the "meme" in more detail in a later essay in this collection, when we turn to consider the utility of this idea in explaining cultural and intellectual evolution. However, at this stage, it is important to note some major difficulties for the concept of the "meme" itself, as well as its application to anything to do with belief in God, or human culture in general.

---

[51] On which see John A. Ball, "Memes as Replicators." *Ethology and Sociology* 5 (1984): 145–61.

[52] *A Devil's Chaplain*, 145.

The first difficulty for Dawkins' vision of "universal Darwinism" is that it is inadequately grounded in the evidence. In his preface to Susan Blackmore's *Meme Machine* (1999), Dawkins points out the problems that the "meme" faces if it is to be taken seriously within the scientific community:[53]

> Another objection is that we don't know what memes are made of, or where they reside. Memes have not yet found their Watson and Crick; they even lack their Mendel. Whereas genes are to be found in precise locations on chromosomes, memes presumably exist in brains, and we have even less chance of seeing one than of seeing a gene (though the neurobiologist Juan Delius has pictured his conjecture of what a meme might look like).

Dawkins talking about memes often seems rather like believers talking about God – an invisible, unverifiable postulate, which helps explain some things about experience, but ultimately lies beyond empirical investigation.

It is rather difficult to know quite what to make of Dawkins' point that "the neurobiologist Juan Delius has pictured his conjecture of what a meme might look like." Most of us have seen countless attempts to depict God in visits to art galleries or exhibitions. Two examples that readily come to mind are Michelangelo's famous fresco on the ceiling of the Sistine Chapel (1511–12) of God creating Adam, or William Blake's celebrated watercolor known as *The Ancient of Days* (1794).[54] So is Dawkins suggesting that being able to picture the meme somehow verifies the concept? Or makes it scientifically plausible? Delius' proposal that a meme will have a single locatable and observable structure as "a constellation of activated neuronal synapses" is purely conjectural, and has yet to be subjected to rigorous empirical investigation.[55] It's one thing to speculate about what something might look like; the real question is whether it is there at all.

The glaring contrast with the gene will be obvious. Genes can be "seen" and their transmission patterns studied under rigorous empirical conditions. What started off as hypothetical constructs inferred from systematic experiment and observation ended up being observed themselves. The gene was initially seen as a theoretical necessity, in that no other mechanism could explain the relevant observations, before being accepted as a real entity on account of the sheer weight of evidence. But what about memes? The simple fact is that they are, in

---

[53] *A Devil's Chaplain*, 124.

[54] I make use of both these illustrations in a popular work: Alister McGrath, *Creation*. London: SPCK, 2004.

[55] Juan D. Delius, "The Nature of Culture." In *The Tinbergen Legacy*, edited by M. S. Dawkins, T. R. Halliday, and R. Dawkins, 75–99. London: Chapman & Hall, 1991.

the first place, *hypothetical constructs*, inferred from observation rather than observed in themselves; in the second place, *unobservable*; and in the third place, more or less *useless* at the explanatory level. This makes their rigorous investigation intensely problematic, and their fruitful application somewhat improbable.

And what about the mechanism by which memes are allegedly transmitted? One of the most important implications of the work of Crick and Watson on the structure of DNA was that it opened the way to an understanding of the mechanism of replication. So what physical mechanism is proposed in the case of the meme? How does a meme cause a memetic effect? Or, to put the question in a more pointed way: How could we even begin to set up experiments to identify and establish the structure of memes, let alone to explore their relation to alleged memetic effects?

Dawkins' argument for both the *existence* and *function* of the meme is based on a proposed analogy between biological and cultural evolution. The argument can be set out as follows:

Biological evolution requires a replicator, now known to actually exist, namely the *gene*.
So, by analogy:
Cultural evolution also requires a replicator, which is hypothesized to be the *meme*.

It is a brave and bold move. But is it right? Does this analogy actually work? And what is the hard, observational evidence for memes, which demands that we accept this hypothetical concept as a necessary and fruitful means of explaining cultural development?

As has often been demonstrated, analogical argumentation is an essential element of scientific reasoning.[56] The perception of an analogy between A and B is often the starting point for new lines of inquiry, opening up new and exhilarating frontiers. Yet that same perception has often led to scientific dead ends, including the long-abandoned ideas of "calorific" and "phlogiston." As Mario Bunge points out, analogies have a marked propensity to mislead in the sciences.[57] So is this posited analogy between gene and meme in the first place *real*, and in the second *helpful*?

The real issue is the limits of analogical argumentation in the natural sciences, which becomes particularly significant in the case of evolutionary theory. The implicit assumption seems to be that, since the transmission of

---

[56] Daniel Rothbart, "The Semantics of Metaphor and the Structure of Science." *Philosophy of Science* 51 (1984): 595–615.
[57] Mario Bunge, *Method, Model, and Matter*. Dordrecht: D. Reidel, 1973, 125–6.

culture and the transmission of genes are analogical processes, the well-developed concepts and methods of neo-Darwinism can explain both. Yet it is an analogy that has been proposed, not demonstrated. And the limits of argument by analogy are well known to any historian of science – think, for example, of the fruitless quest for "the ether," resulting from the belief that light and sound were analogous.

A more fundamental point is that the Darwinian paradigm seems ill-adapted to deal with cultural or intellectual development – a matter to which we shall return in more detail in a later chapter. Although that is now my considered judgment after twenty-five years researching in the development of intellectual and cultural history, I will fully concede that at an earlier stage in my career, I believed that the "memetic" approach had real potential as an explanatory model for historical theology in general, and the issue of doctrinal development in particular.

My own interest in intellectual history developed at more or less the same time as Dawkins first set out the "meme"-theory. When I first encountered the idea of the "meme" in 1977, I found it immensely exciting. Here was something which was potentially open to rigorous evidence-based investigation, offering new possibilities for the study of intellectual and cultural development. Why was I so optimistic about the idea? I was in the process of beginning what would be one of my lifetime concerns: the history of ideas. My particular interest lay in how religious ideas develop over time, and the factors that lead to their development, modification, acceptance, or rejection, and – at least in some cases – their slow decline into oblivion.

The "meme," I thought at the time, would allow me to develop robust and reliable models for intellectual and cultural development, firmly grounded in observational evidence. Yet, as I began to develop my research, I found myself coming up against serious obstacles in practically every area of intellectual activity I investigated. One was that the meme didn't really explain anything. It was an interesting redundancy, which added little, if anything, to the predictive and analytical power of other models. I shall return to this point presently.

The second difficulty is that Darwinism itself seems very poorly adapted to account for the development of culture, or the overall shape of intellectual history. When I researched the rise of atheism during its "Golden Age" (1789–1989),[58] I was struck by the purposefulness of the contemporary retrieval of the older atheisms of writers such as Xenophanes or Lucretius. These ideas were deliberately reappropriated. Their revival did not just happen; it was *made to happen* in order to achieve a specific goal. The

---

[58] See Alister E. McGrath, *The Twilight of Atheism*. New York: Doubleday, 2004.

process was strongly teleological, driven by precisely the purpose and intentionality that Darwinian orthodoxy excludes from the evolutionary process. The same point can be seen in the emergence of the Renaissance. The critical point to appreciate is that the origins, development, and transmission of Renaissance humanism and modern atheism – while admittedly subject at significant junctures to the contingencies of the historical process – was nevertheless *deliberate, intentional*, and *planned*. If Darwinism is about copying the instructions (genotype), Lamarckism is about copying the product (phenotype). We shall return to this point in the next essay, as it merits much more detailed discussion.

The patterns of development I found in the history of the Renaissance – and, I must add, in most of the other intellectual and cultural phenomena I have studied – is, in Dawkins' terms, that of the *blending* of memes, and a clear pattern of intellectual causality which forces us to use a Lamarckian, rather than neo-Darwinian, understanding of the evolutionary process – assuming, of course, that evolutionary biology has any relevance to the development of culture, or to the history of ideas. The use of such terms as "Darwinian" and "Lamarckian" to describe cultural development may just be downright misleading, implying a fundamental analogy where none – other than the passage of time and the observation of change – really exists.

Although now a quarter of a century old, the "science" of memetics has failed to generate a productive research program in mainstream cognitive science, sociology, or intellectual history. It remains speculative and empirically underdetermined. Here is Simon Conway Morris's judgment on the matter: memes seem to have no place in serious scientific reflection.[59]

> Memes are trivial, to be banished by simple mental exercises. In any wider context, they are hopelessly, if not hilariously, simplistic. To conjure up memes not only reveals a strange imprecision of thought, but, as Anthony O'Hear has remarked, if memes really existed they would ultimately deny the reality of reflective thought.

Undeterred, Dawkins developed his meme-concept in another direction: a virus of the mind. "Memes," Dawkins tells us, can be transmitted "like viruses in an epidemic."[60] As with the meme, the key to the "God as virus" hypothesis is *replication*. For a virus to be effective, it must possess two qualities: the

---

[59] Simon Conway Morris, *Life's Solution: Inevitable Humans in a Lonely Universe.* Cambridge: Cambridge University Press, 2003, 324.
[60] *A Devil's Chaplain*, 121.

ability to replicate information accurately, and to obey the instructions which are encoded in the information replicated in this way.[61] Once more, belief in God was proposed as a malignant infection contaminating otherwise pure minds. And again, the whole idea founders on the rocks of the absence of experimental evidence, and the circularity of self-referentiality.

It is meaningless to talk about one kind of virus being "good" and another "evil." In the case of the host–parasite relationship, this is simply an example of Darwinian evolution at work. It's neither good nor bad. It's just the way things are. If ideas are to be compared to viruses, then they simply cannot be described as "good" or "bad" – or even "right" or "wrong." This would lead to the conclusion that all ideas are to be evaluated totally on the basis of the success of their replication and diffusion – in other words, their success in spreading, and their rates of survival. And again, if all ideas are viruses, it proves impossible to differentiate on scientific grounds between atheism and belief in God. The mechanism proposed for their transfer does not allow their intellectual or moral merits to be assessed. Those merits must be determined on other grounds, where necessary going beyond the limits of the scientific method to reach such conclusions.

But what is the experimental evidence for these hypothetical "viruses of the mind"? In the real world, viruses are not known solely by their symptoms; they can be detected, subjected to rigorous empirical investigation, and their genetic structure characterized minutely. In contrast, the "virus of the mind" is hypothetical; posited by a questionable analogical argument, not direct observation; and is totally unwarranted conceptually on the basis of the behavior that Dawkins proposes for it. Can we observe these viruses? What is their structure? Their "genetic code"? Their location within the human body? And, most importantly of all, given Dawkins' interest in their spread, what is their mode of transmission?

We could summarize the problems under three broad headings.

1 Real viruses can be seen – for example, using cryo-electron microscopy. Dawkins' cultural or religious viruses are simply hypotheses. There is no observational evidence for their existence.
2 There is no experimental evidence that ideas are viruses. Ideas may seem to "behave" in certain respects *as if* they are viruses. But there is a massive gap between analogy and identity – and, as the history of science illustrates only too painfully, most false trails in science are about analogies which were mistakenly assumed to be identities.

---

[61] *A Devil's Chaplain*, 135.

3 The "God as virus" slogan is shorthand for something like "the patterns of diffusion of religious ideas seem to be analogous to those of the spread of certain diseases." Unfortunately, Dawkins does not give any evidence-based arguments for this, and prefers to conjecture as to the impact of such a hypothetical virus on the human mind. He also seems to overlook the point that atheism would also be an example of such a "virus of the mind," subject to the same limitations and criticisms as the God-virus. However, Dawkins' touching belief that atheism is a scientifically proven fact blinds him to the obvious deficiency in his thinking at this point. Once more, Dawkins has fallen into the trap of self-referentiality: other people's beliefs are caused by viruses; mine are the result of cool, clinical, objective reasoning.

The "thought contagion" metaphor has been developed most thoroughly by Aaron Lynch,[62] who makes the crucially important point that the way in which ideas spread has no necessary relation to their validity or "goodness." As Lynch puts it:[63]

> The term "thought contagion" is neutral with respect to truth or falsity, as well as good or bad. False beliefs can spread as thought contagions, but so too can true beliefs. Similarly, harmful ideas can spread as thought contagions, but so too can beneficial ideas ... Thought contagion analysis concerns itself primarily with the mechanism by which ideas spread through a population. Whether an idea is true, false, helpful, or harmful are considered mainly for the effects they have on transmission rates.

Neither Dawkins' concept of the "meme" or the "virus of the mind" helps us validate or negate ideas, or understand or explain patterns of cultural development. As most working in the area of cultural development have concluded, it is perfectly possible to postulate and study cultural evolution while remaining agnostic to its mechanism. "All we need to do is recognize that cultural inheritance exists, and that its routes are different from the genetic ones."[64]

---

[62] Aaron Lynch, *Thought Contagion: How Belief Spreads through Society*. New York: Basic Books, 1996.

[63] Aaron Lynch, "An Introduction to the Evolutionary Epidemiology of Ideas." *Biological Physicist* 3, No. 2 (2003): 7–14.

[64] Stephen Shennan, *Genes, Memes and Human History: Darwinian Archaeology and Cultural Evolution*. London: Thames & Hudson, 2002, 63. Shennan cites the work of Luca Cavalli-Sforza and Marcus Feldman in support: *Cultural Transmission and Evolution: A Quantitative Approach*. Princeton, NJ: Princeton University Press, 1981.

Does Theology Impoverish Our View of the Universe?

One of Dawkins' persistent complaints about religion is that it is aesthetically deficient. Its view of the universe is limited, impoverished, and unworthy of the wonderful reality known by the sciences.[65]

> The universe is genuinely mysterious, grand, beautiful, awe-inspiring. The kinds of views of the universe which religious people have traditionally embraced have been puny, pathetic, and measly in comparison to the way the universe actually is. The universe presented by organized religions is a poky little medieval universe, and extremely limited.

The logic of this bold series of assertions is actually rather difficult to follow, and its factual basis seems astonishingly slight. The *Nuremberg Chronicle* (1493) offers us a good illustration of prevailing ideas around this time. The "medieval" view of the universe may indeed have been more limited and restricted than modern conceptions. Yet this has nothing to do with religion, either as cause or effect. It reflected the science of the day, largely based upon Aristotle's treatise *de caelo* ("on heaven"). If the universe of religious people in the Middle Ages was indeed "poky," it was because they trusted the best cosmologists of the day to tell them what it was like. This, they were assured, was scientific truth, and they accepted it. They took it on trust. They were naive enough to assume that what their science textbooks told them was right. Precisely that trust in science and scientists which Dawkins commends so uncritically led them to weave their theology around someone else's view of the universe. They didn't know about such things as "radical theory change in science," which causes twenty-first century people to be cautious about investing too heavily in the latest scientific theories, and much more critical of those who base worldviews upon them.

The implication of Dawkins' unsubstantiated criticism is that a religious view of reality is deficient and impoverished in comparison with his own. There is no doubt that this consideration is an important factor in generating and maintaining his atheism. Yet his analysis of this issue is disappointingly thin and unpersuasive. One of the common themes of much religious writing in the English language from about 1550 to 1850 is that the scientific investigation of the grandeur and glory of nature leads to an enhanced appreciation of the glory of God.[66] Although I see no reason to impute such a base motive to such writers, it was in their interest to exaggerate the beauty and wonders of

---

[65] Richard Dawkins, "A Survival Machine." In *The Third Culture*, edited by John Brockman, 75–95. New York: Simon & Schuster, 1996.

[66] An excellent example being the earlier works of John Ruskin. See Michael Wheeler, *Ruskin's God*. Cambridge: Cambridge University Press, 1999.

the created order, so that a correspondingly greater vision of God might be had. The very slight historical evidence that Dawkins brings forward in support of his extravagant excoriation of religious visions of reality, whether in *Unweaving the Rainbow* or elsewhere, amounts to little more than an observation that our understanding of the vastness and complexity of the universe has increased in recent years.

A Christian approach to nature identifies three ways in which a sense of awe comes about in response to what we observe:

1 An immediate sense of wonder at the beauty of nature. This is evoked *immediately*. This "leap of the heart" that William Wordsworth described on seeing a rainbow in the sky occurs *before* any conscious theoretical reflection on what it might imply. To use psychological categories, this is about *perception*, rather than *cognition*. I can see no good reason for suggesting that believing in God diminishes this sense of wonder. Dawkins' argument at this point is so underdetermined by evidence and so utterly implausible that I fear I must have misunderstood it.

2 A derived sense of wonder at the mathematical or theoretical representation of reality which arises from this. Dawkins also knows and approves of this second source of "awed wonder," but seems to imply that religious people "revel in mystery and feel cheated when it is explained."[67] This is clearly incorrect. The point at issue is whether a purely mimetic approach to reflection is adequate to do justice to the real world. If theory is understood simply as *mimesis*, we are unable to explain the sense of wonder that is occasioned by nature itself, or by art forms.[68]

3 A further derived sense of wonder at what the natural world points to. One of the central themes of Christian theology is that the creation bears witness to its creator, "The heavens declare the glory of the Lord!" (Psalm 19:1). For Christians, to experience the beauty of creation is a sign or pointer to the glory of God, and is to be particularly cherished for this reason. Dawkins excludes any such transcendent reference from within the natural world.

Dawkins suggests that a religious approach to the world misses out on something.[69] Having read *Unweaving the Rainbow* through several times, I still haven't worked out what this is. A Christian reading of the world denies nothing of what the natural sciences tell us, except the naturalist dogma that reality is limited to what may be known through the natural sciences. If anything, a Christian engagement with the natural world adds a richness which I find quite absent from Dawkins' account of things, offering a new motivation for the study

---

[67] Dawkins, *Unweaving the Rainbow*, xiii. See also his extended discussion, ranging from traditional religions to New Age movements, at 114–79.

[68] See the important discussion in Arthur C. Danto, *The Transfiguration of the Commonplace: A Philosophy of Art*. Cambridge, MA: Harvard University Press, 1981, 1–32.

[69] *Unweaving the Rainbow*, xii.

of nature. After all, John Calvin (1509–64) commented on how much he envied those who studied physiology and astronomy, which allowed a direct engagement with the wonders of God's creation. The invisible and intangible God, he pointed out, could be appreciated through studying the wonders of nature.

Dawkins' most reflective account of "mystery" is found in *Unweaving the Rainbow*, which explores the place of wonder in an understanding of the sciences. While maintaining Dawkins' core hostility to religion, the work acknowledges the importance of a sense of awe and wonder in driving people to want to understand reality. Dawkins singles out the poet William Blake as an obscurant mystic, who illustrates why religious approaches to mystery are pointless and sterile. Dawkins locates Blake's many failings in an under-standable – but misdirected – longing to delight in a mystery:[70]

> The impulses to awe, reverence and wonder which led Blake to mysticism ... are precisely those that lead others of us to science. Our interpretation is different but what excites us is the same. The mystic is content to bask in the wonder and revel in a mystery that we were not "meant" to understand. The scientist feels the same wonder, but is restless, not content; recognizes the mystery as profound, then adds, "But we're working on it."

So there isn't actually a problem with the word or the category of "mystery." The question is whether we choose to wrestle with it, or take the lazy and complacent view that this is conveniently off-limits.

Traditionally, Christian theology has been well aware of its limits, and has sought to avoid excessively confident affirmations in the face of mystery. The leading schools of faith have insisted that faith is ultimately a longing, trust, and conviction directed away from ourselves towards its ultimate ground and goal – something that can never be totally or adequately grasped or represented, yet whose reliability is beyond question. Yet the recognition of intellectual limits does not entail conceptual despair or the stifling of the reflective theological enterprise. Christian theology has thus never seen itself as totally reduced to silence in the face of divine mysteries. Nor has it prohibited intellectual wrestling with "mysteries" as destructive or detrimental to faith. As the nineteenth-century Anglican theologian Charles Gore rightly insisted:[71]

> Human language never can express adequately divine realities. A constant tendency to apologize for human speech, a great element of agnosticism, an awful sense of unfathomed depths beyond the little that is made known, is always present to the mind of theologians who know what they are about, in conceiving or expressing God. "We see," says St. Paul, "in a mirror, in terms of a riddle"; "we

---

[70] *Unweaving the Rainbow*, 17.
[71] Charles Gore, *The Incarnation of the Son of God*. London: John Murray, 1922, 105–6.

know in part." "We are compelled," complains St. Hilary, "to attempt what is unattainable, to climb where we cannot reach, to speak what we cannot utter; instead of the mere adoration of faith, we are compelled to entrust the deep things of religion to the perils of human expression."

A perfectly good definition of Christian theology is "taking rational trouble over a mystery" – recognizing that there may be limits to what can be achieved, but believing that this intellectual grappling is both worthwhile and necessary. It just means being confronted with something so great that we cannot fully comprehend it, and so must do the best that we can with the analytical and descriptive tools at our disposal.

A mystery, in the end, is something that we know we can never fully represent, even though we believe that we have managed – whether by our own efforts or by grace – to gain something of an understanding of its depths. Mystery does not imply irrationality; it implies vastness, with inevitable implications for a limited human intellect. It's a recognizable caricature of the idea of "mystery." But it's still a caricature. For Christian theology, a mystery is something which is real, true, and possesses its own rationality – yet which the human mind finds it impossible to grasp fully.

Some years ago, I started learning Japanese. I didn't get very far. The language uses two syllabaries, a complex series of ideographs that I found extremely hard to master, a vocabulary which bears little relation to any of the languages that I knew, and a syntax that seemed completely illogical to my western way of thinking. In short: I couldn't make sense of it. But my failure to grasp the Japanese language represents a failure on my part. Those who know the language assure me that it is rational and intelligible; it's just that I can't get my mind around it.

And it's not just an issue in the area of theology. Any scientific attempt to engage with the immensity of nature – such as the seemingly vast time scale of Darwinian evolution or the emergence of the cosmos – faces the same problems. The idea of a "mystery" is entirely appropriate in the natural sciences. Dawkins himself knows this, as is clear from his derisive comment on postmodern critics of the sciences:[72]

> Modern physics teaches us that there is more to truth than meets the eye; or than meets the all too limited human mind, evolved as it was to cope with medium-sized objects moving at medium speeds through medium distances in Africa. In the face of these profound and sublime mysteries, the low-grade intellectual poodling of pseudo-philosophical poseurs seems unworthy of adult attention.

My point precisely.

There is no way that the idea of "mystery" can be equated with "irrationality," except in the sense that it may be counter-intuitive and beyond full

---

[72] A Devil's Chaplain, 19.

comprehension. A mystery may lie beyond the present capacity of human reason to grasp it; that does not mean it is contrary to reason, as Thomas Aquinas emphasized. The human mind is just too limited to grasp the totality of such a reality, and we must therefore do what we can, while recognizing our limits. We're not God, and hence find what John Donne called "the immense weight of divine glory" difficult to cope with.

Yet Dawkins' critique of theology at this point must surely point to the need to revalidate and restate an authentically Christian natural theology – that is to say, an understanding of the world which celebrates its beauty, admires its complexity, and seeks to understand both what that world is in itself, and what it points to. We shall return to this point presently, as we turn to engage the issues raised by natural theology.

On the basis of the analysis offered in this essay, I believe that it is perfectly legitimate to proceed with the scientific theology project. Dawkins raises a number of important issues, some of which rest on what are obviously misunderstandings. For example, his concept of faith as "blind trust, in the absence of evidence, even in the teeth of evidence"[73] is simply unsustainable, and fails to take account of the role of probabilistic judgments in the sciences, particularly the concept of "abduction to the best explanation." Much of Dawkins' criticism is aimed at straw men, shooting past the fundamental themes of a scientific theology.

Yet not all the points Dawkins raises are based on misreadings or misrepresentation. In particular, he raises two fundamental themes which must be addressed by a scientific theology, partly because it is a public intellectual endeavor, and partly because the issues themselves are of genuine theological importance. In view of their strategic importance for a scientific theology, they will be considered in subsequent essays of this book.

1 Given Dawkins' emphasis on the sciences' "bold and brilliant vision of the universe as grand, beautiful, and awe-inspiring," there is a clear need to revalidate and reconceptualize natural theology, avoiding the theological dead ends that have plagued such enterprises in the past.
2 To what extent, if any, can "universal Darwinism" account for the development of Christian theology? Exploration of this issue would not only be of theological importance; it would also help determine whether the Darwinian paradigm has the universal significance that Dawkins attaches to it.

With this agenda in mind, we turn immediately to engage with the first of these issues: the question of whether the beauty and wonder of nature can adequately be captured by a religious worldview. It is a classic theme of natural theology, a topic that we will explore further in the two following essays.

---

[73] Richard Dawkins, *The Selfish Gene*, 2nd edn. Oxford: Oxford University Press, 1989, 198.

CHAPTER 3

A University Sermon: On Natural Theology

Th'unwearied Sun from day to day
Does his Creator's power display;
And publishes to every land
The work of an Almighty hand.

Thus wrote Joseph Addison in 1712, by concluding an article in the *Spectator* magazine on the intellectual and spiritual excitements of natural theology with an "Ode" which – perhaps rather to its author's surprise – has found its way into the hymnbooks of the English language. Addison's prose and poetry alike took the form of reflection on Psalm 19:1 – "the heavens declare the glory of God." His words pose a question which continues to intrigue us, perhaps because it has never been definitively answered: to what extent do the wonders of the natural world – whether we think of the starlit night sky that Addison could see so clearly from his rooms in Magdalen College, or the rainbows that so excited the Romantic poets – point beyond themselves, to something or to *someone* beyond the world that we can see, hear, and touch?

Since history began, people have been enthralled by the wonder of the sky at night. Few have failed to be overwhelmed by the solemn stillness of the star-studded heavens. The great astronomers of ancient Assyria and Babylon traced the slow movement of the planets through the heavens, wondering if they might somehow shape the mystery of human destiny. The ancient Greeks saw patterns in the stars, and named these constellations after their heroes – Orion the great hunter, Pegasus the flying horse, and Andromeda the doomed heroine. The heavens themselves were mirrors of the great events that had shaped history in the past, and had the potential to shape it again in the future.

Yet not all experienced a sense of wonder when contemplating the starlit heavens. For some, the lonely pinpoints of light against the dark velvet of the night speak of loneliness and pointlessness. Those same stars have witnessed generations rising and falling. Human empires rise and fall; the same stars shone down on them all. The same stars shone while generation after generation flourished, and passed into the dust. Like Tennyson's *Brook*, they remind us of the brevity of human life:

> For men may come and men may go,
> But I go on for ever.

The heavens thus heighten our sense of transience, forcing us to ask whether this life is all that we can hope for. Is there more to life than we know? And can the silent witness of those distant stars help us to find it?

The Rubáiyát of Omar Khayyám, one of the finest works of Persian literature, gives expression to a deep sense of despondency evoked by contemplating the heavens. Khayyám's intellectual interests were wide-ranging, and his astronomical calculations were far ahead of his time. Yet his reflections on the heavens appear to have been sobering, rather than uplifting. We are powerless to change our destiny. The sun, moon, and stars declare both our transience and apparent inability to change our situation.

> And that inverted bowl we call "the Sky,"
> Whereunder crawling cooped we live and die,
> Lift not thy hands to It for help – for It
> Rolls impotently on as Thou or I.

The stars can thus be a melancholy symbol of the vastness of the universe, and our utter insignificance within it. Perhaps the slowly orbiting planets are the secret masters of our destiny, influencing us in ways we could not even begin to understand, let alone to resist. The stars may evoke an unspeakable sense of yearning for something that seems unattainable – a sense of longing for something significant, which the night sky can heighten, yet not satisfy. Maybe the stars point to something mysterious, something unfathomable, which somehow lies beyond them. Something seems to lie beyond the whispering orbs of the night. But what? And how is it to be known?

Questions like these have intrigued people since the human race began to think. Maybe these are pointless questions, the musings of people who cannot cope with the sobering thought of mortality and meaninglessness. Yet maybe we are *meant* to think such thoughts. Maybe the spectacle of the night sky is *meant* to trigger off such ambivalent and unsettling patterns of reflection within us – and by doing so, open the door on a new way of thinking and living. We seem to have been created to ask questions – to try to make sense of what we see around us, and how we fit into the greater scheme of things.

As we reflect on the wonder of the universe, we find questions being raised in our minds that both challenge and excite us. There seems to be some inbuilt longing for purpose which drives us to look for clues to the meaning of the universe. We contemplate the glory of the night sky, wondering if the silent beauty of the stars might cast light on the riddle of human destiny. *L'opinion est comme une patrie* (Claire de Duras). Our view of life, our way of looking at the world, our way of conceiving reality, is the means of opening a door to where we truly belong, to our native land. Is our real homeland out there somewhere, beyond this world? We appreciate the beauty of a glorious sunset, while wondering if the sense of beauty it awakens within us is somehow a pointer to another and more wonderful world that we have yet to discover. Shelley put it like this in a poem of 1824:

> The desire of the moth for the star,
> Of the night for the morrow,
> The devotion to something afar
> From the sphere of our sorrow.

We might thus listen as a distinguished astronomer lectures on the remarkable ordering of the cosmos, and wonder if this might lead us to discover the mind of God. The World War II pilot and poet John Gillespie Magee (1921–41) saw flying high above the earth as an image of a deeper journey:

> I have slipped the surly bonds of earth
> And danced the skies on laughter-silvered wings ...
> Put out my hand and touched the face of God.

Might our hopes and fears allow us to do the same? Or are we like the moth who feels drawn to the distant light of a star, but has no hope of ever reaching this distant and lonely goal?

The sense of wonder evoked by the starry skies or the rainbow thus acts as a pointer to something deeper, something beyond our grasp, yet for which we long with what can easily become a painful, sickening yearning. This "wistful, soft tearful longing" (Matthew Arnold), surrounded by a misty indefiniteness, is fundamentally a longing to be reconnected with something in the universe from which we now feel cut off, to be on the inside of some door which we have always seen from the outside. This sense of longing is not so much a rational judgment grounded in the ordering of the universe, as an imaginative encounter with the world, opening up the question of its deeper meaning. As George MacDonald argued, this kind of encounter with reality "is aroused by facts, is nourished by facts, seeks for higher and yet higher laws in those facts; but refuses to regard science as the sole interpreter of nature, or the laws of science as the only region of discovery." Science may give us access to truth; but can it illuminate meaning? This anxiety about the limits of the natural sciences in our quest for meaning is echoed in the famous 1820 poem "Lamia," in which John Keats (1795–1821) complained of the effect of reducing the beautiful and awesome phenomena of nature to the basics of scientific theory. Such a strategy, he argued, is aesthetically impoverishing, emptying nature of its beauty and mystery, and reduces it to something cold and clinical.

> Do not all charms fly
> At the mere touch of cold philosophy?
> There was an awful rainbow once in heaven:
> We know her woof, her texture; she is given
> In the dull catalogue of common things.
> Philosophy will clip an Angel's wings.

In his important work *Unweaving the Rainbow* (1998), Richard Dawkins takes issue with Keats. Dawkins regards Keats' poetry as typical anti-scientific nonsense, which rests on the flimsiest of foundations. A good dose of basic scientific thinking would have sorted him out in no time.

> Why, in Keats' "Lamia," is the philosophy of rule and line "cold," and why do all charms flee before it? What is so threatening about reason? Mysteries do not lose their poetry when solved. Quite the contrary; the solution often turns out more beautiful than the puzzle and, in any case, when you have solved one mystery you uncover others, perhaps to inspire greater poetry.

Dawkins illustrates this point by drawing attention to the consequences of Newton's analysis of the rainbow:

> Newton's dissection of the rainbow into light of different wavelengths led on to Maxwell's theory of electromagnetism and thence to Einstein's theory of special relativity.

The points that Dawkins makes are important and valid. Perhaps the road from Newton to Maxwell and thence to Einstein was not quite as easily discerned and followed as Dawkins' prose suggests, but the connection certainly exists. And if the unweaving of the rainbow led to the discovery of such greater mysteries (presumably perfectly capable of being expressed poetically, if poets could get their minds around the rather difficult ideas involved), then how can anybody suggest it was a foolish or improper thing to do?

For Dawkins, things are admirably clear. Scientists tell the truth, occasionally in less than inspiring prose; poets, on the other hand, dislike and distrust science, and generally know nothing about it. Dawkins clearly believes that Keats argues that knowing how the rainbow works will destroy its beauty, so that we will not be able to appreciate it any more. It would be like telling a small child that there is no Santa Claus. How silly! Anyone can see that the rainbow remains just as beautiful if we know how it works. In fact, we can appreciate its beauty to the full. Keats wrote these words while he was a young man. When he grew up, he might have become wiser, and learned more about the sciences along the way. According to Dawkins, "Keats believed that Newton has destroyed all the poetry of the rainbow by reducing it to the prismatic colours. Keats could hardly have been more wrong."

Dawkins' refutation of Keats has understandably won many plaudits from some of his fellow scientists, who have welcomed his dismissal of critics who claim that science's tedious and plodding message robs nature of her beauty and inspiration. Yet I cannot help but feel that an important point has been overlooked here. For Dawkins' response to Keats is unassailable *if and only if* Keats' concern was to excoriate the scientific investigation of nature and take refuge in the safety of a premodern world. When Keats is read against the background of the Romantic movement, however, the critique he offers of the natural sciences begins to take on a quite different meaning. Far from refuting Keats, Dawkins in fact confirms precisely the fears that Keats expressed. Let me explain.

The key to Keats' concern lies in his reference to "clipping" an angel's wings. For Keats, as for the classic tradition in general, the natural world is a gateway to the realm of the transcendent. The human reason could grasp at least something of the real world, enabling the imagination to reflect on what it signified beyond itself. Keats (and the Romantic movement at large) prized the human imagination, seeing this as a faculty which allowed insights into the transcendent and sublime. Reason, in contrast, kept humanity firmly anchored to the ground, and threatened to prevent it from discovering its deeper spiritual dimensions. For this reason, we need to treasure C. S. Lewis' enigmatic remark that, "while reason is the natural organ of truth, imagination is the organ of meaning."

For Keats, a rainbow is *meant* to lift the human heart and imagination upwards, intimating the existence of a world beyond the bounds of experience. For Dawkins, the rainbow remains firmly located within the world of human experience, possessing no transcendent dimension. The fact that it can be explained in purely natural terms is taken to deny that it can have any significance as an indicator of a beyond. The angel that was, for Keats, meant to lift our thoughts heavenwards has had its wings clipped; it can no longer do anything save mirror the world of earthly events and principles.

Dawkins' curt, vigorous dismissal of religion or any human quest for the transcendent corresponds precisely to what Keats feared. Despite Dawkins,

Keats does not appear to have had major problems with scientific explanations of the rainbow. His criticisms were directed against those who denied that, precisely because the rainbow could be analyzed scientifically, it could not have any *symbolic* or imaginative significance, both heightening the human yearning for a transcendent realm and hinting at means of its resolution. Dawkins' outright and premature dismissal of any such aspect of life entails a reductionist materialism which denies and eliminates any transcendent dimension to life as some kind of quackery, superstition, or confidence trick (to pick up on just a few of the simplistic anti-religious slogans that grace his writings).

It is a matter for profound regret that Dawkins makes no attempt to empathize with Keats – to try to understand the fear that Keats expresses and its wider resonance within western culture. Keats reacted against precisely such a materialism, which he feared would rob human life of its purpose and meaning. There seems to be a certain inbuilt obtuseness on Dawkins' part here – a studied refusal to take Keats' concerns seriously, dismissing him as a muddled poet who just needed to take Physics 101 to get his weird ideas sorted out.

But why is it that the human mind is able to discern the patterning of the world? Why is it that there appears to be some correspondence between the rationality of the cosmos and our own rationality? If there were not, the universe would remain a mystery to us. Why is it that we are able to represent the structuring and ordering of the world in the language of mathematics, when this is supposedly the free creation of the human mind?

For the Christian, the answers to all these questions converge: because we have been created with the ability to peer into the mind of God. If our reasoning has its source in God, it has the potential to lead us to its fountainhead. Even though it may be attenuated through our weakness and frailty, our created reason retains its God-given ability to guide us to its creator. This stream is both a sign and a navigable channel, which can both point us and take us to its source. And just as that flow of water cannot detach itself from its fountainhead, so the human mind possesses a created capacity to guide us home to God. The resonance between reason, the world, and God is no accident; it is an integral aspect of the Christian doctrine of creation.

The human mind, some argue, is superbly capable of defending itself against thoughts that it finds troubling. There is always one more portcullis to lower, another drawbridge to raise, to prevent the intrusion of threatening ideas – such as personal extinction and the meaninglessness of the cosmic void. Yet it can equally be argued that the mind is finely tuned to discerning signals of transcendence, patterns within the world which point to our origins and destiny lying in God. On this view, God has created us to relate to him, and if we do not do so, we lose sight of our true goal and joy. Without God, we are unfulfilled, precisely because we have been created with a God-shaped gap within us, which cries out to be filled with the luxurious presence of our creator. God has thus fashioned us in such a way that we may begin to gain at least a glimpse of the divine nature and being from the world around us.

This point was made at some length by Bonaventura (1217–74), a medieval philosopher and theologian with a keen eye for the importance of the creation as a guide to its creator:

> All the creatures of this sensible world lead the soul of the wise and contemplative person to the eternal God, since they are the shadows, echoes and pictures, the vestiges, images and manifestations of that most powerful, most wise and best first principle, of that eternal origin, light and fulness, of that productive, exemplary and order-giving Art. They are set before us for the sake of our knowing God, and are divinely given signs. For every creature is, by its very nature, a kind of portrayal and likeness of that eternal Wisdom.

If the world is indeed created, it follows that the beauty, goodness, and wisdom of its creator are reflected, however dimly, in the world around us. All of us have known a sense of imaginative delight at the beauty of the natural world. Yet this is but a shadow of the beauty of its creator. It is a good image, but not the thing itself. The sense of profound, sickening longing that we so often experience when confronted with beauty is not located within nature, but is mediated through it. We see what is good, and realize that something still better lies beyond it. And what lies beyond is not an abstract, impersonal, and unknowable force, but a personal God who has created us in order to love and cherish us.

We have been made to relate to God – to know him. That is one of the most fundamental themes of the Christian faith. Without God, human existence will seem unfulfilled and empty. The creation has the potential to point to its creator. Yet it lacks the ability to satisfy our deepest longings. As Lewis put it in developing his natural theology of longing: "The human soul was made to enjoy some object that is never fully given – nay, cannot even be imagined as given – in our present mode of subjective and spatiotemporal experience." We have been made to long for God, and only the living God can fulfill the longings that he himself has created to lead us back to him.

Suppose, then, that the deep sense of yearning for something that really satisfies us is actually a longing for God – a longing that we are *meant* to experience, and a longing that is *meant* to lead us to its true source and goal in God. Might not this longing accidentally become attached to lesser goals within this world? Might our quest for beauty become an end in itself, yet break our hearts because it fails to deliver what we had anticipated? This point was made in a University Sermon preached in this church sixty years ago in 1941 by Lewis, who commented thus on my theme:

> The books or the music in which we thought the beauty was located will betray us if we trust to them; it was not in them, it only came *through* them, and what came through them was longing. These things – the beauty, the memory of our own past – are good images of what we really desire; but if they are mistaken for the thing itself they turn into dumb idols, breaking the hearts of their worshippers. For they are not the thing itself; they are only the scent of a flower we have not found, the echo of a tune we have not heard, news from a country we have not visited.

The beauty of the night skies or a glorious sunset is an important pointer to the origins and the ultimate fulfillment of our heart's deepest desires. But if we mistake the signpost for what is signposted, we will attach our hopes and longings to lesser goals, which cannot finally quench our thirst for meaning. This enigmatic thought was expressed lyrically by the Russian writer and Orthodox priest Gregory Petrov in his "Hymn of Thanksgiving," written shortly before his death in a Soviet labor camp in 1940:

> O Lord, how lovely it is to be your guest.
> Breezes full of scents; mountains reaching to the skies;
> Waters like boundless mirrors, reflecting the sun's golden rays and the scudding clouds.
> All nature murmurs mysteriously, breathing the depth of tenderness.
> Birds and beasts of the forest bear the imprint of your love.
> Blessed is mother earth, in your passing loveliness, which awakens our yearning for the happiness that will last for ever,
> In the eternal native land where, amid beauty that will never grow old, the cry rings out: Alleluia!

Petrov clearly found immense consolation in these thoughts. The natural world which surrounded the inhuman and degrading life of the labor camp pointed to a future homeland free of oppression and pain. The forests, mountains, and lakes around the camp signaled a future hope, which illuminated and transfigured his present situation.

We began this sermon by reflecting on the deep sense of wonder evoked within us by the sight of the night sky. The brilliance of the stars has always been able to unlock some of the heart's deepest fears and hopes, bringing to light the hidden longings that are part of our human condition. So what might these feelings mean? Do they mean anything at all? Shelley saw the moth's desire for the star as a powerful symbol of the heart's desire for something which was both distant yet compelling, a means of sustaining hope for the future and distracting us from our present "sphere of sorrow." Our dreams, longings, and myths are laden with meaning. The power of the human imagination is itself a clue to our true identity. Perhaps the most interesting advocate of a "natural theology of the imagination" is J. R. R. Tolkien. In his poem "Mythopoeia" Tolkien pointed out how our imaginations constantly confront us with that great question of our origin, which becomes reconceived as the question of our destiny: "Whence came the wish, and whence the power to dream?"

Many have found that the awesome sight of the star-studded heavens evokes a sense of wonder, an awareness of transcendence, which is charged with spiritual significance. Yet the distant shimmering of stars does not itself create this sense of longing; it merely exposes what is already there. They are catalysts for our spiritual insights, revealing our emptiness and compelling us to ask whether and how this void might be filled. Might our true origins and destiny somehow lie beyond those stars? Might there not be a homeland, from which we are presently exiled, and to which we secretly long to return? Might not our accumulation of discontentment and disillusionment with our present existence be a pointer to another land, where our true destiny lies, and which is able to make its presence felt now in this haunting way? Suppose that this is not where we are meant to be, but that a better land lies to hand? We don't belong here. We have somehow lost our way. Would not this make our present existence both strange and splendid? Strange, because it is not where our true destiny lies; splendid, because it points ahead to where that real hope might be found.

This is the essence of the Christian hope. We have been made to relate to God, and our true joy lies in the fulfilment of that God-given potential. It is not something that we are required to achieve or fulfil on our own. It may seem to us that we are engaged on a quest for meaning and truth; in fact, the truth is engaged on a quest for us, and has drawn close to us. The God who created us has entered into our history and drawn close to us, whispering our names in the night, and waiting and longing for us to respond to him. The God who longs to fulfil us awaits us, inviting us to open the door of our lives so that he may enter in.

CHAPTER 4

Towards the Restatement and Renewal of a Natural Theology: A Dialogue with the Classic English Tradition

One of the most distinctive features of my "scientific theology" project is its insistence that natural theology has a critical role to play in developing a critical realist, non-foundational theology, capable of defending its own inherent rationality, while at the same time offering an explanation of rival traditions. In championing such alternatives to the Enlightenment paradigm, Alasdair MacIntyre argues that it is possible to make strong realist claims for the rationality and truth of tradition-specific claims *without* falling into some version of an outmoded Enlightenment foundationalism. Traditions offer access to truth, even though a recognition of the tradition-mediated character of such rationalities must engender at least a degree of caution as to how these are developed.[1]

> Implicit in the rationality of such enquiry there is indeed a conception of a final truth, that is to say, a relationship of the mind to its objects which would be wholly adequate in respect of the capacities of that mind. But any conception of that state as one in which the mind could by its own power know itself as thus adequately informed is ruled out; the Absolute Knowledge of the Hegelian system is from this tradition-constituted standpoint a chimaera.

---

[1] Alasdair MacIntyre, *Whose Justice? Which Rationality?* London: Duckworth, 1988, 360–1. For further comment on this important point, see Jean Porter, "Tradition in the Recent Work of Alasdair MacIntyre." In *Alasdair MacIntyre*, edited by Mark C. Murphy, 38–69. Cambridge: Cambridge University Press, 2003.

So is there a standard of justification which can be adduced which is independent of any tradition, or which somehow transcends such traditions?[2] It is at this point that a natural theology, in the sense in which we have been using this term, becomes of major explanatory importance. In my view, natural theology – rightly *understood* and rightly *applied* – has the potential to function as precisely such a tradition-transcending category of judgment or justification.[3] For a scientific theology, natural theology is to be understood as "the enterprise of seeing nature as creation, which both presupposes and reinforces fundamental Christian theological affirmations." This natural theology is able to offer important insights as to why rival traditions exist, especially in offering a coherent explanation of why certain themes are common to most traditions.

The Christian doctrine of creation is thus of meta-traditional significance. The scientific tradition, for example, finds itself having to presuppose the uniformity and ordering of creation; Christian theology offers an account of this. The scientific tradition recognizes that the natural world has a rationality which human rationality can discern and systematize; Christian theology, however, offers an explanation of why this is the case.[4] On both of MacIntyre's criteria, the Christian tradition is able to set forth a plausible claim to represent a robust and resilient account of reality. It is both particular and public – grounded in a specific view of reality, yet capable of engaging with issues of public truth, avoiding any form of self-imposed imprisonment within an intellectual ghetto which has so impoverished the apologetic potential of some recent theological proposals.

The essential point here is that this natural theology posits that something of God may be known outside the Christian tradition. The possibility of truth is grounded, not merely in the existence of a God, but in the existence of the *Christian* God – that is, the God who is specifically revealed, known, and worshipped within the Christian tradition – who is held to have created the world and humanity, and has not left us "without witness" to the divine presence and activity (Acts 14:16). The impetus to quest for God is, according to Paul's Areopagus sermon, itself grounded in the creative action of God (Acts 17:26–7).[5]

Yet I do not regard the importance of natural theology as being restricted to its capacity to address some of the weighty epistemological issues concerning

---

[2] See the very helpful discussion in Jennifer A. Herdt, "Alasdair MacIntyre's 'Rationality of Traditions' and Tradition-Transcendental Standards of Justification." *Journal of Religion* 78 (1998): 524–46.

[3] For the argument, see McGrath, *A Scientific Theology 2: Reality*, 72–97. I shall not repeat the extensive argument brought forward at that point.

[4] See the detailed discussion in McGrath, *A Scientific Theology 1: Creation*, 196–218.

[5] See the excellent analysis in Bertil Gärtner, *The Areopagus Speech and Natural Revelation*. Uppsala: Almqvist & Wirksells, 1955, 170–202.

reliable knowledge in the aftermath of the wreck of the fundamental Enlightenment concept of a universal rationality. It seems to me that natural theology represents a potential ground of dialogue between Christian theology, natural philosophy, the natural sciences, literature, and art. Natural theology has been a Cinderella for much of the twentieth century. Is it now time for its status and potential to be transformed? Might it yet upstage its sisters at Prince Charming's theological ball?

This significant role allotted to natural theology within the scientific theology project has provoked much discussion among my reviewers and correspondents. While many have regarded "scientific theology" as reopening the question of the dogmatic location and apologetic potential of natural theology, others have wondered whether this represents an error of judgment. For even its more sympathetic observers, the fortunes of this particular theological discipline reached their nadir in the twentieth century. Karl Barth's onslaught against the whole enterprise, although not totally persuasive, nevertheless raised so many formidable problems that its supporters found themselves forced onto the defensive, on the whole being forced to parry Barth's criticisms rather than encouraged to articulate a positive vision of their project. The whole enterprise of natural theology is today regarded with a mixture of suspicion and incredulity. Why bother doing this, when it cannot and should not be done? It seems, in the view of many, to be little more than a waste of time.

I regard these concerns as significant, and will engage with them more extensively in a larger work on natural theology now in preparation. It is my belief that the term "natural theology" has become tainted, contaminated by association, in that it is now identified with one specific approach within a spectrum of possibilities, conceptually linked to the Enlightenment project. The style of natural theology that I propose to develop occupies a somewhat different place on this spectrum of possibilities. It is based on a trinitarian, incarnational ontology, and is located within the scope of a specifically Christian vision of reality, rather than the somewhat generalized theistic worldview of English Deism and the Enlightenment, which prioritized human reason over other faculties, supremely the imagination.

In this essay, I propose to explore some aspects of the current problems many experience with natural theology, in preparation for this larger work dedicated to this theme.

Natural Theology: An Autobiographical Reflection

In the summer of 1995, I was in the process of moving house and office, taking up my position as Principal of Wycliffe Hall, Oxford. It was a time of physical and spiritual disruption, during which my colleagues and I had to transfer my large personal library from one part of the college to another, and I was left to rearrange its dusty contents in my new study. As so often happens at these moments, I discovered books that I never knew I had possessed, filed under the wrong heading or – a common event in my case – having fallen down the back of very inadequate bookcases.

As I unpacked, I came across Stanley Jaki's Fremantle Lectures, delivered at Balliol College, Oxford in April and May 1977. I had been unable to attend the five original lectures myself, due to prior commitments; however, having heard good reports of them, I had subsequently bought the published version, intending to get round to reading it sometime. But somehow, that "sometime" seemed to have been postponed to the point at which I seemed to have quite lost sight of my original intention. Other matters pressed in on me, and Jaki seems to have been forgotten – most likely, through having been lost in my hopelessly inadequate library system.

It had been a long morning, and I felt I deserved a break. I took Jaki outside into the warm summer sun and sprawled out on a bench in Wycliffe Hall's gardens. I flicked through the pages, scanning Jaki's discussion of the origins of science, set out in the first lecture. Suddenly, I sat bolt upright and read a passage again. It was Jaki's evaluation of the significance of Francis Bacon's *Novum Organum* (1620), a landmark work that I had read several times. But Jaki's comments came like a thunderstorm on an oppressively humid summer afternoon, clearing the air and allowing a gentle, cool breeze to refresh and renew me. These are his words.[6]

> The new organon of science was not in the voluminous fumbling of Bacon with mostly irrelevant facts, but in the conviction shared long before him of the fact that since the world was rational it could be comprehended by the human mind, but as the product of the Creator it could not be derived from the mind of man, a creature.

Jaki's words were perhaps a little unfair to Bacon (who, after all, stressed the importance of analyzing facts and not just accumulating them). Yet they crystallized a whole series of thoughts that had been troubling me for some time over the principled limits of natural theology. It was as if someone else had given me the words to express what was fundamentally at fault with the great English tradition of natural theology, bringing into sharp conceptual focus something which had up to that point been slightly vague, always just beyond the horizon of my capacity to capture or express it.

At one level, the point that Jaki was making was a theological commonplace – the classical Thomist view that, while divine revelation was not contrary to

---

[6] Stanley L. Jaki, *The Origin of Science and the Science of its Origin*. Edinburgh: Scottish Academic Press, 1978, 21.

reason, it nonetheless transcended it. The human mind is unable by itself to attain divine truth; yet when such truth is disclosed, it was found to be commensurate with reason. Yet Jaki had subtly redirected this, giving it a pointed application. Yes, the human mind is able to discern the underlying rationality of the world. Yes, it is justified in holding that in discerning such rationality it is responding to a rationality with which the universe has always been saturated, not projecting our own preconceptions of such order into an irrational world. But – and it is a major "but" – we are not justified in seeing this as reflecting or revealing the "mind of God" without prior authorization or enablement, both of which lie beyond the competency of human reason. For natural theology to be "theology" in any meaningful sense of the word, a robust conceptual link must be established between "the world" and "God's creation."

Yet while such a link may be optimistically proposed by the human mind, it cannot be validated or authenticated by that same human mind. Natural theology is caught up in a hermeneutical circle, in which it must presuppose its conclusions. Nature is not an epistemically autonomous entity, capable of shaping human thought; it is itself an interpreted entity, having been shaped by inquiring minds, and often merely adapted to their modes of thought. Nature, far from being the basis of a universal philosophy, itself requires to be given a conceptual foundation by a philosophy, which it can then merely reinforce, yet not establish in the first place. If a natural theology is to have any credibility after the epistemic failures of modernism, it must be repositioned and reconceptualized as having its proper location and scope within the community of faith, not outside it.

Jaki's thoughts were thus a catalyst to a process of reflection which ultimately left his words far behind, and became independent of them. As my own thinking on natural theology has partly been shaped by a conscious sense of standing within the classic English tradition of natural philosophy, it is entirely appropriate to explore some of its difficulties with natural theology with specific reference to this tradition. Although most of the ideas lying behind my approach to natural theology predated my reading of Jaki, his words crystallized my perceptions, allowing me to develop a framework within which I could both critique the classic English natural theology tradition, from Richard Bentley through to William Paley, while at the same time renew it through theological repositioning and reconceptualization.

Traditionally, natural theology has been defined as "the enterprise of providing support for religious beliefs by starting from premises that neither are nor presuppose any religious beliefs" (William Alston).[7] Yet as I wrestled

---

[7] William P. Alston, *Perceiving God: The Epistemology of Religious Experience.* Ithaca, NY: Cornell University Press, 1991, 289. See also Alvin J. Plantinga, "Reason and Belief in God." In *Faith and Rationality*, edited by Alvin Plantinga and Nicholas

with the whole question of the nature, scope, and limits of natural theology, I could not see how belief in God could be separated from reflection on nature itself. There seemed to me to be a compelling parallel with Thomas Aquinas' "five ways," which do not represent conclusive "proofs" of God's existence *ab initio*, but are actually explorations of the explanatory dividend resulting from faith in God. Belief in God allows the world to be seen and interpreted in certain ways, which reinforce an existing faith in God, but are unlikely to create that faith in the first place.

Similarly, natural theology is not about discovering persuasive grounds of faith outside the bounds and scope of revelation, but a demonstration that, when nature is "seen" through the lens of the Christian revelation, the outcome is imaginatively compelling and rationally persuasive. In other words, natural theology *presupposes* the Christian view of the world, and makes an appeal to two groups of individuals:

1 *Those outside the church*, who are invited to see the world in this way, and appreciate the aesthetic power and rational satisfaction that results. If natural theology leads to faith, it is not primarily by rational persuasion, but by an act of imaginative empathy, in which the audience is asked to imagine a way of seeing things which proves to be deeply meaningful, and then told that this is, in fact, the way things are. Imaginative appeal thus leads to a longing that things should be like this, followed by a realization that this is indeed the case.

2 *Those within the church*, who are invited to see the world as God's creation, and experience the deepened sense of understanding and aesthetic appreciation that is consequent upon this realization. The world becomes seen as a lens through which God may be refracted, or a means of ascent towards God. The Christian gospel is here seen to resonate with the deeper structures of the world, with important apologetic and spiritual consequences.

It is important at this point to stress that natural theology is about discernment – about a certain way of seeing the world. It is not about escaping from this world, in order to encounter another, supernatural order. Natural theology positions us within this history and within this natural order, and tells us to expect to discern God within what we observe there. For those who have the eyes of faith to see, God is present and acts within historical events and aspects of nature.

Natural Theology as Discernment

The Old Testament frequently depicts divine communication or disclosure as taking place within the realm of nature, being mediated through natural

Wolterstorff, 16–93. Notre Dame, IN: University of Notre Dame Press, 1983, where natural theology is interpreted as an attempt to prove or demonstrate the existence of God.

processes, events, and entities. The sound of the wind rustling the leaves of trees; the sight of the stars at night; the awesome power of a storm – all are held to be vehicles of divine disclosure. It is not that God is "in" such things; it is that they act as pointers or prisms, through which the divine may be discerned. A classic example of nature disclosing the transcendent is found in Jeremiah's reaction to a rod of almond blossom (Jeremiah 1:11–12), which becomes a conduit for divine revelation and disclosure. The verbal similarity between *saqed* ("almond tree") and *soqed* ("watchfulness") forms the basis of an epiphanic experience.[8] The issue is that of discernment – understood by the Old Testament to be a divine gift, enabling the recipient to see nature as a channel for the transcendent.

To illustrate this point more thoroughly, we may consider the Old Testament account of Samuel hearing the voice of God (1 Samuel 3:1–16) – an excellent example of the category of the transcendent – and the issues that this raises. The call of Samuel in the temple at Shiloh is one of the best-known narratives in the Old Testament. Samuel hears his name being spoken during the night three times. On the first three occasions, he believes that Eli is calling him, and runs to find him. On the fourth occasion, Samuel correctly interprets the calling of his name as coming from God, following Eli's suggestion to interpret the event in this manner. Although the debate over the literary genre of the passage is far from closed, it seems fair to designate this as an example of a prophetic call narrative.[9]

Sadly, most scholarly accounts of this passage fail to see that the central issue is *discernment*.[10] The decisive thing is that an event within nature is viewed in a new manner, and seen to possess a new significance which may ultimately transcend the natural order. Walter Moberly rightly summarizes the central concern as follows:[11] "God then speaks to Samuel. But His speaking instantly poses the central issue of the story, that is discernment. For when God speaks,

---

[8] For a good account of the semantic and religious issues, see Walter G. Williams, "Jeremiah's Vision of the Almond Rod." In *A Stubborn Faith: Papers on Old Testament and Related Subjects Presented to William Andrew Irwin*, edited by Edward C. Hobbs, 90–9. Dallas: Southern Methodist University Press, 1956.

[9] Murray Newman, "The Prophetic Call of Samuel." In *Israel's Prophetic Heritage: Essays in Honor of James Muilenburg*, edited by B. W. Anderson and W. J. Harrelson, 86–97. London: SCM Press, 1962. The interesting thesis of Robert K. Gnuse, *The Dream Theophany of Samuel: Its Structure in Relation to Ancient Near Eastern Dreams and Its Theological Significance*, Lanham, MD: University Press of America, 1984, should be noted, although the absence of the specific word "dream" makes his thesis problematic.

[10] A luminous exception is the highly insightful account of R. W. L. Moberly, "To Hear the Master's Voice: Revelation and Spiritual Discernment in the Call of Samuel." *Scottish Journal of Theology* 48 (1995): 443–68, which replays close study.

[11] Moberly, "To Hear the Master's Voice," 458–9.

Samuel does not recognize the voice as God's voice." So what are the implications of this? Moberly points out that the call of God may not be recognizable as such, in that it is mediated in and through the natural realm. In this case, "the voice of God, while not being reducible to that which is human, may be inseparably linked with the human." The voice of God sounds like the voice of Eli.

On the first three occasions, Samuel assumes that the natural sound he has heard has a natural referent, and behaves accordingly. Samuel interprets a natural phenomenon as having a natural referent, and as a result goes to wake Eli. Why? Because "Samuel did not yet know the Lord; the word of the Lord had not yet been revealed to him" (1 Samuel 3:7). The turning point of the narrative takes place when Eli offers an alternative interpretive framework. Confronted with the evident failure of the most obvious such framework, Samuel is invited to consider a transcendent explanation of a natural phenomenon (1 Samuel 3:9).[12]

Natural theology is about seeing nature in such a way that it points beyond itself to a transcendent reality, without itself constituting that reality. Nature is not itself supernatural; yet the supernatural is disclosed in and through the natural. The relevance of the point about the call of Samuel to any Christian engagement with nature will therefore be clear. We are invited, as ones who are part of the natural order and who stand within that realm of nature, to see nature as pointing beyond itself to the realm of the transcendent. Moments of epiphany do not require us to stand outside the realm of nature, nor need they be mediated through what might be called "supernatural" means. Christian theology has long recognized that the divine may be disclosed through the mundane; that God may be known through things of this world.

It is therefore important to lay down a fundamental challenge to any approach to natural theology which assumes that God is absent from the natural world, and fails to speak through its genres. Revelation is not supernatural, as this unhelpful term is traditionally understood. As the story of Samuel and countless other biblical narratives make clear, divine revelation does not take place in the heavens, but here on earth, in the midst of the commonplaces of life. Perhaps Charles Williams' idea of "arch-nature" deserves more careful consideration than it has traditionally received. God is present in this world, and makes himself known in the world of human experience, inspiring a sense of awe, mystery, and wonder. The whole point of the Christian doctrine of revelation is that God elicits such a response from humanity through self-revelation adapted or "accommodated" (Calvin) to the familiar realities of this world, in order to form a bridge between earth and heaven, nature and grace. It also accentuates the importance of

---

[12] For further discussion, see Jacques Briend, *Dieu dans l'écriture*. Paris: Cerf, 1992.

discernment – the God-given faculty of discerning God's presence and action within nature.

This, of course, raises the question: who may discern God in this way? Is this a public matter, in which all will see God within nature on the basis of fundamental shared assumptions of human reason and culture? Or does it require us to see nature in a certain specific, perhaps counter-cultural, manner? During the "Golden Age" of English natural theology, it was widely assumed that anyone viewing the wonders of nature would infer the existence of their creator. In view of the importance of this period for our reflections on the dogmatic location and intellectual scope of natural theology, we may consider it in more detail.

The Golden Age of English Natural Theology

Natural theology, understood as a means of finding one's way to religious belief without recourse to any instruments of ecclesial authority through reflection on the natural order, began to blossom in England during the seventeenth century, partly in response to political and intellectual developments which had created unease, occasionally suspicion, of traditional Christian approaches to revelation.

Several factors appear to have shaped this new interest in "natural theology" (often referred to at the time as "physical theology," from the Greek *physis* = nature) and "natural religion" at this time in England.[13] We may note three.

1 The rise of biblical criticism called into question the reliability or intelligibility of scripture, and hence generated interest in the revelatory capacities of the natural world.
2 A growing distrust of ecclesiastical authority, which led some to explore sources of knowledge which were seen to be independent of ecclesiastical control, such as an appeal to reason or to the natural order.
3 A dislike of organized religion and Christian doctrines caused many to seek for a simpler "religion of nature," in which nature was valued as a source of revelation.

In some ways, these developments can be seen as confirming anxieties famously expressed by Karl Barth concerning the eighteenth-century worldview – that it represented an assertion of human autonomy over and against divine self-revelation.[14] "Natural theology," as understood by Barth,

---

[13] See Richard S. Westfall, "The Scientific Revolution of the Seventeenth Century: A New World View." In *The Concept of Nature*, edited by John Torrance, 63–93. Oxford: Oxford University Press, 1992.

[14] For Barth's general assessment of this development, see his important essay on humanity in the eighteenth century: Karl Barth, *Die protestantische Theologie im 19.*

embodies the characteristic tendency of sinful humanity to affirm its epistemic and soteriological independence. Humanity could discover and relate to God under terms of its own choosing, rather than those mandated by the Christian proclamation. If knowledge of God can be achieved independently of God's self-revelation in Christ, then it follows that humanity can dictate the place, time, and means of its knowledge of God.[15]

The fundamental assumption underlying this approach is that nature can be "read" in such a way to disclose the existence and, within limits, the nature of God *without* the need for any specifically theological or religious assumptions. To use a textual metaphor: the "book of nature" can be read without the need for theistic presuppositions. The "two books" tradition tended to minimize the need for interpretation, generally regarding the natural world as publicly accessible, and not requiring any hermeneutical devices other than human reason.[16] Nature is thus to be regarded as a "universal and public manuscript" (Sir Thomas Browne), capable of being interpreted and appreciated on the basis of assumptions which were not specific to the Christian tradition, but which were rather part of the common intellectual and cultural fabric of western civilization. The Christian tradition could thus be subverted, marginalized, ignored, or selectively appropriated in any engagement with nature, according to the taste of the interpreter.

The background to the emergence of this style of natural theology is, however, rather more complex than Barth allows, particularly in relation to the emergence of English natural theology over this period – something that Barth's linguistic and geographical horizons may have prevented him from fully appreciating. It is undoubtedly true that the "autonomy" motif was significant for Deists and others in England at this time wishing to promote a certain style of natural theology. Yet it is not difficult to discern another motif: growing anxiety concerning the reliability of the specifics of the Christian revelation, and especially specific concerns about the authority of the Bible, reflecting changes in the English cultural scene at this time.[17] The primary motivation for undertaking

---

Jahrhundert: Ihre Vorgeschichte und ihre Geschichte, 2nd edn. Zurich: Evangelischer Verlag, 1952, 16–59. On the importance of the "autonomy" theme, see Christof Gestrich, *Neuzeitliches Denken und die Spaltung der dialektischen Theologie: Zur Frage der natürlichen Theologie*. Tübingen: Mohr, 1977.

[15] On this general point, see Regin Prenter, "Das Problem der natürlichen Theologie bei Karl Barth." *Theologische Literaturzeitung* 77 (1952): 607–11.

[16] For a discussion, see Kenneth J. Howell, *God's Two Books: Copernican Cosmology and Biblical Interpretation in Early Modern Science*. Notre Dame, IN: University of Notre Dame Press, 2002.

[17] For the best study of this development, see Henning Graf Reventloh, *The Authority of the Bible and the Rise of the Modern World*. London: SCM Press, 1984.

natural theology within English Christianity during the late seventeenth and eighteenth centuries was not *dogmatic*, but *apologetic*. The church itself did not reject revelation; it realized that it needed to relate the gospel to a culture which no longer felt inclined to accept this notion. Natural theology rapidly became an apologetic tool of no small importance.

This perceptible acceleration of interest in natural theology was partly – though not totally – due to a perception within the English Christian church that an appeal to the regularity of nature would be much more effective and productive in the public arena than reliance on a sacred text which was increasingly regarded with suspicion. Natural theology was thus seen as an especially promising apologetic tool in a cultural situation which had witnessed significant erosion in the esteem in which Christianity's sacred texts were held. If an appeal to the Bible no longer carried weight, might an appeal to that more public text of nature itself prove decisive? It was ultimately a forlorn hope. But that crushing sense of disappointment, as it turned out, took some considerable time to crystallize.

If one can speak of a "golden age of natural theology" this may reasonably be argued to occupy a period of a century and a half, beginning in the late seventeenth century, and ending in the first half of the nineteenth. It is not difficult to understand why. The rise of the Newtonian worldview gave natural theology a new lease of life, as the celebrated "Boyle Lectures" make clear.

The Boyle Lectures and the Problem of Heterodoxy

Shortly before his death in 1691, Robert Boyle – unquestionably one of England's greatest scientists of that age[18] – bequeathed a sum of money which was to endow a series of lectures, to be devoted to "proving the Christian Religion against notorious Infidels." The lectures rapidly became the bulwark of the Church of England's campaign against the rise of skepticism within society at large. Boyle himself seemed to see natural theology as the outcome, not the foundation, of his faith.[19] Yet he was not unaware of the apologetic implications of such a natural theology, and its relevance to the worsening situation of the Church of England at that time.

---

[18] There is a huge literature. See especially J. J. MacIntosh, "Robert Boyle's Epistemology: The Interaction between Scientific and Religious Knowledge." *International Studies in the Philosophy of Science* 6 (1992): 91–121.

[19] On which see the excellent study of Jan W. Wojcik, *Robert Boyle and the Limits of Reason*. Cambridge: Cambridge University Press, 1997. Note also the older study of Harold Fisch, "The Scientist as Priest: A Note on Robert Boyle's Natural Theology." *Isis* 44 (1953): 252–65.

The Boyle Lectures, delivered over the period 1692–1732, are widely regarded as the most significant public demonstration of the "reasonableness" of Christianity in the early modern period, characterized by that era's growing emphasis upon rationalism and its increasing suspicion of ecclesiastical authority.[20] These sermons are an absolute delight to a historical theologian, such as myself. They provide a snapshot of a lost and bygone era, when it was still possible to offer a publicly persuasive "confutation of atheism" – the title of the first series of Boyle Lectures, delivered in 1692 by Richard Bentley, which inaugurated the golden years of natural theology.[21]

In his substantial and important introduction to a recent reprint of the original Boyle Lectures, Andrew Pyle – a distinguished intellectual historian of the seventeenth century[22] – notes that the lectures signally failed in their objects.[23] "As the eighteenth century progressed, the 'reasonable' Christianity of the Boyle lecturers came to look increasingly flimsy and vulnerable." Their abandonment was inevitable; they had had their day, and had come to be a liability rather than an asset to the apologetic task of the church. Far from persuading their audiences of the intellectual robustness of the Christian faith, they had come to sow the seeds of doubt. Two particular points emerged as problematic.

In the first place, this approach seemed to lead to Deism, rather than to orthodox Christianity. God tends to be presented and understood as the extension of accepted human ideas of justice, rationality, and wisdom. This apologetic approach does not necessarily lead *away* from Christianity; nevertheless, it is certainly not well disposed towards Christian specifics. Alarmingly, some of the most influential Boyle lecturers were Arians, committed to a thoroughly rationalist understanding of Christ.[24] The common sense underlying the "natural theology" developed by William Whiston and Samuel Clark extended to their christology. Natural theology, it seemed, when left to its own devices, seemed to lead into the byways of heterodoxy.[25]

---

[20] *The Boyle Lectures (1692–1732): A Defence of Natural and Revealed Religion, being an Abridgement of the Sermons preached at the Lectures founded by Robert Boyle*, 4 vols. Bristol: Thoemmes Press, 2000.

[21] John Gascoigne, "From Bentley to the Victorians: The Rise and Fall of British Newtonian Natural Theology." *Science in Context* 2 (1988): 219–56. See also David Berman, *A History of Atheism in Britain*. London: Routledge, 1988, 1–47.

[22] See especially his excellent *Dictionary of Seventeenth-Century British Philosophers*. Bristol: Thoemmes Press, 2000.

[23] Andrew Pyle, "Introduction," in *The Boyle Lectures*, Vol. 1, vii–liii.

[24] Maurice Wiles, *Archetypal Heresy: Arianism Through the Ages*. Oxford: Oxford University Press, 1996, 62–134.

[25] This is, of course, precisely the concern expressed by Calvin in his *Institutes*.

Secondly, whatever the intentions of its advocates, this approach to natural theology actually eroded the conceptual space traditionally occupied by God. The amalgam of Newtonian natural philosophy and certain forms of Anglican theology proved popular and plausible in England during a period of political instability and uncertainty. Nevertheless, it was an unstable amalgam – more of a convenient, temporary convergence of vested intellectual and social interests, rather than a resilient, integrated, conceptual fusion. It was not long before the "estrangement of celestial mechanics and religion" began to set in.[26] The somewhat problematic enterprise of "celestial mechanics" increasingly seemed to suggest that the world was a self-sustaining mechanism which had no need for divine governance or sustenance for its day-to-day operation.

An appeal to natural theology might therefore be argued, on historical grounds, to lead to a form of Christianity which seriously distorted the traditional orthodox understanding of the nature of God, and especially the critical issue of God's continuing involvement in the world – in other words, the concept of providence. Natural theology came to be associated with a mechanistic worldview and a significantly reduced conception of God, in which "providence" is evacuated of much, if not all, of its traditional meaning. This danger is particularly clear from William Whiston's 1707 Boyle Lectures, which reinterpreted providence in terms of the regularity of the cosmic mechanism.[27]

By the end of the eighteenth century, a growing concern can be discerned within orthodox Christian circles in England, to the effect that the "natural theology" commended by the Boyle Lectures seemed to point only towards a generalized conception of God. The identification of this generic divinity with the more specific Christian understanding of God rested more on inherited cultural assumptions and memories than on argument or evidence. Yet the rise of Deism and other heterodox intellectual movements at this time made problematic any direct correlation between the divinity inferred from reflection on nature and the God disclosed in scripture and proclaimed by the church. Although the historical evidence is complex, the classic style of natural theology appears to have been appropriated just as much by those arguing for a return to a "religion of nature" as by those who hoped to defend institutionalized Christian beliefs, and may thus have been a threat as much as an ally to orthodox Christianity at this time.

---

[26] See the important study of H. H. Odom, "The Estrangement of Celestial Mechanics and Religion." *Journal of the History of Ideas* 27 (1966): 533–58.

[27] See the important general discussion in D. C. Kubrin, "Newton and the Cyclical Cosmos: Providence and the Mechanical Philosophy." *Journal for the History of Ideas* 28 (1967): 325–46.

William Paley and the Divine Watchmaker

In the first years of the nineteenth century, natural theology underwent a new development, based on a subtle transposition of its themes. In the enthusiastic hands of William Paley, archdeacon of Carlisle, arguments once deployed in relation to the *physical* world were now given a new lease of life, by being transposed to the *biological* level. Paley's *Natural Theology; or Evidences of the Existence and Attributes of the Deity, Collected from the Appearances of Nature* (1802) had a profound influence on popular English religious thought in the first half of the nineteenth century, and is known to have been read by Charles Darwin. Although most commentators have stressed its apologetic function, it is important also to note its consequent social role. As Frank Turner rightly notes, a fundamental goal of natural theology around this time was "to avoid social turmoil by repudiating the claims of atheism and materialism."[28]

Nature, Paley argues, shows signs of "contrivance" – that is, purposeful design and fabrication. Nature bears witness to a series of biological structures which are "contrived" – that is, constructed with a clear purpose in mind. "Every indication of contrivance, every manifestation of design, which existed in the watch, exists in the works of nature." Indeed, Paley argues, nature shows an even greater degree of contrivance than the watch. He is at his best when dealing with the immensely complex structures of the human eye and heart, each of which can be described in mechanical terms. Anyone using a telescope, he points out, knows that the instrument was designed and manufactured. Who, he wonders, can look at the human eye, and fail to see that it also has a designer?

There are significant theological difficulties with Paley's approach. Long before Darwin's theory of natural selection made its appearance, causing Paley's approach hitherto unimagined difficulties, a growing body of informed theological opinion was urging the abandoning of his ideas, or their significant modification. In 1852, John Henry Newman was invited to give a series of lectures in Dublin on "the idea of a university." This allowed him to explore the relation between Christianity and the sciences, and especially the "physical theology" of William Paley. Newman was scathing about Paley's approach, lambasting it as "a false gospel." Far from being an advance on the more modest apologetic approaches adopted by the early church, it represented a degradation of those views.

The nub of Newman's criticism of Paley's natural theology can be summarized in a sentence: "it has been taken out of its place, has been put too prominently

---

[28] Frank M. Turner, *Contesting Cultural Authority: Essays in Victorian Intellectual Life*. Cambridge: Cambridge University Press, 1993, 119.

forward, and thereby has almost been used as an instrument against Christianity."[29] Paley's "physical theology" was a liability, and ought to be abandoned before it discredited Christianity.[30]

> Physical Theology cannot, from the nature of the case, tell us one word about Christianity proper; it cannot be Christian, in any true sense, at all ... Nay, more than this; I do not hesitate to say that, taking men as they are, this so-called science tends, if it occupies the mind, to dispose it against Christianity.

Seven years before Darwin had subverted Paley's approach on scientific grounds through his theory of natural selection, Newman – widely regarded as the most important English theologian of the nineteenth century – had repudiated Paley as an outdated theological liability.

What is interesting is that there is no awareness on Newman's part of a new crisis of faith about to be precipitated by Darwin's work. His argument, which predates Darwin's *Origin of Species*, rests solely on his belief that Paley's approach fails in what it sought to deliver, and traps Christian theology in an apologetic which can only go disastrously wrong. It was not the first time Christian apologetics had taken a disastrous wrong turn; an immediate correction was, in Newman's view, long overdue.

So what is the concern that lies behind Newman's antipathy to Paley? Perhaps the simplest explanation has to do with the concept of God which results from Paley's emphasis on "contrivance." For Newman, Paley's image of God as the divine artificer of the world reduced God to its level. Where was any sense of transcendence, mystery, or glory? Paley's image might appeal to the human reason. But what about the human imagination? Or the human emotions? Did not Paley tend to proclaim a somewhat cold, distant, mechanical God, a lawgiver rather than a savior? We can see similar concerns expressed a hundred years earlier by High Church critics of the Boyle Lectures. Paley may have succeeded in persuading a generation of readers that the existence of a creator God could be established by an empirical argument to design. Yet that defense of the existence of God was at the cost of modifying or abandoning many things that more traditional Christians regarded as essential to their faith.

Newman was deeply concerned that the notion of a transcendent God, who could never be fully comprehended by human reason, was being compromised by a decidedly weaker notion of divinity. For Paley, God was an explanation; for Newman, God was the supreme desire of the human heart, who was to be

---

[29] John Henry Newman, *The Idea of a University*. London: Longmans, Green, 1907, 450–1.

[30] Ibid, 454.

worshipped and adored. Paley defended the credibility of a lesser God than that which Christianity proclaimed. For Newman, any authentic vision of the Christian God arrested people in their tracks. God, if truly known, compelled a response of worship, adoration, and existential transformation. Paley, he believed, left people with little more than a vague sense of intellectual satisfaction, to be compared with that experienced after the successful completion of a crossword puzzle. There is no sense of wonder, no epiphany of transcendence, no glimpse of glory – merely the satisfaction of having solved a diverting conundrum.[31]

The Challenge of Darwinism for Natural Theology

Yet Paley's approach raises a further question which cannot be overlooked by any concerned with the reconstruction of natural theology in the contemporary world – the rise of Darwinism, both as a scientific theory of natural development, and as a worldview in its own right.[32] It will be immediately obvious that the major part of Paley's approach is called into question by Charles Darwin's theory of natural selection. Indeed, Richard Dawkins' *Blind Watchmaker* can be regarded as an extended, appreciative, yet ultimately fatal critique of the fundamentals of Paley's natural theology. Of course, it should be noted that there were many who believed that the obvious deficiencies in Paley's account of biological life – most notably, the notion of "perfect adaptation" – were actually *corrected* rather than *refuted* by Darwin's notion of natural selection.[33] More importantly, a series of writers discarded Paley's interest in specific adaptations (to use a Darwinian term unknown to him), and preferred to focus on the fact that evolution appeared to be governed by

[31] Others found Paley's approach unsatisfactory for somewhat different, though conceivably related, reasons. John Ruskin insisted that the goal of any engagement with nature could not simply be understanding, or grasping the fact that some divinity existed. The study of nature was about the pursuit of wisdom. See Michael Wheeler, *Ruskin's God*. Cambridge: Cambridge University Press, 1999, 197–205.

[32] There is a huge literature dealing with the challenges posed by Darwin to Christian faith, or the settled social assumptions of Victorian England. Two helpful studies are especially useful in setting the scene: Adrian J. Desmond, *The Politics of Evolution: Morphology, Medicine, and Reform in Radical London, Science and Its Conceptual Foundations*. Chicago: University of Chicago Press, 1989; Peter J. Bowler, *The Non-Darwinian Revolution: Reinterpreting a Historical Myth*. Baltimore: Johns Hopkins University Press, 1988.

[33] James R. Moore, *The Post-Darwinian Controversies: A Study of the Protestant Struggle to Come to Terms with Darwin in Great Britain and America, 1870–1900*. Cambridge: Cambridge University Press, 1979.

certain quite definite laws – a clear application to biology of the notion of "secondary causality" within the world, developed in the Middle Ages by Thomas Aquinas. Others sought to adapt Paley's text so that it might "harmonize with modern science."[34] Yet none of these moves ultimately proved to be sufficient to reverse the emerging consensus of that age: natural theology – at least, as conceived by Paley – had failed.[35]

It is important to appreciate that Darwin's theory of natural selection causes difficulties at several levels for natural theology. While some scholars have argued that the rise of Darwinism in the later nineteenth century forced, or at least encouraged, the abandonment of natural theology at that time,[36] this is historically indefensible and theologically unwarranted. The reality is far more complex. If Darwinism forced anything onto the agenda of natural theology, it was the need to transition from a view of divine creation which held that everything was created in its present, fixed form to one which acknowledged that development of some sort had taken place within the natural order.

Perhaps the most obvious casualty of Darwin's theology of natural selection is Paley's account of the origins of the marvelous intricacies of nature – such as the amazingly complex structure of the human eye. What Paley ascribed to special divine creation, Darwin put down to natural selection over extended periods of time. Late Victorian intellectual culture was well aware of the importance of the rise of scientific naturalism, and its implications for religious belief.[37] More recently, the importance of this point has again been emphasized. As Richard Dawkins points out in *The Blind Watchmaker* and *Climbing Mount Improbable*, complex things – such as the human eye – evolve from simple beginnings, over long periods of time.[38]

> Living things are too improbable and too beautifully "designed" to have come into existence by chance. How, then, did they come into existence? The answer, Darwin's answer, is by gradual, step-by-step transformations from simple beginnings, from primordial entities sufficiently simple to have come into existence by

---

[34] See the 1880 revision of the text, "with such alternations in the illustrative part of the text as are required by the progress of science since the author's time": *Paley's Natural Theology*. London: SPCK, 1880.

[35] For the crystallization of this perception, see Turner, *Contesting Cultural Authority*, 101–27.

[36] See, for example, the somewhat disappointing analyses of the American situation in Cynthia Eagle Russett, *Darwin in America: The Intellectual Response, 1865–1912*. San Francisco: W. H. Freeman, 1976, 43. For an important corrective, see Jon H. Roberts, *Darwinism and the Divine in America: Protestant Intellectuals and Organic Evolution, 1859–1900*. Madison: University of Wisconsin Press, 1988, 117–45.

[37] See Turner, *Contesting Cultural Authority*, 131–200.

[38] *The Blind Watchmaker*, 43.

chance. Each successful change in the gradual evolutionary process was simple enough, *relative to its predecessor*, to have arisen by chance. But the whole sequence of cumulative steps constitutes anything but a chance process.

What might seem to be a highly improbable development needs to be set against the backdrop of the huge periods of time envisaged by the evolutionary process. Dawkins explores this point using the image of a metaphorical "Mount Improbable." Seen from one angle, its "towering, vertical cliffs" seem impossible to climb. Yet seen from another angle, the mountain turns out to have "gently inclined grassy meadows, graded steadily and easily towards the distant uplands."[39]

Yet it is a second aspect of Darwinism that has proved arguably more problematic for classic natural theology – the immense wastefulness of the process, and the suffering that seems to be part of the natural order. Why do things have to be like this? Why could not God have used a more humane, efficient means of achieving an intended outcome? (I speak from a Christian point of view; the idea of "purpose" or any "goal" within nature is intensely controversial, especially within evolutionary biology.)[40] Richard Dawkins speaks for many when he argues that a Darwinian world has no goal or purpose, and we delude ourselves if we think otherwise. The universe is neither good nor evil, and cannot be considered to be moving towards any specific goal.[41]

> In a universe of blind physical forces and genetic replication, some people are going to get hurt, other people are going to get lucky, and you won't find any rhyme or reason in it, nor any justice. The universe we observe had precisely the properties we should expect if there is, at bottom, no design, no purpose, no evil and no good, nothing but blind pitiless indifference.

Dawkins may certainly be challenged on this, especially in relation to his flawed and problematic derivation of atheism from the natural sciences, including evolutionary biology.[42] But his concerns, and the general anti-theistic worldview he constructs in response to his reading of things, are widespread in scientific culture and beyond.

Yet it is not merely the Darwinian elimination of teleology that is problematic for Paley's natural theology. What of the suffering and waste that the

---

[39] *Climbing Mount Improbable*, 64.

[40] See such works as Michael Ruse, *Darwin and Design: Does Evolution Have a Purpose?* Cambridge, MA: Harvard University Press, 2003.

[41] Richard Dawkins, *River out of Eden: A Darwinian View of Life*. London: Phoenix, 1995, 133.

[42] See Alister E. McGrath, *Dawkins' God: Genes, Memes and the Meaning of Life*. Oxford: Blackwell, 2004, especially 49–81.

mechanism of natural selection proposes? Is there not a serious issue here concerning the goodness of a God who permits (or determines) that life shall emerge and develop in this way? The once unimaginable immense wastefulness of the Darwinian mechanism is difficult to reconcile with a natural theology along the lines of the original Boyle Lectures. As Michael Buckley pointed out some time ago, the decision by French apologists of the seventeenth century to place an emphasis upon the perfection of God (which they hoped would facilitate proofs of God's existence) had the most unfortunate result of exacerbating the difficulties raised for faith by the existence of suffering in the world.[43] How could a perfect, good God allow such things to happen? Any natural theology which makes an appeal to God's wisdom, perfection, or goodness is likely to end up making the existence of imperfections within nature a *disconfirmation* of faith, where once it was little more than an anomaly or puzzle.

"It is a happy world after all," William Paley declared. "In a spring noon, or a summer evening, on whatever side I turn my eyes, myriads of happy beings crowd upon my view." The Cumbrian landscape contained nothing but things that delighted the eye. Yet the hidden Malthusian process of the extinction of species by competition for survival undermines Paley's natural theology in just the same way as the larger problem of evil poses a challenge to belief in God more generally. It is not surprising that some of those who welcomed aspects of Darwin's thoughts on evolution found its darker side more troubling.[44] Nature was a battleground for survival; the penalty for failure was extinction.

It is well known that one of the most fundamental impulses leading to the development of the natural sciences in the sixteenth and seventeenth centuries was the belief that to study nature at close quarters was to gain a deeper appreciation of the wisdom of God.[45] As the great botanist John Ray (1628–1705) – author of the celebrated work *The Wisdom of God Manifested in the Works of Creation* (1691) – put it in 1660:

> There is for a free man no occupation more worthy and delightful than to contemplate the beauteous works of nature and honour the infinite wisdom and goodness of God.

---

[43] Michael J. Buckley, *At the Origins of Modern Atheism*. New Haven, CT: Yale University Press, 1987.

[44] See especially Daniel P. Todes, *Darwin without Malthus: The Struggle for Existence in Russian Evolutionary Thought*. Oxford: Oxford University Press, 1989. For other aspects of the question, see Robert Young, "Malthus and the Evolutionists: The Common Context of Biological and Social Theory." *Past and Present* 43 (1969): 109–45; Scott A. Kleiner, "The Logic of Discovery and Darwin's Pre-Malthusian Researches." *Biology and Philosophy* 3 (1988): 293–315.

[45] For some reflections, see John Hedley Brooke, *Science and Religion: Some Historical Perspectives*. Cambridge: Cambridge University Press, 1991.

The rise of Darwinism has revealed the hidden cost of that beauty, and made that honoring somewhat more problematic – so much so, in fact, that any idea that nature is "good" is openly challenged within evolutionary ethics.[46]

The Darwinian account of natural selection highlights the suffering, destructiveness, and wastefulness of the natural order, filtering out those who are less adapted for survival than their rivals. Darwin himself was appalled by the seeming immorality of the natural process, and its negative implications for the character of the God who created such a process. "I cannot persuade myself," Darwin wrote, "that a beneficent and omnipotent God would have designedly created the *Ichneumonidae* with the express intention of their feeding within the living bodies of caterpillars."

David Hull, reflecting on the intellectual challenges posed by the Darwinian worldview, notes how it is "rife with happenstances, contingency, incredible waste, death, pain and horror." Citing the findings of researchers Peter and Rosemary Grant, who studied the finches of the Galapagos Islands, Hull argues that the patterns of development they observed would prevent anyone except a signed-up sado-masochist to develop a natural theology. How, he asks, can such a God be said to care about his creatures? Such a God seems to be "wasteful, indifferent, almost diabolical" – hardly the sort of God that any normal person might want to pray to.[47]

An excellent example of this same concern can be seen in Charles Sherrington's reflections on the implications of the liver fluke for a natural theology. In his Gifford Lectures on natural theology, delivered at the University of Edinburgh during the academic year 1936–7, Sherrington invited his audience to follow the life cycle of this parasite. It begins its life in water, where it infests water-snails, keeping them alive long enough so that they can mature. At this point, they leave the body of the dying snail, and make their way to the edge of the pond, waiting for grazing animals – such as sheep or cattle – to ingest them. They then make their way to the animal's liver, where they mature, eventually laying eggs that make their way down the animal's liver duct, into the wet pasture, and back into the pond. And so the whole cycle begins again, as yet another water-snail is infected with the parasites. So what does this tell us about the goodness of God, or the beauty of nature? Sherrington cannot offer an explanation, because he does not believe an explanation is to be had.[48]

---

[46] See the excellent analysis in George C. Williams, "Mother Nature Is a Wicked Old Witch!" In *Evolutionary Ethics*, edited by Matthew H. Nitecki and Doris V. Nitecki, 217–31. Albany: State University of New York Press, 1995.

[47] David L. Hull, "God of the Galapagos." *Nature* 352 (1992): 485–6.

[48] Charles S. Sherrington, *Man on His Nature*. Cambridge: Cambridge University Press, 1940, 266.

[This] is a story of securing existence to a worm at cost of lives superior to it in the scale of life as humanly reckoned. Life's prize is given to the aggressive and inferior of life, destructive of other lives at the expense of suffering in them, and, sad as it may seem to us, suffering in proportion as they are lives high in life's scale. The example taken is a fair sample of almost countless many.

While one may doubtless admire the ingenuity of liver flukes in securing their existence in this way, it is not the easiest of things to attribute this resourcefulness to beneficent divine design. What about the unfortunate water-snails? There have been a number of responses from Christian writers to the apologetic challenge faced from Darwinism. Yet a close reading of these responses reveals a significant departure from the neat, simplistic affirmations of the tradition of natural theology from Boyle to Paley. The observation that the universe is evolving is met with the idea of a providentially directed progression towards its ultimate divine goal. One of the most celebrated, though admittedly problematic, such approaches is due to Pierre Teilhard de Chardin, the French Jesuit paleontologist.[49] A more promising approach, however, is to be found in the works of John F. Haught. We shall examine this approach in a little detail, as it is much more distinctively Christian than many of the traditional Deist or theist apologetic responses of the past, raising important questions as to whether a theist or Deist approach to natural theology can be sustained in a changed cultural environment.

Incarnation, Trinity, and Natural Theology

In his 2003 Boyle Lecture – which renewed the tradition of engaging with issues in science and religion in the tradition of the original lecture series – Haught addressed the question of how a natural theology might be developed and justified within the parameters of a Darwinian worldview.[50] Haught sets out a vision for a "reconfiguration of natural theology after Darwin" based on "nature's narrative openness to the promise of an ever-renewing Future." It is an approach which he set out in earlier works,[51] and which merits continued

---

[49] For reflections on the implications of Teilhard's thought for the place of the church in the world, see the recent discussion of David Grumett, "Church, World and Christ in Teilhard De Chardin." *Ecclesiology* 1 (2004): 87–103.

[50] John F. Haught, "The Boyle Lecture 2003: Darwin, Design, and the Promise of Nature." *Science and Christian Belief* 17 (2005): 5–20.

[51] John Haught, *The Promise of Nature*. Mahwah, NJ: Paulist Press, 1993; *God after Darwin: A Theology of Evolution*. Boulder: Westview, 2000.

attention. One of its features is the reworking of the traditional notion of providence, here understood as taking "the form not so much of design and fine-tuning as the perpetual dawning of a new future for the world." Amplifying this point, Haught comments: "An infinitely compassionate and resourceful Future can be the ultimate redemptive repository of the entire series of cosmic occurrences no less than of those episodes that make up our individual lives."

Haught recognizes the difficulties raised for natural theology by the apparent wastage and pointless suffering of the natural order, and seeks to engage with these concerns in a number of ways. In particular, he makes the entirely correct point that Christian theology is not confronted with fundamentally new problems in dealing with the suffering associated with the "Darwinian recipe"; it is an extension of a familiar problem (natural suffering and animal pain) which theology has addressed in the past. Yet this "recipe" undermines any Paleyesque attempt to argue from the present order of creation to God. The plausibility of Paley's understanding of nature – which is basically a biological extension of Boyle's appeal to the physical aspects of nature – is undermined by Darwinism. As Haught points out:

> The idea of divine providence has generally been associated closely with a divine "plan," "purpose," or "design," but there seems to be little in the Darwinian charting of life's journey that corresponds to such cozy concepts. Cataloging signs of divine design was the backbone of Robert Boyle's natural theology and the famous lectures he endowed. But, were he here with us today, Boyle himself might agree that after Darwin any natural theology built solely or primarily on the notion of design is hardly destined to prosper.

For such reasons, Haught recommends that we reconceive natural theology. We must not limit our reflections to the apparent design of the present natural order, but also look forward to its transformation. "Instead of focusing only on the fact of living design, which can be accounted for scientifically in terms of the Darwinian recipe, a revived natural theology will focus on nature's openness to the future." Haught develops this through the image of a "self-emptying God" who "participates fully in the world's struggle and pain."[52]

> The picture of an incarnate God who suffers along with creation [affirms] that the agony of living beings is not undergone in isolation from the divine eternity, but is taken up everlastingly and redemptively into the very "life-story" of God.

It is a thoroughly incarnational, trinitarian vision of God, which I respect and admire, which clearly offers Christians a framework by which they may view

---

[52] *God after Darwin*, 49–50.

and even make limited sense of the complex Darwinian picture of an emergent, suffering world. It parallels, in important respects, the approach offered by Wolfhart Pannenberg, who argues for a creative exploration of the impact of a trinitarian doctrine of creation for a right understanding of "nature," along with an incorporation of the insights of the *logos* doctrine of the ancient church.[53]

But there is a highly significant point to be made here. The original Boyle Lectures were based on a direct appeal to the natural order, from which certain theistic conclusions were drawn on the basis of certain assumptions which might well be deemed to be common to all people. A natural theology, in Boyle's sense of the term, is based on an appeal to nature and a set of shared communal assumptions which leads an audience to the Christian revelation. What Haught offers us is an appeal to nature and a very specifically *Christian* set of assumptions, through which nature is to be viewed. Boyle's vision of natural theology is based on common sense; Haught argues (surely rightly) that many specifically Christian ideas – including that of a suffering, incarnate God – are "offensive to our customary sense of what should pass muster as ultimate reality,"[54] and may thus be seen as contrary to this same common sense. The belief that there is a creator God remains widely dispersed within at least parts of western culture,[55] even though it is no longer universally held or its dominant mood. Earlier Boyle Lectures regarded this as a truth of natural reason. For this reason, these natural theologies often lacked a distinctively Christian identity, often having a decidedly Deist tone. In marked contrast, however, the doctrines of the Trinity and incarnation are not merely specific to Christianity; they are widely regarded as running contrary to natural reason.

The approach to natural theology and theodicy which Haught offers in response to the challenges posed by Darwinism include the following four elements, all of which are distinctive to Christianity:

1 The notion of a "suffering God,"[56] which runs counter to a philosophically preconceived notion of divinity, based on the concept of divine perfection.

---

[53] Wolfhart Pannenberg, "God and Nature." In *Toward a Theology of Nature: Essays on Science and Faith*, 50–71. Louisville, KY: Westminster/John Knox Press, 1993, quote at 65–6.

[54] *God after Darwin*, 50.

[55] For example, think of John Calvin's insistence that knowledge of God the creator was common to all people, whether within the church or outside it: Edward A. Dowey, *The Knowledge of God in Calvin's Theology*. New York: Columbia University Press, 1952.

[56] See William C. Placher, *Narratives of a Vulnerable God: Christ, Theology, and Scripture*. Louisville, KY: Westminster/John Knox Press, 1994. More generally, see Terence E. Fretheim, *The Suffering of God: An Old Testament Perspective*. Philadelphia: Fortress, 1984; Joseph M. Hallman, *The Descent of God: Divine Suffering in History and Theology*. Minneapolis: Fortress, 1991.

2 The concept of the incarnation,[57] which establishes a link between God and creation which goes beyond the act of original origination and subsequent supervenience to include the idea of divine entry and habitation within the natural order.

3 The doctrine of the Trinity,[58] which includes the notion that the "spirit of God" indwells the created order,[59] thus establishing a further connection between God and the creation.

4 A concept of the "economy of salvation" which sets the idea of a creator God in a trinitarian perspective, and emphasizes the notion of activity, directionality, and purpose within salvation history.[60]

These will cause no difficulty to the orthodox Christian; they (especially the fourth) are not, however, assumptions that will find much support within the community of professional evolutionary biologists, and those in the wider culture who take their intellectual cues from this constituency and their scientific popularizers.

The type of natural theology advocated by Haught thus diverges radically from that of seventeenth or eighteenth-century England in one highly significant respect: namely, that natural theology is not seen as an independent means of establishing the existence and character of God, but as a legitimate activity undertaken within the Christian community of faith, on the basis of its distinctive assumptions. It is an activity which takes place *intra muros ecclesiae* in the light of the faith of the church. While natural theology may indeed be used for apologetic purposes in relation to the culture at large, it is not to be seen as establishing Christian faith. That faith is already established, and its distinctive parameters give rise to "natural theology" within the content of the Christian revelation, not as its alternative or substitute. Natural theology depends upon revelation if it is indeed to be "theology."

---

[57] See T. F. Torrance, *The Incarnation: Ecumenical Studies in the Nicene-Constantinopolitan Creed AD 381*. Edinburgh: Handsel Press, 1981; Wolfgang A. Bienert, "Zur Logos-Christologie des Athanasius von Alexandrien in *Contra Gentes* und *De Incarnatione*." In *Papers Presented to the Tenth International Conference on Patristic Studies*, edited by E. A. Livingstone, 402–19. Louvain: Peeters, 1989.

[58] See, for example, Stephen T. Davis, Daniel Kendall, and Gerald O'Collins. *The Trinity: An Interdisciplinary Symposium on the Trinity*. Oxford: Oxford University Press, 1999. We shall return to a more detailed discussion of this matter later in this volume.

[59] A view found especially in Jürgen Moltmann, *Gott in der Schöpfung: Ökologische Schöpfungslehre*. Munich: Kaiser Verlag, 1985. Moltmann interprets creation as an operation of the Trinity with a special emphasis on the Spirit as the means by which God not merely acts in creation, but is actively present within it. See further his *Der Geist des Lebens: Eine ganzheitliche Pneumatologie*. Munich: Kaiser Verlag, 1991.

[60] See J. Patout Burns, "Economy of Salvation: Two Patristic Traditions." *Theological Studies* 37 (1976): 598–619.

If this approach is correct, it entirely subverts the natural theology tradition of the Enlightenment. To discover God through nature, nature must be "read" in a way that ultimately presupposes Christian conclusions. The presuppositions determine the outcome. And here we find our answer to the concerns that Barth so forcefully expressed. If natural theology is reconceived and repositioned, Barth's objections lose their force. At the heart of this process of reconception is an insistence that natural theology is not an autonomous intellectual exercise conducted from outside the Christian tradition, but a legitimate consequence of the Christian vision of reality. Natural theology presupposes the core doctrines of the Christian faith, which impels the theologian to view nature through the lens of a trinitarian vision of God. Natural theology is the proper outcome of faith, not its foundation; its consequence, not its presupposition. And this, it will be noted, provides a response to Barth's concerns about natural theology subverting divine revelation.

Responding to Barth: Natural Theology as a Specifically Christian Undertaking

Natural theology is to be undertaken from the standpoint of faith, making explicit and extensive use of the distinctive ideas of Christian theology. In making such a fundamental realignment of theological parameters, the Christian tradition repositions the whole enterprise of natural theology, shifting it from an autonomous intellectual exercise outside the community of faith to a discipline that arises and is undertaken within the context of the Christian revelation.[61] While I would argue that this conceptual relocation is intrinsic to the theological vision articulated in the "scientific theology" project, I am also clear that Barth's criticisms of the traditional approach have shaped my thinking at this point. They represent legitimate concerns, which merit a response for the sake of the theological vigilance that is a core obligation of the community of faith.

It is clear that a number of factors shape Barth's anxieties concerning natural theology, including his belief in the theological destructiveness of the reasser-tion of human autonomy,[62] and his perennial fear that theology might be reduced to anthropology.[63] These are not unreasonable concerns, although it

---

[61] For my earlier proposals on the need for such repositioning, see Alister E. McGrath, *A Scientific Theology 1: Nature*. Grand Rapids, MI: Eerdmans, 2001, 241–305.

[62] Bruce L. McCormack, *Karl Barth's Critically Realistic Dialectical Theology: Its Genesis and Development, 1909–1936*. Oxford: Clarendon Press, 1997, 241–88. See also John Macken, *The Autonomy Theme in the Church Dogmatics of Karl Barth and His Critics*. Cambridge: Cambridge University Press, 1990.

[63] Karl Barth, *Die christliche Theologie im Entwurf*. Munich: Kaiser Verlag, 1927, 81–7.

must be noted that Barth's somewhat negative attitude towards the understanding of the social and psychological aspects of the human condition leads him to develop a theology of revelation which is ultimately inattentive to the question of how human beings recognize revelation *as such*, and use constructs in its analysis. This makes it difficult for Barth to engage with the important question of the provisionality of theoretical responses to revelation. Perhaps more seriously, it has negative implications for Barth's attitude towards the natural sciences.[64] Barth's failure to engage in dialogue with leading physicists surely represents one of the greatest missed opportunities in twentieth-century theology.

Barth's concerns about natural theology can be met by reconceptualizing natural theology as an intellectual undertaking within the community of faith, on the basis of its central doctrinal commitments. This point has been made repeatedly by Thomas F. Torrance, widely regarded as Barth's leading twentieth-century British interpreter, and a systematic theologian of the first rank.[65] Torrance's most important analysis of the positive role of natural theology is to be found in the discussion of "The Transformation of Natural Theology," which formed part of the 1978 Richards Lectures, given at the University of Virginia at Charlottesville.[66] Torrance rejects "natural theology of the traditional kind," by which he understands that approach to natural theology which "is pursued as an independent system on its own, antecedent to positive or revealed theology."[67] I myself follow a similar approach in *A Scientific Theology*, noting Barth's concerns, yet insisting these can be met by repositioning natural theology.

Tradition, Interpretation, and the Discovery of God: Natural Theology and Meno's Paradox

Earlier in this essay, we noted some concerns about traditional approaches to natural theology that were well established by the end of the nineteenth

---

[64] A point made by Ray S. Anderson, "Barth and a New Direction for Natural Theology." In *Theology Beyond Christendom: Essays on the Centenary of the Birth of Karl Barth*, edited by John Thompson, 241–66. Allison Park, PA: Pickwick Publications, 1986.

[65] See in particular T. F. Torrance, "The Problem of Natural Theology in the Thought of Karl Barth." *Religious Studies* 6 (1970): 121–35. For further discussion, see Alister E. McGrath, *Thomas F. Torrance: An Intellectual Biography*. Edinburgh: T&T Clark, 1999.

[66] Published as T. F. Torrance, *The Ground and Grammar of Theology*. Charlottesville: University of Virginia Press, 1980.

[67] Ibid, 93.

century – for example, the challenges posed by Darwin's account of the origin of species. During the twentieth century, however, a new concern emerged, partly in response to the realization of the non-universality of western modes of thought. Up to that point, there appears to have been a widespread belief that nature could be interpreted on the basis of a shared set of universal beliefs. Nature, to revert to the "two books" metaphor, was as an open book, capable of being more or less unequivocally interpreted as the handiwork of a creator God.

Yet the passage of time has called into question any such conclusion. The idea that nature interprets itself as the creation of God has run into the sands. The "book of nature" can be read and interpreted in many ways, and it is intensely problematic to speak of its "right" or "necessary" interpretation. The idea that nature can be seen as God's creation remains a possibility among many others; the older idea that belief in God as creator is the inevitable outcome of an unbiased process of reflection is no longer regarded as plausible.[68] A growing awareness of the importance of culturally inherited assumptions has pointed to the earlier tendency to interpret nature as God's creation as ultimately residing in a network of cultural beliefs, shaped by the Christian faith of the past. With the erosion of such beliefs over time, the apparently self-evident reading of nature as creation becomes increasingly counter-intuitive.

As Norbert R. Hanson has constantly emphasized, we do not simply "see" things; we see them *as* something. Observation is a theory-laden process, in which we bring theoretical preconceptions to the act of observation.[69] If nature was self-interpreting, this might not be a matter of great significance. However, there is a growing realization that nature is an *interpretandum*, something that requires interpretation, not an *interpretans*, something that actually interprets. While theoretical frameworks used to interpret nature may be grounded in observation of the natural order, they are not unambiguously determined

---

[68] For a detailed analysis, see Alister E. McGrath, *A Scientific Theology 1: Nature*. London: Continuum, 2001, 81–133.

[69] See the classic discussion in N. R. Hanson, *Patterns of Discovery: An Inquiry into the Conceptual Foundations of Science*. Cambridge: Cambridge University Press, 1961. Many examples can be given to illustrate the importance of such frameworks – for example, the naming of colors, which in some cultures involves the merging of green and blue. Here, a culturally determined theoretical framework determines what is "seen": M. H. Bernstein, "Color Vision and Color Naming: A Psychophysiological Hypothesis of Cultural Difference." *Psychological Bulletin* 80 (1973): 257–87. The development of color perception is often accounted for in evolutionary terms, as in Evan Thompson, *Colour Vision: A Study in Cognitive Science and the Philosophy of Perception*. London: Routledge, 1995.

by that order. To see nature as creation, assumptions must be brought to the process of interpretation which belong within the Christian tradition. It proves to be highly problematic to develop a "neutral" or "tradition-independent" approach to natural theology, in that a *hermeneutic of nature* is presupposed by the act of interpreting nature. Wilhelm Dilthey was right in insisting that we all approach all texts with certain preunderstandings, and Rudolph Bultmann equally rightly held that there is no such thing as "presuppositionless exegesis."[70] The problem is that the traditional approach to natural theology, evident in the original Boyle Lectures, seems to have been unaware of this awkward point. The "book of nature" is read on the basis of a series of presuppositions, some inherited from our culture, some from our personal history, and some from covert influences we have yet to identify or understand. The grand vision of "natural theology" as a public undertaking, capable of commanding consent by virtue of a secure set of culturally plausible assumptions, has clearly receded into the distant past. How can a culture which has lost its cultural memory of God expect to find a God in nature? How can it seek something when it doesn't know what it is actually looking for?

There are strong hints of "Meno's paradox" here: unless the searcher has a prior understanding of what is being sought, it seems that inquiry is impossible.[71] The response offered to this by Plato in the *Meno* – namely, that we already have within our souls the answers to such questions, so that arriving at the answers is a matter of retrieving them from within – has been the subject of much criticism.[72] Yet it is the point underlying the paradox – rather than Socrates' attempt to resolve it – that is of relevance to natural theology. If one has no concept of God, how can belief in this God be elicited from reflection on nature? How can God be *discovered*, when this God is not directly disclosed empirically within nature?

---

[70] See the classic essay: Rudolf Bultmann, "Is Exegesis without Presuppositions Possible?" In *The Hermeneutics Reader: Texts of the German Tradition from the Enlightenment to the Present*, edited by Kurt Mueller-Vollmer, 241–8. Oxford: Blackwell, 1986. For critical comment, see Joseph Fitzmyer, "Historical Criticism: Its Role in Biblical Interpretation and Church Life." *Theological Studies* 50 (1989): 249–52; Roger A. Johnson, *The Origins of Demythologizing: Philosophy and Historiography in the Theology of Rudolf Bultmann*. Leiden: Brill, 1974.

[71] *Meno* 80d–e. For discussion, see Gail Fine, *Plato on Knowledge and Forms: Selected Essays*. Oxford: Oxford University Press, 2003, 44, 50–1. See also the diverging account in Panagiotis Dimas, "True Belief in the Meno." *Oxford Studies in Ancient Philosophy* 14 (1996): 1–32. Dimas' approach runs counter to the current orthodoxy, by proposing that Plato wishes to move beyond Socrates' account of knowledge.

[72] See, for example, Roslyn Weiss, *Virtue in the Cave: Moral Inquiry in Plato's Meno*. New York: Oxford University Press, 2001, 95–100. Weiss herself takes the view that this argument is something of a farce, best suited for convincing the gullible.

C. S. Lewis attempted to respond to this issue at several points in his works, particularly the sermon "The Weight of Glory." As Lewis there points out, we are confronted with the paradox that our desire for "this far-off country," though intense, is uninformed; as a result, "we cannot tell it because it is a desire for something that has never actually appeared in our experience. We cannot hide it because our experience is constantly suggesting it, and we betray ourselves like lovers at the mention of a name."[73] Yet even those lacking a Christian perspective can still appreciate the importance of this issue. Maurice Merleau-Ponty's ontology can be seen as an attempt to overcome Meno's paradox, in particular the question of how we need to know what we are looking for, if we are to find it.[74] The plausibility of "natural theology" in western culture, particularly England, rested on the subtle transformation of cultural memories into self-evident propositions through the passage of time.

The point will be familiar to readers of Alasdair MacIntyre. In his 1988 Gifford Lectures, published as *Three Rival Versions of Moral Inquiry*, MacIntyre argues that philosophy in general and ethics in particular cannot proceed by means of reasoning from neutral, self-evident facts accepted by all rational persons.[75] He points out that many intellectuals of the late Victorian period believed exactly that, confusing the customs of their time with universal truths. For MacIntyre, the solution to moral and philosophical problems does not, and cannot, lie in an appeal to an allegedly universal conception of rational or moral judgment,[76] but in working within the tradition that supplies the framework of judgment for those posing those philosophical and moral problems.[77] Conceptions of both rationality and morality are shaped and transmitted by traditions, which can be thought of as functioning in a manner similar to the *polis* of ancient Greece.[78] The classic English tradition of natural theology,

---

[73] C. S. Lewis, "The Weight of Glory." In *Screwtape Proposes a Toast*, 94–110. London: Collins, 1965, quote at 97.

[74] See the important study of M. C. Dillon, *Merleau-Ponty's Ontology*. Bloomington: Indiana University Press, 1988.

[75] Alasdair MacIntyre, *Three Rival Versions of Moral Inquiry: Encyclopedia, Genealogy, and Tradition*. Notre Dame, IN: University of Notre Dame Press, 1990. The 1990 Aquinas Lecture is also of importance in developing this point: see Kent Reames, "Metaphysics, History, and Moral Philosophy: The Centrality of the 1990 Aquinas Lecture to MacIntyre's Argument for Thomism." *The Thomist* 62 (1998): 419–43.

[76] See the comments and analysis of the Enlightenment paradigm in Thomas Nagel, *The View from Nowhere*. New York: Oxford University Press, 1986.

[77] Craig Allen Beam, "Gadamer and MacIntyre: Tradition as a Resource of Rationality." *Kinesis* 25 (1998): 15–35.

[78] For a similar use of this approach in Stanley Hauerwas' work, see Arne Rasmusson, *The Church as Polis: From Political Theology to Theological Politics as Exemplified by Jürgen Moltmann and Stanley Hauerwas*. Lund: Lund University Press, 1994.

we might therefore observe, proves to be dependent on a series of tradition-mediated assumptions which were mistakenly supposed to be natural truths of reason.

The secular traditions of western culture do not themselves legitimate a godly "reading" of nature; this, however, must not be interpreted as meaning that such an interpretation of nature is illegitimate. It is simply an affirmation that these specific traditions of rationality, deriving from the Enlightenment, do not naturally lead to this interpretation. More importantly, it allows us to make the crucially important point that the enterprise of natural theology rests on a tradition-specific rationality. Reading nature as God's creation is tradition specific, not a universal option. It requires a certain net to be cast over our experience of the world, and a certain quite definite framework to be brought to its interpretation.

Returning to Meno's paradox: to the extent that this "paradox" expresses a genuine difficulty (as opposed to merely playing a heuristic role in clarifying the process of inquiry), a scientific theology resolves this by proposing that the God which natural theology "finds" in the world is already known and characterized by the specifics of the Christian tradition, grounded in revelation. The Christian tradition provides the presuppositions by which exegesis of the "book of nature" takes place. An integral aspect of the scientific theology project is the recognition that this enables an important debate over which of the rival intellectual traditions offers the "best fit" or the "best explanation" of what may be observed within nature, while at the same time realizing that nature itself lacks the epistemic authority and clarity to settle this question on its own terms.

As I stressed throughout the first volume of A Scientific Theology, nature requires interpretation – and such interpretations are mediated by specific traditions. There is no "right," "objective," or "universal" way to read nature. The whole enterprise of natural theology thus depends on a tradition-specific interpretation of nature, which sees nature as God's creation. But the Christian tradition brings far more to bear on its reading of nature than the sole, single insight that the world is God's creation – which, after all, could be taken as a Deist, rather than Christian, insight. For a natural theology to be Christian, it presupposes and articulates such notions as the Trinity and the incarnation – and thus moves decisively away from the "common sense" Deism of the Enlightenment.

Cognitive and Perceptual Approaches to Natural Theology

A further point at which a reconceived natural theology needs to break free from the influence of the Enlightenment is in the latter's emphasis on the rational character of a knowledge of God on the part of a detached observer of nature. The debate over "natural theology" in the last three hundred years has been framed largely (but not exclusively) in terms that are characteristic of the thought-world of that period. Human beings are understood to be observers of the universe around them, an enterprise which is undertaken on the basis of assumptions inherited from Descartes and Kant, which tend to detach the conscious observer from what is given in our experience of the world. On this way of construing the world, natural theology is an essentially cognitive activity, concerned with "making sense" of things – in other words, rational reflection on the world, particularly how it may be represented, and how tensions arising within our theoretical representation of reality may be contained within the limits of this theory.[79] The immensely complex and variegated reality of nature is thus reduced to the abstraction of theory, with the risks and opportunities that this brings in its wake.

This immediately gives rise to a highly significant question. Given that the natural order is, on the basis of either a scientific or theological account of its origins, *contingent*,[80] how can nature be the basis of any form of reliable knowledge? It is instructive to compare the very different attitudes of Jean-Paul Sartre and Iris Murdoch to contingencies, the former adopting an attitude of "horror to the contingent."[81] For Murdoch, this represents a failure to accept the realities of the human situation in particular, and the world in general. The world is just too complex to fit our systems. Whereas, for Sartre, the defeat of reason by the particularities of contingency is an affront to human dignity, to Murdoch it represents a gateway to the sublime, through the realization of our limited yet significant place within the greater order of things. For the Christian theologian, Murdoch *must* be right: we cannot hope to master nature or God, and accept the limits under which we operate – not as a craven act of submission, but as the acceptance of an insight which informs our entire understanding of what it is, in the first place, to be human, and in the second, to be a human within the natural order as a whole.

Traditional approaches to natural theology, generally shaped by the Enlightenment, treat human beings as observers of nature, seeking to offer an explanation and theoretical representation of what they observe. It is an entirely natural approach for thinkers steeped in the Cartesian and Kantian

---

[79] For an extensive reflection on the nature and limits of theory in theological reflection, see Alister E. McGrath, *A Scientific Theology 3: Theory*. Grand Rapids, MI: Eerdmans, 2003.

[80] This point is stressed particularly by T. F. Torrance: see, for example, his *Divine and Contingent Order*. Oxford: Oxford University Press, 1981.

[81] See Peter J. Conradi, *The Saint and the Artist: A Study of the Fiction of Iris Murdoch*, 3rd edn. London: Harper Collins, 2001, 133–8.

traditions of the Enlightenment to take. It rests implicitly on the Cartesian distinction between *res cognitans* and *res extensa*, which is typically expressed in the idea of an observing subject reflecting on an external object. Humanity observes nature, and reflects on how it is best to be understood.

Prior to Kant, there was a general assumption that God could be considered as an entity within nature, or detached from it, and that the scientific study of nature might provide evidence for (or perhaps merely consistent with) God's existence and attributes. As we saw earlier, this was a fundamental assumption of the original Boyle Lectures. The traditional approach to natural theology was also grounded on the assumption – once more, characteristic of the Boyle Lectures – that humans already are, or could become, non-participatory observers of nature. These assumptions led to human observers becoming elevated to subjects and God demoted to an object by the rise of science in the seventeenth and eighteenth centuries.

Both Kant and Hume challenged this traditional approach. Hume effectively eliminates God from any description of nature, achieving a parsimonious account of observations that might otherwise have been taken as pointing towards God's existence, or regarded as confirmation of selected divine attributes.[82] Kant argued that God was not a knowable object or phenomenon, but a transcendent reality only accessible by faith. What can be known of nature is constrained by *a priori* human ideas and categories, which are capable of assimilating *phenomena*, but not the whole transcendental reality (*noumena*) that lies behind or alongside them. Kant's approach thus erects a theologically impervious barrier between nature and God, preventing human inquiries into nature from reaching any meaningful conclusions concerning God.[83] While William Paley was able to overlook such awkward arguments (if, indeed, he was aware of them at all) in formulating his natural theology, his more recent successors have had to be considerably more cautious in their approach.

Yet this strongly cognitive approach to natural theology overlooks or marginalizes the fact that cognition is an embodied, situated activity. Human beings are part of nature, located within it. While the Christian tradition has always posited a rigorous theological distinction between humanity and the remainder of the natural world, this does not alter the fact that our process of reflection on that world takes place within the context of our being agents within it. Heidegger's notion of "being-in-the-world"

---

[82] Wesley C. Salmon, "Religion and Science: A New Look at Hume's *Dialogues.*" *Philosophical Studies* 33 (1978): 143–76.

[83] A point perhaps best seen in his reflections on the ontological argument: Otto Samuel, "Der ontologische Gottesbeweis bei Karl Barth, Immanuel Kant und Anselm von Canterbury." *Theologische Blätter* 14 (1935): 141–53.

articulates the insight that the condition of our creating disengaged representations of reality is that we should already be engaged in coping with that world, dealing with it as an experienced reality. Similarly, Maurice Merleau-Ponty stressed that perception and representation take place within the context of an embodied agent purposefully engaging with the world. Merleau-Ponty is critical of the approaches of Descartes and Kant, who he argues to have detached the conscious subject from the world that is given in experience. "The perceiving mind is an incarnated mind." This leads him to reject those "doctrines which treat perception as a simple result of the action of external things on our body."[84]

Similar concerns abound in the writings of John Dewey, who emphasizes the limits of the empirical method. As Dewey puts it, boldly and succinctly: "What is really 'in' experience extends much further than that which at any time is known."[85] Knowledge is a simplification of experience, which attempts to reduce a complex, subtle, and at times apparently chaotic world to manageable ideas. The attraction of the approach will be evident; so, however, are its dangers. For Dewey, "the great vice of philosophy is an arbitrary 'intellectualism'," which he defines as:[86]

the theory that all experiencing is a mode of knowing, and that all subject matter, all nature, is in principle, to be reduced and transformed till it is defined in terms identical with the characteristics presented by refined objects of science as such. The assumption of "intellectualism" goes contrary to the facts of what is primarily experienced. For things are objects to be treated, used, acted upon and with, enjoyed and endured, even more than things to be known. They are things *had* before they are things cognized.

Applying these insights to natural theology – something that Dewey would not entirely have commended, of course[87] – we can see a fundamental criticism being directed against the traditional way of understanding this whole enterprise. There is a danger of an "intellectual" engagement with nature, which sees it simply as something to be understood through a process of abstraction. Such an "intellectualism," Dewey argues, "is so foreign to the facts of primary

---

[84] Maurice Merleau-Ponty, "Un inédit de Maurice Merleau-Ponty." *Revue de métaphysique et de morale* 4 (1962), 401–9.

[85] John Dewey, *Experience and Nature*, 2nd edn. New York: Dover, 1958, 20.

[86] Ibid, 21.

[87] This is not to say, however, that Dewey overlooked the transcendent, as some of his interpreters believed to be the case. For an important correction of this misconception, see Victor Kestenbaum, *The Grace and Severity of the Ideal: John Dewey and the Transcendent*. Chicago: University of Chicago Press, 2002.

experience that it not only compels recourse to non-empirical method, but it ends in making knowledge, conceived as ubiquitous, itself inexplicable."[88] While not denying the importance of such habits of abstraction and reflection, Dewey insists on recognizing the dangers of the method. "When intellectual experience and its material are taken to be primary, the cord that binds experience and nature is cut."[89]

The challenge, then, is to develop a Christian approach to nature – that is to say, a natural theology or a theology of nature – which is not limited to intellectual or explanatory aspects. Natural theology cannot be restricted to reflecting on a sense of awe in the presence of nature, but disregarding that awe in its headlong rush to understand what is being experienced. A fundamental reconnection between experience and understanding, between perception and cognition, is to be sought. On a Christian understanding of things, a truly natural theology appeals to the human imagination, not simply the human reason.

The fundamental theme of any "natural theology" is the affirmation of an intellectual pathway from the natural to the spiritual, from nature to God. This does not preclude ensuing debate and discussion over the apologetic question of what those paths might be, nor the theologically significant evaluation of the interaction of the human and the divine in this quest. Is this to be seen as the unaided journey of the autonomous human mind, or as the graceful guidance of a God who, like a city on a hill, guides humanity towards their source and goal as a moth is drawn to a lamp? This is one of the most fundamental themes of the "natural theology of the imagination" set out by J. R. R. Tolkien, especially in his landmark poem "Mythopoeia."[90] Part of the theological enterprise is to place the discipline of natural theology on a conceptual map, calibrating its capacities and correlations, both rational and imaginative, and locating it along the coordinates of time and eternity on the one hand, and human achievement and divine grace on the other.

When seen from the perspective of faith, the world is indeed charged with the glory and grandeur of God. Natural theology, when properly done, does not merely leave us with new academic insights. It forces us to our knees in admiration of the God who has made us spectators in this theatre of the divine glory, having captured our imaginations with glimpses of glory, not simply persuaded our minds with impressions of rationality.

---

[88] *Experience and Nature*, 22.

[89] Ibid, 23.

[90] For the text of the poem, see J. R. R. Tolkien, *Tree and Leaf*. London: Harper Collins, 2001, 83–90. See further Verlyn Flieger, *Splintered Light: Logos and Language in Tolkien's World*, revd. edn. Kent, OH: Kent State University Press, 2002, 49–56.

CHAPTER 5

Stratification: Levels of Reality and the Limits of Reductionism

The discussion of the scientific (*wissenschaftlich*) status of Christian theology continues unabated.[1] Is there, as many Enlightenment writers believed, a universal method, capable of being applied to theology as much as to any other intellectual discipline? Can the gap between *Naturwissenschaften* and *Geisteswissenschaften* be bridged? Is there one scientific methodology capable of functioning as both foundation and ground of adjudication across all disciplines – including the natural sciences, social sciences, and humanities? The Enlightenment regarded the advances of the natural sciences as paradigmatic for human knowledge as a whole, and sought to consolidate and rationalize every aspect of human knowledge on the basis of a unified methodology. Critics of the Enlightenment – such as Giambattista Vico (1688–1744), Johann Georg Hamann (1730–88), and Johann Gottfried Herder (1744–1803) – sought to distance the humanities from the natural sciences in order to rebuff any such rationalist attempt to bring about the unification of human knowledge.[2]

In part, this hostility towards the methodology of the natural sciences in the specific case of Christian theology rests on a belief, common to many contem-

---

[1] For important discussions, see works such as Hermann Diem, *Theologie als kirchliche Wissenschaft: Handreichung zur Einübung ihrer Probleme*. Munich: Kaiser, 1951; Gerhard Sauter, *Theologie als Wissenschaft: Aufsätze und Thesen*. Munich: Kaiser, 1971; Wolfhart Pannenberg, *Wissenschaftstheorie und Theologie*. Frankfurt am Main: Suhrkamp Verlag, 1977; Rudolf Langthaler, *Theologie als Wissenschaft: ein Linzer Symposium*. Frankfurt am Main: Lang, 2000. It must be noted that the German term *wissenschaftlich* does not mean specifically pertaining to the *natural* sciences, but rather to the systematic exploration of knowledge in general.

[2] See especially Isaiah Berlin, *Three Critics of the Enlightenment: Vico, Hamann, Herder*. Princeton, NJ: Princeton University Press, 2000.

porary theologians, that theology possesses both a distinct methodology and a unique subject matter, making its assimilation to other scientific methodologies deeply problematic.

The concept of *stratification* provides an answer to this critically important question. It is not a new concept; a case can be made for at least some of its aspects being anticipated in antiquity.[3] The idea also began to emerge as significant in German-language philosophy in the opening decades of the twentieth century. Max Scheler (1874–1928) set out a "stratified" theory of ethics in his 1916 work *Der Formalismus in der Ethik*. In this work, Scheler distinguished five levels (*Schichten*) of human emotions, arguing for their distinctiveness, while maintaining their interconnectedness.[4] Scheler's work stimulated others to adopt a stratified approach, particularly to human nature. In 1938 Erich Rothacker set out a stratified approach to anthropology.[5] Although the concept of stratification was used primarily in the 1930s to discuss aspects of human psychology, it was clear that the concept had the potential to illuminate culture in general.

Stratification in Nicolai Hartmann

In a series of publications, Scheler's pupil Nicolai Hartmann (1882–1950) argued for the need for a critical ontology, sensitive to the complex, variegated nature of reality.[6] This, he argues, must be grounded in fundamental human experience, not superimposed on the basis of preconceived categories.[7] While Hartmann has no difficulty with the Kantian notion of critical reflection, he insists that any processes of categorization must be rigorously grounded in

---

[3] See, for example, Hans Wagner, "Die Schichtentheoreme bei Platon, Aristoteles und Plotin." *Studium Generale* 9 (1957): 283–91.

[4] Max Scheler, *Der Formalismus in der Ethik und die materiale Wertethik: Neuer Versuch der Grundlegung eines ethischen Personalismus*, 4th edn. Bern: Francke, 1954, 332–45. For comment on Scheler, see Arne Jaitner, *Zwischen Metaphysik und Empirie: Zum Verhältnis von Transzendentalphilosophie und Psychoanalyse bei Max Scheler, Theodor W. Adorno und Odo Marquard*. Würzburg: Königshausen & Neumann, 1999.

[5] Erich Rothacker, *Die Schichten Der Persönlichkeit*, 4th edn. Bonn: Bouvier, 1948.

[6] See, for example, Nicolai Hartmann, *Zum Problem der Realitätsgegebenheit*. Berlin: Pan-Verlagsgesellschaft, 1931; *Zur Grundlegung der Ontologie*, 3rd edn. Meisenheim am Glan: Anton Hain, 1948. For the best study in English, see W. H. Werkmeister, *Nicolai Hartmann's New Ontology*. Tallahassee: Florida State University Press, 1990.

[7] Nicolai Hartmann, *Neue Wege der Ontologie*, 4th edn. Stuttgart: Kohlhammer, 1964, 18.

experience, rather than being detached from it. On the basis of his reflection on human experience, Hartmann offers a fourfold stratification of reality, as follows.[8]

First stratum: inorganic being, including the categories of matter, substantiality, and causality.
Second stratum: organic being, including the categories of metabolism, assimilation, and self-reproduction.
Third stratum: mental being (*seeliges Sein*), including the categories of consciousness and pleasure.
Fourth stratum: spiritual being, including the categories of thought, knowledge, and personality.

Two points emerge on considering Hartmann's stratified ontology. First, it clearly is an *ontology*. Although Rudolf Carnap had also proposed a hierarchically organized *Konstitutionsystem*, he did not regard this as fundamentally ontological, but merely a heuristic process of categorization.[9] In contrast to this deontological conception of cognition, Hartmann insists that such categorization corresponds to the way things actually are. Second, some aspects of his categorization now seem as improbable as Kant's, largely on account of Hartmann's slightly vague knowledge of modern physics, and subsequent scientific advance.[10] Yet the idea of stratification was shown to be philosophically promising, even if Hartmann's particular understanding of it did not lead to significant outcomes.[11]

Since then, the idea has been given a much more rigorous grounding, especially in relation to the natural sciences. This important conceptual tool allows us to affirm the ontological unity of reality, while recognizing that this unity expresses itself at different levels, each demanding a form of engagement

---

[8] Nicolai Hartmann, *Kleinere Schriften*, 3 vols. Berlin: De Gruyter, 1955, Vol. 1, 99–101.

[9] Rudolf Carnap, *Der logische Aufbau der Welt*. Hamburg: Felix Meiner Verlag, 1998, 102–7.

[10] Paul Feyerabend expressed concern at this point, especially in relation to Hartmann's weak grasp of quantum theory and the concept of relativity: see Paul K. Feyerabend, "Professor Hartmann's Philosophy of Nature." *Ratio* 5 (1963): 91–106. For further comment, which does not entirely absolve Hartmann of such criticisms, see Ingvar Johansson, "Hartmann's Nonreductive Materialism, Superimposition, and Supervenience." *Axiomathes* 12 (2001): 195–215.

[11] I do not mean to imply that it was philosophically sterile. As Werner Lichter has shown, Hartmann's analysis offers some creative insights into the relation of ontology and epistemology, particularly through the notions of the *Realsphäre* and the *Idealsphäre*. See Werner Lichter, *Die Kategorialanalyse der Kausaldetermination: Eine kritische Untersuchung zur Ontologie Nicolai Hartmanns.* Bonn: Bouvier, 1964.

which is determined by the distinctive identity of the area of reality under investigation. The form of critical realism that I adopt in the "scientific theology" project insists that the world must be regarded as differentiated and stratified. Each individual science deals with a different stratum of this reality, which in turn obliges it to develop and use methods of investigation adapted and appropriate to this stratum. Stratum *B* might be grounded in, and emerge from, Stratum *A*. Yet despite this relation of origin, the same methods of investigation cannot be used in dealing with these two different strata. These methods must be established *a posteriori*, through an engagement with each of these strata of reality.

Stratification in Roy Bhaskar

In developing such ideas, I found myself drawing particularly on the work of Roy Bhaskar, whose ideas I discovered in 1998.[12] Bhaskar offers a critical realist account of the relation of the natural and social sciences which affirms their methodological commonalities, while respecting their distinctions, particularly when these arise on account of their objects of investigation.[13]

> Naturalism holds that it is possible to give an account of science under which the proper and more or less specific methods of both the natural and social sciences can fall. But it does not deny that there are significant differences in these methods, grounded in real differences in their subject matters and in the relationships in which these sciences stand to them ... It is the nature of the object that determines the form of its possible science.

We see here a clear recognition of each science being determined by the nature of its object, and being obligated to respond to it *kata physin*, in a manner which is appropriate to its distinctive nature.[14]

Bhaskar is stridently opposed to any form of reductionism – the rather crude and wooden approach which seems to collapse everything into one allegedly fundamental level. Such reductionist positions are surprisingly common, despite their obvious difficulties. Bhaskar argues that, because level *A* is rooted in and

---

[12] I explain how this came about in *A Scientific Theology 2: Reality*, xv–xvi.

[13] Roy Bhaskar, *The Possibility of Naturalism: A Philosophical Critique of the Contemporary Human Sciences*, 3rd edn. London: Routledge, 1998, 3.

[14] At this point, it is worth pointing out that the great Victorian art critic and cultural historian John Ruskin adopted the pen-name "Kata Physin" for a series of articles he wrote at the age of eighteen for *Loudon's Magazine* on "The Poetry of Architecture." The basic theme is very simple: the need to respect, preserve, and appreciate things for what they are.

emerges from level B, it does not follow that level A is therefore "nothing but" level B. Emergent strata possess features that are "irreducible" – that is, which cannot be conceived solely in terms of lower levels.

For Bhaskar, biology cannot be "reduced" to chemistry or physics, precisely because the biological stratum possesses characteristics which go beyond those of the stratum in which it is rooted. If it were possible to explain the origins of biological life in chemical or physical terms, that would not amount to the reduction of biology to either of these disciplines.

This idea of the stratification of reality is one of the most distinctive features of a scientific theology, allowing it to posit diversity within unity in terms of the way in which reality is investigated and depicted. In developing this idea further, I will initially explore the significant correlations between stratification and the concept of "emergence," noting particularly their implications for attempts to offer reductionist accounts of theology or the natural sciences. I will then note the difficulties that the notion of stratification causes for methodological uniformitarianism of the Enlightenment, focusing particularly on Heinrich Scholz's important but ultimately indefensible application of the Cartesian idea of *mathesis universalis* to philosophy and theology.

Stratification, Emergence, and the Failure of Reductionism

The concept of "emergence" has come to play a highly significant role in contemporary scientific discussions, ranging from the classic question of the origins of life to the limits of predictability in the sciences.[15] The burgeoning field of complexity science is often characterized by the slogan "the whole is greater than the sum of its parts." The whole idea of emergence has generated a new debate and a new literature,[16] calling into question many of the seemingly settled assumptions of classical physics, upon which so many reductionist views of the world are ultimately grounded.[17]

---

[15] See the classic discussion in Harold J. Morowitz, *The Emergence of Everything: How the World Became Complex*. Oxford: Oxford University Press, 2002. There is also much important material in Stuart A. Kauffman, *Investigations*. Oxford: Oxford University Press, 2000.

[16] See especially John H. Holland, *Emergence: From Chaos to Order*. Oxford: Oxford University Press, 2000.

[17] For reflections on the theological significance of biological emergence, see Arthur Peacocke, "Complexity, Emergence, and Divine Creativity." In *From Complexity to Life: On the Emergence of Life and Meaning*, edited by Niels Henrik Gregersen, 187–205. Oxford: Oxford University Press, 2003.

The term "emergence" is often used in a weak sense.[18] It is becoming increasingly clear that many complex systems are computationally intractable – that is to say, that predictive calculations of the development of such systems are so complex and problematic that one can do little other than watch how they evolve. Mark Bedau draws a fine distinction between weak and strong senses of the term emergent. A high-level phenomenon is *weakly* emergent with respect to a low-level domain when truths concerning that phenomenon are *unexpected* given the principles governing the low-level domain. Or, to put this another way, the causal dynamics of the whole system are completely determined by those of its individual parts – but the mathematical calculation of the relationship is so complex that we have to resort to simulation rather than predictive calculation. Such a system would then be "algorithmically incompressible," following the language of Gregory Chaitin and others.[19]

This naturally raises the question of whether there are limits to our capacity to compute. This notion was famously explored by Rolf Landauer, who stressed that, since computation ultimately rested on a physical basis, it was subject to the laws of physics and the resources available in the universe.[20] In practice, it is questionable whether such a limit can be rigorously derived in this manner, or whether it actually makes much difference to many traditional applications of mathematics.[21] Yet the notion does raise certain difficulties for reductionism, particularly any dismissal of the idea that there are organizing principles that only come into play once a certain threshold of complexity has been achieved. For example, conventional non-relativistic quantum mechanics is perfectly capable of describing the behavior of the everyday world in terms of a small number of known quantities – the charge and mass of the electron, the charges and masses of atomic nuclei, and Planck's constant – in terms of equation [1], which may be amplified as equation [2], as follows:

$$ i\hbar \frac{\partial}{\partial t} |\Psi> = \mathcal{H} |\Psi> \qquad [1] $$

[18] M. A. Bedau, "Weak Emergence." In *Philosophical Perspectives: Mind, Causation, and World*, edited by James Tomberlin, 375–99. Oxford: Blackwell, 1997.

[19] Gregory J. Chaitin, *Information-Theoretic Incompleteness*. Singapore: World Scientific, 1992.

[20] Rolf Landauer, "Computation and Physics: Wheeler's Meaning Circuit?" *Foundations of Physics* 16 (1986): 551–64: "The calculative process, just like the measurement process, is subject to some limitations. A sensible theory of physics must respect these limitations and should not invoke calculative routines that in fact cannot be carried out."

[21] For some excellent reflections, see Seth Lloyd, "Ultimate Physical Limits to Computation." *Nature* 406 (2002): 1047–54.

where

$$\mathcal{H} = -\sum_{j}^{N_e} \frac{\hbar^2}{2m} \nabla_j^2 - \sum_{\alpha}^{N_i} \frac{\hbar^2}{2M_\alpha} \nabla_\alpha^2$$

$$-\sum_{j}^{N_e}\sum_{\alpha}^{N_i} \frac{Z_\alpha e^2}{|\vec{r}_j - \vec{R}_\alpha|} + \sum_{j \ll k}^{N_e} \frac{e^2}{|\vec{r}_j - \vec{r}_k|} + \sum_{\alpha \ll \beta}^{N_j} \frac{Z_\alpha Z_\beta e^2}{|\vec{R}_\alpha - \vec{r}_\beta|}. \qquad [2]$$

The symbols Z_α and M_α respectively designate the atomic number and mass of nucleus α, R_α designates the location of this nucleus, e and m are the electron charge and mass, r_j is the location of nucleus j, and is the reduced Planck's constant, sometimes also referred to as Dirac's constant. As Robert Laughlin – awarded the Nobel Prize in physics in 1998 – and David Pines point out, these equations "are, for all practical purposes, the Theory of Everything for our everyday world."[22] Yet the equation has only been solved accurately for small numbers of particles, and cannot be solved to any degree of accuracy when the number of particles exceeds about ten. "No computer existing, or that ever will exist, can break this barrier because it is a catastrophe of dimension."

On the other hand, a high-level phenomenon could be said to be *strongly emergent* with respect to a low-level domain when truths concerning that phenomenon are not *deducible* even in principle from truths in the low-level domain. On this approach, whole systems may possess properties that cannot be reduced, even in principle, to the accumulated properties of its individual components. When a system reaches certain levels of complexity, novel causal powers emerge which are absent from its constituent parts.[23] Strong emergence is the notion of emergence that is most common in philosophical discussion of emergence, and is the notion invoked by the "British emergentists" of the 1920s.[24] The most important emergentist texts of this period – such as C. D. Broad's *The Mind and Its Place in Nature* (1923) – argued strongly that "new and theoretically unpredictable modes of behaviour" could appear in biological systems. While some of these older statements of the approach

---

[22] Robert B. Laughlin, and David Pines, "The Theory of Everything." *Proceedings of the National Academy of Sciences USA* 97 (2000): 28–31.

[23] The concept of "novelty" is of considerable interest at this point. See Robert Klee's discussion of "Empedoclean" and "Democritean" forms of explanation: Robert Klee, "Micro-Determinism and Concepts of Emergence." *Philosophy of Science* 51 (1984): 44–63.

[24] See the important review by Brian P. McLaughlin, "The Rise and Fall of British Emergentism." In *Emergence or Reduction? Essays on the Prospects of Non-Reductive Physicalism*, edited by A. Beckermann, H. Flohr, and J. Kim, 49–93. Berlin: de Gruyter, 1992.

must be approached with considerable caution, there are many recent discussions of the matter which insist that the emergent laws of biology are simply not reducible to the laws of physics which operate at the microscopic level.[25]

Examples of such properties of emergence are legion, both in molecular biology and condensed matter physics. Is life itself an emergent concept? There are very few scientists who would dispute that the phenomenon of life is at the very least a weakly emergent phenomenon. And what about consciousness, often cited as another example of the same phenomenon?[26] More importantly, it could be argued that Darwinian evolution, far from being the grand "theory of everything" that popularizers such as Richard Dawkins suggest,[27] is actually an emergent phenomenon, which only comes into play once a certain state of complexity has been reached. There is thus a "Darwinian horizon" before which the development of life does not proceed by the standard Darwinian paradigm.

In quantum theory, attention has recently been paid to the notion of "quantum protectorates," arising from certain higher organizing principles.[28] Robert Laughlin and David Pines point out there appears to be an unacknowledged tendency towards a reductionist mindset on the part of many natural scientists, which causes them to resist any notion of higher principles:

> The fact that the essential role played by higher organizing principles in determining emergent behavior continues to be disavowed by so many physical scientists is a poignant comment on the state of modern science. To solid-state physicists and chemists, who are schooled in quantum mechanics and deal with it every day in the context of unpredictable electronic phenomena such as organogels, Kondo insulators, or cuprate superconductivity, the existence of these principles is so obvious that it is a cliché not discussed in polite company. However, to other kinds of scientist the idea is considered dangerous and ludicrous, for it is fundamentally at odds with the reductionist beliefs central to much of physics. But the safety that comes from acknowledging only the facts one likes is fundamentally incompatible with science. Sooner or later it must be swept away by the forces of history.

As long ago as 1972, Philip W. Anderson – awarded the Nobel Prize in physics in 1977 – noted the uncritical acceptance of reductionism within the sciences,

---

[25] See here the often-cited claim that the enzymatic efficiency of a protein is an emergent property: Pier Puigi Luisi, "Emergence in Chemistry: Chemistry as the Embodiment of Emergence." *Foundations of Chemistry* 4 (2002): 183–200.

[26] For some important reflections, see Philip Clayton, *Mind and Emergence: From Quantum to Consciousness*. Oxford: Oxford University Press, 2004.

[27] Richard Dawkins, "Universal Darwinism." In *Evolution from Molecules to Men*, edited by D. S. Bendall, 403–25. Cambridge: Cambridge University Press, 1983.

[28] For a survey of the issues, see Laughlin and Pines, "The Theory of Everything."

while pointing out that "the ability to reduce everything to simple fundamental laws does not imply the ability to start from those laws and reconstruct the universe."[29] This whole enterprise, he argued, "breaks down when confronted with the twin difficulties of scale and complexity."

This acknowledgment of the stratified structuring of reality, and a growing awareness of the complex interactions between the strata, is not limited to thinking about emergence. The distinctive approach of the "scientific theology" project is based on the explicit recognition of the stratification of reality, as expressed in the hierarchical structure of the sciences. Each level of reality brings into existence "entirely new laws, concepts, and generalizations." As Anderson points out, it is possible to "array the sciences roughly linearly in a hierarchy, on the basis of the assumption that the elementary sciences of science X obey the laws of science Y":

X	Y
many-body physics	elementary particle physics
chemistry	many-body physics
molecular biology	chemistry
cell biology	molecular biology
*	*
*	*
psychology	physiology
social sciences	psychology

Yet, as Anderson stresses, this does *not* mean that "science X is 'just applied Y'." At each stage, new behaviors emerge. The contrast with scientific reductionism will be obvious. Thus Harvard biologist Edward O. Wilson, one of the founders of sociobiology, argues that social behavior is to be explained by the principles of biology, biology by the principles of chemistry, and chemistry by the principles of physics. Eventually, all higher disciplines will be reduced to nothing but the laws of chemistry and physics.[30] Similarly, Nobel Laureate Francis Crick has argued that the goal of the sciences is to reduce all knowledge to the laws of chemistry and physics: "The ultimate aim of the modern movement in biology is in fact to explain all biology in terms of physics and chemistry."[31] But, despite this bold rhetoric, this simply cannot be done, for precisely those reasons set out by Anderson.

---

[29] Philip W. Anderson, "More Is Different." *Science* 177 (1972): 393–6.

[30] Edward O. Wilson, *Sociobiology: The New Synthesis*. Cambridge, MA: Harvard University Press, 1975.

[31] Francis Crick, *Of Molecules and Men*. Seattle: University of Washington Press, 1966, 10.

To give an example from many-body physics:[32] the properties of a single, isolated gold atom can be completely understood on the basis of the Schrödinger equation and the laws of quantum mechanics. Yet the vast assemblies of gold atoms that make up metallic gold behave on the basis of principles which cannot be thus predicted. The collective behavior of materials demonstrates all too clearly the inadequacy of approaches that believe it is possible to reduce everything to the level of the atomic.

A wide variety of methodologies are deployed across the spectrum of these disciplines. Physics, evolutionary biology, and psychology each have their own vocabularies, methods, and procedures, and engage with nature at their own distinctive levels. This point has long been understood, and is not controversial. For example, consider Robert Oppenheimer's comments:[33]

> Every science has its own language ... Everything the chemist observes and describes can be talked about in terms of atomic mechanics, and most of it at least can be understood. Yet no one suggests that, in dealing with the complex chemical forms which are of biological interest, the language of atomic physics would be helpful. Rather it would tend to obscure the great regularities of biochemistry, as the dynamic description of gas would obscure its thermodynamic behaviour.

The merits of the point that Oppenheimer wishes to make would be recognized by any working scientist. Each science develops a vocabulary and a working method which is appropriate or adapted to its object. The more complex that object, the more levels of explanation are required. A classic example is the human body, which can be investigated at a series of levels – anatomical, physiological, and psychological – each of which illuminates one aspect of the greater whole, but none of which is adequate by itself to give a full account. There is no generalized scientific methodology, no *mathesis universalis*, which can be applied without variance and uncritically to all sciences. While certain general principles may be argued to lie behind the specific approaches found in any given natural science, the point is that the nature of the field to be investigated shapes the approach to be adopted. In that each science deals with a different object, it is under an obligation to respond to that object according to its distinctive nature. The methods which are appropriate to the study of one object cannot be abstracted and applied uncritically and universally. Each science develops procedures which it deems or discovers to be appropriate to

---

[32] Piers Coleman, "Many-Body Physics: Unfinished Revolution." *Annales de l'Institut Henri Poincaré* 4 (2003): 1–22.

[33] J. Robert Oppenheimer, *Science and the Common Understanding*. Oxford: Oxford University Press, 1954, 87.

the nature of its own particular object in which it "has solved its own inductive problem of how to arrive at a general conclusion from a limited set of particular observations."[34]

This general point, of such fundamental theological importance, can be illustrated from quantum mechanics. Werner Heisenberg's uncertainty principle represents the theoretical outcome of the application of the principle that we must encounter reality on its own terms, and accept the limitations which this entails. Electrons, Heisenberg insists, are not *anschaulich*, in that they cannot be "perceived." The question of how this affected the manner in which they were studied now became a matter of critical importance, in that the procedures of measurement and observation – which were virtually unproblematic in classical physics – encountered fundamental difficulties in relation to quantum phenomena.[35] If these phenomena are to be investigated, the fundamental limitations imposed upon the processes of observation and measurement by the nature of the quantum entities must be respected. Entities are known only in ways that correspond to their idiosyncratic identities, which must be acknowledged and respected.

A scientific theology believes that such a stratification of reality is both demanded by *a posteriori* reflection on the scientific enterprise, and by the Christian vision of the nature of the world. A unitary understanding of reality, such as that mandated by a Christian doctrine of creation, thus does not demand that each human intellectual discipline should adopt identical methods for their tasks, but that they should accommodate themselves to the distinctive natures of those aspects of reality which they attempt to represent and depict. Every level of reality demands to be investigated on its own terms, which are established *a posteriori* by reflection on the way things are, not determined *a priori* in advance of any such interpretation. A scientific theology thus insists on the need to reject the methodological uniformitarianism which the Enlightenment sought to impose on all disciplines, and instead to appreciate that ontology determines epistemology.[36] To repeat the formula that is of decisive importance to the whole enterprise of scientific theology: what something *is* determines both *how it is to be known* and *the extent to which it can be known*.

In the case of Christian theology, one of the most significant twentieth-century advocates of methodological uniformitarianism has been Heinrich Scholz. In what follows, we shall consider his use of the concept of *mathesis*

---

[34] A. D. Ritchie, *Studies in the History and Methods of the Sciences*. Edinburgh: Edinburgh University Press, 1963, 7.

[35] Werner Heisenberg, "Über den anschaulichen Inhalt der quantentheoretischen Kinematik und Mechanik." *Zeitschrift für Physik* 43 (1927): 172–98.

[36] For Bhaskar's discussion of the "epistemic fallacy" of the Enlightenment, see Roy Bhaskar, *A Realist Theory of Science*, 2nd edn. London: Verso, 1997, 16.

universalis, originally set out by René Descartes, and its impact on his landmark debate with Karl Barth over the methods and norms of Christian theology.

Mathesis Universalis: Heinrich Scholz and the Flawed Quest for Methodological Uniformity

It will be obvious that our analysis up to this point in this essay raises many of the issues to be debated in one of the most celebrated theological engagements of the early twentieth century: the debate between Heinrich Scholz and Karl Barth over whether theology can indeed be considered to be *wissenschaftlich*. As I believe my approach to theology casts light on at least some aspects of the debate, I shall begin by exploring the distinctive features and importance of Scholz's approach to theology, which draws heavily on his understanding of the methods of the natural sciences.

Scholz (1884–1956) was one of the most remarkable German theologians and philosophers of religion of the twentieth century.[37] Born in Berlin as the son of the pastor Hermann Scholz, he studied theology and philosophy at the University of Berlin under such luminaries as Adolf von Harnack and Alois Riehl, specializing in systematic theology and the philosophy of religion.[38] Although his initial call was as a professor of the philosophy of religion and systematic theology at Breslau (1917–21), he subsequently was called to chairs of philosophy at Kiel (1921–8) and Münster (1928–43). In 1938 he took up a newly founded chair of mathematical logic and foundations at Münster, the first such chair to be established in Germany.[39]

---

[37] For studies, see Matthias Fallenstein, *Religion als philosophisches Problem: Studien zur Grundlegung der Frage nach der Wahrheit der Religion im religionsphilosophischen Denken von Heinrich Scholz*. Frankfurt am Main: Lang, 1981; Arie Leendert Molendijk, *Aus dem Dunklen ins Helle: Wissenschaft und Theologie im Denken von Heinrich Scholz: mit unveröffentlichten Thesenreihen von Heinrich Scholz und Karl Barth*. Amsterdam: Rodopi, 1991; Georg Pfleiderer, *Theologie als Wirklichkeitswissenschaft: Studien zum Religionsbegriff bei Georg Wobbermin, Rudolf Otto, Heinrich Scholz und Max Scheler*. Tübingen: J. C. B. Mohr (Paul Siebeck), 1992; Eberhard Stock, *Die Konzeption einer Metaphysik im Denken von Heinrich Scholz*. Berlin: de Gruyter, 1987.
[38] See the useful biographical comments of D. Schellong, "Heinrich Scholz in memoriam." *Evangelische Theologie* 18 (1958): 1–5.
[39] For the importance of this development for the institutionalization of mathematical logic in Germany, see Volker Peckhaus, "Hilbert, Zermelo und die Institutionalizierung der mathematischen Logik in Deutschland." *Berichte zur Wissenschaftsgeschichte* 15 (1992): 27–38. Ernst Zermelo held a lectureship in mathematical logic in 1908; Scholz was the first holder of an official chair in the subject.

The complex relation of faith and reason was a subject of considerable importance for Scholz, and he returned to this topic at a number of points during his career.[40] During his time at Münster, Scholz became increasingly persuaded that mathematical logic had a decisive role to play in any theoretical discipline, and laid increasing emphasis upon the necessity of logical formalization in the philosophy of religion.[41] Hans Hermes – initially Scholz's student, and subsequently his successor in the chair at Münster – recalls that this growing appreciation of the importance of mathematical logic was due to Scholz's chance reading of Whitehead and Russell's *Principia Mathematica*, which forced him to the conclusion that all theoretical sciences rested upon logical foundations.[42] The form of logic best adapted to exploring the intellectual integrity of any theoretical discipline was that set out by Whitehead and Russell.

Where others were content to appeal to traditional forms of logic, based on natural language, for such purposes, Scholz insisted that only the formalized language of mathematics – which he increasingly referred to as "Leibniz language (*Leibniz-Sprache*)" – was appropriate.[43] Leibniz's project of an "ideal language" involved the development of a *lingua characteristica* which could at the same time function as a *calculus ratiocinator*.[44] Since Leibniz's experimentations with *characteristica universalis*, there have been numerous attempts to find the perfect language, free from the imperfections and ambiguities of natural languages.[45] Ludwig Wittgenstein initially adopted a logic-based approach, defining the world as a set of complex statements (*Tatsache*) composed of individual statements (*Sachverhalte*). The limitations of this account of language led him to move towards an approach which was more sensitive to the manner in which natural language was actually used,

---

[40] Fallenstein, *Religion als philosophisches Problem*, 53–4.

[41] T. Mahlmann, "Was ist Religion in der Religionsphilosophie von Heinrich Scholz?" In *Religion im Denken unserer Zeit*, edited by W. Härle and E. Wölfel, 1–33. Marburg: N. G. Elwert, 1986.

[42] Hans Hermes, "Heinrich Scholz. Die Persönlichkeit und seine Werk als Logiker." In *Heinrich Scholz: Drei Vorträge*, 25–45. Münster: Aschendorff, 1958.

[43] For Scholz's discussion of "Leibniz language," see Heinrich Scholz, "Was ist Philosophie? Der erste und der letzte Schritt aud dem Wege zu ihrer Selbstbestimmung." In *Mathesis Universalis: Abhandlungen zur Philosophie als strenger Wissenschaft*, edited by Hans Hermes, 341–87. Darmstadt: Wissenschaftliche Buchgesellschaft, 1961, especially 373–7.

[44] For an analysis of this notion, and its possible impact on Frege, see E. H. W. Kluge, "Frege, Leibniz and the Notion of an Ideal Language." *Studia Leibnitiana* 12 (1980): 140–54.

[45] See especially Umberto Eco, *The Search for the Perfect Language*. Oxford: Blackwell, 1995.

based on the concept of the playing of a "language-game."[46] Scholz clearly hoped to be able to develop an approach to theoretical engagement with the world which allowed for a uniformity of approach and mode of representation, which he regarded as the inevitable and proper outcome of the *mathesis universalis*. His interest in Leibniz's approach to language led Scholz to develop an approach to metaphysics which combined a logically reformulated ontology with a ontologically founded logic to yield a "scientific metaphysics," set out in detail in his 1941 work *Metaphysik als strenge Wissenschaft*.

The particular approach adopted in this late work can be seen to reflect Scholz's criticisms of German idealism, particularly as he sets them out in his 1917 work *Das Wesen des deutschen Geistes*.[47] The wartime provenance of this work may lead Scholz to make certain overstatements and take some disturbing argumentative short cuts; nevertheless, the general thrust of the work is clear. German idealism is characterized by a latent hostility towards the natural sciences, a rejection of the advances made by the Enlightenment, and a tendency towards irrationality.[48] Such concerns were widely expressed within philosophical circles around this time.[49] Scholz regarded idealism as representing a retreat from central Enlightenment values, including clarity (the terms *Klarheit* and *Deutlichkeit* feature prominently in his analysis of this point). We can see here a reflection of the Cartesian emphasis on the necessity of "clear and distinct ideas." "Everything that is not already clear is excluded from discussion by the 'ideal of clarity [*Deutlichkeitsideal*]'; and, correspondingly, everything that conforms to this presupposition is elevated, and accorded a position of highest value."[50]

This emphasis upon the critical importance of "clear and distinct ideas" constitutes the backdrop to Scholz's reflections on scientific (*wissenschaftlich*) method. Descartes deployed the notions of clarity and distinctiveness for a variety of purposes, especially in relation to the establishment of evidential standards, and generalizations concerning the logical status of axioms in deductive systems.[51] For Descartes, ideas are not self-evidently true because they are clear and distinct; rather, the self-evident truths that constitute the

---

[46] For some of the many issues this raises, see Umberto Eco, *The Limits of Interpretation*. Bloomington: Indiana University Press, 1990.

[47] Heinrich Scholz, *Das Wesen des deutschen Geistes* Berlin: Grote'sche Verlagsbuchhandlung, 1917.

[48] Ibid, 49–73.

[49] See, for example, the concerns expressed by Carl Schmitt, *Politische Romantik*. Berlin: Duncker & Humblot, 1919, 24.

[50] Scholz, *Das Wesen des deutschen Geistes*, 68.

[51] Ronald Rubin, "Descartes' Validation of Clear and Distinct Apprehension." *Philosophical Review* 86 (1977): 197–208.

foundation of any deductive system are necessarily clear and distinct in themselves.[52] Some such idea underlies the foundationalism found in Descartes himself, Leibniz, and Spinoza. This is not to say that all these writers were satisfied with the outcome of the application of this principle. Thus, in his *Tractatus de Intellectus Emendatione*, Spinoza appears to equivocate over the merits of the approach, without being able to offer a satisfactory alternative.[53]

It is clear that Scholz was deeply influenced by the theoretical advances of the natural sciences in stressing the importance of clarity, and demonstrating the importance of mathematics in representing the world. Scholz clearly aligns himself with the notion of *mathesis universalis* – the seventeenth-century slogan which articulated a universal scientific method, patterned on the deductive method of mathematics, which can be seen reflected in Tarski's equation of the methodology of the deductive sciences with that of mathematics itself.[54] The term *mathesis universalis* was invented by Descartes to designate a system of thought which would reveal the "order and disposition of the objects toward which our mental vision must be directed if we would find out any truth."[55] From the outset, there was an explicit association between the idea of a universal methodology and mathematics, not least in terms of the incorrigibility, clarity, and universality of its ideas.

Scholz thus argues that, in order to be intellectually defensible, philosophy must be regarded as *ein Inbegriff aller mathematisierbaren Wissenschaften* – something that includes all the disciplines that can be expressed mathematically. Such an approach contrasts sharply with idealist approaches to reality, which Scholz believes to be virtually casual in their argumentation, and fail to take the issue of intellectual control seriously.[56] How can philosophical statements be validated, and held to be accountable?

Given these concerns, it is hardly surprising that Scholz should have noticed their implications for Christian theology. Scholz had a genuine concern for the future of both the Christian faith and theology, and had no doubt that the nineteenth century had raised some fundamental difficulties, especially in

---

[52] Stanley Tweyman, "Truth, No Doubt: Descartes' Proof that the Clear and Distinct Must Be True." *Southern Journal of Philosophy* 19 (1981): 237–58.
[53] I here follow the analysis of Diane Steinberg, "Method and the Structure of Knowledge in Spinoza." *Pacific Philosophical Quarterly* 79 (1998): 152–69.
[54] On which see Volker Peckhaus, *Logik, Mathesis universalis und allgemeine Wissenschaft: Leibniz und die Wiederentdeckung der formalen Logik im 19. Jahrhundert.* Berlin: Akademie Verlag, 1997.
[55] For the background, see Luis Arenas, "Matemáticas, método y *mathesis universalis* en las Regulae de Descartes." *Revista de Filosofia* 8 (1996): 37–61.
[56] See, for example, Scholz, "Was ist Philosophie?," 355–9.

relation to theological method, that simply could not be ignored.[57] His analysis of the "modern crisis of religion" rested partly on his appreciation of the importance of the challenges raised by Ernst Troeltsch in his *Absoluteness of Christianity*, and more generally on his growing awareness of the need for religious or theological clarity – for precision in theological argumentation, particularly in relation to doctrinal statements, and for defensible definitions of religion.[58]

The theological implications of Scholz's approach were set out with uncompromising clarity in his 1931 paper "How is it possible for an evangelical theology to be a science [*Wissenschaft*]?"[59] In this paper, Scholz argued that a science must be able to state its propositions as axioms or fundamental propositions, and thence as theorems which were deduced from these axioms.[60] It can be seen immediately that this represents a form of foundationalism, in which knowledge is understood to be grounded on a set of "basic beliefs" which do not themselves require demonstration or justification. These basic beliefs function as axioms – that is to say, self-evident truths which may be used to derive other beliefs (provided that the means used ensures that their truth is preserved in subsequent beliefs).

Scholz went on to argue for five further conditions which had to be fulfilled before the scientific (*wissenschaftlich*) status of a subject could be accepted. Two of these are of decisive importance:

1 The "proposition postulate," which insisted that any *Wissenschaft* must be capable of affirming "propositions" [*Sätze*] or making "statements [*Aussage*], the truth of which is affirmed."

2 The "control postulate," which holds that any truth-claims made by theological statements must be open to testing. Otherwise, Christian theology would be

---

[57] For a useful discussion of the nature of these concerns, see Pfleiderer, *Theologie als Wirklichkeitswissenschaft*, 144–59.

[58] On which see ibid, 159–92. For the significance of Troeltsch for a "theological science," see Gerhard Sauter, "Der Wissenschaftsbegriff der Theologie." *Evangelische Theologie* 35 (1975): 283–309. Sauter argues (p. 305) that Troeltsch's 1898 paper "Über historische und dogmatische Methode in der Theologie" sets up a fundamental tension between the empirical methodology of the science of history and the authority-dependent statements of Christian dogmatics, thus sharpening the issues that Scholz came to view as decisive. See Ernst Troeltsch, "Über historische und dogmatische Methode in der Theologie," in *Gesammelte Schriften*. Tübingen: Mohr, 1922, Vol. 2, 729–53.

[59] Heinrich Scholz, "Wie ist eine evangelische Theologie als Wissenschaft möglich?" *Zwischen den Zeiten* 9 (1931): 8–51. For the background, see Molendijk, *Aus dem Dunklen ins Helle*, 341–6. Note that the English translation of this title is problematic: the English terms "Protestant" and "evangelical" are both possibilities.

[60] Scholz, "Wie ist eine evangelische Theologie als Wissenschaft möglich?," 24.

reduced to a series of subjective statements by individual believers, which could not be subjected to critical evaluation.[61] Although he was clear that theological statements could not be verified, in the strict sense of the term, Scholz nevertheless believed that they must be held to be accountable in some manner.

It was inevitable that Scholz's insistence upon methodological consistency and universality, however appropriately qualified, would lead him into controversy with Karl Barth. Scholz's 1931 article was prompted by Barth's insistence that Christian theology was *wissenschaftlich* in that it responded to its object in an appropriate manner. It was not acceptable, Barth insisted, to develop a universal method, capable of being applied across disciplines; rather, it was necessary to identify the unique object of Christian theology, and respond in a manner which was consonant with its distinctive characteristics. Although the rudiments of this idea can be seen in earlier writings, the idea is set forth with particular clarity in the 1927 *Christliche Dogmatik*.

In this important work, Barth launched an attack on the views of Hans Heinrich Wendt, who had argued that *wissenschaftlich* knowledge did not depend upon the specific nature of its subject matter. A more or less identical method was appropriate to all intellectual disciplines.[62] Wendt here follows the general neo-Kantian consensus of the period, and did not see himself as making particularly controversial or outrageous statements. It was not a universal viewpoint, and was opposed by Martin Kähler among others, who held that the object of a discipline must determine its methods.[63] Nevertheless, his views prompted Barth to launch a sustained attack on the notion of a universal *wissenschaftlich* method, using Wendt as a foil. In doing so, Barth was concerned primarily to defend the distinctive identity of theology as a discipline.

For Barth, it was essential to respect the unique subject matter of Christian theology, and respond accordingly.[64] The means of establishing the objective truth, the type of epistemic connection (*die Art des Erkenntniszusammenhangs*), the critical norm, and possibility of proof in any discipline (*Gebiet*) must all be determined by the distinctiveness of the relevant object (*Eigenart des betreffenden Gegenstandes*), rather than forcing this object to conform to predetermined

---

[61] Ibid, 48.

[62] Hans Heinrich Wendt, *System der christlichen Lehre*. Göttingen: Vandenhoeck & Ruprecht, 1907, 2–3.

[63] See Martin Kähler, *Die Wissenschaft der christlichen Lehre*. Leipzig: Deichert, 1893, 5.

[64] Karl Barth, *Die christliche Theologie im Entwurf*. Munich: Kaiser Verlag, 1927, 115.

concepts of method and science (*Wissenschaftlichkeit*). Barth thus holds that ontology determines epistemology. For such reasons, Barth feels able to reject foundationalism completely.[65] We must, he insists, recognize "the fundamentally non-foundational character of the dogmatic method (*das grundsätzlich Ungründsatzliche der dogmatischen Methode*)"[66] – a phrase which is impossible to render neatly in English, and whose sense is completely missed by the official translation of the *Church Dogmatics*, which translates this as the "fundamental lack of principle in the dogmatic method."[67]

So how does using the natural sciences as *ancilla theologiae* cast light on this debate? A scientific theology argues that its ideas, like those of the natural sciences, represents an *a posteriori* response to a distinct existing reality, which it attempts to describe, represent, and communicate. The distinctiveness of the object of a science must be reflected in the methodology of that science. The Enlightenment tended to assume that all sciences were committed to using the same working methods and assumptions; a scientific theology insists that the distinctive identity of the object of a science is reflected in its response to that object.

To suggest that theology is a distinct discipline with its own integrity might at first sight appear to call into question any unitary conception of knowledge, or any conception of "the real," as opposed to an aggregate of discrete realities. This is an issue of considerable importance; indeed, it could be argued that any attempt to construct a unitary conception of reality or of human knowledge must be able to offer a satisfactory response to this concern.

Barth is surely right to argue that it is impossible and illegitimate to lay down *a priori* what conditions must apply to theology as the science (*Wissenschaft*) of God, or to assume that norms and working assumptions drawn from other disciplines can be transposed to theology without doing violence to its integrity. The point at issue is made well by T. F. Torrance, who

---

[65] For an excellent study, see Dirk-Martin Grube, *Unbegründbarkeit Gottes? Tillichs und Barths Erkenntnistheorien im Horizont der gegenwärtigen Philosophie*. Marburg: Elwert Verlag, 1998, 88–161.

[66] *Die kirchliche Dogmatik*, 30 vols, *Studienausgabe*. Zurich: Theologischer Verlag, 1988–99, I/2, 972. See also his earlier comment: "Gibt es nun für die Dogmatik keine voraussetzende Grundanschauung, sondern als Fundament und Zentrum nur das selbst voraussetzende und in der Kraft seines Inhalts sich selbst bestätigende Wort Gottes, dann kann es offenbar kein dogmatisches System geben. Gerade das richtig verstandene Materialprinzip der Dogmatik zerstört den Begriff eines dogmatischen Systems im Keime." *Die kirchliche Dogmatik* I/2, 970–1.

[67] Karl Barth, *Church Dogmatics*, 14 vols. Edinburgh: T&T Clark, 1957–75, Vol. I/2, 869.

can be seen as developing Barth's notion of "theological science" in a positive yet critical manner:[68]

> Scientific procedure will not allow us to go beyond the boundary set by the object, for that would presume that by the inherent powers of our own "autonomous reason" we can gain mastery over it. We have to act within the limits imposed by the nature of the object, and avoid self-willed and undisciplined speculative thinking. It would be uncontrolled and unscientific procedure to run ahead of the object and prescribe just how it shall or can be known before we actually know it, or to withdraw ourselves from actual knowing and then in detachment from the object lay down the conditions upon which valid knowledge is possible.

Torrance's point is that the natural sciences make it clear that we cannot settle questions of scientific knowledge *a priori*. Instead, we must recognize, in the first place, that such knowledge is *a posteriori*, and, in the second, that it is conditioned by the specific nature of the scientific discipline and its object. Torrance's concern here is reinforced through the postmodern recognition that there is no "universal rationality," no universal method or foundations, which allow us to lay down in advance what form a discipline should take, still less to apply the methods and foundations of another intellectual tradition to Christian theology.

So what may we conclude from this exploration of the partial methodological convergence of Christian theology and the natural sciences? Perhaps most interestingly, that it is Barth (who had virtually no interest in the natural sciences) who develops a theological trajectory that most reflects their working methods and assumptions. Although Scholz had a genuine interest in, and knowledge of, the natural sciences, he nevertheless appears to have imposed the Enlightenment assumption of the universality of method on his subject matter, failing to notice how the natural sciences insisted upon the priority of ontology over epistemology. What something *is* determines both the manner in which it may be known and the extent to which it may be known. This insight is fundamental to the concept of a "scientific theology," as I have developed this in recent years.

A scientific theology insists that we are under an obligation to respond coherently to reality. Theology should be seen as a response to reality – a deliberate and principled attempt to give a faithful and adequate account of the way things are, subject to the limits placed upon human knowledge on account

---

[68] T. F. Torrance, *Theological Science*. Oxford: Oxford University Press, 1969, 26. For a study of Torrance, see Alister E. McGrath, *T. F. Torrance: An Intellectual Biography*. Edinburgh: T&T Clark, 2000.

of our status as sinful creatures, and our location in history. To put this another way, it is *responsible*, in two senses of that term:

1 It represents a *response to reality*. We do not create our theological concepts through our free and unrestrained mental activity, but recognize and respond to a situation which already exists, independent of and prior to our reflections.
2 It is *accountable* for its insights and themes – that is to say, there are criteria against which it may be judged; there is a community who may judge how faithful that theology is as a positive yet critical affirmation of its insights and beliefs; and ultimately, in the Christian way of viewing things, a God who will hold the theologian accountable for the manner in which God's character and nature are rendered.

The notion of theology as a scientific discipline which gives an account of its apprehension of reality is thoroughly traditional. In more recent times, the substantial theological project of Karl Barth has given this new significance. For Barth, theology is an exercise in *Nachdenken*, a following through of the objectivity of reality which exists prior to any operation of the human mind. Our reflections disclose and illuminate the structures of this reality, but do not call that reality or its structures into being. We are not speaking of a human mind imposing order in any way it pleases, but of a principled attempt to recognize and represent the way things are. It is, perhaps, a very traditional way of thinking about theology, but one that is given new plausibility through an engagement with the history and philosophy of the natural sciences.

Now let us agree that, just because the natural sciences see things this way, it does not mean that theology is bound to follow suit. But it does point out how the scientific community's principled attentiveness to the complexity of reality obliges us to set aside the "one-size-fits-all" simplifications of the Enlightenment project, and acknowledge the epistemological implications of the ontological finality of reality. The way things are determines both how we know them and what can be known of them. And that must surely be a theological maxim characteristic of the Christian tradition, which should not need to be reminded of this by outsiders – still less to have to relearn so basic a lesson concerning the grounds and grammar of its faith.

CHAPTER 6

The Evolution of Doctrine? A Critical Examination of the Theological Validity of Biological Models of Doctrinal Development

One of the most remarkable developments within western cultural history of the last century has been the assimilation of the idea of cultural and intellectual change to a Darwinian evolutionary paradigm. Indeed, it has become so influential within western culture that it has become incorporated into much orthodox Christian thinking.[1] The language of "doctrinal evolution" and the related vocabulary of "a theological genetic code" has become commonplace in contemporary academic theology. For example, consider the following helpful account of doctrinal development, taken from the most recent edition of *First Things*, an influential orthodox Christian journal:[2]

> There is a discernible pattern of Christian truth, a pattern derived from the apostolic witness and maintained across time as the *depositum fidei*, or what the New Testament calls "the faith once delivered to the saints." This pattern is embedded, like a genetic code, in the inspired text of Scripture itself.

---

[1] This is not to say that all theologians use this paradigm: to mention only one example, Edward Schillebeeckx's account of doctrinal development makes virtually no use of the concept. See Daniel P. Thompson, "Schillebeeckx and the Development of Doctrine." *Theological Studies* 62 (2001): 303–21.
[2] *First Things*, No. 155 (August/September 2005): 68.

The widespread use of the imagery and vocabulary of evolutionary biology in both academic and popular theology raises the question of whether this way of speaking and thinking is to be understood as fundamentally *rhetorical* or *analogical*. Is this use of Darwinian ideas *verbal* or *conceptual*? In other words, has Christian theology merely appropriated the vocabulary of the Darwinian paradigm as a convenient way of speaking about the conceptually distinct phenomenon of intellectual development, or is this way of speaking itself a reflection of a deeper conviction that the development of ideas, especially that of Christian doctrine, actually conforms to this evolutionary paradigm? Since this is such an important issue for Christian theology in general, this essay sets out to explore in some detail the extent to which Darwinism can be considered a legitimate conceptual tool for the exploration and explanation of the development of Christian doctrine.

The concept of the development of Christian doctrine is of no small theological and apologetic importance. Even before I began to study theology with academic seriousness in 1976, I had been interested in the whole issue of the history of human cultural development, particularly the development of the natural sciences and their associated theories, and the models proposed to account for them. My own intellectual fascination with the field of cultural evolution was catalyzed by my early research in historical theology – specifically, the intellectual origins of the Reformation and the development of the doctrine of justification – which pointed to a complex process of doctrinal development, strongly shaped by local factors, which did not fit easily into any existing models of doctrinal development. What determines how religious ideas develop over time? What factors have at least a degree of control over their development, modification, acceptance, or rejection, and – at least in some cases – their slow decline into oblivion?[3]

The first stage in the process of investigation of the situation was to identify precisely what patterns of progression could be observed, irrespective of whether these were confirmative or disconfirmative of existing theories of development. Taken as a whole, these patterns – which I cannot hope to summarize in this essay – seemed incapable of explanation on the basis of any existing models of doctrinal development proposed by Christian theologians, even though some of their individual aspects were amenable to such theoretical assimilation.

---

[3] For some of the issues involved, see Alister E. McGrath, *The Intellectual Origins of the European Reformation*, 2nd edn. Oxford: Blackwell, 2003; *Iustitia Dei: A History of the Christian Doctrine of Justification*, 3rd edn. Cambridge: Cambridge University Press, 2005. The first editions of these works were published in 1987 and 1986, respectively.

Nature as a Source of Theological Models

The Christian church has constantly been engaged in a process of self-criticism and self-evaluation, as it interrogates itself as to whether its existing modes of thought are indeed adequately grounded in the realities of divine revelation, or whether they are indeed the best possible representations of a divine self-disclosure that is ultimately resistant to being reduced to human words and concepts. It is a theme that is especially associated with Protestantism, in pursuit of its fundamental ethos of constant self-examination, given the need for fidelity to the biblical foundations of faith. *Ecclesia reformata, ecclesia semper reformanda.* Yet the recognition that the quest for doctrinal authenticity involves a critical dialogue with the past is a shared assumption of most Christian theologians, and is not a distinguishing mark of Protestantism.[4]

It is easy to see how this demand for constant theological vigilance is intimately connected with the notion of the development of doctrine, in that the church's internal dialogue and self-critique inevitably (if slowly) leads to a realization that, in some cases, yesterday's attempts to conceptualize the essence of faith needed improvement, perhaps through being too closely tied to the prevailing assumptions of the day, or perhaps through focusing excessively on only one aspect of a complex question. Doctrinal development is the inevitable and proper outcome of the theological watchfulness demanded by the church. There is thus a sense in which Christian orthodoxy is something that is *made*, as succeeding generations inherit ways of speaking about God and Christ which they rightly respect, yet equally rightly wish to subject to examination.

Rather than passively accept the ways that previous generations interpreted a particular biblical passage or dogmatic concept, the church is called to "put everything to the test, and hold on to what is found to be good" (1 Thessalonians 5:21). This is most emphatically not being disrespectful towards the past; it is about maintaining the dialogue that began in the past, continues today, and will not end until the close of history. Is this really the best way of telling the truth of faith? Is this really the most comprehensive account of who God is, and what God has done? Is this really the least conceptually extravagant way of representing the identity of Christ? These questions must be asked *and answered* as part of the church's "discipleship of the mind."

---

[4] See the important contribution of Yves Congar, "La 'réception' comme réalité ecclésiologique." *Revue des sciences philosophiques et théologiques* 56 (1972): 369–403. More recently, John Thiel has developed a "retrospective" model of doctrinal development, which traces the continuity of tradition from present to past, rather than as (traditionally) from past to present: John E. Thiel, *Senses of Tradition: Continuity and Development in Catholic Faith.* Oxford: Oxford University Press, 2000, 84–95.

The issues attending the concept of doctrinal development are well known,[5] as is their potential apologetic importance. Was the "faith once delivered to the saints" (Jude 3) itself a fully developed system of doctrine, or the seed from which such a system might grow?[6] Or was it more in the way of a fundamental relationship with God, based and focused upon Christ, requiring and anticipating significant theological elaboration?[7] Most Christian writers would give broad assent, with inevitable qualifications, to the general position mapped out by Charles Gore in his 1891 Bampton Lectures. Dealing with the question of the relationship of the New Testament witness to Christ, and the subsequent elaboration and consolidation of those ideas in the doctrines of the church, Gore argues for a natural, organic emergence of the Chalcedonian Definition.[8] The whole process is governed by the gradual emergence of "a corporate consciousness" which is in the process of "gaining clearer expression." This, he insists, distinguishes this process of doctrinal development from an alternative way of conceiving it – namely, "the survival of the fittest formulas."

The astute reader will realize immediately that Gore is here referring to the application of Darwinian evolutionary ideas to the development of doctrine – something that Gore regarded as totally inappropriate. Others, however, would see this as the entirely apposite theological application of a legitimate biological analogy.[9] And this is the question that concerns us in this essay:

---

[5] For helpful analysis of the main issues, see Pierre Rousselot, "Petit théorie du développement du dogme." *Recherches de science religieuse* 53 (1965): 355–90; Aidan Nichols, *From Newman to Congar: The Idea of Doctrinal Development from the Victorians to the Second Vatican Council.* Edinburgh: T&T Clark, 1990.

[6] While Thomas Aquinas does not use the phrase "doctrinal development," he can certainly be said to have undergone "development" in his theological views, particularly in the period between the writing of the *Commentary on the Sentences* and the *Summa Theologiae* – see, for example, the brilliant analysis in A. F. von Guten, "In principio erat verbum: une évolution de Saint Thomas en théologie trinitaire." In *Ordo sapientiae et amoris: image et message de Saint Thomas d'Aquin,* edited by Carolos-Josaphat Pinto de Oliveira, 119–41. Fribourg: Editions Universitaires, 1993. Yet one can speak cautiously of "doctrinal development" in a deeper sense within Aquinas' writings, as pointed out by Christopher Kaczor, "Thomas Aquinas on the Development of Doctrine." *Theological Studies* 62 (2001): 283–302.

[7] For some penetrating reflections on such issues, see Rowan Williams, "Doctrinal Criticism: Some Questions." In *The Making and Remaking of Christian Doctrine,* edited by Sarah Coakley and David A. Pailin, 239–64. Oxford: Clarendon Press, 1993.

[8] Charles Gore, *The Incarnation of the Son of God.* London: John Murray, 1922, 85–7.

[9] One of the most significant influences on this trend was James Baldwin's 1909 declaration that Darwinism could be applied with profit to most areas of the humanities: James M. Baldwin, *Darwin and the Humanities.* Baltimore: Review Publishing, 1909.

what biological analogies may be proposed for the phenomenon of doctrinal development, and how appropriate are they? Theology, like all disciplines, makes extensive use of models and analogies in its undertakings. Many of these are drawn from the natural world. The use of parables in the preaching of Jesus of Nazareth itself may be singled out as an especially luminous and theologically significant use of analogies drawn from the world of nature.[10] There is an entirely legitimate debate over whether Jesus uses aspects of the natural world – such as the germination of seeds[11] – in a theologically opportunistic way, or whether there is some deeper structure within nature that can be held to undergird such an appeal.

But the point is simple and ultimately independent of how these questions are answered – namely, that the routine workings of the biological world have, when rightly interpreted, the capacity to be theologically illuminating. The growth of a seed, so readily examined and appreciated, becomes the lens through which other, more puzzling and enigmatic observations can be approached. Among these is the development of Christian doctrine. Might the observed complexities of the emergence of orthodoxy be compared to the germination and growth of a seed? And might this also illuminate the emergence of alternatives to orthodoxy?

The Notion of Doctrinal Development

The question of whether Christian doctrine can be said to "develop" caused many people considerable unease in the nineteenth century.[12] In an era when the conceptual foundations of Christianity were being called into question

---

[10] There is a huge literature: see, for example, Arland J. Hultgren, *The Parables of Jesus: A Commentary.* Grand Rapids, MI: Eerdmans, 2000. For a particularly helpful analysis of some central themes, see Kurt Erlemann, *Das Bild Gottes in den synoptischen Gleichnissen.* Stuttgart: Kohlhammer, 1988.

[11] John Dominic Crossan, "Seed Parables of Jesus." *Journal of Biblical Literature* 92 (1973): 244–66; Zeba Antonin Crook, "The Synoptic Parables of the Mustard and the Leaven: A Test-Case for the Two-Document, Two-Gospel, and Farrer-Goulder Hypotheses." *Journal for the Study of the New Testament* 78 (2000): 23–48.

[12] For a basic overview of the cultural background which made this such a sensitive issue, see Howard R. Murphy, "The Ethical Revolt against Christian Orthodoxy in Early Victorian England." *American Historical Review* 60 (1955): 800–17; Robert Lee Wolff, *Gains and Losses: Novels of Faith and Doubt in Victorian England.* London: John Murray, 1977; Bernard V. Lightman, *The Origins of Agnosticism: Victorian Unbelief and the Limits of Knowledge.* Baltimore: Johns Hopkins University Press, 1987.

with unprecedented vigor and rigor,[13] the idea that at least some fundamental Christian doctrines had undergone change was seen as further undermining the already fragile credibility of the church's witness. In part, this alarm over the possibility of change was due to the absolute certainty that an earlier generation of theologians, especially within Roman Catholicism, had asserted the unchangeability of the fundamentals of faith.

For the noted Catholic apologist Jacques-Bénigne Bossuet (1627–1704), the matter was not worthy of serious debate. The catholic deposit of faith was the same yesterday, today, and forever. Protestant innovation and heretical degradation – religious categories that tended to elide in Bossuet's judgment – could be identified without undue difficulty, precisely because they represented change.[14] The critique of this essentially static understanding of tradition by the French Reformed jurist Pierre Jurieu (1637–1717) was simply brushed aside as irrelevant.[15] In an age dominated by deductive modes of thought, the notion of doctrinal change or development was understood to imply prior error or imperfection, and thus be an apologetic liability.

It was a view that simply could not be sustained – or, rather, that could only be maintained by a deliberate decision to ignore the disconcerting counter-factuals of church history. During the 1830s and 1840s, the Catholic Tübingen School, including writers such as J. S. Drey and J. A. Möhler, developed an organic approach to doctrinal development, which likened the process to the natural growth of a biological seed.[16] Related ideas developed elsewhere in the German-speaking world, with Protestant church historians increasingly coming to recognize the explanatory merits of an organic approach to their discipline, as opposed to the more wooden and constraining ideological frameworks used by earlier writers – as, for example, in the case of F. C. Baur's procrustean attempt to impose a Hegelian dialectical mechanism upon the historical process.[17]

---

[13] See the analyses in Frank M. Turner, *Contesting Cultural Authority: Essays in Victorian Intellectual Life*. Cambridge: Cambridge University Press, 1993, 38–100; James Moore, "Theodicy and Society: The Crisis of the Intelligentsia." In *Victorian Faith in Crisis: Essays in Continuity and Change in Nineteenth-Century Religious Belief*, edited by Richard J. Helmstadter and Bernard Lightman, 153–86. Basingstoke: Macmillan, 1990.

[14] See especially Renate Struman, "De la perpétuité de la foi dans la controverse Bossuet–Julien (1686–1691)." *Revue d'histoire ecclésiastique* 37 (1941): 145–89; Richard F. Costigan, "Bossuet and the Consensus of the Church." *Theological Studies* 56 (1995): 652–72.

[15] On Jurieu, see Debora Spini, *Diritti di Dio, diritti Dei popoli: Pierre Jurieu e il problema della sovranità, 1681–1691*. Turin: Claudiana, 1997.

[16] For the best analysis, see Hans Geisser, *Glaubenseinheit und Lehrentwicklung bei Johann Adam Möhler*. Göttingen: Vandenhoeck & Ruprecht, 1971.

[17] Wilhem Maurer, "Das Prinzip der Organischen in der evangelischen Kirchengeschichtsschreibung des 19. Jahrhunderts." *Kerygma und Dogma* 8 (1962): 256–92.

It is widely held that the beginnings of an attempt in the English-speaking world to respond to the rather more complex patterns disclosed by the history of Christian thought are to be found in the sermon preached by John Henry Newman before the University of Oxford on February 2, 1843.[18] In this university sermon, Newman used the text of the day – "But Mary kept these things, and pondered them in her heart" (Luke 2.19) – to draw a distinction between the (to him) theologically unthinkable idea of "new truths" and the rather more palatable notion of "further insights." His dialogue partner in this brief engagement with historical theology was Joseph Butler, whose celebrated *Analogy of Religion* had proposed a process of gradual progress in theology, tantamount – or so it seemed to some – to acknowledging the emergence of new articles of faith.

At this point, we must note that Newman's interest in historical theology appears to have been occasioned, and to no small extent shaped, by the somewhat intemperate and theologically simplistic ecclesiastical polemics of the era, reflecting the deeply divisive debates within the Church of England arising from the growth of the Oxford Movement. This is especially evident in two of Newman's landmark works of the 1830s: the *Lectures on Justification* and *Arians of the Fourth Century*. Newman here uses historical theology as little more than a thinly veiled foil for his own theological and ecclesiological agenda, which is firmly wedded to the realities of the Church of England in the 1830s.

In each case, Newman's enemy is not so much the stated subject of his inquiry – whether Arians or Luther – but Protestantism in general, and evangelicalism in particular. Equally, in each case the scholarship is flawed, even to the point of involving what I must regrettably describe as deliberate misrepresentation.[19] Rowan Williams, in his excellent study of Arius, points out the severe limitations of Newman's historical scholarship:[20]

For an assessment of Baur's approach, see Ulrich Köpf, ed., *Historisch-kritische Geschichtsbetrachtung. Ferdinand Christian Baur und seine Schüler.* Sigmaringen: Verlag Thorbecke, 1994.

[18] John Henry Newman, "The Theory of Developments in Religious Doctrine," in John Henry Newman, *Conscience, Consensus and the Development of Doctrine*, edited by James Gaffney. New York: Doubleday, 1992, 6–30. Although Newman shows affinity with the Tübingen school, especially with Möhler, in this sermon, there is no compelling evidence of direct dependence on Möhler in this respect.

[19] For this point, see Alister E. McGrath, "Newman on Justification: An Evangelical Anglican Evaluation." In *Newman and the Word*, edited by Terrance Merrigan and Ian T. Ker, 91–108. Louvain: Peters, 2000.

[20] Rowan Williams, *Arius: Heresy and Tradition.* London: Darton, Longman, & Todd, 1987, 4–5.

One must charitably say that Newman is not at his best here: a brilliant argument, linking all sorts of diverse phenomena, is built up on a foundation of complacent bigotry and historical fantasy. However, setting aside for the moment the distasteful rhetoric of his exposition, it should be possible to see something of what his polemical agenda really is. *The Arians of the Fourth Century* is, in large part, a tract in defence of what the early Oxford Movement thought of as spiritual religion and spiritual authority.

In both his *Arians of the Fourth Century* and *Lectures on Justification,* Newman's critique of Protestantism is subtle and largely indirect, tending to proceed by "eccentric, superficial and prejudiced"[21] historical analysis of the past, on the basis of an assumed linkage between disliked individuals of the past (Arius and Luther) and the evangelicalism of the 1830s.

Yet Newman's skewed use of the history of Christian doctrine must not allow us to overlook one simple fact: his recognition that some of the fundamental ideas of Christianity had indeed undergone discernible change over the vast period of the existence of the church. In 1845 Newman published his celebrated *Essay on the Development of Christian Doctrine.* Its most signal contribution to the study of the development of doctrine was not any specific, explicit theory of how doctrine develops; rather, it was the tacit acknowledgment that such change had indeed taken place.[22] It is the insistence upon the *fact* of doctrinal development, not any specific *theory* or model of this process, that is the distinguishing mark of Newman's seminal work:[23]

> From the necessity, then, of the case, from the history of all sects and parties in religion, and from the analogy and example of Scripture, we may fairly conclude that Christian doctrine admits of formal, legitimate, and true developments, that is, of developments contemplated by its Divine Author.

Yet Newman nonetheless found himself under an intellectual obligation to suggest some means of conceptualizing this process of development. He was decidedly unhappy with the idea of a progressive revelation, by which advances in human reason led to the emergence of new understandings of divine truth, allowing the inferior judgments and conclusions of earlier generations

---

[21] Ibid, 6.

[22] In this, I concur completely with Nicholas Lash, *Change in Focus: A Study of Doctrinal Change and Continuity.* London: Sheed & Ward, 1973, 88. For alternative reflections, see Hugo Meynell, "Newman on Revelation and Doctrinal Development." *Journal of Theological Studies* 30 (1979): 138–52.

[23] John Henry Newman, *Essay on the Development of Doctrine.* London: Longmans, Green, 1909, 74.

to be set to one side as outmoded and obsolete.[24] But what other options existed? Fortunately, he found an idea in Butler's *Analogy* which seemed to offer a happier alternative.[25]

"The whole natural world and government of it," says Butler, "is a scheme or system; not a fixed, but a progressive one; a scheme in which the operation of various means takes up a great length of time before the ends they tend to can be attained. The change of seasons, the ripening of the fruits of the earth, the very history of a flower is an instance of this; and so is human life. Thus vegetable bodies, and those of animals, though possibly formed at once, yet grow up by degrees to a mature state. And thus rational agents, who animate these latter bodies, are naturally directed to form each his own manners and character by the gradual gaining of knowledge and experience, and by a long course of action. Our existence is not only successive, as it must be of necessity, but one state of our life and being is appointed by God to be a preparation for another; and that to be the means of attaining to another succeeding one: infancy to childhood, childhood to youth, youth to mature age."

Newman interprets Butler to draw the conclusion that God's providential ordering of the world is not fixed, but progressive from his observations of the world (the ripening of fruit, the maturing of animals, and so forth).[26] The analogy for the development of doctrine is thus organic, not intellectual, to be likened to the growing of a plant rather than the emergence of new forms of logic or theological ideas.

It was an attractive idea, which proved immensely influential, not least because of its resonance with the appealing category of "the organic." Even those who had ingrained ecclesiastical misgivings about the idea were aware of its intuitive plausibility and potential explanatory potential.[27] Yet it was an idea whose full flowering would be catalyzed in ways Newman could not have

---

[24] As Ker and others have pointed out, Newman nevertheless seems to revert to some such understanding: Ian T. Ker, "Newman's Theory: Development or Continuing Revelation?" In *Newman and Gladstone*, 145–60. Dublin: Veritas Publications, 1978.

[25] Newman, *Essay on the Development of Doctrine*, 74.

[26] As Owen Chadwick rightly points out, Butler's reasoning does not actually permit this conclusion to be reached on the basis of any such inference: Owen Chadwick, *From Bossuet to Newman: The Idea of Doctrinal Development*. Cambridge: Cambridge University Press, 1957, 93–5.

[27] See, for example, Ambroise Gardeil, *Le Donné révélé et la théologie*, 2nd edn. Paris: Editions du Cerf, 1932, which notes the merits of the model – especially the idea of the church as gardener – while expressing concern about potential modernist abuse of the model. See further H. D. Gardeil, *L'Oeuvre théologique du père Ambroise Gardeil*. Etiolles par Soisy-sur-Seine: Le Saulchoir, 1956.

anticipated, for reasons unknown to him in 1845. Within two decades, Charles Darwin's theory of natural selection began to transform the manner in which the matter of doctrinal development was conceptualized. If one could speak of evolution within the biological world, could not the same – or at least an analogous – process be discerned within the world of ideas? Darwinism rapidly began its subtle and pervasive transformation from a tool of biological explanation to a more general view of reality.[28]

The impact of such lines of thought was particularly evident in Germany, where the growing academic acceptance of Darwinism in the late 1860s led to certain significant theological developments.[29] The intellectual milieu of writers such as Albrecht Benjamin Ritschl was shaped by the advance of evolutionary theory, and its application – sometimes tentative, sometimes aggressive – to issues of intellectual history.[30] Similar trends emerged in Great Britain and the United States.[31] The idea of the organic development of ideas – as expounded by the Tübingen School and Newman – was clearly felt to require substantial intellectual clarification, even where this forced revision of existing understandings of the issues. Given the growing impact of Darwinism throughout the western world in the late nineteenth century and beyond, it was perhaps inevitable that growing acceptance of the phenomenon of doctrinal development would begin to be conceptualized in unambiguously Darwinian terms. Nineteenth-century cultural evolutionarists – such as Sir Edward B. Tylor – were committed to a "doctrine of progress," in

---

[28] For some of the problems that such developments create for historical definitions of "Darwinism," see David Hull, "Darwinism as a Historical Entity: A Historiographic Proposal." In *The Darwinian Heritage*, edited by David Kohn, 773–812. Princeton, NJ: Princeton University Press, 1985.

[29] See Alfred Kelly, *The Descent of Darwin: The Popularization of Darwinism in Germany, 1860–1914*. Chapel Hill: North Carolina University Press, 1981. For its impact in France, see Yvette Conry, *L'Introduction du Darwinisme en France au XIXe siècle*. Paris: Vrin, 1974.

[30] For an excellent overview of the situation and issues, see Rudolf Otto, "Darwinismus von Heute und Theologie." *Theologische Rundschau* 5 (1902): 483–96; 6 (1903): 183–99, 229–36; 7 (1904): 1–15. On Ritschl, see James Richmond, *Ritschl: A Reappraisal*. London: Collins, 1978, 19–20. For the wider impact on Darwinism, especially when coupled with Marxism, see Richard Weikart, *Socialist Darwinism: Evolution in German Socialist Thought from Marx to Bernstein*. San Francisco: International Scholars Publications, 1999.

[31] See Thomas F. Glick, *The Comparative Reception of Darwinism*. Austin: University of Texas Press, 1972; Alvar Ellegård, *Darwin and the General Reader: The Reception of Darwin's Theory of Evolution in the British Periodical Press, 1859–1872*. Chicago: University of Chicago Press, 1990.

which the human situation was confidently predicted to improve through the constant replacement of inferior beliefs by those which were considered to be superior.[32]

This essay aims to ask a simple question: to what extent is this appeal to biological analogies in the description and analysis of intellectual development justified?

"Universal Darwinism" and the Development of Culture

Richard Dawkins has been one of the most outspoken advocates of the application of Darwinism to human cultural development as a whole.[33] For Dawkins, Darwinism is simply too big a theory to be limited to the biological domain. "Universal Darwinism" possesses an explanatory capacity which is capable of being extended far beyond these limits.[34] Perhaps the most celebrated, and certainly the most controversial, application of Darwinian theory is to be found in evolutionary psychology.[35]

Dawkins here reflects a consensus within a significant section of the evolutionary biological community in the opening decade of the twenty-first century. The Darwinian paradigm, it is argued, offers a magisterial explanatory model, capable of accounting for developments far beyond the realm of the purely biological. This markedly upbeat assessment contrasts sharply with the situation a century ago. At the beginning of the twentieth century, the notion of "cultural evolution" temporarily began to lose its appeal, in my view largely because of growing anxiety within professional biological circles

---

[32] See the excellent analysis by Stephen K. Sanderson, *Social Evolutionism: A Critical History*. Oxford: Blackwell, 1992. On this view, monotheism was regarded as "superior" to polytheism, and was therefore held to be a "higher" form of religious expression.

[33] See especially Richard Dawkins, *River out of Eden: A Darwinian View of Life*. London: Phoenix, 1995. His earlier works should also be consulted, especially *The Selfish Gene*, 2nd edn. Oxford: Oxford University Press, 1989.

[34] See especially Richard Dawkins, "Universal Darwinism." In *Evolution from Molecules to Men*, edited by D. S. Bendall, 403–25. Cambridge: Cambridge University Press, 1983.

[35] See Lance Workman and Will Reader, *Evolutionary Psychology: An Introduction*. New York: Cambridge University Press, 2004. For its application to archeology, see Steven J. Mithen, *The Prehistory of the Mind: The Cognitive Origins of Art, Religion, and Science*. New York: Thames & Hudson, 1999. On evolution and archeology, see Stephen Shennan, *Genes, Memes and Human History: Darwinian Archaeology and Cultural Evolution*. London: Thames & Hudson, 2002.

concerning the plausibility of the Darwinian evolutionary schema.[36] However, in the period following World War II, the neo-Darwinian synthesis began to emerge, and proved intellectually resilient.[37] This created new interest in the possibility of cultural evolutionary theory, which was given a new injection of energy by the work of Julian H. Steward and Leslie A. White.[38]

The recovery of interest in the application of paradigms drawn from evolutionary biology to cultural development has led to cultural evolutionary theory fragmenting. While some writers have retained the cultural evolutionism of Steward and White,[39] others have branched out in alternative directions. In their *Evolution of Human Societies* (1987), Allen W. Johnson and Timothy K. Earle use a series of case studies to produce explanatory models that relate human social organization with economic activity, human demography, and subsistence activities.[40] Other approaches that have emerged recently include evolutionary ecology,[41] sociobiology,[42] and coevolution or cultural Darwinism.[43]

---

[36] For a good account, see R. J. Berry, *Neo-Darwinism*. London: Edward Arnold, 1982.

[37] The best study of this development is probably David J. Depew and Bruce H. Weber, *Darwinism Evolving: Systems Dynamics and the Genealogy of Natural Selection*. Cambridge, MA: MIT Press, 1996.

[38] The landmark works are: Leslie A. White, *The Science of Culture: A Study of Man and Civilization*. New York: Farrar, Straus, 1949; *The Evolution of Culture: The Development of Civilization to the Fall of Rome*. New York: McGraw-Hill, 1959; Julian H. Steward, *Theory of Culture Change: The Methodology of Multilinear Evolution*. Urbana: University of Illinois Press, 1963.

[39] See, for example, Elman R. Service, *Primitive Social Organization: An Evolutionary Perspective*, 2nd edn. New York: Random House, 1971; *Origins of the State and Civilization: The Process of Cultural Evolution*. New York: W. W. Norton, 1975; Marvin Harris, *Cultural Materialism: The Struggle for a Science of Culture*. New York: Random House, 1979.

[40] Allen W. Johnson and Timothy K. Earle, *The Evolution of Human Societies: From Foraging Group to Agrarian State*, 2nd edn. Stanford, CA: Stanford University Press, 2000.

[41] Eric A. Smith and Bruce Winterhalder, *Evolutionary Ecology and Human Behavior*. New York: Aldine de Gruyter, 1992.

[42] Kim Hill and A. Magdalena Hurtado, *Aché Life History: The Ecology and Demography of a Foraging People*. New York: Aldine de Gruyter, 1996. For a general survey of this important area, see J. van der Dennen, David Smillie, and Daniel R. Wilson, eds., *The Darwinian Heritage and Sociobiology*. Westport, CT: Praeger, 1999.

[43] Robert D. Boyd and Peter J. Richerson, *Culture and the Evolutionary Process*. Chicago: University of Chicago Press, 1985; William H. Durham, *Coevolution: Genes, Culture, and Human Diversity*. Stanford, CA: Stanford University Press, 1991.

But can any aspect of cultural or intellectual development legitimately be analyzed on the basis of a Darwinian model of evolution? Does not this involve the elevation of a contingent scientific theory, not without its difficulties, to the status of a universal truth,[44] by which all else may be judged? It is important to explore whether the development of ideas or culture in general can indeed be accounted for on such a mechanism, before turning to deal with the specific case of the development of doctrine.

At first sight, the case for proposing that cultural evolution is Darwinian is eminently plausible.[45] Darwin himself often used analogies drawn from the world of culture to illuminate his theory of natural selection. In particular, he was clearly intrigued by the parallels between biological and linguistic evolution[46] – a theme that would be explored with enthusiasm during the later nineteenth century,[47] before being abandoned as something of a dead end.

More recently, however, the possibility of a neo-Darwinian mechanism for cultural evolution has been the subject of fresh discussion.[48] A recent study argues that the fundamentals of a Darwinian mechanism can be discerned within cultural development, thus reopening the possibility that Darwinian evolutionary theory may have a much wider applicability than once thought:[49]

> The comparison [between cultural evolution and] *The Origin* is more than just an intellectual exercise or historical curiosity. It is of considerable significance to biologists if the core evolutionary processes at the heart of their discipline govern an aspect of human life – culture – that is often contrasted with biology. This is

---

[44] Dawkins, for example, concedes that Darwinism may be displaced by an alternative in the future: Richard Dawkins, *A Devil's Chaplain*. London: Weidenfeld & Nicolson, 2003, 81. Dawkins suggests that it may be possible to isolate a "core Darwinism" which is relatively resistant to this kind of historical erosion.

[45] For what follows, see Alex Mesoudi, Andrew Whiten, and Kevin N. Laland, "Is Cultural Evolution Darwinian? Evidence Reviewed from the Perspective of *The Origin of Species*." *Evolution* 58 (2004): 1–11.

[46] Parallels that continue to be explored: see Hans Aarsleff, *From Locke to Saussure: Essays on the Study of Language and Intellectual History*. Minneapolis: University of Minnesota Press, 1982; R. S. Wells, "The Life and Growth of Language: Metaphors in Biology and Linguistics." In *Biological Metaphor and Cladistic Classification*, edited by H. H. Hoenigswald and L. F. Wiener, 39–80. Philadelphia: University of Pennsylvania Press, 1987.

[47] Note especially the contribution of Sir Edward B. Tylor in works such as *Researches into the Early History of Mankind and the Development of Civilization*. London: John Murray, 1865.

[48] See especially M. I. Sereno, "Four Analogies between Biological and Cultural/Linguistic Evolution." *Journal of Theoretical Biology* 151 (1991): 467–507.

[49] Mesoudi, "Is Cultural Evolution Darwinian?," 1.

not only because the theory, tools and findings of biological evolution may generalize to other disciplines, rendering the study of evolution far broader and more important than currently conceived, but also because biological evolution would have to be regarded as interwoven into a lattice of interacting evolutionary processes, for which hierarchical, multiple-level or multiple process models will be required.

The development of human culture, it is argued, demonstrates variation, competition, inheritance, and the accumulation of successive cultural modifications over time. A reasonable case for Darwinian cultural evolution thus seems to have been established.

The evolutionary psychologist Donald T. Campbell (1916–96) developed such ideas as early as 1960,[50] and introduced the term "mnemone" to refer to the cultural replicators that his theory required.[51] This line of thought was taken further by the anthropologist F. T. Cloak. In an important article of 1968, expanded in 1975, Cloak proposed that culture evolved through an essentially Darwinian mechanism, and set out how ethological methods might be applied to culture-specific behavior.[52] He drew a distinction between "i-culture" (the set of cultural instructions that are contained in the nervous system) and "m-culture" (relationships in material structures which are maintained by such instructions, or changes in material structures which come about as a result of these instructions):

> An i-culture builds and operates m-culture features whose *ultimate function* is to provide for the maintenance and propagation of the i-culture in a certain environment. And the m-culture features, in turn, environmentally affect the composition of the i-culture so as to maintain or increase their own capabilities for performing that function. As a result, each m-culture is shaped for its *particular* functions in that environment.

The serious exploration of the question of the mechanism of cultural evolution is generally thought to have begun in 1981, when Cavalli-Sforza and

---

[50] Donald T. Campbell, "Blind Variation and Selective Retention in Creative Thought as in Other Knowledge Processes." *Psychological Review* 67 (1960): 380–400.

[51] Donald T. Campbell, "A General 'Selection Theory' as Implemented in Biological Evolution and in Social Belief-Transmission-with-Modification in Science." *Biology and Philosophy* 3 (1988): 413–63. The term was introduced by Campbell in 1974; this article sets out a later exposition of the notion.

[52] F. T. Cloak, "Is a Cultural Ethology Possible?" *Human Ecology* 3 (1975): 161–81. An earlier version of this article appeared in *Research Previews* 15 (1968): 37–47. For another perspective, see L. L. Cavalli-Sforza, "Cultural Evolution." *American Zoologist* 26 (1986): 845–55.

Feldman proposed a quantitative approach which permitted the analysis of the dynamics of change within a fixed population of specified forms of cultural traits.[53] This study suggested that some form of non-Darwinian process was implicated, at least in part, suggesting that it might be necessary to propose a mechanism of "cultural evolution" which was distinct from natural selection.

A quite distinct approach was developed around the same time by Lumsden and Wilson. Building on the earlier work of Cloak, they proposed that human cultural transmission was fundamentally determined genetically, through a unit they termed the "culturgen."[54] This concept was derived from the notion of the "artifact," already widely used in archeology to refer to operational units of culture. According to Lumsden and Wilson, genetic and cultural evolution are interconnected. While culture is ultimately shaped by biological processes, those biological processes are simultaneously modified in response to ensuing cultural change.

Are Human Ideas and Values Outside the Darwinian Paradigm?

Interest in the application of Darwinian orthodoxy to the evolution of culture has been immense.[55] This has not, however, led to the emergence of a consensus, rigorously informed by analysis of the evidence.[56] The reason for this is not particularly difficult to identify. Darwinism – especially in the form of the standard neo-Darwinian synthesis – proposes a relatively small number of causal mechanisms to explain what may be observed within the natural world. Yet does this mean that humanity stands above these mechanisms,

---

[53] L. Cavalli-Sforza and M. W. Feldman, *Cultural Transmission and Evolution: A Quantitative Approach*. Princeton, NJ: Princeton University Press, 1981.

[54] Charles J. Lumsden and Edward O. Wilson, *Genes, Mind and Culture: The Coevolutionary Process*. Cambridge, MA: Harvard University Press, 1981; *Promethean Fire: Reflections on the Origin of the Mind*. Cambridge, MA: Harvard University Press, 1983.

[55] The case of "evolutionary economics" is of especial interest: see Geoffrey M. Hodgson, "Darwinism in Economics: From Analogy to Ontology." *Journal of Evolutionary Economics* 12 (2002): 259–81.

[56] See, for example, the variety of opinions discussed in Herbert D. G. Maschner, *Darwinian Archaeologies*. New York: Plenum, 1996. For a survey of some of the issues, see Robin Allott, "Evolution and Culture: The Missing Link." In *The Darwinian Heritage and Sociobiology*, edited by J. M. G. van der Dennen, D. Smillie, and D. R. Wilson, 67–81. Westport, CT: Praeger, 1999.

able to resist forces that are determinative for other species? Are humans the splendid exceptions to the processes that shape the contours of other forms of biological life?[57]

The question is far from trivial, given the growing body of evidence that suggests that animal populations – especially certain primates, such as chimpanzees – are capable of constructing what might reasonably be referred to as a "culture."[58] However, the question is made deeply problematic by the fact that there is little agreement among anthropologists on precisely what is meant by the term "culture" as it is applied to human social groups, let alone whether the term can be extended beyond humans to other species.[59] If "culture" is defined as "variation acquired and maintained by social learning," then the phenomenon is widespread within nature, and by no means peculiar to humans. Yet cumulative cultural evolution is rare: there are only a few well-documented cases in which cultural change accumulates over many generations, leading to the evolution of behavior that no individual could invent.[60]

Christophe Boesche, for example, has argued that it is legitimate to speak of "chimpanzee culture."[61] While noting that many anthropologists and psychologists would resist any such suggestion, Boesche points out that the differences in cultural evolution between humans and chimpanzees can be primarily attributed to two factors. In the first place, humans possess a more complex

---

[57] There is a substantial literature on the acquisition and the possibility of the transmission of socially acquired behavior in certain animal populations. See, for example, E. Avital and E. Jablonka. "Social Learning and the Evolution of Behavior." *Animal Behavior* 48 (1994): 1195–9.

[58] See Cecilia M. Heyes and Bennett G. Galef, *Social Learning in Animals: The Roots of Culture.* San Diego, CA: Academic Press, 1996; Wendy Barnaby, "Evolution of Social Behaviour Patterns in Primates and Man." *Interdisciplinary Science Reviews* 23 (1998): 95–8.

[59] For a detailed consideration of this point, see Bradd Shore, *Culture in Mind: Cognition, Culture, and the Problem of Meaning.* Oxford: Oxford University Press, 1998.

[60] Robert D. Boyd and Peter J. Richerson, "Why Culture Is Common, but Cultural Evolution Is Rare." In *Evolution of Social Behaviour Patterns in Primates and Man,* edited by W. G. Runciman, J. Maynard Smith, and R. I. M. Dunbar, 77–93. Oxford: Oxford University Press, 1996.

[61] Christophe Boesch, "The Emergence of Cultures among Wild Chimpanzees." In *Evolution of Social Behaviour Patterns in Primates and Man,* edited by W. G. Runciman, J. Maynard Smith, and R. I. M. Dunbar, 251–68. Oxford: Oxford University Press, 1996; "Three Approaches for Assessing Chimpanzee Culture." In *Reaching into Thought: The Minds of the Great Apes,* edited by A. E. Russon, K. A. Bard, and S. T. Parker, 404–29. New York: Cambridge University Press, 1996.

language, allowing cultural dissemination to take place over greater lengths of time and spatiality. Human culture also incorporates cumulative cultural evolution or the "ratchet effect" (by analogy with the device that keeps things in place while the user prepares to advance them further). This permits cumulative modifications to occur that give rise to increasingly elaborate cultural practices. At present, there seems to be no directly comparable analogue within chimpanzee culture.

Richard Dawkins, perhaps the most celebrated popularizer of Darwinian orthodoxy and aggressive advocate of "universal Darwinism," insists that, at least in two respects, humans do not conform to the mechanisms that shape the biosphere. In the first place, human beings have developed culture – something that he asserts has no direct counterpart within other evolved species.[62] Secondly, and perhaps more significantly, Dawkins proposes an important – indeed, a decisive – distinction between humanity and every other living product of genetic mutation and natural selection. *We alone are able to resist our genes.* Where E. O. Wilson and others had insisted that human beings came within the scope of the methods of sociobiology, Dawkins excludes them from its purview. It is as if Dawkins wishes to place as much clear, blue water as possible between himself and sociobiology at this critical point.

While some writers – such as Julian Huxley – tried to develop an ethical system based on what they regarded as Darwinian evolution's more progressive aspects, Dawkins regards this as misguided.[63] Natural selection may be the dominant force in biological evolution; this does not for one moment mean that we need to endorse its apparent ethical implications.[64] Dawkins is adamant that human beings are *not* the prisoners of their genes or memes, but are capable of rebelling against such a genetic tyranny:[65]

> We have the power to defy the selfish genes of our birth and, if necessary, the selfish memes of our indoctrination. We can even discuss ways of deliberately cultivating and nurturing pure, disinterested altruism – something that has no place in nature, something that has never existed before in the whole history of

---

[62] Dawkins, *The Selfish Gene*, 189.

[63] See here Paul L. Farber, *The Temptations of Evolutionary Ethics*. Berkeley: University of California Press, 1994, 136. Farber comments that Huxley's "ethics was a projection of his values onto the history of man," so that his "naturalism assumed the vision he pretended to discover."

[64] There are, of course, important questions that arise from such a suggestion. See Donald Symons, "On the Use and Misuse of Darwinism in the Study of Human Behavior." In *The Adapted Mind*, edited by J. H. Barkow, L. Cosmides, and J. Tooby, 137–59. Oxford: Oxford University Press, 1992.

[65] *The Selfish Gene*, 200–1. The first edition (1976) ended at this point; the second edition (1989) added two additional chapters.

the world. We are built as gene machines and cultured as meme machines, but we have the power to turn against our creators. We, alone on earth, can rebel against the tyranny of the selfish replicators.

(Note that Dawkins introduces the term "meme" here, as a "cultural replicator" analogous to the gene, as a genetic replicator. We shall have more to say about this new type of replicator later in this essay.)

On this view of things, humanity appears to have evolved to the point at which we are able to rebel against precisely the genetic processes that brought us here in the first place. Only humanity has evolved brains which are capable of, in the first place, understanding how we came to being here, and in the second, subverting the process that may – according to Darwinian orthodoxy – at some very distant point lead to our being displaced, perhaps by some superior primate.

But this raises an important point concerning the applicability of any Darwinian paradigm to the evolution of culture, or of ideas. If Dawkins is right – and his critics would certainly contest this – then the unique capacity of humanity to defy the forces that shape other participants in the evolutionary process must raise questions concerning whether the Darwinian paradigm can actually be applied to human artifacts – such as ideas, values, or practices – given the interactive nature of what is evolving and the evolutionary process itself. My concern is that there is a degree of inconsistency between Dawkins' advocacy of "universal Darwinism" and his specific views concerning the place of humanity within the evolutionary process, in that the latter seem to limit, while not necessarily excluding, the former.

Yet these reflections naturally lead to another area which needs careful examination: of the various evolutionary paradigms available to us, is Darwinism actually the most appropriate to model cultural development? Alternative approaches abound, such as that found in the writings of Christopher Hallpike, who calls for a reappropriation of "the old idea of evolution as the manifestation of latent potential."[66] For Hallpike, the "directional features of social evolution" may be accounted for on the basis of "the structural properties of certain common institutions," rather than any neo-Darwinian account of evolution.

Darwinism, Lamarckianism, or What? The Indeterminate Mechanism of Cultural Evolution

In the light of Dawkins' vigorous assertion of the capacity of humanity to subvert its genes, it is necessary to ask whether a Darwinian mechanism really

---

[66] Christopher R. Hallpike, *The Principles of Social Evolution*. Oxford: Clarendon Press, 1986, 23.

can be seriously proposed for intellectual or cultural evolution. Certainly, plausible analogies between the processes of biological and cultural evolution may be proposed.[67] And it can indeed be shown that the history of culture demonstrates change, competition, and the capacity to transmit and accumulate information. Yet this is not, in itself and of itself, enough to point to a Darwinian model of cultural development. For example, some have identified a fundamental dichotomy between biological approaches, which focus on all the information that is transmitted among members of a group, and more psychological approaches in which the main concern is the cognitive and learning mechanisms by means of which such information is transmitted.[68]

The problem is, in part, that any export of biological models to the social domain is fraught with difficulty, and potentially misleading.[69] These models are laden with assumptions characteristic of their specific domains, and simply cannot be parachuted into another realm of inquiry and analysis without due modification and revision. While there are indeed many superficial similarities between biological and cultural evolution, attempts to develop these analogies have not been entirely successful.[70] Yet there is an additional difficulty: at least at certain levels, cultural evolution appears to conform more to a Lamarckian than to a Darwinian paradigm – assuming, of course, that the use of these biological analogies has any applicability to the more complex question of cultural evolution.

Darwinism consists of two elements: random variation within a generation, which is subjected to the process of natural selection. Lamarckism denotes a family of views associated with the French evolutionist Jean-Baptiste de Lamarck (1744–1829), who proposed that changes acquired during the lifetime of an organism are passed on to its offspring. The idea that phenotypic changes can be passed on to the genotype is now widely discredited as a mechanism for explaining biological evolution. But what about cultural evolution?[71]

---

[67] See especially Daniel C. Dennett, *Darwin's Dangerous Idea: Evolution and the Meaning of Life.* New York: Simon & Schuster, 1995.

[68] See, for example, Michael Tomasello, "Do Apes Ape?" In *Social Learning in Animals: The Roots of Culture,* edited by C. Heyes and B. Galef, 319–46. New York: Academic Press, 1996; Bennett G. Galef, "Social Enhancement of Food Preferences in Norway Rats: A Brief Review." In *Social Learning in Animals: The Roots of Culture,* edited by C. Heyes and B. Galef, 49–64. New York: Academic Press, 1996.

[69] A point repeatedly stressed by Stephen Jay Gould. See, for example, his *Life's Grandeur: The Spread of Excellence from Plato to Darwin.* London: Jonathan Cape, 1996.

[70] Richard Pocklington and Michael L. Best, "Cultural Evolution and Units of Selection in Replicating Text." *Journal of Theoretical Biology* 188 (1997): 79–87.

[71] There are some perceptive comments in Richard Dawkins, *The Extended Phenotype: The Gene as the Unit of Selection.* Oxford: Freeman, 1981, 112.

A crucial issue is that of *intentionality* in cultural development. Although Lamarck gave priority to habit rather than conscious will in giving rise to biological adaptation, he clearly held that adaptation could result from intentions and inclinations, as his comments in a lecture of 1800 indicate:[72]

> The bird of the shore that dislikes swimming, and which none the less needs to approach the water to find its prey, is continually exposed to sinking in the mud; but wishing to avoid the immersion of its body, its feet will get into the habit of stretching and lengthening. The effect of this, for those birds which continue to live in this manner over generations, will be that the individuals will be raised up on stilts, on long naked legs, that is to say, legs bare of feathers up to the thigh and often beyond.

Habits are here understood to be the outcome of intention or volition. Later writers in the Lamarckian tradition gave greater emphasis to this aspect of Lamarck's thought, leading to the perception that evolution could, at least in some respects and to some extent, be considered as a consciously directed process.

If a Darwinian evolutionary algorithm applies to cultural development, it is essential to demonstrate that there is an independent dynamic to cultural change which cannot be accounted for on the basis of goal-directed activity of individual human beings or social groups. To explore the role of intentionality in cultural evolution, we shall consider a case study of major significance that demonstrates unequivocal signs of intentional development: the European Renaissance.

Cultural Evolution: A Historical Case Study

The Renaissance is widely regarded as one of the most remarkable developments in the evolution of western culture. Its origins are widely agreed to lie in Italy during the thirteenth century, although its full blossoming would take place during the following two centuries.[73] The movement gradually spread from Italy into northern Europe, causing significant changes wherever it took hold. Its impact on the worlds of ideas, architecture, literature, language, and the arts was immense. To note one example: the Gothic style of architecture gave way to the classical style, impacting significantly on western European urban landscapes.[74]

---

[72] Jean-Baptist de Lamarck, *Zoological Philosophy: An Exposition with Regard to the Natural History of Animals*. Chicago: University of Chicago Press, 1984, 415.

[73] There is a huge literature. For a useful introduction, see Charles G. Nauert, *Humanism and the Culture of Renaissance Europe*. Cambridge: Cambridge University Press, 1995.

[74] See, for example, Norbert Huse, Wolfgang Wolters, and Edmund Jephcott, *The Art of Renaissance Venice: Architecture, Sculpture, and Painting, 1460–1590*. Chicago: University of Chicago Press, 1990; James S. Ackerman, *Distance Points: Essays in Theory and Renaissance Art and Architecture*. Cambridge, MA: MIT Press, 1991.

So why did this happen? What explanation may be given for this radical and highly creative redirection of European culture at this time? Since the origins and development of the movement are so well understood, it represents an ideal – indeed, even a critical – case for the application of the Darwinian paradigm outside its specific scientific domain.

The European Renaissance was a brilliant, multifaceted movement, whose scintillating cultural dynamics were determined by the interactions of a complex series of interacting communities and individuals. Recent research has demonstrated the importance of networks of humanist writers – often referred to as "sodalities" – in coordinating the spread of the ideals of the Renaissance, and placing them on a secure intellectual foundation.[75] Yet there is little doubt about the overall intellectual basis of the Renaissance. Since the pioneering work of P. O. Kristeller, the fundamental agenda of the Renaissance has been widely accepted to be the critical reappropriation of the culture of ancient Rome (and, to a lesser extent, Athens).[76] The Renaissance was about the pursuit of eloquence, with classical norms and resources being seen as integral to this task.[77]

Perhaps stimulated by the presence of the remains of classic civilization in Italy, Renaissance theorists advocated the recovery of the rich cultural heritage of the past – the elegant Latin of Cicero; the eloquence of classical rhetoric; the splendor of classical architecture; the philosophies of Plato and Aristotle; the republican political ideals which inspired the Roman constitution.[78] Renaissance writers set about deliberately and systematically adopting these principles, and applying them to their own situation. Even though many aspects of classical culture were specifically grounded in, and shaped by, the history and religion of ancient Rome, these were disregarded. Classical temple designs, originally based on and influenced by ancient Latin religious beliefs, were detached from those mythological foundations and used for Christian purposes.

---

[75] Eckhart Bernstein, "From Outsiders to Insiders: Some Reflections on the Development of a Group Identity of the German Humanists between 1450 and 1530." In *In Laudem Caroli: Renaissance and Reformation Studies for Charles G. Nauert*, edited by Charles G. Nauert and James V. Mehl, 45–64. Kirksville, MO: Thomas Jefferson University Press, 1998.

[76] See the classic study of Roberto Weiss, *The Renaissance Discovery of Classical Antiquity*. Oxford: Blackwell, 1988. There are also important observations in Paul Oskar Kristeller, *Renaissance Thought: The Classic, Scholastic, and Humanistic Strains*. New York: Harper & Row, 1961.

[77] See the classic essay of H. H. Gray, "Renaissance Humanism: The Pursuit of Eloquence." In *Renaissance Essays*, edited by P. O. Kristeller and P. P. Wiener, 199–216. New York: Harper & Row, 1966.

[78] For the general issue, see Ronald G. Witt, *In the Footsteps of the Ancients: The Origins of Humanism from Lovato to Bruni*. Leiden: Brill, 2000.

The essential point about the Renaissance "pursuit of eloquence" is that it was *intentionally* modeled on a previous era in the history of culture, which was reappropriated with certain objectives and criteria. This clearly points to a Lamarckian, rather than Darwinian, model of evolution – assuming, of course, that either of these biological analogues actually has any direct bearing upon the process of cultural evolution. The origins, development, and transmission of Renaissance humanism – while subject to the inevitable happenstance of history – was *deliberate, intentional,* and *planned.* If Darwinism is about copying the instructions (genotype), Lamarckism is about copying the product (phenotype). Lamarck, not Weismann, would seem to offer the better account of cultural evolution in this case.

It might reasonably be objected that this case study is atypical, and cannot be considered as representative of the complex patterns of human cultural development as a whole. Yet this criticism cannot be sustained without great difficulty, in that the reappropriation of previous cultural modalities appears to be a significant regular feature of cultural development. In the arts, for example, the pre-Raphaelite movement can be seen as a deliberate, systematic program of reappropriation of the tactile values of an earlier generation. In the case of Christian theology, the early Reformation period can equally well be seen as a programmatic endeavor to reappropriate the patterns of biblical interpretation of an earlier era, which early Protestants regarded as more authentic than those of the medieval period.[79]

This pattern of deliberate reappropriation within human cultural evolution is generally recognized. The philosopher of biology David Hull concedes the important role played by intentionality in human social evolution; nevertheless, he argues that this is not sufficient to permit the process to be designated as "Lamarckian":[80]

> The trouble with terming sociocultural evolution "Lamarckian" is that it obscures the really important difference between biological and sociocultural evolution – the role of intentionality. In sociocultural evolution, Lamarckian correlations exist between the environmental causes and the conceptual effects, but the mechanism responsible for these correlations is not the least Lamarckian. Rather, it is the conscious striving of intentional agents.

Hull's argument depends both on a somewhat skewed and truncated understanding of cultural development, inadequately informed by history, based on

---

[79] For a study of the complex patterns of reappropriation involved in the Reformation, see McGrath, *Intellectual Origins of the European Reformation.*

[80] David L. Hull, "The Naked Meme." In *Learning, Development and Culture: Essays in Evolutionary Epistemology,* edited by H. C. Plotkin, 273–327. New York: Wiley, 1982, quote at 312.

the fundamental assumption that Lamarck excluded volition and intention from his account of the acquisition and transmission of adaptions, which is clearly incorrect. Happily, Hull revisited the question subsequently, and offered a more informed engagement with the issue, conceding that sociocultural evolution could after all be considered Lamarckian in certain respects.[81]

But my point does not depend on the problematic issue of how one chooses to define "Lamarckism."[82] The central point is that the pivotal role of intentionality within sociocultural evolution cannot be adequately or plausibly adapted to a Darwinian model of evolution. Elements of a Darwinian account of evolution may certainly be applicable to cultural evolution, or the phenomenon of doctrinal development – for example, competition between ideas. Yet it is clear that any suggestion that cultural evolution can be explained completely and exclusively in terms of this single, universal set of principles is unsustainable. At the very least, this hypothesis requires modification by domain-specific auxiliary explanations.

Directing Evolution: Antonio Gramsci and the Manipulation of Cultural Development

The importance of these concerns about the applicability of the Darwinian paradigm to the development of culture becomes clearer in the light of the cultural analysis offered by the Italian Marxist cultural theoretician Antonio Gramsci (1891–1937). Gramsci is especially important to any discussion of cultural evolution on account of his assertion of the malleability of culture, and the identification of means by which the evolution of culture could be shaped and directed by those in appropriate positions of influence.[83] While accepting the general Marxist analysis of how society functioned, Gramsci believed that this failed to give due account to the role played by ideology, and its impact upon the shaping of communal beliefs and attitudes. This might not have

---

[81] See his preface "Lamarck among the Anglos," in Lamarck, *Zoological Philosophy*, xl–lxvi, especially lx. He develops such themes further in his later essay "Taking Memetics Seriously: Memetics Will Be What We Make It." In *Darwinizing Culture: The Status of Memetics as a Science*, edited by Robert Aunger, 43–67. Oxford: Oxford University Press, 2000.

[82] See the comment of Susan J. Blackmore, *The Meme Machine*. Oxford: Oxford University Press, 1999, 62: "The question 'Is cultural evolution Lamarckian?' is best not asked."

[83] For a thorough exploration of Gramsci's approach, see Alberto Burgio and Antonio A. Santucci, eds., *Gramsci e la rivoluzione passiva*. Rome: Editori Riuniti, 1999.

been of great importance in pre-revolutionary Russia; it was, however, of critical significance if a Marxist revolution were to take place in western Europe.

Gramsci drew a sharp distinction between "domination" (the direct coercion of society) and "hegemony" (the ideological control of society and manipulation of its notion of consent). For Gramsci, it was possible to manipulate the ideas of a society in such a way that the culture, ideas, and morality of its dominant groups come to appear as the natural order of things, despite the fact that these values have been created in order to justify the interests of the dominant groups. Gramsci thus identified the importance of churches, schools, cultural associations, and the family as agencies by which ideas and attitudes were shaped. He also stressed the importance of the intellectual in creating a "counter hegemony" – that is, a plausible and attractive view of reality which opposed the prevailing notions of "common sense," which in turn had been manufactured and manipulated by the leaders of society.[84]

Underlying Gramsci's careful analysis of the development of popular culture is the belief that the revolutionary model developed by Lenin in the Soviet Union would not work in the nations of western Europe, including his own native Italy. The Russian Revolution was the work of a tiny elite in a generally backward country with no experience of democracy. In the West, it was essential to generate a mass consciousness which would predispose the population towards revolution, with intellectuals playing a leading role in this process of transformation. The western European working classes seemed to have little interest in revolution, and Gramsci argued that this must reflect their intellectual manipulation through popular culture, shaped by dominant social groupings with their own interests in mind:[85]

> Dominant groups in society, including fundamentally but not exclusively the ruling class, maintain their dominance by securing the "spontaneous consent" of subordinate groups, including the working class, through the negotiated construction of a political and ideological consensus which incorporates both dominant and dominated groups.

So how is the present order of things to be overthrown? Gramsci argues that this must take place through radical cultural change, in which a "counter hegemony" arises which challenges the prevailing "common sense." If the dominant groupings maintain their position through the voluntary assimilation

---

[84] Antonio Gramsci, *Gli intellettuali e l'organizzazione della cultura*, 6th edn. Milan: Giulio Einaudi Editore, 1955, 95–128. Note especially the significant role attached to journalists at 129–66.

[85] Dominic Strinati, *An Introduction to Theories of Popular Culture*. London: Routledge, 1995, 165.

of their worldview on the part of the dominated, then the only means by which this stranglehold may be broken is through the articulation and propagation of a counter-worldview – a popular culture – which will ultimately gain the ascendancy.[86]

Gramsci's theoretical reflections on the evolution of culture thus allow the possibility of that evolution being directed and manipulated by those in positions of power. For Gramsci, culture is fundamentally a human creation, shaped and fashioned by those with positions of power and influence. It is directed intentionally and purposefully by those with the necessary motivation and capacity to do so. On this account of cultural evolution, a Darwinian analogy is simply inappropriate. Certain aspects of the evolution of culture may indeed be illuminated by this paradigm; at other points, however, the analogy simply cannot cope with the way in which the evolutionary process is directed and manipulated from within, with certain definite goals in mind – even if some outcomes of that process of manipulation may be unintentional and unforeseen, being subject to the happenstance of the contingencies of history.

Thus far, we have considered using biological models to discuss cultural evolution as a whole, regarding the more specific domain of the development of ideas as a subset of this broader phenomenon. Alongside the traditional model of doctrinal development being like the growth of a plant, we have considered the more precise Darwinian paradigm. Yet the application of this paradigm to the phenomenon of intellectual or cultural development, though possessed of a superficial plausibility, turns out to be rather less persuasive than might be expected. Certain individual aspects of that process of emergence can be rationalized on the basis of a Darwinian evolutionary framework; others cannot.

Many within the academic community regard the Darwinian schema as a universal paradigm for every aspect of cultural change. Yet, as we have seen, there are considerable difficulties in applying a Darwinian framework to cultural or intellectual evolution. The Darwinian evolutionary paradigm has been developed in other ways in order to allow it to engage with cultural and intellectual development. One of the most important of these is due to Richard Dawkins, who proposed the "meme" as a way of explaining the mechanism of cultural evolution.[87] As this has had such a major impact on discussion of the development of ideas, at least at the popular level, it is clearly essential that we deal with it in this essay.

---

[86] David Harris, *From Class Struggle to the Politics of Pleasure: The Effects of Gramscianism on Cultural Studies.* London: Routledge, 1992.

[87] See, for example, the economic approach found in S. Bikhchandani, D. Hirshleifer, and I. Welch, "Learning from the Behavior of Others: Conformity, Fads, and Informational Cascades." *Journal of Economic Perspectives* 12 (1998): 151–70. For an early

The Memetic Approach to Intellectual Evolution

On a Darwinian account of cultural evolution, the maintenance of cultural variation requires the *transmission* of information from one human brain to another, and the *preservation* of such information within a community. Darwinian accounts of the persistence of information tend to stress the role of natural selection in favoring such preservation.[88] But what account may be offered of transmission of ideas? Is there such a thing as a "cultural replicator"? And if so, how does it function? If such a cultural replicator could be identified, and its mechanism clarified, an important theoretical doorway would be thrown open on the inner workings of the development of culture. A conceptually robust theory could be brought to bear on areas of human activity which hitherto had largely resisted successful explanation. The identification of the nature, location, and mechanism of such cultural replicators would therefore be of enormous significance to intellectual historians and cultural theorists. If this quest for a cultural replicator were to be successful, a new conceptual energy would be injected into the philosophy of "universal Darwinism," giving it a new lease of explanatory life. In this section, we shall consider a highly significant development, which once seemed to many to open a Darwinian gateway to the world of ideas and culture.

In his landmark work *The Selfish Gene*, Richard Dawkins introduced the concept of the "meme" as a way of understanding cultural evolution, and allowing a biological analysis to be offered of the development of ideas throughout history. The process of the transmission of ideas could be explained within a Darwinian paradigm by proposing that cultural change can be accounted for in terms of the selection, variation, and inheritance of a particulate replicator. When I first encountered this idea in 1977, I found it immensely exciting. It seemed obvious that this was something which enabled the whole process of intellectual history to become open to rigorous evidence-based investigation, offering new and exciting possibilities for the study of intellectual and cultural development. The thought that evolutionary biology

---

exploration of the merits of an "epidemiology of representations," see Dan Sperber, "Anthropology and Psychology: Towards an Epidemiology of Representations." *Man* 20 (1985): 73–89. A more expansive account of this approach is to be found in Sperber's later work, *Explaining Culture: A Naturalistic Approach*. Oxford: Blackwell, 1996. It must be stressed that this "epidemiology of representations" is not equivalent to Richard Dawkins' notoriously inadequate notion of "viruses of the mind," as set out in *A Devil's Chaplain*, 128–45.

[88] See, for example, A. R. Rogers, "Does Biology Constrain Culture?" *American Anthropologist* 90 (1989): 819–31; Robert D. Boyd and Peter J. Richerson, "Why Does Culture Increase Human Adaptability?" *Ethology and Sociobiology* 16 (1996): 125–43.

might both illuminate such developments and offer new and rigorously grounded models for the evolution of human ideas and culture seemed compelling to me back at that time. There seemed every possibility that light would be thrown on some matters that were at present shrouded in obscurity and confusion. Others clearly felt the same; Stephen Shennan recalls reflecting at exactly that same time on how the notion of the meme might illuminate the study of the evolution of human society.[89] It was a wonderful time to be alive – and still better to be young!

Dawkins' breezy 1976 presentation of the meme-hypothesis was presented in a typically swashbuckling style, reflecting the popularizing agenda of *The Selfish Gene*. With characteristic panache, Dawkins argues that humanity is distinguished from other evolved beings on account of the existence of culture:[90]

> Most of what is unusual about man can be summed up in one word: "culture." I use the word not in its snobbish sense, but as a scientist uses it. Cultural transmission is analogous to genetic transmission in that, although basically conservative, it can give rise to a form of evolution.

Dawkins' readers would, of course, be relieved to hear that the word culture is not being used in a pejorative or judgmental sense – as, for example, in Matthew Arnold's definition of culture as "contact with the best which has been thought and said in the world" – but "as a scientist uses it." But how *does* a scientist use this term?

Dawkins' discussion of the meme is compromised from the outset by his failure to engage seriously with the complex phenomenon of culture. As his critics have relentlessly pointed out, there is no "single, unsnobbish, scientific conception of culture."[91] More importantly, Dawkins overlooks the fact that an entire discipline of the sciences is predominantly concerned with precisely this question of the definition and exploration of the development of human culture – namely, anthropology.[92] As Maurice Bloch commented, the "exasperated reaction of many anthropologists to the general idea of memes" reflects the apparent ignorance of the proponents of the meme-hypothesis of the discipline of anthropology, and its major successes in the explanation of

---

[89] Shennan, *Genes, Memes and Human History*, 7–8.

[90] Dawkins, *The Selfish Gene*, 189.

[91] Adam Kuper, "If Memes Are the Answer, What Is the Question?" In *Darwinizing Culture: The Status of Memetics as a Science*, edited by Robert Aunger, 175–88. Oxford: Oxford University Press, 2000.

[92] For an introduction, see Adam Kuper, *Culture: The Anthropologists' Account*. Cambridge, MA: Harvard University Press, 1999.

cultural development – without feeling the need to develop the idea of a "meme."[93] The alternative models of cultural evolution developed within the scientific discipline dedicated to precisely this area of investigation are conveniently overlooked by those evolutionary biologists wishing to extend the competency of their discipline from the biological to the cultural.[94]

The plausibility of Dawkins' argument for memes is further undermined by his uncritical use of evidence in its support, which is particularly troubling in the case of his discussion of whether there exists a meme for suicide:[95]

Just as a gene for suicide sometimes spreads itself by a roundabout route (e.g., in social insect workers, or parental sacrifice), so a suicidal meme can spread, as when a dramatic and well-publicized martyrdom inspires others to die for a deeply loved cause, and this in turn inspires others to die, and so on (Vidal, 1955).

The casual reader might suppose that this final reference was to an evidence-based study of the social dynamics of patterns of suicide, or perhaps an early anticipation of the notion of a suicide-meme. In fact, it turns out to be an early fictional work by the novelist Gore Vidal. *Messiah* is a prophetic novel that makes deft use of the modernist technique of the journal within the memoir. In this novel, Vidal tells the story of a former undertaker who preaches that "death is good," who becomes the Christ-like center of a new world religion. On the face of it, this would seem to be something of an error of scientific judgment on Dawkins' part, comparable to a social scientist appealing to Alfred Hitchcock's film *The Birds* (1963) as the basis of a discussion about ornithology.

Setting these concerns about Dawkins to one side, it may be agreed that the key notion of a cultural or intellectual replicator is an essential element of any Darwinian account of evolution.[96] The question of whether it is possible to identify and study cultural replicators, directly analogous to genes, had been raised before Dawkins published *The Selfish Gene*. The evolutionary psychologist Donald T. Campbell had already developed such ideas as early as 1960, using the term "mnemone" to refer to the cultural replicators he proposed to

---

[93] Maurice Bloch, "A Well-Disposed Social Anthropologist's Problem with Memes." In *Darwinizing Culture: The Status of Memetics as a Science*, edited by Robert Aunger, 189–203. Oxford: Oxford University Press, 2000.

[94] For examples of such models, see Michael Carrithers, *Why Humans Have Cultures: Explaining Anthropology and Social Diversity*. Oxford: Oxford University Press, 1996; Maurice Bloch, *How We Think They Think: Anthropological Approaches to Cognition, Memory, and Literacy*. Boulder: Westview, 1998.

[95] Dawkins, *The Extended Phenotype*, 111.

[96] Additionally, a distinction must be drawn between the "replicator" and its "inter-actor."

underlie cultural evolution.[97] One model that was clearly of importance to Dawkins as he wrote *The Selfish Gene* was that due to F. T. Cloak, which drew a fundamental distinction between i-culture and m-culture.

Important though such earlier attempts to develop Darwinian models of cultural evolution might have been, they were eclipsed by Dawkins' popularizing of both the specific term "meme" and his particular notion of a cultural replicator. In part, this was on account of the neater and more memorable terminology Dawkins developed. Yet another factor was the greater popular reach of his writings, which allowed a much wider reading public to become aware of the potential of essentially biological analogues for cultural development. As a result, Dawkins' pioneering work generated considerable discussion of the idea of the meme.[98] The term now even appears in the *Oxford English Dictionary*, although it must be pointed out that this represents nothing more than a lexicographical acknowledgment of the common popular usage of the term, having no bearing on whether it is a serious or legitimate scientific notion.

Dawkins introduced the word "meme" in 1976 as an abbreviation of the term "mimeme," derived from the Greek *mimesis* ("imitation"). A meme, he declared, was "a unit of cultural transmission, or a unit of imitation." The meme is thus the cultural analogue of the biological gene. It was a potent idea, throwing open the possibility of allowing evolutionary biology to explain and clarify other areas in which some form of "evolution" might be said to have taken place – such as the development of doctrine.

Dawkins provides the first major statement of the concept of the meme in *The Selfish Gene* (1976). Dawkins explains that he had long been interested in the analogy between cultural and genetic information. Noting the contributions of Cloak and others, Dawkins argued that "Darwinism is too big a theory to be confined to the narrow context of the gene." For this reason, he turned to the meme, which he believed offered a scientifically rigorous account of the diffusion and replication of ideas. In much the same way as genes propagate themselves in the gene pool, memes propagate themselves by

---

[97] Donald T. Campbell, "A General 'Selection Theory' as Implemented in Biological Evolution and in Social Belief-Transmission-with-Modification in Science." *Biology and Philosophy* 3 (1988): 413–63. The term was introduced by Campbell in 1974; this article sets out a later exposition of the notion.

[98] For some popular accounts of this approach, see Susan J. Blackmore, *The Meme Machine*. Oxford: Oxford University Press, 1999; Richard Brodie, *Virus of the Mind: The New Science of the Meme*. Seattle: Integral Press, 1996. Other definitions of the meme include "culturally transmitted instructions" and "actively contagious ideas": see Dennett, *Darwin's Dangerous Idea*, 352–69; Aaron Lynch, *Thought Contagion: How Belief Spreads through Society*. New York: Basic Books, 1996.

"leaping from brain to brain" in a somewhat undefined and conceptually elusive manner, which can nonetheless be called "imitation."[99] As examples of cultural artifacts that are replicated in this way, Dawkins identifies such things as catch-phrases, fashions, aspects of architecture, songs, and belief in God.[100]

Yet there is an obvious and serious problem here. In proposing the meme, Dawkins seemed to his more critical readers to offer as an explanation what actually needed to be explained. The examples that Dawkins offers of memes are all what Cloak terms "m-culture" – in other words, things which arise through the impact of ideas on the environment. This makes this understanding of the meme readily applicable to cultural evolution, as it allows an engagement with something observable. It is not, however, particularly Darwinian. On the basis of the examples offered by Dawkins, the analogue is not between memes and *genes*, but between memes and *phenotypes*. The parallel between the propagation of genes in the gene pool and memes in a (hypothetical) meme pool is thus quite inappropriate. Furthermore, the evolutionary paradigm entailed by this 1976 concept of the meme was not Darwinian, but Lamarckian.

Dawkins recognized these problems almost immediately, and modified his ideas in his next major popular work, *The Extended Phenotype* (1982). His original account of the meme, he conceded, was defective; it required correction.[101]

I was insufficiently clear about the distinction between the meme itself, as replicator, and its "phenotypic effects" or "meme products" on the other. A meme should be regarded as a unit of information residing in a brain (Cloak's "i-culture"). It has a definite structure, realized in whatever medium the brain uses for storing information ... This is to distinguish it from phenotypic effects, which are its consequences in the outside world (Cloak's "m-culture").

This clarification removed one fundamental difficulty with the concept of the meme. On any standard neo-Darwinian account, genes give rise to phenotypes. There is no question of phenotypical causation of genetic traits. To put it in a nutshell: genes are *selected, not instructed*.[102] (The rival Lamarckian view requires that acquired bodily changes can subsequently be inherited – in other

---

[99] *The Selfish Gene*, 192.
[100] *The Selfish Gene*, 193.
[101] *The Extended Phenotype*, 109.
[102] For an excellent presentation of this point, see Gary Cziko, *Without Miracles: Universal Selection Theory and the Second Darwinian Revolution*. Cambridge, MA: MIT Press, 1995.

words, that genes are instructed.)[103] Dawkins, who vigorously defends this "central dogma" of Darwinian orthodoxy, had thus put himself in a potentially indefensible position, in that *The Selfish Gene* appeared to imply that it was phenotypes that were inherited – thus pointing to a Lamarckian evolutionary mechanism.

The new position set out in *The Extended Phenotype* represents a significant move away from the 1976 view, which embraced cultural artifacts and ideas. The meme is now clearly defined as the units of information which *give rise to* cultural artifacts and ideas. What Dawkins originally defined as memes – things like "catchy tunes" – are now regarded as "meme products." The meme is to be understood as the instructions, not the product that arises from the application or execution of those instructions. This may have re-solved one difficulty; it nevertheless created others. Most importantly, it raised the question of how anyone could empirically distinguish memes themselves from the resulting meme products.[104] Indeed, it is important to note that a number of supporters of the meme-hypothesis continue to regard artifacts themselves as memes.[105]

A further issue here concerns the timescale of cultural evolution. As Daw-kins constantly emphasizes, major genetic developments take place over huge periods of time, vastly exceeding the lifetime of any "gene vehicle" or popula-tion of organisms. Cultural developments, in contrast, are now so rapid that they generally take place within the lifetime of individual human beings; in the past, they might be spread out over several generations. The continuity and stability offered by the gene has no necessary memetic counterpart, on account of the vastly reduced timescale, which renders such a memetic stabilizing mechanism unnecessary. Cultural evolution takes place over single human generations, whereas biological evolution demands a much greater timespan.

The meme, then, was proposed as a cultural analogue to the gene. But what force does this biological analogy possess outside its own specific field of

---

[103] Readers not familiar with this "central dogma" of Darwinism – originally pro-posed by August Weismann (1834–1914) – should read the highly accessible account provided in John Maynard Smith, *The Theory of Evolution*. Cambridge: Cambridge University Press, 1995, 76–85.

[104] At a popular level, it may be noted, Dawkins' meme concept is generally misun-derstood, in that it continues to be discussed in terms of his 1976 definition, set out in the widely read *Selfish Gene*, rather than its 1982 revision, as presented in the some-what less widely read *Extended Phenotype*. On this latter view, memes are *not* cultural artifacts, such as ideas or tunes, but whatever transmits them.

[105] For example, see Blackmore, *The Meme Machine*; Rosaria Conte, "Memes through (Social) Minds." In *Darwinizing Culture: The Status of Memetics as a Science*, edited by Robert Aunger, 83–119. Oxford: Oxford University Press, 2000.

application? As has often been demonstrated, analogical argumentation is an essential element of scientific reasoning.[106] The perception of an analogy between A and B is often the starting point for new lines of inquiry, opening up new and exhilarating frontiers. Yet that same perception has often led to scientific dead ends, including the long-abandoned ideas of "calorific" and "phlogiston."[107] As Mario Bunge points out, analogies have a marked propensity to mislead in the sciences.[108] So is this posited analogy between gene and meme in the first place *real*, and in the second *helpful*?

Now genes can be "seen," and their transmission patterns studied under rigorous empirical conditions. But what about memes, as Dawkins defined them in 1982? The simple fact is that they are, in the first place, *hypothetical constructs*, inferred from observation rather than observed in themselves, and in the second place, *unobservable*. This makes their rigorous investigation intensely problematic, and fails to enable a *meme* and an *idea* to be satisfactorily distinguished.

Such is the force of this point that other writers in the field seem to have abandoned the idea of the meme as a unit of replication, and replaced it as a basic unit of mental representation or content. John Ball, for example, suggests that all the contents of the human mind – including what might reasonably be thought of as Skinnerian conditioning – must be thought of as a "meme."[109]

More troublingly, the flawed analogy between gene and meme becomes so overextended that it simply collapses under the evidential tensions that it creates. There is a widespread feeling that the forceful pressing of the alleged analogy between "memes" and "genes" is deliberately intended to distract attention from the significance of the evident disanalogies between them, or the awkward fact that the use of the term tends to provoke more definitional quarrels than it resolves evidential disagreements. A gene is an observable entity that is well defined at the biological, chemical, and physical levels. Biologically, the gene is a distinct portion of a chromosome; chemically, it consists of DNA; physically, it consists of a double-helix, with a sequence of nucleotides which represent a "genetic code" that can be read and interpreted. What are memes? Where are they located? How are they to be described biologically, chemically, and physically?

---

[106] Daniel Rothbart, "The Semantics of Metaphor and the Structure of Science." *Philosophy of Science* 51 (1984): 595–615.

[107] John Worrall, "Fresnel, Poisson and the White Spot: The Role of Successful Predictions in the Acceptance of Scientific Theories." In *The Uses of Experiment: Studies in the Natural Sciences*, edited by David Gooding, Trevor Pinch, and Simon Schaffer, 135–57. Cambridge: Cambridge University Press, 1989.

[108] Mario Bunge, *Method, Model, and Matter.* Dordrecht: D. Reidel, 1973, 125–6.

[109] John A. Ball, "Memes as Replicators." *Ethology and Sociology 5* (1984): 145–61.

If we are to believe that the same evolutionary algorithm governs biological and cultural evolution, the ontological questions raised by this proposal cannot be ignored. A "meme," if it is to be scientifically evaluated, cannot be allowed to remain at the level of a vague, heuristic device, deriving its limited plausibility by force of a questionable analogy. Their ontology demands clarification. "Memes are rather shadowy entities, which acquire a certain solidity only by virtue of a metaphorical relationship with genes."[110] Are memes *really* there? On any responsible account of scientific explanation, memes cannot remain arbitrary units of analysis, invoked to describe the world when other modes of description already exist, and have proved their worth; we need to know precisely what kind of things they are claimed to be, and what scientific evidence makes their existence at least plausible, and preferably necessary.

David Hull and Susan Blackmore both argue that it is not necessary to have a clear, precise definition of a meme,[111] pointing out that purely operational definitions of genes were perfectly adequate to allow the notion to be scientifically productive in the early twentieth century. Blackmore reasonably points out that the theory of natural selection made enormous advances long before the underlying chemistry was understood, yet unwisely goes on to claim that, for all our ignorance about how memes are stored and transmitted, "we certainly know enough to get started." Yet the ontological question can neither be marginalized nor indefinitely postponed. Before memetics can be taken seriously, making the critical transition from popular pseudo-science to mainstream academic science, memes need to be defined in such a way that their identity can be confirmed and clarified. At present, a loose, general case has been made for a broad analogy between biological and cultural evolution. Yet the analogy is not sufficiently precise nor persuasive to elicit the concept of the meme as a necessary explanation of those limited parallels, nor as an explanation that may be judged superior to the many others already developed within anthropology and other disciplines.

Yet the indeterminate ontology of memes is only the first of a series of concerns about the proposed analogy between memes and genes. What about the mechanism by which memes are transmitted? One of the most important implications of the work of Crick and Watson on the structure of DNA was that it opened the way to an understanding of the mechanism of replication. What physical mechanism is proposed in this case? How does a

---

[110] Kuper, "If Memes Are the Answer, What Is the Question?," 185.
[111] Blackmore, *The Meme Machine*, 56; David Hull, "Taking Memetics Seriously: Memetics Will Be What We Make It." In *Darwinizing Culture: The Status of Memetics as a Science*, edited by Robert Aunger, 43–67. Oxford: Oxford University Press, 2000.

meme cause a memetic effect? Or, to put the question in a more pointed way, how could we even begin to set up experiments to identify and analyze memes, even before we begin to explore their relation to alleged memetic effects?

Now if memetics was a legitimate evidence-based science, comparable to genetics, there would be no particular difficulty at this point. It might be argued that the memetic observer of cultural evolution is in a situation similar to Darwin in the 1850s: observing patterns which seemed to demand some kind of inherited transmission of traits, even though there was no existing explanation for such a mechanism. Or that the present state of knowledge of memes is similar to that of genes in the early twentieth century – namely, purely operational definitions of genes proved adequate to explain the empirical evidence, until further advances could be made. Yet I see no reason for suggesting that memetics offers even a plausible description, let alone an explanation, for the evolution of human culture. While Darwin accumulated a mass of observational evidence in favor of his theories, memetics has yet to make any significant advances on this front. Yet there is a possibly insurmountable problem in the form of argument used to advance this agenda.

The real issue is the limits of analogical argumentation in the natural sciences, which becomes particularly significant in the case of evolutionary theory. "Evolution is to analogy as statues are to birdshit" (Steve Jones). The implicit assumption seems to be that, since the transmission of culture and the transmission of genes are analogical processes, the well-developed concepts and methods of neo-Darwinism can explain both. Yet it is an analogy that has been proposed, not demonstrated. And the limits of argument by analogy are well known to any historian of science.[112] Quantum theory is an excellent example of a scientific discipline bedeviled by problems arising from the bad use of analogies.[113] And when we move outside the relatively well-defined world of physics into the chaos of human culture, analogies often develop a life of their own, unchecked by the rigid demands of evidence-based argument in the harder sciences.

In the case of the gene, the early case for some physical factor for the transmission of hereditary information was based on the Mendelian demonstration of the precision of such transmission, and the self-evident fact that there were no other means by which such information could be stored, transmitted, and retrieved. The case of cultural evolution is completely

---

[112] An excellent example is to be had in the notion of the "luminiferous ether," posited by analogy with sound: see Tetu Hirosige, "The Ether Problem, the Mechanistic World View, and the Origins of the Theory of Relativity." *Historical Studies in the Physical Sciences* 7 (1976): 3–82.

[113] Mario Bunge, "Analogy in Quantum Theory: From Insight to Nonsense." *British Journal for the Philosophy of Science* 18 (1967): 265–86.

different. All human cultures possess means by which information may be transmitted within existing populations and to subsequent generations, none of which appear to be genetically determined but rather to be the outcome of cultural and technological developments such as books, traditions, institutions, and oral traditions.[114] The notion of a "meme" is functionally redundant, forcing its defenders to make a case by analogy with the gene – yet to downplay the empirically determined biological, chemical, and physical parameters of the gene, which are now an essential aspect of molecular genetics. Its plausibility is determined by an analogical argument, not by evidence and observation. Yet the analogy is flawed and inappropriate, possessed of a capacity to mislead, rather than inform, discussion of the basics of cultural evolution.

The gene *had* to be proposed, in that without the assumption of the physical transmission of inherited traits over vast periods of time, Darwinism was rendered incoherent. In the absence of anything even remotely resembling the overwhelming biological evidence that Darwin brought forward in support of his ideas, there is simply no need to propose a "meme," in that the dynamics of cultural development can be explained perfectly well without proposing such an idea.

Dawkins' canonical memetic statements have been upheld in two major recent publications – Daniel Dennett's *Darwin's Dangerous Idea* (1995) and Susan Blackmore's *The Meme Machine* (1999) – each of which offers a defense of the notion, and its more general application to cultural evolution.[115] Although Blackmore's exposition of the idea is characterized more by aspiration than evidence-based reasoning, Dennett sounds a welcome note of caution:[116]

> The prospects for elaborating a rigorous science of memetics are doubtful, but the concept provides a valuable perspective from which to investigate the complex relationship between cultural and genetic heritage.

Others are more skeptical, arguing – assisted in no small way by Dennett's astonishing lack of rigorous critical thinking at this point – that his account

---

[114] There is a huge literature, including works such as Niklas Luhmann, *Love as Passion: The Codification of Intimacy*. Stanford, CA: Stanford University Press, 1998; Vera Schwarcz, *Bridge across Broken Time: Chinese and Jewish Cultural Memory*. New Haven, CT: Yale University Press, 1998; John Lowney, *The American Avant-Garde Tradition: William Carlos Williams, Postmodern Poetry, and the Politics of Cultural Memory*. Lewisburg, PA: Bucknell University Press, 1997.

[115] For a sympathetic account, see Kevin N. Laland and Gillian R. Brown, *Sense and Nonsense: Evolutionary Perspectives on Human Behaviour*. Oxford: Oxford University Press, 2002, 197–239.

[116] Dennett, *Darwin's Dangerous Idea*, 369.

of the meme is simply philosophically incoherent.[117] The concept of the meme is so vague and undefined, so empirically indeterminate, that there exist no means by which it can be verified or falsified. And there, for most, the matter rests.

Perhaps the most significant criticism of the meme-concept is that the study of cultural and intellectual development can proceed, and as a matter of fact *has proceeded*, perfectly well without it. It is not necessary to propose a "replicator" to account satisfactorily for cumulative adaptive evolution.[118] Economic and physical models – especially information transfer – have proved their worth in this context. The contrast between meme and gene is, once more, painfully obvious: the gene *had* to be postulated, as there was simply no other way of explaining the observational evidence concerning the patterns of transmission of inherited traits. The meme is, to put it bluntly, explanatorily redundant. It is an "explanation" that is not required to explain the phenomena, and which itself rests upon a perilously superficial evidential foundation.

Economic models, which treat ideas as "information cascades" or consumer durables, are rather more persuasive and helpful than the unverified meme-concept. These models incorporate the "competition" and "extinction" motifs of Darwinian theory, without necessarily endorsing its theories on the origins of innovations. For example, an economic "theory of fads" is considerably more convincing as an explanation of patterns of thought adoption and dispersal than Dawkins' meme.[119] Cultural evolution and intellectual development can often be better understood in terms of a physical, rather than a biological analogue – such as the transmission of information on random

---

[117] See the devastating critique in M. R. Bennett and P. M. S. Hacker, *Philosophical Foundations of Neuroscience*. Oxford: Blackwell, 2003, 432–5.

[118] A point stressed by Robert Boyd and Peter Richerson. See especially their paper "Memes: Universal Acid or a Better Mousetrap?" In *Darwinizing Culture: The Status of Memetics as a Science*, edited by Robert Aunger, 143–62. Oxford: Oxford University Press, 2000. For an interesting application of Boyd and Richerson's approach to cultural history, see W. G. Runciman, "Greek Hoplites, Warrior Culture, and Indirect Bias." *Journal of the Royal Anthropological Society* 4 (1998): 731–51. Runciman has also used such an approach to make sense of the rapid spread of Christianity in the third century, offering "a selectionist analysis explicitly focused on the particular historical environment," while not doubting "the existence of universal psychological capacities and dispositions." See W. G. Runciman, "The Diffusion of Christianity in the Third Century AD as a Case-Study in the Theory of Cultural Selection." *European Journal of Sociology* 45 (2004): 3–21.

[119] S. Bikhchandani, D. Hirshleifer, and I. Welch, "A Theory of Fads: Fashion, Custom, and Cultural Change as Informational Cascades." *Journal of Political Economy* 100 (1992): 992–1026.

networks.[120] Dawkins now seems to be distancing himself from any suggestion that he offered the meme-concept as an *explanation* of human culture in general.[121]

Of course, it may be pointed out that the notion of a cultural replicator does not require to be abandoned merely because one highly influential interpretation of the idea appears to be of limited value in explaining the phenomena of cultural development. Yet it is entirely fair to respond that Dawkins' notion of the meme embodies most of the elements that any such theory of cultural replication demands.

So what is the relevance of this theory to doctrinal development? At this stage, I can only report that it appears to have at best limited relevance, and is potentially unsafe as a means for illuminating the phenomenon of the development of doctrine. Although I entertained what I now must concede to be unrealistically high hopes for the idea of a particular cultural replicator back in 1978, when I began my detailed study of the development of doctrine, it is now clear that this is at present an unreliable conceptual framework for elucidating the phenomenon of cultural evolution, and is likely to remain so.

Doctrinal Development: Are There Islands of Theological Stability?

Does evolution – whether biological or doctrinal – show a tendency to converge on certain favored outcomes? Many writers who adopt the standard Darwinian paradigm argue for the essentially random and contingent nature of the evolutionary process. For example, Stephen Jay Gould insists that "almost every interesting event of life's history falls into the realm of contingency."[122] It is pointless to talk about purpose, historical inevitability, or direction. From its beginning to its end, the evolutionary process is governed by contingencies. "We are the accidental result of an unplanned process ... the fragile result of an enormous concatenation of improbabilities, not the predictable product of any definite process."[123]

---

[120] See, for example, D. J. Watts, "A Simple Model of Information Cascades on Random Networks." *Proceedings of the National Academy of Sciences* 99 (2002): 5766–71. The implications of this as an analogue for the transmission of ideas in a cultural system will be obvious.

[121] *A Devil's Chaplain*, 127.

[122] Stephen Jay Gould, *Wonderful Life: The Burgess Shale and the Nature of History*. New York: Norton, 1989, 290.

[123] Ibid, 101–2.

As Gould famously put this point, using the characteristically 1990s analogy of a video tape, if we were to replay the tape of evolutionary history, we would not see the same thing happen each time. The influence of contingency is such that what happens is the product of happenstance. "Alter any early event, ever so slightly and without apparent importance at the time, and evolution cascades into a radically different channel." The same, he argued, applies to human history as a whole, which is shaped by unpredictabilities. He argues, for example, that the entire course of American history was changed by the actions of Joshua Lawrence Chamberlain, who led a decisive bayonet charge in the battle of Gettysburg in the American Civil War.[124] Gould argues that without this small event the South might have won the war. How different might world history have been if that were the case?

At this point, we cannot avoid noting the sensitive issue of Stephen Jay Gould's decidedly ambivalent standing within the evolutionary biology community.[125] Many would argue that he placed too much emphasis on drift and historical contingency, and neglected the themes that adaptationists regard as significant in selectionist theories.[126] Yet there is no doubt that contingency is an issue in evolution. So how might the role of contingency in the evolutionary process – whether biological, cultural, or intellectual – be examined? How might we begin to gain an understanding of the doubtless complex interaction of the contingencies of history and the (presumably) universal processes which underlie and shape the changing contours of the biological and cultural worlds? In what follows, we shall explore these matters in more detail.

---

[124] It is a good example. Readers wanting to know more about Chamberlain will enjoy reading Alice Rains Trulock, *In the Hands of Providence: Joshua L. Chamberlain and the American Civil War*. Chapel Hill: University of North Carolina Press, 1992.

[125] John Maynard Smith, *New York Review of Books*, November 30, 1995, 46: "Because of the excellence of his essays, he has come to be seen by non-biologists as the preeminent evolutionary theorist. In contrast, the evolutionary biologists with whom I have discussed his work tend to see him as a man whose ideas are so confused as to be hardly worth bothering with, but as one who should not be publicly criticized because he is at least on our side against the creationists." Smith argues that Gould "is giving non-biologists a largely false picture of the state of evolutionary theory." Or see Ernst Mayr, *Toward a New Philosophy of Biology: Observations of an Evolutionist*. Cambridge, MA: Belknap, 1988, 534–5, who argues that Gould and his colleagues "quite conspicuously misrepresent the views of [biology's] leading spokesmen."

[126] See, for example, the reassertion of the merits of adaptationist approaches in George C. Williams and Randolph Nesse, "The Dawn of Darwinian Medicine." *Quarterly Review of Biology* 66 (1991): 1–22.

Contingency, History, and Adaptation in the Evolutionary Process

The role of contingency in the evolutionary process has been the subject of careful experimental study. Perhaps one of the most often-cited studies of relevance was carried out in Richard Lenski's laboratory at Michigan State University in East Lansing. Lenski and co-workers followed the development of twelve separate populations of *E. coli* over 24,000 generations – long enough to explore the manner in which history, contingency, and adaptation shaped the organism's development.[127] As Simon Conway Morris points out, the experiments allowed at least a partial evaluation of the relative impacts of chance, history, and adaptation in evolution:[128]

> After the 1,000 generations of maltose-based existence the historical component was strongly reduced, and correspondingly there was a strong degree of convergence, that is, different routes led to the same end-point ... And the role of chance? In this evolutionary experiment, at least, it was of negligible importance. The simple conclusion is that history does not go away, but is swamped by the effects of convergence.

In evolutionary biology, the phrase "convergent evolution" is used to describe the process whereby organisms not closely related independently acquire similar characteristics while evolving in separate and sometimes varying ecosystems.[129] For Conway Morris, the apparent ubiquity of convergence within the evolutionary process opens up the most interesting, and potentially controversial, question concerning biological evolution: its possible *inevitability*. Not simply that the process of evolution itself is inevitable, but that certain of its outcomes seem predetermined.

Conway Morris' argument is an important reminder that, although contingency plays a role in the evolutionary process, it must not be assumed that this means that evolution is fundamentally based on chance. It has often been

---

[127] For a very recent survey of the work, see Richard E. Lenski, "Phenotypic and Genomic Evolution During a 20,000-Generation Experiment with the Bacterium Escherichia Coli." *Plant Breeding Reviews* 24 (2004): 225–65. See also Richard E. Lenski and Michael Travisano, "Dynamics of Adaptation and Diversification: A 10,000-Generation Experiment with Bacterial Populations." *Proceedings of the National Academy of Sciences, USA* 91 (1994): 6808–14.

[128] Simon Conway Morris, *Life's Solution: Inevitable Humans in a Lonely Universe.* Cambridge: Cambridge University Press, 2003, 132.

[129] There is a huge literature. For a useful survey focusing on one specific ecosystem, see Eviatar Nevo, *Mosaic Evolution of Subterranean Mammals: Regression, Progression, and Global Convergence.* Oxford: Oxford University Press, 1999.

pointed out that biological evolution is far from the random process that some might suggest. While recognizing that many have indeed drawn the conclusion that Darwinism was a "theory of chance," Richard Dawkins insists that this amounts to something of a misrepresentation of the situation. "Chance is a minor ingredient in the Darwinian recipe, but the most important ingredient is cumulative selection which is quintessentially *non*-random."[130] Evolution can thus be seen as the outcome of the non-random survival of randomly varying replicators, with the emphasis placed upon the regularity of selection rather than the happenstance of variation. For Dawkins, evolution is better thought of as non-random. "Core Darwinism," he argues, should be defined as the "minimal theory that evolution is guided in adaptively non-random directions by the non-random survival of small random hereditary changes."[131]

We have already seen that the supposition that there is any sort of analogy between doctrinal development and biological evolution is intensely problematic. Nevertheless, the exploration of intellectual possibilities of this kind remains immensely important. In this section, I propose to explore whether there is any sense in which certain doctrinal developments can be thought of as inevitable.

The possibility that the evolution of certain doctrinal forms is inevitable has long been noted within the literature. In recent years, it has been raised with particular clarity by New Testament scholar Morna D. Hooker. In a careful and reflective analysis of the complex relationship between the witness to the person of Jesus of Nazareth in the New Testament documents and the christological formula of the Council of Chalcedon, Hooker expresses her conviction that this must be regarded "as an inevitable development."[132] This raises the all-important question of how we are to understand the process of doctrinal development so that it may engage with the question of whether Chalcedon indeed was an "inevitable development," as well as the related question of what other doctrinal formations should be added to this category.

It is essential to concede from the outset that contingency plays a major role in the specifics of doctrinal development. Had Pelagius not been irritated by moral laxity in the Roman church of the late fourth century, would there have

---

[130] Richard Dawkins, *The Blind Watchmaker: Why the Evidence of Evolution Reveals a Universe without Design*. London: Longman, 1986, 49.

[131] *A Devil's Chaplain*, 81. This does not, by the way, imply that all evolutionary change is adaptive.

[132] Morna D. Hooker, "Chalcedon and the New Testament." In *The Making and Remaking of Christian Doctrine*, edited by Sarah Coakley and David A. Pailin, 73–93. Oxford: Clarendon Press, 1993, 90. Hooker makes it clear that the historical inevitability of the Chalcedonian Definition does not mean that it is necessarily to be thought of as "a proper development."

been a Pelagian controversy, with the ensuing clarification of the doctrine of grace? What if Decius had not demanded sacrifice to the gods as a thanksgiving that the world did not end in 247? Might there then have been no Donatist controversy, and subsequently no clarification of early Christian ecclesiology? What if the first son of Hans Luder and Margarette Lindemann had died in a mining accident? If there had been no Martin Luther, would there have been a Reformation – at least, in the form we know it?

The exploration of counter-factuals makes it clear that the development of Christian doctrine has been impacted by the unpredictable contingencies of history. As has often been pointed out, this neither subverts nor marginalizes any theology of doctrinal development which appeals to divine providence; providence, it must be appreciated, cannot be equated with predictability. The essential point is that, as seen from the human perspective of the historian of thought, the development of Christian doctrine appears to be the result of "an enormous concatenation of improbabilities" (Gould). Gould's interest in cultural development led to his using cultural artifacts – such as the spandrels of Cathedral of San Marco, Venice – as analogues of biological evolution.[133] This point serves to highlight the potential analogy between evolution in the domains of the biosphere and broader aspects of human culture, including theology. Yet it also raises another, more intriguing, question. Might evolution, in both these domains, actually be rather more directed than at first seems the case? Might there not be a case for suggesting that the emergence of certain possibilities might be *inevitable*?

Stephen Jay Gould argues that the role of contingency in biological evolution is so substantial that the tape will disclose different patterns on replay. Gould describes this thought experiment as follows in his magisterial *Structure of Evolutionary Theory* (2002):[134]

I call this experiment "replaying life's tape." You press the rewind button and, making sure you thoroughly erase everything that actually happened, go back to

---

[133] Stephen Jay Gould and Richard C. Lewontin, "The Spandrels of San Marco and the Panglossian Paradigm: A Critique of the Adaptationist Programme." *Proceedings of the Royal Society of London* B 205 (1979): 581–98. Gould and Lewontin here use a spandrel as a metaphor for characteristics that were originally side effects rather than being true adaptations to the environment. The point being made is that, just as spandrels are architectural byproducts, or automatic consequences, of building something in a certain way, so certain evolutionary developments may well be non-adaptive. This has generated a substantial debate, which is not without relevance for the development of doctrine. See T. A. Graham, "Constraints and Spandrels in Gould's *Structure of Evolutionary Theory*." *Biology and Philosophy* 19 (2004): 29–43.

[134] Stephen Jay Gould, *The Structure of Evolutionary Theory*. Cambridge, MA: Belknap, 2002, 1019–20.

any time and place in the past – say, to the seas of the Burgess Shale. Then let the tape run again and see if the repetition looks at all like the original. If each replay strongly resembles life's actual pathway, then we must conclude that what really happened pretty much had to happen. But suppose that the experimental versions all yield sensible results strikingly different from the actual history of life? What could we then say about the predictability of self-conscious intelligence? Or of mammals? Or of life on land? Or simply of multicellular persistence for 600 million difficult years?

It is, of course, an experiment that cannot be carried out, save in the rather restrictive laboratory of the human mind. But is it right? Is the process of intellectual development really so subject to the happenstance of history?

To appreciate the issue in relation to intellectual development, consider the following question. If Darwin had never existed, would what we now term the "Darwinian theory of evolution" have emerged? This is unquestionably an idea, linked with certain specific events, observations, and personalities embedded within a historically contingent situation. So what would have happened if the *Beagle* had foundered off the coast of Patagonia, with the loss of all hands – including the ship's naturalist? The answer, from a scientific perspective, is clear. The emergence of this way of thinking was not dependent upon the contingencies of Darwin's existence. It was something of an inevitability. And Gould agrees:[135]

> I will grant one point to scientific colleagues and freely allow that if Charles Darwin had never been born, a well-prepared and waiting scientific world, abetted by a cultural context more than ready for such a reconstruction of nature, would still have promulgated and won general acceptance for evolution in the mid-nineteenth century. At some point, the mechanism of natural selection would also have been formulated and eventually validated.

Equally, he argues that the Renaissance would still have unfolded if Michelangelo had never been born. But in each case the historical specifics would not have been the same. The richly interesting patterns of how evolutionary theory was established and accepted, or how the Renaissance originated and developed, would have been different.

We have already noted that Gould's emphasis on historical contingency is regarded with suspicion by many within the professional community of evolutionary biologists. At this point, we must also consider Leigh van Valen's critique of Gould's use of the "tape of life" metaphor. What would happen, he asks, if we were to replay the tape of evolutionary history, as

---

[135] Stephen Jay Gould, *The Structure of Evolutionary Theory.* Cambridge, MA: Belknap, 1342.

Gould suggested?[136] Van Valen concedes immediately, following Gould, that the first thing that an observer would be likely to notice was the differences between the two versions of the tape. The contingencies of history are such that the outcomes are different in each case. But on closer examination, the situation would prove to be more complex than Gould allowed. Despite the differences, similarities would emerge:

> Play the tape a few more times, though. We see similar melodic elements appearing in each, and the overall structure may be quite similar ... When we take a broader view, the role of contingency diminishes. Look at the tape as a whole. It resembles in some ways a symphony, although its orchestration is internal and caused largely by the interactions of many melodic strands.

Although the details will be different, van Valen argues that similarities and convergences are to be expected.

A similar approach is taken by Simon Conway Morris, whose pioneering work on the Burgess Shale was taken up by Stephen Jay Gould.[137] Although both Gould and Conway Morris recognize the role of contingency in the evolutionary process, they evaluate its importance in significantly different ways. For Gould, "the awesome improbability of human evolution" is a result of contingency in adaptive evolution. Conway Morris argues that if our planet were even slightly different from the way it actually is, then life might never have emerged. Although this seems similar to Gould's emphasis on historical contingency, it is important to note that Conway Morris emphasizes the way in which physical events create opportunities for life to emerge and adapt, where Gould instead emphasized the idiosyncratic nature of adaptation itself.

In *Life's Solution*, Conway Morris argues that the number of evolutionary endpoints is limited. "Rerun the tape of life as often as you like, and the end result will be much the same."[138] *Life's Solution* builds a forceful case for the predictability of evolutionary outcomes, not in terms of genetic details but rather their broad phenotypic manifestations. Conway Morris's case is based on a remarkable compilation of examples of convergent evolution, in which two or more lineages have independently evolved similar structures and functions. The examples range from the aerodynamics of hovering moths and hummingbirds, to the use of silk by spiders and some insects to capture prey.

---

[136] Leigh M. van Valen, "How Far Does Contingency Rule?" *Evolutionary Theory* 10 (1991): 47–52.

[137] For his correction of Gould at points of importance, see Simon Conway Morris, *The Crucible of Creation: The Burgess Shale and the Rise of Animals*. Oxford: Oxford University Press, 1998.

[138] Morris, *Life's Solution*, 282.

The force of Conway Morris's critique of Gould cannot be overlooked. While contingency is a factor in the overall evolutionary mechanism, it plays a significantly less decisive role than Gould allows. Evolution regularly appears to "converge" on a relatively small number of possible outcomes. Convergence is widespread, despite the infinitude of genetic possibilities, because "the evolutionary routes are many, but the destinations are limited." Certain destinations are precluded by "the howling wildernesses of the maladaptive," where the vast majority of genotypes are non-viable, thus precluding further exploration by natural selection. Biological history shows a marked tendency to repeat itself, with life demonstrating an almost eerie ability to find its way to the correct solution, repeatedly. "Life has a peculiar propensity to 'navigate' to rather precise solutions in response to adaptive challenges."[139]

In making this important point, Morris offers a non-biological analogy to help his readers grasp his point. He appeals to the discovery of Easter Island by the Polynesians, perhaps 1,200 years ago.[140] Easter Island is one of the most remote places on earth, at least 3,000 kilometers from the nearest population centers, Tahiti and Chile. Yet though surrounded by the vast, empty wastes of the Pacific Ocean, it was nevertheless discovered by Polynesians. Is this, asks Morris, to be put down to chance and happenstance? Possibly. But probably not. Morris points to the "sophisticated search strategy of the Polynesians" which made its discovery inevitable. The same, he argues, happens in the evolutionary process: "Isolated 'islands' provide havens of biological possibility in an ocean of maladaptedness." These "islands of stability" give rise to the phenomenon of convergent evolution.[141]

So can these "islands of stability" be predicted? Can one identify in advance, so to speak, points on which various evolutionary processes converge? Morris is properly cautious at this point. After all, the scientific method is about *a posteriori* analysis, not *a priori* prediction. "Hindsight and foresight are strictly forbidden ... we can only retrodict and not predict."[142] Evolutionary theory may offer an account of what has been observed and is being observed – but cannot predict future specifics. Yet the notion of islands of biological stability is perfectly valid, and can be retrodicted on the basis of what is already known about parameters believed to be involved in the evolutionary process. Perhaps the identity of *individual* "islands of stability" cannot be predicted; yet the

---

[139] Morris, *Life's Solution* 225.

[140] Ibid, 19–21. The island was also "discovered" by Admiral Roggeveen on Easter Day, 1722.

[141] Ibid, 127.

[142] Ibid, 11–12. Morris here cites approvingly from the standard Darwinian account of the "Game of Life," as set out by Temple Smith and Harold Morowitz, "Between Physics and History." *Journal of Molecular Evolution* 18 (1982): 265–82.

general phenomenon could be broadly predicted, and the identity of specific "islands" *retrodicted* on the basis of such an understanding of the forces of contingency, history, and adaptability entailed in the evolutionary process.

So might this observation have relevance to the phenomenon of doctrinal development? Once more, it is necessary to emphasize the need to proceed with caution when using biological analogies of any kind in dealing with general cultural issues, including the development of ideas. Yet this being said, an important possibility emerges – namely, that the nature of the Christian faith is such that "islands of theological stability" may be expected to emerge, nucleating around certain core themes or notions, such as the identity of Jesus Christ. We shall explore such issues in what follows.

Contingency, History, and Adaptation in the Development of Doctrine

Simon Conway Morris's broad vision of the evolutionary process emphasizes the phenomenon of convergence. Why do these islands of biological stability exist, despite the infinitude of genetic possibilities? Conway Morris's answer is simple: although "the evolutionary routes are many, the destinations are limited." Certain of these destinations are ruled out by "the howling wilder-nesses of the maladaptive." The evolutionary process thus navigates towards the viable, in response to the environment in which this development takes place.

There are, of course, alternative explanations. Some more radical evolutio-nary psychologists have suggested that cultural traits arise in response to the environmental stimulus of the mind. Where others might place an emphasis on factors such as cultural transmission in catalyzing or directing the process of cultural evolution, writers such as John Tooby and Leda Cosmides argued that this arises through the stimulation of innate mental content by potentially simple environmental factors.[143] Cultural traits are already present within the human brain; environmental stimuli are required for these to be expressed or manifested. From this perspective, cultural evolution is best described in terms of the dynamics of recall, not of transmission.

The development of doctrine shows important parallels with this process. The process of doctrinal development was certainly catalyzed by a series of unpredictable events. The development of ecclesiology owed much to the historical contingencies of the relationships of indigenous Berbers and

---

[143] John Tooby and Leda Cosmides, "The Psychological Foundations of Culture." In *The Adapted Mind*, edited by J. H. Barkow, L. Cosmides, and J. Tooby, 19–136. Oxford: Oxford University Press, 1992.

Roman settlers in western North Africa in the third and fourth centuries. This historically contingent situation did much to focus attention on the nature of the Christian community, forcing clarification of certain core issues. Yet Conway Morris's analysis demonstrates the conceptual shallowness of proposing that the historical specifics of the Donatist controversy "caused" the emergence of an Augustinian doctrine of the church. Rather, it may be viewed as the contingent historical occasion that catalyzed the emergence of this way of thinking. If it had not emerged then, it would have done so at another time, in another place. It was a development waiting to happen.

Equally, the development of christology during the patristic period was shaped by a number of historical contingencies, including imperial Roman politics. Yet these contingencies cannot be regarded as determining the shape of the Christian understanding of Jesus Christ. They were rather the contingent occasions for the exploration of the identity and significance of Christ. Had these contingencies not forced discussion of the issues, others would in due course.

So what general forces might operate within the process of doctrinal development? Without proposing any specific theory of the manner in which these interact, or the priority that is to be assigned to each, it is entirely possible to identify four broad factors that need to be incorporated into any viable theory of the development of doctrine. While these could easily be illustrated by a close reading of various episodes in the development of doctrine, it is exceptionally easy to fail to see the wood because of the trees – to become so concerned about the fine details of individual case studies that we fail to see the "big picture" underlying them.

(1) First, we must note the role of the contingencies of history. The word "contingency" is here taken to designate unpredictabilities. Things happen which, from a human standpoint, seem to be random or unpredictable. While the observed contingencies of history can often be retrodicted with at least a degree of success, they cannot be predicted individually in advance of their occurrence. For the Christian, there is no tension between this notion of "contingency" and the concept of divine providence. The fact that something cannot be predicted has virtually no bearing on whether it is providentially directed.

The point here, however, is that the contingencies of history act as stimuli to the development of certain aspects of Christian thought which were already intrinsic to its very nature. The need to "unpack" some specific aspect of the Christian tradition was forced upon the church by historical circumstances – but there is a sense in which this process of unpacking was ultimately an inevitability, given the nature of the historical process. Sooner or later, the historical circumstances needed for the precipitation of clarification and consolidation would have arisen. More significantly, it is not merely the need to unpack the tradition that can be seen as potentially inevitable; the nature of what was being unpacked was such that it could only be developed or reformulated in a limited number of legitimate manners, even allowing for the tendency for Piagetian assimilation to existing social, intellectual, religious, or cultural norms.

(2) This naturally focuses attention on the internal structures and dynamics of the Christian tradition, as embodied in the church. As the development of christology in the first four centuries suggests, the ideas of Christianity can be developed in a number of directions. Yet not all such developments are equally adaptive. Some possess a superior degree of internal consistency, external correspondence, and popular appeal than others. The critical question is whether the internal structures of the Christian church, given specificity by the institution of the church, in themselves and of themselves create a propensity for conceptual development and elaboration to proceed in certain specific directions, almost predetermined by the parameters of that tradition.

From the outset, there was a realization that there were limits to the community of faith, especially in relation to the boundaries of belief. Augustine of Hippo spoke of such limits as "hedges," which surrounded and enfolded the pastures of the New Testament. These limits were not arbitrary, but were elicited and informed by the content of the Christian faith itself. Early Christian debates about the location of the center and the periphery of the church were grounded on the assumption that these were shaped internally by the contours of the Christian tradition, even if external modification was possible in the light of historical contingencies.

(3) This process of reflection was driven by the relentless human desire to understand, explore, and correlate.[144] The process of doctrinal development arises precisely because human beings are rational creatures, and feel impelled, both morally and intellectually, to give an account of things. What is the best way of conserving the "givens" of faith? What are their implications? How can they be elaborated without being distorted or overextended, in order that their significance may be more fully appreciated? The Christian church set out on a voyage of intellectual discovery no less programmatic and no less significant than the mariners of Polynesia, which eventually led them to discover Easter Island. As Simon Conway Morris rightly pointed out, its discovery was a virtual inevitability, precisely because of their sophisticated search strategies.[145] The intellectual voyage of exploration and elaboration conducted within the Christian tradition was driven by a similar series of search strat-

---

[144] For the inevitability and legitimacy of doctrine within the Christian community, see the extended discussion in Alister E. McGrath, A Scientific Theology 3: Theory, 3–76.

[145] Morris, Life's Solution, 19–21.

egies, all designed to aid systematic theological development and greater apologetic potential. Such a series of strategies could not fail to throw up a number of potential candidates for intellectual legitimation as doctrine, not just theology – in other words, as the authorized public statements of belief of the Christian community, not just the private opinions of individuals.[146]

There is at most a weak analogy here with the neo-Darwinian mechanism of the development of adaptations. However, the force of that analogy is severely weakened by the fact that the church *intentionally* conducts such a search. The historical specifics may well rest on contingencies. For example, we have noted how the Donatist and Pelagian controversies were, as far as can be established, evoked by historical particularities, specific to certain places and times. But this cannot be taken to mean that these historical contingencies "caused" the Augustinian doctrine of the church or of grace. The historical context may well have evoked the debate, by forcing the need for clarification on the church and mapping out the areas to be explored. It may also have created an environment characterized by a predisposition to accept one idea rather than another, or to accentuate one aspect of the issue, where others might otherwise have been emphasized. Yet Christian doctrines are ultimately about the controlled, re-flective unfolding of the inner logic of the Christian tradition.

(4) A process of competition, in which rival candidates for such public authorization are evaluated, often over an extended period of time. There is an obvious parallel here with the Darwinian mechanism of natural selection. However, the analogy is not exact. The issue is that, when a variety of options are available and a choice must be made, some options are going to be discarded or closed down. It is a familiar routine, which can be explained as much on economic as on Darwinian grounds. The common feature to all is the existence of a filter, which determines which options are selected and which wither and fail.

These broad patterns will be familiar to anyone who has worked in the field of the development of Christian doctrine. Though requiring elaboration and development to cope with the phenomena under consideration, the basic features are relatively clear and settled. Yet, if this is indeed the case – or something approximating to it – Conway Morris's notion of "islands of stability" becomes a potentially helpful way of visualizing some aspects of the phenomenon of doctrinal development. Given the dynamics of this phe-nomenon, is not convergent evolution something of an inevitability? In other words, is there not a certain inevitability to the emergence of certain ways of conceiving the Christian doctrine of God or the person of Christ, even if this

---

[146] For the distinction, see Alister E. McGrath, *The Genesis of Doctrine*. Oxford: Blackwell, 1990.

process of unfolding and exploration is catalyzed by historical contingencies? While issues of historical context will not go away, they are perhaps "swamped by the effects of convergence."[147]

The emergence of the Chalcedonian Definition of Christ illustrates this trend remarkably well. The dynamics of the Christian tradition are such that some such understanding of the identity of Jesus Christ was inevitable. The starting point, and the theological and doxological constraints of the Christian tradition, were such that there was nothing accidental about the emergence of the doctrine of the "two natures" of Christ.[148] The specific course of the emergence of this doctrine was undoubtedly influenced by the seeming contingencies of history. Yet that does not entail that the doctrine itself was contingent, one of a number of possible outcomes, determined solely by the happenstance of history. It is as if it was built into the fabric of the Christian tradition, merely waiting to be formulated in the best possible manner. On examining the kerygmatic, doxological, and theological components of the Christian tradition, it is difficult to avoid the suspicion that it was hardwired for this development, merely awaiting the historical circumstances that crystallized its formulation.

There is thus a case to be made for suggesting that the Chalcedonian Definition represents a clear case of the triumph of convergence over contingency in the process of the development of doctrine. The starting point for such development, and the constraints exercised upon it, lead to a strictly limited number of evolutionary outcomes. This hypothesis requires further testing and clarification, and it is my intention to provide this over the coming years.

Yet even at this early stage, a further question emerges as significant. Is every aspect of that definition to be seen as an adaptive development? What of the specific form of the Chalcedonian formula, which uses the categories of contemporary Greek metaphysics in such a manner and to such an extent that it has become somewhat problematic for at least some in the contemporary church? Is this also to be seen as a case of convergence?

Chalcedon, Metaphysics, and Spandrels: Evolutionary Perspectives on the Chalcedonian Definition of Faith

On the evolutionary approach that we have been considering, the use of contemporary Greek metaphysical categories in the formulation of the Christian

---

[147] Conway Morris, *Life's Solution*, 132.

[148] For some of the issues, see Larry W. Hurtado, *Lord Jesus Christ: Devotion to Jesus in Earliest Christianity*. Grand Rapids, MI: Eerdmans, 2003; Richard Bauckham, *God Crucified: Monotheism and Christology in the New Testament*. Grand Rapids, MI: Eerdmans, 1998.

understanding of Jesus Christ is to be seen essentially as a *spandrel*, to use the vocabulary of Stephen Jay Gould – that is to say, a byproduct of the evolutionary process, rather than an adaptive development in its own right. The core development is a specific conceptual clarification of the relationship of divinity and humanity, particularity and universality, in the person of Jesus Christ. The use of Greek metaphysical categories to elaborate this relationship was a contingent, non-adaptative development, which can theoretically be dissociated from the true adaptation seen in the core development of the Chalcedonian dogma.

As many readers of this essay will be unfamiliar with Gould's concept of the spandrel, I shall explain it in more detail, drawing on a classic statement of the notion.[149] Gould points out how many of the world's buildings include spandrels – that is, "tapering triangular spaces formed by the intersection of two rounded arches at right angles" – which are often filled with complex decorative designs. The dome of the cathedral of San Marco in Venice is an excellent example:

> Each spandrel contains a design admirably fitted into its tapering space. An evangelist sits in the upper part flanked by the heavenly cities. Below, a man representing one of the four biblical rivers (Tigris, Euphrates, Indus, and Nile) pours water from a pitcher in the narrowing space below his feet.

Gould argues that the same feature is found in the chapel of King's College, Cambridge. A fan-vaulted roof demands such "tapering triangular spaces" as a byproduct of its design. It is a feature that is an architectural necessity, yet has the capacity to be transformed into an aesthetic object in its own right:

> Every fan-vaulted ceiling must have a series of open spaces along the midline of the vault, where the sides of the fans intersect between the pillars. Since the spaces must exist, they are often used for ingenious ornamental effect. In King's College Chapel in Cambridge, for example, the spaces contain bosses alternately embellished with the Tudor rose and portcullis.

So why are these aesthetically pleasing spandrels there? They are beautifully designed, and their design might be taken to imply that the building was constructed around them, or that their role was primary. The decoration is not the goal of the construction of the spandrel; the spandrel is required by the structure of the building itself, which is subsequently put to a decorative use which is incidental to its function. As Gould stresses, any building with certain

---

[149] For what follows, see Stephen Jay Gould and Richard C. Lewontin. "The Spandrels of San Marco and the Panglossian Paradigm: A Critique of the Adaptationist Programme." *Proceedings of the Royal Society of London* B 205 (1979): 581–98.

architectural features has to have such spaces if the structure is to be stable. The genius of the architects is seen in their ability to make such functional spaces beautiful by inserting ornamentation which is strictly unnecessary from a physical point of view:

> The spaces arise as a necessary byproduct of fan vaulting; their appropriate use is a secondary effect. Anyone who tried to argue that the structure exists because the alternation of rose and portcullis makes so much sense in a Tudor chapel would be inviting the same ridicule that Voltaire heaped on Dr. Pangloss: "Things cannot be other than they are ... Everything is made for the best purpose. Our noses were made to carry spectacles, so we have spectacles. Legs were clearly intended for breeches, and we wear them."

In the case of San Marco, the beautiful ornamentation of the spandrels is essentially a byproduct of the design process. The need for such spaces is determined by the structure of the building; the specific form they take is determined by the designer. The constraint comes first; the design of the spandrel is secondary:

> The design is so elaborate, harmonious, and purposeful that we are tempted to view it as the starting point of any analysis, as the cause in some sense of the surrounding architecture. But this would invert the proper path of analysis. The system begins with an architectural constraint: the necessary four spandrels and their tapering triangular form. They provide a space in which the mosaicists worked; they set the quadripartite symmetry of the dome above.

The point I wish to make here is that not every aspect of the Chalcedonian Definition of Christ is to be regarded as an adaptive development. The use of Greek metaphysical categories was a natural means of supporting its core insights, given the assumptions of that day and age. But their use is secondary, being incidental to the core development itself. They can be replaced by other supportive structures, more appropriate for a new environment, without losing the central conceptual development relating to the person of Christ.

Reverting to Gould's analogy: the fundamental insight of Chalcedon concerns the architecture of the Christian vision of Christ. The pillars are set in place. Yet the manner of their intersection allows various manners of intellectual ornamentation or conceptual elaboration. This is *secondary* to the establishment of the fundamental christological architecture, which creates conceptual space for metaphysical elaboration. Yet that elaboration is a matter of contingency, whereas the fundamental intellectual architecture is determined by the internal dynamics of the Christian tradition. It is therefore, as Karl Rahner rightly pointed out, entirely possible to maintain this core structure of the Chalcedonian Definition while regarding the Hellenistic metaphysics that accompanies it as a historical contingency, one particular way of ornamenting the spandrel, while leaving open the possibility of alternatives, better adapted to the cultural circumstances of their day and age. It is widely accepted that the decision to adopt the specific metaphysical categories associated with the Nicene theology was partly determined by historical contingencies.[150] This would leave the church in subsequent eras free to chose which metaphysical categories were best adapted to the contingencies of their periods, rather than limiting them to those definitively set out at Nicea. Rahner, for example, argued for the recognition of corrective replacements of historically conditioned theological formulations, and in his later writings pressed for the translation of traditional formulae into contemporary thought forms and modes of expression.[151]

Simon Conway Morris, as we have seen, emphasizes that the evolutionary process navigates towards the viable, in response to the environment in which this development takes place.[152] While I have stressed the limitations and liabilities of any approach to doctrinal development which uncritically assumes that it is analogous to Darwinism, it seems clear that this aspect of Conway Morris's analysis offers a fascinating insight into one aspect of the process of the clarification and development of doctrine. The question of whether there exist "islands of doctrinal stability" is of such fundamental theological and historical importance that it demands to be investigated thoroughly by intellectual historians. This essay cannot hope to undertake such an analysis, and represents little more than the preliminary exploration of possibilities. But the signs are promising. This is unquestionably one of the most important areas of contemporary theological exploration – both historical and systematic – and deserves detailed evaluation in the future by those competent in both the fields of historical theology and evolutionary biology.

---

[150] Avery Dulles, *The Survival of Dogma: Faith, Authority and Dogma in a Changing World.* New York: Crossroad, 1982.

[151] Karl Rahner, "Chalkedon – Ende oder Anfang?" In *Das Konzil von Chalkedon: Geschichte und Gegenwart*, edited by Alois Grillmeier and Heinrich Bacht, 3–49. Würzburg: Echter-Verlag, 1951–4. See also his "Überlegungen zur Dogmenentwicklung." In *Schriften zur Theologie*, 11–50. Einsiedeln: Benziger Verlag, 1960.

[152] Morris, *Life's Solution*, 225.

CHAPTER 7

Assimilation in the Development of Doctrine: The Theological Significance of Jean Piaget

Revelation takes place within the structures of this world. The traditional distinction between "natural" and "revealed" theology does not actually concern the *location* of revelation, but the manner in which divine agency requires to be implicated in its discernment. As Karl Barth rightly pointed out, for revelation to be received as *revelation*, it must be *interpreted* as revelation. Time and time again, the Bible represents divine disclosure as taking place within the regular order of things, in which God uses events or agencies located within nature and history. The case of the calling of Samuel, which we considered in an earlier chapter, is an excellent illustration of this point. We do not need to be removed from nature or history in order to hear God, or know about God. That divine address takes place in the here and now. God speaks through nature, rather than bypassing it – a fundamental Christian principle, which finds its ultimate affirmation in the incarnation of the Son of God (John 1:14; Romans 1:3; Hebrews 2:14; 4.14–15). The incarnation can be seen as a freely chosen inhabitation of human categories by God (Philippians 2:6–7).

Only a Gnostic reading of the world allows us to bypass, ignore, or deny God's decision, abundantly affirmed within scripture, to speak to humanity through the realities of human history and the natural order. It is a matter of grace that God chooses to speak to us and relate to us in this way – a point which, though characteristic of Christian theology in general, was given particular emphasis by John Calvin in his notion of "accommodation."[1]

---

[1] See Ford Lewis Battles, "God Was Accommodating Himself to Human Capacity." *Interpretation* 31 (1977): 19–38; David F. Wright, "Accommodation and Barbarity in

The question of how the human mind adapts to its environment is of enormous importance to a scientific theology. So how, we may ask, does the mind respond to revelation? Such questions tend to be set to one side as theologically irrelevant, and potentially dangerous, by those within the Barthian tradition. Does this not reduce theology to anthropology or psychology?[2] It is a fair question; but asking it does not negate the location of revelation within the historical order.

An understanding of the characteristics of human perception – the process by which we make sense of the information we receive from our environment – may thus inform us in our reflections concerning how we know God. Once this decisively important point is conceded, it becomes critically important to ask how humanity responds to something new, in that this process of response may bring about theologically significant modifications, perhaps even distortions, to our grasp of divine revelation.

All human perception begins in this world. It involves natural perceptual faculties, and the subjective perceptual experiences of phenomena of natural and supernatural origin overlap. There is therefore no strong reason to assume that perception of the "natural" world, perception of the "divine in the natural world," and perception of the "divine through direct revelation" are underpinned by different psychological processes. These general principles are likely to be common to all forms of perception. While perception of distinct types of phenomena may be differentiated in specific details, the general principles are likely to remain the same. If this is the case, then the general principles which underlie the formation of human ideas are of relevance to an informed understanding of the emergence of the corporate ecclesial understanding of the "vision of God" which we call "doctrine."

John Calvin's Old Testament Commentaries." In *Understanding Poets and Prophets*, edited by A. Graeme Auld, 413–27. Sheffield: JSOT Press, 1993. For the principle in general, see Stephen D Benin, *The Footprints of God: Divine Accommodation in Jewish and Christian Thought*. Albany: State University of New York Press, 1993.

[2] Emil Brunner's questioning of Barth's disengagement with the realities of the human cognitive situation (evident in the 1934 debate over natural theology) needs to be heard here. Brunner's marginalization in recent theological analysis leaves me puzzled: there is no doubt that his insights need to be reassessed and reappropriated by any concerned with the dynamics of the human response to God's revelation. I shall offer an extended engagement with Brunner on this point in my forthcoming monograph on natural theology.

Piaget on "Reflective Abstraction"

With this general point in mind, we may turn to consider the landmark contribution made to our understanding of cognitive development by the Swiss psychologist Jean Piaget (1896–1980). Although Piaget is often referred to as a "developmental psychologist," he himself resisted such a designation, however understandable, preferring to speak of his method as "genetic epistemology." Piaget's empirical approach to the question of cognitive development stands in stark contrast to its rivals – the belief that knowledge takes the form of innate ideas (which Piaget terms *préformation des idées*),[3] or that such knowledge is environmentally determined.[4] Piaget's ideas were often ignored within the English language world during the 1940s and 1950s, largely due to the dominance of behaviorism in American academia.[5]

Although Piaget is best remembered for his taxonomy of "stages of development," which resulted from years of careful observation of how children acquire a knowledge of the external world,[6] this is not the point which concerns us in this essay. The real question of importance is how human beings develop their cognitive structures through which they represent reality.

For Piaget, there exists a process of "reflecting abstraction" (*l'abstraction réflechissante*) through which human beings interact with their environment. Human beings are not born with such structures, nor do they absorb them passively from their environment: they construct them through a process of

---

[3] An idea now particularly associated with Noam Chomsky, who argues that some form of "universal grammar" is encoded within the human mind, resulting from Darwinian evolution. See, for example, Noam Chomsky, *Knowledge of Language: Its Nature, Origin, and Use.* New York: Praeger, 1986. For a discussion, see the important study of Fiona Cowie, *What's Within?: Nativism Reconsidered.* Oxford: Oxford University Press, 2002.

[4] For some purely environmental accounts of learning, see Clark L Hull, *Principles of Behavior: An Introduction to Behavior Theory.* New York: Appleton-Century, 1943. After World War II, American psychology came to be dominated by the behaviorism of B. F. Skinner. For a convenient summary of his views, see B. F. Skinner, "The Experimental Analysis of Behavior." *American Scientist* 45 (1957): 343–71.

[5] The situation is actually slightly more complex than this. For an analysis of criticisms of Piaget, see Michael Chapman, *Constructive Evolution: Origins and Development of Piaget's Thought.* Cambridge: Cambridge University Press, 1988, especially 331–80.

[6] See Jean Piaget, *Le Langage et la pensée chez l'enfant.* Neuchâtel: Delachaux and Niestle, 1923; *La Naissance de l'intelligence chez l'enfant.* Neuchâtel: Delachaux & Niestle, 1936; *La Construction du réel chez l'enfant.* Neuchâtel: Delachaux & Niestle, 1937. That this taxonomy is now regarded by many as questionable does not affect the issues raised in this study.

interaction (which Piaget terms "equilibration"), in which an equilibrium is achieved between assimilation and accommodation.[7] Assimilation may be defined as the "act of incorporating objects or aspects of objects into learned activities," where accommodation is "the modification of an activity or ability in the face of environmental demands."[8] These interact in an adaptive process which permits new information or observation to be fitted into already existing cognitive structures, leading to equilibration, in which a balance is maintained "between assimilation (using old learning) and accommodation (changing behavior; learning new things)."[9]

To use a familiar analogy, assimilation and accommodation can be compared to swings of a developmental pendulum, which advances our understanding of the world and our competency in it. According to Piaget, these two elements interact dynamically, aiming to achieve a balance between the structure of the mind and the environment. The process of equilibration eventually leads to a certain congruency between the mind and its environment, suggesting that a workable or adequate model of the universe has been attained.

Assimilation can be thought of as applying an existing scheme of thought to a new situation, initiating a process of comparison and evaluation. At times, that may lead to the realization that the old way of thinking is not capable of coping with what is being observed, forcing a modification of this scheme – in other words, accommodation. Contrary to what some studies of Piaget assert, the early Piaget assumed that reasoning originates in *interpersonal argumentation*. The process of cognitive development takes place within a social context, in which interaction with others plays an important role in catalyzing the process of reflection.[10] Piaget can thus be thought of as developing a *via media* between methodological individualism and sociological holism.[11]

Piaget's ideas have been subject to a number of criticisms, particularly following the famous 1975 debate on "language and learning" between Piaget and Chomsky at the Royaumont Abbey, which was generally regarded as

---

[7] For Piaget's own reflections on the importance of this approach, and some problems in defining and investigating it, see Jean Piaget, "Problems of Equilibration." In *Topics in Cognitive Development 1*, edited by M. H. Appel and L. S. Goldberg, 3–14. New York: Plenum, 1977.

[8] As defined by Guy R. Lefrançois, *Theories of Human Learning*, 3rd edn. Pacific Grove, CA: Brooks/Cole Publishers, 1995, 329–30.

[9] Ibid, 335.

[10] Richard F. Kitchener, "Piaget's Social Epistemology." In *Social Interaction and the Development of Knowledge*, edited by J. I. M. Carpendale and U. Miller, 45–66. Mahwah, NJ: Lawrence Erlbaum Associates, 2004.

[11] See the analysis of Mario Bunge, "Ten Modes of Individualism – None of Which Works – and Their Alternatives." *Philosophy of the Social Sciences* 30 (2000): 384–406.

marking a victory for Chomsky.[12] Other frequently encountered criticisms include the suggestion that Piaget tended to assume that development took place in a social vacuum, ignoring the importance of social learning.[13]

So why are Piaget's insights on the development of human cognition of any relevance to exploring the theological phenomenon of doctrinal development? The answer becomes clear if we begin to think in terms of the "mind of the church" – a corporate mind which began by being steeped within the assumptions of Judaism, and was subject to local influence by other existing schemes of thought as it expanded into other regions of the Mediterranean – for example, the Hellenistic worldview of the great city of Alexandria, with its philosophically conceived notions of divinity which were destined to have such a significant impact on Christian theological reflection in that region.[14]

Our growing knowledge of the intellectual and social complexity of both first-century Palestinian Judaism and late classical antiquity has made many of the generalizations of earlier generations of scholars somewhat problematic, and it is clearly important to avoid making incautious overstatements at this point. Nevertheless, it is entirely proper to make the point that these frameworks, however variegated, can be thought of as establishing existing patterns of thought – the habits of thinking into which people naturally fell. The intellectual, cultural, and cultic contexts of early Christianity often shaped notions of what was a self-evidently correct paradigm for the interpretation of Jesus Christ and the gospel proclamation.

This allows us to begin to use the three central Piagetian notions of assimilation, accommodation, and equilibration in an attempt to make sense of some observed patterns in the history of Christian doctrine. To explore this issue further, we shall briefly outline a few case studies in doctrinal development, and indicate how Piaget's empirically derived categories cast light on them. We may begin by considering the emergence of Ebionitism in early Christianity.

---

[12] Massimo Piattelli-Palmarini, "Ever since Language and Learning: Afterthoughts on the Piaget–Chomsky Debate." *Cognition* 50 (1994): 315–46.

[13] Generally, see Peter A. A. Sutherland, *Cognitive Development Today: Piaget and His Critics*. London: Paul Chapman Educational Publishing, 1992.

[14] Although requiring more subtle nuancing at points, the important article of Wolfhart Pannenberg remains of landmark significance here: Wolfhart Pannenberg, "The Appropriation of the Philosophical Concept of God as a Dogmatic Problem of Early Christian Theology." In *Basic Questions in Theology*, 119–83. London: SCM Press, 1971. This needs expansion and modification, particularly in relation to the church's complex relationship with paganism: see Friedrich Prinz, "Die Kirche und die pagane Kulturtradition. Formen der Abwehr, Adaption und Anverwandlung." *Historische Zeitschrift* 276 (2002): 281–303.

Assimilation to Jewish Religious Norms: Ebionitism

The early church fully recognized the importance of articulating the significance of Jesus Christ for the human mind, imagination, emotions, and behavior. In the course of its development, the church had to deal with a number of interpretations of the identity of Jesus Christ which it regarded as failing to do justice to his significance. An improper location of Jesus Christ on a conceptual map would be fatal to Christian evangelism and discipleship.

Yet it was clear that this process of identifying the best conceptual framework within which to locate Jesus Christ was intensely difficult. The initial tendency was to take existing categories, inherited from the social matrices to which early Christians belonged, and treat these as appropriate to the task of conceptualizing the significance of Jesus Christ. The origins of such a trend can be seen inside the New Testament itself, in that the gospels record attempts to make sense of Jesus which are drawn from contemporary Jewish sources – such as a second Elijah, a prophet, and so forth.[15] A particularly interesting example of Jesus being interpreted within cultic paradigms inherited from Judaism (more specifically, Second Temple Judaism) is to be found in the notion of the high priestly ministry of Jesus, as it appears in the New Testament and other early Christian writings.[16]

The early christological development which demonstrates this Piagetian process of assimilation most clearly is Ebionitism. Frustratingly little is known about this movement, despite the fact that it represents such a significant theological landmark.[17] While uncertainties remain concerning the origins of the title of the movement, and some significant historical questions await clarification in the light of the Qumran documents,[18] it is clear that the beliefs of the Ebionites are to be positioned firmly within the matrix of contemporary Judaism. It is misleading to suggest that the Ebionites regarded Jesus of Nazareth as "just a human being," in that they clearly regard him as God's chosen one, and in particular as God's chosen prophet.

---

[15] For an excellent recent survey of the issues contested within early Judean Jewish Christianity, see Larry W. Hurtado, *Lord Jesus Christ: Devotion to Jesus in Earliest Christianity.* Grand Rapids, MI: Eerdmans, 2003, 155–216.

[16] For a survey of many of these issues, see Richard Bauckham, *God Crucified: Monotheism and Christology in the New Testament.* Grand Rapids, MI: Eerdmans, 1998.

[17] For a useful account, see Hans Joachim Schoeps, "Ebionite Christianity." *Journal of Theological Studies* 4 (1953): 219–24. This is based on his earlier study *Theologie und Geschichte des Judenchristentums.* Tübingen: J. C. B. Mohr, 1949.

[18] For an early exploration of the issue, see Joseph A. Fitzmyer, "The Qumran Scrolls, the Ebionites, and Their Literature." *Theological Studies* 16 (1955): 335–72.

So what is the significance of this movement? One of the interesting (and relatively few) points of convergence between Karl Barth and F. D. E. Schleiermacher is that both regard Ebionitism as one of the extreme limits of christological speculation, pressing a Christian understanding of the identity of Jesus to a point beyond which the specifics of the Christian revelation are left behind, and a form of christological naturalism takes over.[19] My concern at this point, however, is to observe that this represents a clear case of Piaget's notion of assimilation – the process by which new observations or ideas are initially fitted within an existing framework.

Piaget stressed that the process of conceptual development is not simply the unfolding of a genetic pattern, nor the importation of existing structures from the intellectual or cultural environment, but is an interactive process in which the adequacy of a conceptual framework is tested out against what is being observed. Ebionitism may be regarded as one of the best examples of theological assimilation, in that Jesus is assimilated to existing Jewish religious models – particularly that of the prophet.

An essential difference between the development of the "mind of the church" and that of an individual is the extended manner in which the process of evaluation of conceptual schemes takes place.[20] While Piaget focuses on how an individual accommodates conceptual schemes to fit observation, any attempt to make sense of the development of Christian doctrine will have to deal with a corporate attempt to achieve equilibrium. This corporate "equilibration" will balance both assimilation and accommodation, aiming to assess the extent to which existing frameworks require modification in the light of observation. The judgment of the church was ultimately that the existing conceptualities of God's presence in and dealings with the world, inherited from Judaism, required modification in the light of their manifest incapacity to cope with its experience and memory of Jesus, as expressed in the oral and written tradition of the church. The old wineskins of Judaism could not cope with the new wine of the gospel events.

Thus Ebionitism. I chose to deal with this historically obscure yet theologically significant heresy precisely because it illustrates the innate tendency towards

---

[19] On Schleiermacher's views on Ebionitism, see Klaus M. Beckmann, *Der Begriff der Häresie bei Schleiermacher*. Munich: Kaiser Verlag, 1959, 36–62. For Barth's judgment, see Paul D. Molnar, "Some Dogmatic Implications of Barth's Understanding of Ebionite and Docetic Christology." *International Journal of Systematic Theology* 2 (2000): 151–74.

[20] The historical aspects of this process are complex, and are best appreciated from a significant essay by Rowan Williams, "Does It Make Sense to Speak of Pre-Nicene Orthodoxy?" In *The Making of Orthodoxy*, edited by Rowan Williams, 1–23. Cambridge: Cambridge University Press, 1989.

assimilation within the development of doctrine. Precisely the same trend can be seen in early Christian reflection on the Pauline doctrine of "salvation by grace," to which we now turn.

Assimilation to Roman Cultural Norms: Pelagianism

Christians are saved, not by works, but by grace (Ephesians 2:5, 8–9). The notions of "salvation by grace" and "justification by faith" are firmly woven into the fabric of the New Testament, especially the Pauline epistles.[21] In recent years, there has been intensive discussion of the Jewish background to this idea, partly in reaction against the perceived inadequacies of Martin Luther's dialectic between law and gospel, and partly as a result of a growing understanding of inter-testamental Judaism.[22] Yet while the "New Perspective" on Paul remains a topic of contemporary interest, at least for the time being, the most significant debate relating to the doctrine of grace is located within a very different cultural milieu: the imperial Roman culture of the late fourth century. In what follows, we shall consider the dynamics of the Pelagian controversy, viewed from a Piagetian standpoint.

One of the most interesting aspects of the Pelagian controversy is the extent to which the Christian proclamation of salvation by grace was assimilated to the prevailing norms of Roman culture, with its distinctive emphases on the rule of law. By the end of the second century, the Latin term *iustitia* had acquired well-established juristic connotations which were to exert considerable influence over future theological interpretation of such notions as *iustitia Dei* – the "righteousness of God," which plays such an important role in the theology of the Pauline epistles.[23] The Ciceronian definition of *iustitia* as *reddens unicuique quod suum est* ("giving someone their due") had become normative.[24] Human beings do certain things, which entitles them to be esteemed in a certain way and

---

[21] For a comprehensive analysis of the development of the Christian understanding of justification, see Alister E. McGrath, *Iustitia Dei: A History of the Christian Doctrine of Justification*, 3rd edn. Cambridge: Cambridge University Press, 2005.

[22] For a recent appraisal of these discussions, see Stephen Westerholm, *Perspectives Old and New on Paul: The "Lutheran" Paul and His Critics*. Grand Rapids, MI: Eerdmans, 2004.

[23] For its significance, see works such as Peter Stuhlmacher, *Gerechtigkeit Gottes bei Paulus*. Göttingen: Vandenhoeck & Ruprecht, 1966.

[24] Cicero, *Rhetoricum libro duo* II, 53: "Iustitia virtus est, communi utilitate servata, suam cuique tribuens dignitatem." Cf. Justinian, *Institutio* I, I: "Iustitia est constans et perpetua voluntas suum unicuique tribuens." On Cicero's fundamental notion of *iustitia*, see D. H. van Zyl, *Justice and Equity in Cicero*. Pretoria: Academica Press, 1991.

rewarded accordingly. Actions and achievements determine a person's status in the eyes of their peers, and what they are entitled to in response. As van Zyl notes:[25]

> The golden thread running through all of Cicero's thought on moral philosophy is the need, and indeed the desire, of all persons to achieve "the greatest good" (*summum bonum*). This is done by leading a virtuous, moral, and ethically acceptable life in accordance with the "cardinal virtues" of wisdom, justice, fortitude, and self-restraint. Its purpose is to bring man back to his true nature (*natura*), in conformity with reason, justice, and equity. In this regard, Cicero is essentially a moralist and an idealist, who links his moral philosophy inextricably with his approach to law and good government as prerequisites for a stable and harmonious society.

In effect, the Ciceronian definition encapsulates the western concept of *iustitia distributiva*, the "due" of each person being established through the *iuris consensus*, and embodied in *ius*.[26] There is a clear tension between this concept of "righteousness" and that found in Old Testament writings. In the first place, there is no fundamental appeal to a covenant between God and humanity as determinative of ethical or legal norms or conventions. More significantly, the Old Testament notion of righteousness possesses strongly soteriological overtones.[27] An appeal to God's righteousness is fundamentally a plea for salvation and deliverance:

> In you, O Lord, do I take refuge, Let me never be put to shame.
> *In your righteousness* deliver me and rescue me.
> (Psalm 31:1)

The Pelagian controversy can be interpreted in many ways,[28] in that it possesses cultural, social, legal, moral, and theological aspects, each of which merits detailed discussion in itself. Yet on reading Julian of Eclanum, perhaps the most culturally sophisticated of the Pelagian writers, one is struck primarily by his thoroughgoing assimilation of the Christian gospel to the social and civil norms of Roman society. For Julian, it was self-evident that the idea of the "righteousness of God" was to be assimilated to prevailing cultural norms.

---

[25] Ibid, 34.

[26] Franz Wieacker, *Römische Rechtsgeschichte: Quellenkunde, Rechtsbildung, Jurisprudenz und Rechtsliteratur.* Munich: C. H. Beck, 1988.

[27] For details, see McGrath, *Iustitia Dei*, 6–21. On Augustine, see ibid, 38–54.

[28] For some very helpful reflections, see Agostino Trapè, *Sant'Agostino: Introduzione alla dottrina della grazia*, 2 vols. Rome: Citta Nuova, 1990.

God gave each their due. Justification was thus about God rewarding the righteous and punishing the wicked.

A central theme in the debate between Augustine and Julian of Eclanum was therefore precisely what the idea of the "righteousness of God" actually entailed.[29] Julian defined divine justice in terms of God rendering to each individual their due, without fraud or grace, so that God would be expected to justify those who merited his grace on the basis of their moral achievements. This approach yielded a doctrine of the justification of the *godly*, whereas Augustine held the essence of the gospel to be the justification of the *ungodly*.

The precise historical details of the conflict need not detain us. The important point is the general trend that it illustrates – namely, the assimilation of the gospel to prevailing cultural or intellectual trends. It must be stressed that this process is normal, not pathological. It is simply the way that human beings adapt to new, puzzling phenomena by attempting to assimilate it to the known, familiar, and trusted. The problem arises if the process stops there, and does not proceed further, leading into the Piagetian processes of accommodation and equilibration.

For Augustine, any assimilation of the "righteousness of God" to the Ciceronian idea of "giving to each their due" (*reddens unicuique quod suum est*) was called into question by many biblical passages, which indicated that this cultural notion of righteousness could not be used without significant adaptation. In countering Julian's concept of *iustitia Dei*, Augustine appealed to the parable of the laborers in the vineyard (Matthew 20:1–16) to demonstrate that *iustitia Dei* primarily refers to God's fidelity to the gospel promises of grace, irrespective of the merits of those to whom the promise was made.

Similar processes can be seen at work during the patristic period, especially in relation to the question of whether God can be said to suffer, or the emergence of the doctrine of the Trinity. In each case, there was a natural tendency to assimilate Christian ideas to those of the prevailing cultural trends – such as Hellenistic philosophy – without necessarily giving due weight to those factors which pointed to the need for accommodation. Such assimilation was often local, causing significant regional variations in how the gospel was proclaimed and conceptualized. That the process continued to be significant at other points in the shaping of Christian thought beyond the patristic period will be clear from the case of Anglo-Saxon England, to which we now turn.

---

[29] For a full discussion, see Alister E. McGrath, "Divine Justice and Divine Equity in the Controversy between Augustine and Julian of Eclanum." *Downside Review* 101 (1983): 312–19. There is also some useful material in F. J. Thonnard, "Justice de Dieu et justice humaine selon Saint Augustin." *Augustinus* 12 (1967): 387–402.

Assimilation to Anglo-Saxon Cultural Norms: Christ as Hero

The establishment of Christianity in the Anglo-Saxon world is known to have been a complex and precarious development, in which the Christian church found itself in competition with well-established forms of paganism, often focusing on the cult of heroes. While the veneration of the values of warrior culture dates back to classical antiquity,[30] they came to play an especially significant role in Old Norse and Anglo-Saxon culture.[31] It was inevitable that a serious tension would arise between these heroic warrior ideals and the Christian virtues of humility, submission, and self-effacement. As might be expected, the advance of Christianity within such a culture took place through local assimilation of Christian ideals to existing cultural norms and expectations.

The "Dream of the Rood" is an Anglo-Saxon poem thought to date from the end of the seventh century, which aims to depict Jesus Christ in terms that will resonate with the heroic ideals of the culture of that era.[32] The poem does more than adapt the Christian proclamation to the language and verse forms of pagan literature of the period; it assimilates Christ to a hero-figure, comparable to those which so enthralled the audiences of the great tribes of that era. The gospel narrative is subtly reworked to make Christ conform to the heroic ideal.[33] The gospel accounts of Christ's passivity before his accusers and on the cross are swept to one side. Christ actively, bravely, and intentionally embraced the cross, as a hero preparing for daring combat. Even the indignity of Christ being stripped of his clothes by his executioners is reworked in order to assimilate him to the heroic ideal: in *The Dream*, Christ strips himself for battle, as an athlete might prepare for a race. When it comes to the crucifixion itself, the poem depicts Christ as a warrior, actively grappling the cross as a hero would wrestle his opponent to the ground. It is the cross that is wounded, not Christ, who dies as a hero, without being defaced in any manner.

---

[30] See especially Gregory Nagy, *The Best of the Achaeans: Concepts of the Hero in Archaic Greek Poetry*, revd. edn. Baltimore: Johns Hopkins University Press, 1999.

[31] *Beowulf* is an especially important witness to these ideals, and their potential difficulties for Christianity: see J. R. R. Tolkien, "Beowulf: The Monster and the Critics." In *The Monster and the Critics and Other Essays*, 5–48. London: Harper Collins, 1997.

[32] Graham Holderness, "The Sign of the Cross: Culture and Belief in *The Dream of the Rood*." *Literature and Theology* 11 (1997): 347–71.

[33] Peter Clemoes, "King and Creation at the Crucifixion: The Contribution of Native Tradition to *The Dream of the Rood*." In *Heroes and Heroines in Medieval English Literature*, edited by Leo Carruthers, 31–43. Cambridge: Brewer, 1994.

There is no doubt that this process of assimilation of the identity and signifi-cance of Christ to the great heroic ideals of the pagan north was checked and countered at several points; reverting to Piagetian terminology, assimilation was forced into accommodation at several points on account of doctrinal considerations.[34] *Quid Hinieldus cum Christo?*[35] Yet the natural tendency is clearly to assimilate Christ to familiar social or cultural exemplars, partly for apologetic purposes, and partly because this was seen as entirely natural. What a culture defines as "natural" or takes to be a matter of "common sense" are social constructions that have a profound influence upon theology,[36] and it is essential that these implicit cultural norms be identified, and their potential impact on doctrinal development (not to mention apologetic approaches) be identified.

The Achievement of Equilibration: Factors Encouraging Theological Accommodation

Our analysis thus far has concentrated on the tendency to assimilate Christian ideas and values to prevailing cultural norms as part of an apologetic strategy. Unlike Islam, which simply displaced previous religious norms, the history of Christianity is characterized more by constructive engagement with such norms, with the ultimate goal of transforming them from within. The apologetic strategy of the church down the ages has been to use the existing milieu as vehicles for the reception of the gospel. Yet, to paraphrase a comment often made in evaluating the theological achievement of Paul Til-lich, a useful apologetic strategy can often be theologically disastrous. There must be limits to assimilation. But how are those limits identified? And what factors prompt revision through accommodation? (At this point, I should remind readers that the term "accommodation" is being used throughout

---

[34] Rosemary Woolf, "Doctrinal Influences on *The Dream of the Rood.*" *Medium Aevum* 27 (1958): 137–53.

[35] "What has Ingeld to do with Christ?" The stories of heroes such as Beowulf and Ingeld helped keep alive the heroic ideals of that culture. So great was the influence of these writings that in 797 Alcuin wrote to bishop Higbald, asking that scripture and the works of the Christian fathers – not pagan myths! – should be read aloud at meals in the monastic refectories.

[36] Clifford Geertz has stressed how the notion of "common sense," far from being a summary of the necessary truths of reason, is actually socially constructed and cultur-ally located. See Clifford Geertz, "Common Sense as a Cultural System." In *Local Knowledge: Further Essays in Interpretative Anthropology,* edited by Clifford Geertz, 73–93. New York: Basic Books, 1983.

this essay in its Piagetian sense of the modification of an activity or ability in the face of environmental demands.)

The history of Christian doctrine makes it clear that a number of factors pointed to the need for such an accommodation, either by *limiting* the extent of assimilation in the first place, or by forcing its revision in the light of a growing awareness of the dangers, incoherency, or inconsistency of this development. This resulted in the process of equilibration – that is, a considered evaluation of possibilities to ensure the maximum correspondence to the observed realities. With Piaget, as with the philosophy of science in general, the principle of "saving the phenomena" is of paramount importance.

While this essay has been particularly concerned with the issue of assimilation in doctrinal development, it is clearly proper to end by noting, however sketchily, those processes that lead to accommodation. Three are of especial importance:

1 The most important point is that theologizing is not a solitary activity, but one that is carried out within the body of the church, in interaction with others. Piagetian theory stresses the importance of social interaction as a means of achieving the process of equilibration.[37] The church's corporate reflection on the nature of doctrine, shaped and informed by its corporate life of prayer and worship, serves to filter out the individualism that is often an integral element of heterodox conceptions of faith.
2 Continuing reflection on the biblical witness, which often, over an extended period of time, suggests that a particular method of conceptualizing the divine nature or the identity of Jesus Christ is sufficiently in tension with scripture to warrant its revision, marginalization, or even rejection. The centuries-long debate over the impassibility of God is a case in point.[38]
3 The inhabitation of the living tradition shaped by the doxological tradition of the church. This cumbersome phrase is intended to make the point that the church's life is shaped to no small extent by its worship. Unless the theologian is to be divorced from the living reality of corporate Christian existence – a development which the professionalization of theology within the academy has, by the way, encouraged – the church's worship will act as a decisively significant constraint and stimulus to theological reflection. To give an obvious but theologically luminous example, an Arian christology simply cannot be

---

[37] Jeremy J. I. M. Carpendale and Ulrich Miller, "Social Interaction and the Development of Rationality and Morality: An Introduction." In *Social Interaction and the Development of Knowledge*, edited by J. I. M. Carpendale and U. Miller, 1–18. Mahwah, NJ: Lawrence Erlbaum Associates, 2004.

[38] On the importance of the biblical witness to this debate, see Terence E. Fretheim, *The Suffering of God: An Old Testament Perspective*. Philadelphia: Fortress, 1984.

accommodated with the church's public worship of Christ.[39] The church's doxological tradition is of decisive importance in the process of theological equilibration within the development of doctrine.

In general terms, one can identify the following processes as active in the early church's attempt to achieve theological formalization of its beliefs:

1 An initial tendency to *assimilate* the gospel to existing, familiar ways of thinking.
2 A growing awareness of the limitations of this assimilation, often through a heightened engagement with biblical counter-factuals or the embodied ideas and values of the liturgical tradition, leading to the recognition of the need for *equilibration*.
3 A subsequent process of *accommodation* in which conceptual adjustments are made to achieve the "best fit" between the phenomena that require to be explained or represented, and the conceptual schemes under exploration.
4 A process of *closure*, in which communal agreement is reached over the best way of representing the situation. In early Christianity, such consensus often took place at grassroots level, but was occasionally formalized by conciliar processes.
5 A subsequent ongoing process of review and reconsideration, involving both assimilation and accommodation, in which the adequacy of the agreed closure is monitored as an act of theological vigilance. Within the Christian tradition, closure is always understood as subject to continuing examination in the light of the evidence.

While it would clearly be quite inappropriate to rely on Piaget in drawing up criteria of authenticity for the development of doctrine, it is clear that he offers us a very helpful framework for making sense of what was actually happening during that process itself, based on empirical reflection. Perhaps Piaget's most important insight, which doctrinal critics must take with the greatest seriousness, is that the process of assimilation is to be seen as *natural*, not degenerate – in other words, that there is an innate human tendency to assimilate Christian ideas to existing patterns, which are often automatically assumed to have self-evident legitimacy. Whether this perception enables us to correct such developments is open to question; however, it certainly allows us to understand them, and alerts historians of doctrine to certain patterns of assimilation of theological importance.

---

[39] A point stressed by Rowan Williams, *Arius: Heresy and Tradition*. London: Darton, Longman, & Todd, 1987.

CHAPTER 8

A Working Paper: The Ordering of the World in a Scientific Theology

1. A brief summary of the basics of pre-Socratic philosophy might run like this. The world is structured; that structure can be discerned by the wise; and having been discerned, that structuring enables us both to understand the world, and live the good life within it. Underlying the ancient quest for wisdom is the notion of the ordering of the world – a fundamental belief that certain definite patterns lie beneath the complex swirling patterns of experience, or that certain deep structures underlie the behavior of stars, animals, and humans. The first step in achieving wisdom is to discern this ordering, and adjust one's thoughts and actions accordingly.

2. For some, this "order" or "structure" is something that we ourselves have created through the imposition of our own agendas and preconceptions, not the discernment of the order of reality. Part of the grand strategy for mastering the universe is to impose our own structures upon a universe which knows no such ordering. To speak of the universe as "ordered" is merely to project our own ideas onto an essentially formless reality. (This approach is superbly represented in the recent work of John Dupré, *The Disorder of Things: Metaphysical Foundations of the Disunity of Science*. Cambridge, MA: Harvard University Press, 1993.) (But we need also to note Michel Foucault, *The Order of Things: An Archaeology of the Human Sciences*. New York: Random House, 1970.) It is a seductive idea, especially for those who long to shape reality in their own image, or project their own values and aspirations onto a conceptually plastic reality. Yet any account of the emergence of the natural sciences raises formidable difficulties for such a dismissal of the ordering of the world. The natural sciences are based on the *perception of explicable regularity to the world, which is capable of being represented*

mathematically. In other words, there is something about the world – and the nature of the human mind – which allows us to discern patterns within nature, for which explanations may be advanced and evaluated. One of the most significant parallels between the natural sciences and religion is a fundamental shared conviction that the world is characterized by regularity and intelligibility. (Good exploration of some of the issues in George Johnson, *Fire in the Mind: Science, Faith and the Search for Order.* New York: Alfred A. Knopf, 1995.)

3. The present paper takes the form of a reflection on the importance of the concept of "order" for a scientific theology. It represents an attempt to show how the theme of the ordering of reality runs throughout the entire theological enterprise, as a *Leitmotif* runs throughout Wagner's *Ring des Nibelungen.* My focus will not be on the importance of order (or the representation of such order) in the natural sciences, concerning which there is already a vast literature, but rather with the teasing out of the central, unifying role that the concept of order plays within systematic theology. These reflections on the critical theological role played by the concept of order will be expanded considerably in a projected "scientific dogmatics."

4. The concept of "order" plays a critical foundational and integrational role in systematic theology. Although the importance of the notion in certain specific areas of theology is generally conceded, there is a need both to explore other theological areas in which the concept plays a central role, and to determine how it gives a conceptual unity across a wide range of theological themes.

The most obvious area of theology in which the idea of "ordering" plays a significant role is the doctrine of creation. The Christian understanding of creation is framed in terms of the ordering of the world, secured through the divine imposition of structure or the conquest of the forces of chaos. Order is imposed through the creation of a specific structure. This can be seen in the first Genesis creation account, where the images of "darkness" and "water" are often regarded as symbols of chaos, which is subsequently ordered through the divine creative action. Elsewhere, chaos is personified as a dragon or monster ("Behemoth," "Leviathan," "Nahar," "Rahab," "Tannim," or "Yam") who must be subdued. This idea is found within the wisdom literature (see Job 3:8; 7:12; 9:13; 40:15–32; Psalm 74:13–15; 139:10–11), but seems to play a more significant role within the prophetic writings (Isaiah 27:1; 51:9–10; Ezekiel 29:3–5; 32.2–8; Habakkuk 3:8–15; Zechariah 10:11). This "ordering" of creation can be interpreted both physically and morally.

5. Yet Christian theology has always declined to see creation in isolation, insisting that it should be set within the context of the entire "economy of salvation." Here again we encounter the theme of order: the trajectory of divine action demonstrates an intrinsic structure. If any theologian may claim credit for the initial unfolding of this notion, it is probably Irenaeus of Lyons.

The essential point here is that God's interaction with the world is "ordered" – that there is an *oikonomia*, an "ordering of the divine household," underlying and undergirding the entire trajectory of salvation from creation through to final consummation. The God who made the world in an ordered manner also acted to redeem it in an ordered manner. In the previous section, we referred to the idea of the "economy of salvation" as an indication of the structured or ordered nature of the actions of God within the world, both in revelation and salvation. The notion of the "economy of salvation" points to salvation being an ordered, intentional process, whose origins, development, and consummation are capable of being mapped onto a single trajectory of divine action.

6. A distinction must be drawn between the ordering of creation and the covenantal ordering of redemption, including that of the community of faith. (Some good points in Rolf Rendtorff, " 'Covenant' as a Structuring Concept in Genesis and Exodus." *Journal of Biblical Literature* 108 (1989): 385–93.) The *ordo creationis* or *ordo entis* is linked with the act of creation, and the *ordo salutis* with the process of redemption. There is a parallel (but not exact) between these ideas and the Thomist notion of *analogia entis* and the Barthian concept of *analogia fidei*.

The transition from creation to covenant is of fundamental importance within the Old Testament, raising fundamental questions concerning the continuity of the relation of natural law and the law of Israel. The concept of salvation is about the "reordering" of creation, and is often conceptualized as the restoration – or the initiation of the process of restoring – of a fractured creation to what God intended it to be. However, it is obvious that the theme of ordering plays an even greater role in a Christian discussion of redemption, in that the means of redemption – not merely its end – are traditionally defined in terms of God's respect for the moral order which God established. The Anselmian dilemma – how can a holy God justly forgive sin? – is fundamentally about the limits of divine operation within the moral ordering established by God at (or through) creation.

7. The eschatological aspects of the economy of salvation should also be noted at this point. Once more, the theme of the restoration of all things to their final intended purpose must be noted. While this ordering can be articulated at a number of levels, the important point to note is the persistent theme of the eschatological renewal of reality. The order that was destroyed, disrupted, or disturbed – depending on the theological emphasis of the interpreter – is restored and renewed at the final consummation.

8. The theme of ordering also emerges as significant in Christian discussion of the incarnation. Especially within the Alexandrian tradition, we find an emphasis on the integrative role of the *logos* within the economy of salvation. The divine rationality which is expressed in the creation of the world is incarnated in Jesus Christ. Or, to put this another way, the *logos* embedded

in creation is embodied in Christ, and is capable of being discerned by the human mind, which is created in the image of God. Scripture affirms that the image of God, after which humanity is created, is rendered (or, better, is made incarnate) in Christ – that is, in a specific historical figure, rather than a conceptual abstraction (Colossians 1:15). The importance of this resonance between the created human mind and the word of God in creation, incarnation, and redemption is upheld by many key patristic writers (e.g., Athanasius, *de incarnatione Verbi* 3; Augustine, *de trinitate* XIV.xii.15).

9. In that the doctrine of the Trinity is derived from reflection on the economy of salvation, it is to be expected that the concept of ordering is reflected in this doctrine. For a writer such as Augustine, the trinitarian configuration of reality is evident at virtually every turn – whether one looks at the ordered creation of the world, or the internal structure of the human mind. The concept of the *vestigial Trinitatis* merits far more careful attention than Barth suggests.

10. The concept of divine order plays an important role in the Old Testament, especially in relation to the theologically significant notion of "righteousness." (Important here is Hans Heinrich Schmid, *Gerechtigkeit als Weltordnung. Hintergrund und Geschichte des alttestamentlichen Gerechtigkeitsbegriffs*. Tübingen: Mohr, 1968.) This concept of righteousness, which has many parallels in ancient wisdom literature, points to a close correspondence between the idea of "righteousness" and "world-order" – an order which is itself ultimately grounded in the divine act of creation. The dominant sense of the Hebrew terms *sedeq* and *sedaqa* appears to be that of "right behavior" or "correct disposition." Things are as they should be; the way things are correspond to the way it is meant to be – either within creation, or within the covenantal community. The world is understood to be ordered in a certain way as a result of its divine creation; to act "rightly" or "correctly" is thus to act in accordance with this patterning of structures and events. (See Alfred Jepsen, "*Sdq* und *sdqh* im Alten Testament." In *Gottes Wort und Gottes Land*, edited by H. G. Reventloh, 78–89. Göttingen: Vandenhoeck & Ruprecht, 1965.)

11. The covenantal application of the idea of ordering can be seen at many points. When God and Israel mutually fulfill their covenant obligations to each other, a state of righteousness can be said to exist (i.e., things are *saddiq*, "as they should be" or "as they are intended to be"). There is no doubt that much of the Old Testament thinking about righteousness is linked with the notion of a covenant between God and Israel, demanding fidelity on the part of both parties if a state of "righteousness" is to pertain. The close connection between the themes of creation and covenant in the Old Testament points to a linking of the moral and salvific orders.

In the Song of Deborah (Judges 5:1–31), which contains many unusual grammatical forms and rare words, God is understood to have acted in "righteousness" by defending Israel when its existence was threatened by an outside agency – in other words, when the order of the covenant was under threat. The term "righteousness" can therefore possess both retributive and salvific aspects, without being reduced to, or exclusively identified with, either concept. Thus God's act of judgment is *retributive* with regard to Israel's enemies, but *salvific* with regard to God's covenant people.

12. At this stage in the history of Israel, the "righteousness" of the covenant does not appear to have been considered to have been under threat from within Israel itself, but merely from external agencies. However, with the establishment of Israel came the rise of prophecy, and the threat posed to the covenant relationship from within Israel itself became increasingly apparent. The eighth-century prophets Amos and Hosea stressed the importance of righteousness on Israel's part if it were to remain in a covenant relation with its righteous God. This insight was expressed by the prophets in terms of the *conditional election* of Israel as the people of God. For the prophets, *sedaqa* was effectively that condition or state required of Israel if its relationship with its God was to continue. Although there are many instances where *sedaqa* can be regarded as corresponding to the concept of *iustitia distributiva*, which has come to dominate western thinking on the nature of justice (despite the rival claims of *iustitia commutativa*), there remains a significant number which cannot.

13. The ordering of the covenant has important moral implications: part of the covenant obligations of Israel is the maintenance or bringing into being of the state of affairs which is appropriate to being the people of God. A particularly significant illustration of this may be found in the Old Testament attitude to the poor, needy, and destitute. The "right order of affairs" is violated, at least in part, by the very existence of such unfortunates. God's *sedaqa* is such that God must deliver them from their plight – an aspect of the Hebrew concept of *sedaqa* which has proved intractable to those who attempted to interpret it solely as *iustitia distributiva*. It is clear that this aspect of the Hebraic understanding of "righteousness" cannot be understood in terms of an impartial judge who administers justice according to which party has broken a universally accepted law.

14. Hermann Cremer (1834–1903) argued that the only way of making sense of the Old Testament usage of *sedaqa* was to assume that, in its most fundamental sense, the term refers to an actual relationship between two persons, and implies behavior which corresponds to, or is consistent with, whatever claims may arise from or concerning either party to the relationship. (Hermann Cremer, *Die paulinische Rechtfertigungslehre im Zusammenhange ihrer geschichtlichen Voraussetzungen*. Gütersloh: Bertelsmann, 1899.) The relationship in question is that presupposed by the covenant between God and Israel, which must be considered as the ultimate norm to which *sedaqa*

must be referred. The Hebrew concept of *sedaqa* thus stands in a conceptual class of its own – a class which Cremer characterized as *iustitia salutifera*. The strongly soteriological overtones of the term *sedaqa* can be illustrated from a number of passages in which "righteousness" and "salvation" are practically equated, particularly in many passages within Deutero-Isaiah:

I will bring my *sedaqa* near, it is not far away, And my salvation will not be delayed. (Isaiah 46:13).

15. From this brief analysis of the Old Testament concept of righteousness, the notion of the ordering of the world is seen to be of central importance to Israel's understanding of its place in the world, and its relationship to its God. Israel's identity is shaped by its relationship to the natural world, and to God. In both cases, the concept of "order" plays a critical role. The covenant between God and Israel orders relationships within Israel, and is understood to have implications for the individual Israelite's relationship with the land, with others, and with God. Order is established, initially through creation, and subsequently through the giving of the covenant. This double act of God as *datum* and *donum* establishes the framework within which Israel acted and thought.

16. There is, of course, an important discussion here as to where the emphasis lies – on the physical order established by God in creation, or the moral and cultic ordering established through the giving of the covenant. Gerhard von Rad argued that the most characteristic insight of the Old Testament was that the Lord was sovereign over history, especially the history of Israel (Gerhard von Rad, "Das theologische Problem des alttestamentlichen Schöpfungsglaubens." In *Gesammelte Studien zum Alten Testament*, 136–47. Munich: Kaiser Verlag, 1958.) In the Old Testament, faith in the Lord is not *Schöpfungsglaube* but *Heilsglaube* – faith in a God who acts within, and is sovereign over, human history. While this debate is legitimate, and highlights Israel's changing theological emphases in relation to its complex history, it does not require the abandonment of the grand structuring of reality which underlies the Old Testament worldview. The concept of order in creation and through covenant is a powerful tool for the crafting of a theology which is faithful to Israel's identity and mission. It clearly has considerable potential to illuminate other aspects of theology as well.

17. The idea of ordering was developed by later writers, often to great effect. The importance of the concept of order to Augustine's theology has long been appreciated. (Excellent summary in Josef Rief, *Der Ordobegriff des jungen Augustinus*. Paderborn: Schoningh, 1962.) Especially in Augustine's earlier writings, the concept of *ordo* proves to be of critical importance to Augustine's concept of God, particularly in relation to issues of justice,

aesthetics, and soteriology. In general terms, Augustine argues that the universe is structured at a number of levels, including a "hierarchy of being" within the order of creation. Within this stratified universe, humanity has a particular place, again reflecting the ordering of the world by God at creation.

18. The importance of the theme of ordering is especially evident in Augustine's concept of God as *iustissimus ordinator* who orders the universe according to the divine will. (Augustine, *de civitate Dei* XI, 17. Note also *de libero arbitrio* I, v, II: "iustum est, ut omnia sint ordinatissima.") The idea of divine "righteousness" (*iustitia*) includes the notion of a physical ordering of all things, and is also reflected in the right ordering of human affairs, and humankind's relationship to its environment. For Augustine, *iustitia* is practically synonymous with the right ordering of human affairs in accordance with the will of God.

19. Augustine's quasi-physical understanding of justice reflects his hierarchical structuring of the order of being: *iustitia* is essentially the ordering of the world according to the order of being, itself an expression of the divine will. God created the natural order of things, and therefore this natural order of things must itself reflect *iustitia*. Thus God created humans as they ought to be (i.e., God created humans *in iustitia*, the correct order of nature). By choosing to ignore this ordering, humans stepped outside this state of *iustitia*, so that their present state may be characterized as *iniustitia*. The trajectory of redemption can therefore be considered to be essentially a "making right" of things – in other words, the restoration of every facet of the relationship between God and humanity. *Iustitia* is thus not conceived primarily in legal or forensic categories, but transcends them, encompassing the "right-wising" of the relationship of God to humankind, of humans to their fellows, and of humans to their environment. This grand vision of the divine purpose to reestablish the harmony of order is fundamental to Augustine's theological trajectory. Augustine's theological influence is such that this way of thinking has had a considerable impact on the western theological tradition.

20. The most significant early medieval discussion of the theological significance of ordering is due to Anselm of Canterbury. Although the concept is explored at a number of points, the theologically most significant of these concerns Anselm's attempt to determine how God's dealings with humanity are based on the moral ordering of the universe, established by God, and reflecting God's nature and identity. Anselm's central concern is to demonstrate that God's righteousness (*iustitia*) is not arbitrary or whimsical, but is grounded in the divinely established moral structure of the universe. Anselm's solution is to ground the idea of the "righteousness of God" in the moral fabric of the universe. The divine ordering of reality, itself established by God and reflecting God's nature and purposes, can be the foundation for a discussion of how

a righteous God is able to redeem sinful humanity. Recognizing that the inner theological logic of incarnation and atonement is of decisive importance, Anselm sets out to demonstrate how the concept of divine order provides a secure foundation for dogmatic reflection.

21. In his major work *Cur Deus homo?* (1098), Anselm offers a new approach to the logic of incarnation and atonement, grounded in the moral ordering of the universe. God is wholly and supremely just. How can he then give eternal life to one who deserves eternal death? How can he justify the sinner? Anselm resolves this dilemma by arguing that God is just, not because God rewards humans according to their merit, but because God does what is appropriate to God, considered as the highest good (*Proslogion*, 10: "Ita iustus es non quia nobis reddas debitum, sed quia facis quod decet te summe bonum"). Far from endorsing prevailing secular accounts of justice, as some less perceptive critics suggested, Anselm aims to disconnect the theological discussion of redemption from preconceived human patterns of distributive or retributive justice, and reconnect it with something much more profound: the moral structuring of God's creation.

22. A similar pattern of engagement and criticism with various secular concepts of justice may be seen in *Cur Deus homo*. The concept of justice which Anselm believes to be most appropriate to characterize God's dealings with humanity is, as in the *Proslogion*, justice understood as action directed towards the highest good. As that highest good includes the redemption of fallen humankind, their salvation may be regarded as an act of divine justice. In the course of the discussion, however, it becomes clear that Anselm understands the concept of *rectitudo* to underlie that of *iustitia*, and to determine its basic meaning.

23. According to Anselm, justice is a "rectitude of will served for its own sake." Similarly, truth must also be defined in terms of metaphysical rectitude (*de veritate*, 12). The foundational notion for Anselm is thus actually *rectitude*, which is understood to have metaphysical dimensions (truth – i.e., the conforming of the human mind to what it ought to be) and moral dimensions (justice – i.e., the conforming of human behavior to what it ought to be.) (See Gottlieb Söhngen, "Rectitudo bei Anselm von Canterbury als Oberbegriff von Wahrheit und Gerechtigkeit," in H. Kohlenberger, ed., *Sola Ratione*. Stuttgart: Frommann, 1970, 71–7.) In both cases, the notion of rectitude is understood as conformity to the divine ordering of creation. Rectitude of the mind and rectitude of the will are both determined by a correct relationship to the divine ordering of creation.

24. Anselm clearly assumes that the three concepts of rectitude, truth, and righteousness are closely linked, and notes the intersection of their meanings in the notion of "rectitude" – the "rightness of things." For Anselm, the fundamental sense of "righteousness" is the moral rectitude of the created order,

established by God at creation, itself reflecting the divine will and nature. This moral ordering of the universe extends to the relationship between humans and God, and humans and their fellows. Anselm appears to use the term *rectitudo* to describe the basic God-given ordering of the universe, and employs the term *iustitia* in a number of derivative senses, each of which may be traced back to the fundamental concept of rectitude. God's moral governing of the universe clearly involves both the divine regulation of the affairs of humans, and also the self-imposed regulation of God's dealings with human dealings. For Anselm, it is not possible to argue that the laws governing each are the same. In its fundamental sense, *iustitia* merely refers to rectitude; it remains to be seen what form this ordering may take with respect to the various aspects of creation. Thus, the justice which regulates the affairs of humans (e.g., the Ciceronian and Justinian principle of *reddens unicuique quod suum est*) cannot be considered to be identical with the justice which regulates God's dealings with humanity.

25. Anselm applies these ideas to the redemption of humanity. Anselm understands the term "original justice" to refer to the initial moral rectitude of humanity within the created order. For Anselm, the basic requirement is that rational creatures be subject to God, accepting and realizing their proper place within the hierarchical moral ordering of creation. This moral ordering of creation, itself an expression of the divine will, allots a specific place to humans, with a concomitant obligation that they submit their rational nature to God. This moral ordering of the universe was violated by humans at the Fall.

For Anselm, the human violation of the moral order of creation means that they are no longer capable of submitting their rational nature to God – and therefore that they are incapable of redeeming themselves. If humanity is to be redeemed, a divine act of redemption is required *which must itself be consonant with the established moral order of the universe*. God, having created the moral order of the universe as an expression of his nature and will, is unable to violate it himself in the redemption of humankind. The rectitude of the established moral order thus requires that God redeem humankind in such a way that God's own nature as *summa iustitia* is not contradicted.

26. In his evaluation of traditional accounts of the redemption of humankind in Christ, Anselm makes it clear that he is not satisfied with their failure to explain *why* God chose to redeem humans – at best, they were merely descriptions of *how* God redeemed them, so offering no explanation for why God should choose to redeem humans in the first place, nor the particular mode of redemption selected. Many late patristic and early medieval discussions of the redemption of humanity were based on the idea of the devil having "rights" over humanity as a consequence of the Fall. It is an idea that Anselm regards as totally unwarranted, and dismisses it accordingly.

Anselm's more fundamental concern is that these traditional approaches present God as acting in a manner that is not consistent with God's character as the one who established the moral fabric of creation in the first place. Why should God disregard or flout the established moral order in the redemption of humanity? Redemption must take place in a manner that is consonant with rectitude – the moral ordering of the universe, established by God, and in turn respected by God.

27. Anselm therefore presents an account of the redemption of humankind, based on the moral rectitude of the created order, which demonstrates both that the redemption of humankind is necessary as a matter of justice, and that this redemption is effected in a manner that is consonant with the divinely established moral ordering of the universe. For Anselm, the moral ordering of the universe was violated by the sin of humans, so that the present state of affairs is that of a privation of justice. As whatever is unjust is a contradiction of the divine nature, it is therefore imperative that the moral rectitude of the created order be restored. God, as *summa iustitia*, is therefore obliged, by God's very nature, to restore the rectitude of the created order by redeeming fallen humankind – *as an act of justice*.

28. Anselm's soteriology depends significantly on his concept of satisfaction, which I do not propose to discuss further. The essential point, however, is that Anselm considers, presumably on the basis of the established satisfaction–merit model of the penitential system of the contemporary church, that the payment of a satisfaction by the God-human would be regarded by his readers as an acceptable means of satisfying the demands of moral rectitude without violating the moral order of creation. For our purposes, this aspect of Anselm's soteriology is subsidiary, the main element being his development of *iustitia Dei* as action directed towards the highest good, and thus embracing the redemption of humankind. Anselm's soteriology is dominated by the understanding of justice as moral rectitude, and it marks a decisive turning point in the medieval discussion of the salvation of humanity.

29. From this brief analysis, it should be clear that the concept of divine ordering has enormous potential as a theological *Leitmotif*. This could be illustrated by exploring its role in the constructive theology of a chronologically and theologically diverse range of writers, such as Thomas Aquinas, John Calvin, various Anglican divines of the early seventeenth century, and Emil Brunner. The concept of ordering allows theology to engage with the following central questions, some of which have ramifications far beyond the community of faith:

1 Natural law as an expression of divine ordering.
2 The covenant as the ordering of the relationship between God and God's people, publicly affirmed in certain covenantal signs or – to anticipate a Christian perspective – sacraments.

3 Atonement: sin as disruption of divine ordering, atonement as proleptic restoration of that ordering by means that are consistent with it.
4 The ordering of the world and the perception of beauty – note especially the aesthetics of Thomas Aquinas, John Ruskin, and Hans Urs von Balthasar.
5 The ordering of the world and the cognition of structure, particularly in the natural sciences.
6 Eschatology as consummation, either in terms of the restoration of the original order of creation and covenant, or the transfiguration of that order.

30. This brief analysis of the place of the concept of order in systematic theology could easily be extended. The point is not simply that the conceptual fabric of Christian theology is shot through with the theme of "ordering"; it is that this theme itself provides a means of integrating the themes of Christian theology, ensuring their internal coherence, and its intrinsic capacity to engage with the structures of the external world. The idea of the "order of things" – embedded in creation, expressed in the covenant, and embodied in Jesus Christ as God incarnate – will play a central role in the projected "scientific dogmatics" now being planned.

CHAPTER 9

A Working Paper: Iterative Procedures and Closure in Systematic Theology

1. Conventional models of systematic theology tend to assume that it follows an essentially linear trajectory: you begin *here* and you end *there*. Your starting point determines your end point, even if you may arrive at that final destination by a circuitous rather than direct route. As is obvious from a survey of modern theology, there are many different starting points (e.g., Schleiermacher, *Glaubenslehre*; Barth, *Dogmatik*; Pannenberg, *Offenbarung als Geschichte*), with their corresponding different ending points.

But is this actually so? Surely not. If we concede the central Reformation principle of *ecclesia semper reformanda*, systematic theology is better thought of as an iterative procedure. In other words, theology is a process of constant comparison and evaluation, leading to modification and further evaluation until a stable situation is achieved. This equilibrium is dynamic, rather than static, in that the iterative procedure of comparison is regarded as continuing, not ending, once such a position of equilibrium has been achieved. Yet it is entirely reasonable to designate the achievement of such a position of equilibrium as "closure." Theology never ends its task; it merely temporarily suspends its operations while it recovers its breadth.

2. Can we think of the community of faith as operating as a Turing machine, proceeding by an agreed iterative procedure (regressive?) until closure is achieved? There are clear and important parallels with iterative procedures for non-linear integral equations – as in the Newton-Raphson method applied to the van der Waals equations for gases, or to polynomial equations. Newton's original presentation of the approach in the *Principia Mathematica* does not seem to make significant use of fluxional calculus – but his discussion of the

solution of Kepler's equation $x - e \sin(x) = M$ may be more representative. (See especially the commentary by John Couch Adams, 1882.) Iterative procedures of this era are probably best seen in Joseph Raphson's works (note the discussion and examples in Tjalling J. Ypma, "Historical Development of the Newton-Raphson Method." *SIAM Review* 37 (1995): 531–51).

Or consider the "method of moments" for resolving complex exponential decay curves, as in my work on fluorescent probes in biological systems (I. Isenberg and R. D. Dyson, "Analysis of Exponential Curves by a Method of Moments, with Special Attention to Sedimentation Equilibrium and Fluorescence Decay." *Biochemistry* 10 (1971): 3233–41; "The Analysis of Fluorescence Decay by a Method of Moments." *Biophysical Journal* 9 (1969): 1337–50.) The basic idea is to find a best theoretical approximation to observed data by a method of empirical fit. This can only be done in an iterative manner, until a stable position is reached which can legitimately be described as a "solution."

So is there a theological equivalent of Newton's iterative algorithm for solving non-linear algebraic equations? Or is theology non-recursive, as in the solution of Diophantine equations (Roger Penrose)? Yet the dynamic nature of the process of reception points to an implicit process of iteration taking place, whether this is formalized or not – or even recognized.

3. On the basis of both historical observation and theoretical reflection, it is proposed that systematic theology operates on the basis of an implicit iterative method, which needs to be made explicit and incorporated into any discussion of theological method. This can be thought of as a process of convergence (= closure) on a region of doctrinal stability, or as ascending a hermeneutical spiral, allowing access to enhanced levels of appreciation and understanding.

4. So where does this iteration begin? What is the appropriate starting point? It can't be nature, as nature requires interpretation to act as a theological resource. Nature needs to be seen as creation, and thus presupposes the interpretive framework of the Christian tradition. Classic Protestantism begins with the Bible. But then how can theology be done prior to the closing of the canon of scripture? Interconnections of community and text, church and Bible? Explicitly accepting the authority of the Bible (which is not problematic) entails the implicit acceptance of the actuality of the church as the community which received that text. The starting point must therefore be the actuality of the church as an institution which embodies Christian tradition – and this "actuality" must be understood to include various levels or strata of revelation, such as texts, sermons, actions, and artifacts.

5. Systematic theology begins with the actuality of the church – an embodied tradition, aware of its own distinct origins, identity, and purpose. The church mediates ideas and values at a number of levels – texts, public rehearsal of faith, public recollection and sacramental representation of events

(bread, wine, and water), and so forth. Although explanation of things is only part of its agenda (the mediation of salvation being presumably rather more important), the church is able to offer an explanation of things which is adequate for its own purposes – and better than that of its rivals. (See MacIntyre on the comparison of competing traditions.) The church represents the Christian tradition embodied in historical actualities and specifics, articulating and inhabiting a life-changing vision of reality. *Gloria enim Dei vivens homo; vita autem hominis visio Dei* (Irenaeus, *adversus haereses* IV.xx.7).

6. The church is already as a ship under way (von Neurath). As it journeys, it maintains and seeks to understand its identity and purpose by reflecting on what it embodies and what it transmits – both *kerygma* and *dogma*. The church exists by acting – through proclamation, reenactment, celebration, outreach, and adoration. Its identity is thus preserved and propagated by a process of handing down and handing over. Note the importance of the idea of tradition in the Pastoral epistles and elsewhere: the emphasis on "guarding the good deposit which was entrusted to you" (2 Timothy 1:14), and Paul's references to "passing down" (1 Corinthians 15:3). "The Church, in her teaching, life and worship, perpetuates and hands on to all generations all that she herself is, all that she believes" (*Verbum Dei*, 8).

7. Thus the process of transmission; but what is transmitted? Clearly, a number of levels of reality: institutions (bishops – note especially points made by Irenaeus, but also in dogmatic constitution *Lumen Gentium*); texts (above all, holy scripture, but note also creeds); buildings (tactile impact of Christian ideas and values: architecture, images, etc.); actions (especially eucharist and baptism); and artifacts (such as icons). Pastoral epistles as especially important in this respect: early Pauline letters especially focus on gospel itself; Pastorals concerned with the preservation and transmission of the gospel to a later generation, aiming to ensure continuity through individuals (Timothy, Titus), structures (bishops, elders, etc.), and ideas (deposit of faith).

8. Key element of what is transmitted: Jesus Christ. Not just as a historical person, but as one whose significance is interpreted and proclaimed. Martin Kähler: "der wirkliche Christus ist der gepredigte Christus." The church is the vehicle of the preaching of Jesus and the apostolic preaching about Jesus. The church *witnesses* to its understanding of Jesus Christ, and its implications for its identity and mission. Three levels of this ministry: the church as planted in the world by the apostles to proclaim Christ; as adhering to the teaching of the apostles about Christ; as carrying on the succession of apostolic ministry of Christ. The church can be said to convey Christ – both in terms of its historical starting point, the substance of its proclamation (gospel), and its recollection and celebration of Christ in bread and wine. Protestants may place the emphasis upon the presence of Christ through the word, and Catholics on

his presence through the sacraments, but these are theologically complementary, even if some make them polemically exclusive. *Ubi Christus ibi ecclesia catholica* (Ignatius of Antioch, *Ep. ad Smyrn.* 8).

9. The church's task is not simply to preserve and transmit this proclamation about Christ, as if its task were simply to maintain theological vigilance and kerygmatic enthusiasm. The church is a reflective practitioner of the proclamation of Christ, ensuring that it is subject to a process of constant reevaluation and reconsideration. On the one hand, it seeks to be faithful to the past; on the other, it seeks to avoid being imprisoned by the past, being aware that an ancient tradition may simply be an old mistake (Cyprian of Carthage, *Epistolae*, lxxi, 3; lxxiii, 13; lxxiv, 9). This dynamic process of revisiting the received tradition in the light of its ultimate foundation and criterion underlies the Reformation notion of *ecclesia semper reformanda*, and the Catholic and Orthodox notion of "living tradition." It also points to an iterative approach to the theological task, as we shall consider presently.

10. Part of the task of the church is to give a theological account of Jesus Christ. The centrality of Jesus Christ is part of the actuality or "givenness" of the Christian tradition; reflection both on the doxological positioning and the theological interpretation of Jesus Christ is part of the discipleship of the mind and heart that is rightly expected of that tradition. It is therefore no accident that the central theological task of the first four centuries of Christian reflection was to locate Jesus Christ on a conceptual map. How is he to be positioned along the coordinates of time and eternity, humanity and divinity, particularity and universality? How can an event which took place at a specific time and place be relevant for all peoples and all times?

11. The history of early Christian engagement with the identity and significance of Jesus Christ can easily be accounted for using the model of adaptation developed on empirical grounds by Jean Piaget. Piaget argued that two elements could be distinguished in the process by which the growing child adapts to the world around. In *assimilation*, what is observed in the outside world is incorporated into the child's mental world without changing the structure of that internal world. The mind adapts new information in such a way that it fits preexisting categories. As a result, the external perceptions are forced into an existing way of thinking, leading to pigeon-holing and stereotyping. In *accommodation*, the mind has to adjust itself to the evidence with which it is confronted and thus adapt to it, which is a somewhat more difficult and painful process. In this case, information resulting from encountering the world does not fit the preexisting categories, forcing the mind to develop new categories to accommodate the new information.

In encountering Christ, the corporate mind of the church was already shaped by a number of categories inherited from Judaism – such as the category of the "prophet." Initially, the development of Christian understandings of Jesus

Christ appeared to consist primarily of assimilation to existing categories. The New Testament shows this process at work – for example, in the gospel reports suggesting Jesus was seen by some as a "new Elijah" – in other words, as a recognizable variant of a familiar category. The early heresy of Ebionitism represents the assimilation of Jesus to an already familiar religious category – the charismatic figure, or *nabi*. (Schleiermacher was right to identify Ebionitism, not Arianism, as one of the four "natural heresies" of Christianity: *Glaubenslehre* §22.)

Yet even the New Testament shows evidence of the process of accommodation, often in response to an irreconcilable tension between observation and theory. An excellent example of this forced revision of existing religious categories is found in Mark's account of the healing of the paralytic (Mark 2:1–12). There is a sense in which the crowds can cope with "Jesus the healer." This can easily be assimilated to existing Jewish categories. But the claim to forgive sins is baffling. The claim seems tantamount to blasphemy. Yet Jesus is able to heal the paralytic, disconfirming this. The outcome is a forced reappraisal of what categories are appropriate to represent Jesus – including the realization that conceptual hand-me-downs are not up to the task. It is no accident that Mark's narrative almost immediately follows this remarkable incident with Jesus' words about the failure of old wineskins to contain new wine (Mark 2.22). The coming of Jesus into human history has introduced something new, something dynamic, that the old ways of thinking were not capable of grasping. The unthinkable was happening. And there were only two ways out of this dilemma – to deny what seemed to be happening, or to rethink the limits of divine possibilities.

12. Yet this trajectory of this line of exploration does not end here. For if a secure link is established between the person of Jesus Christ and the God of Israel, a significant degree of conceptual renegotiation needs to take place. If we are to "think about Jesus as we do about God" (2 Clement 1:1–2), simple handed-down images of God, whether borrowed from the history of Israel or Hellenistic philosophy, will have to be revised. To revert to Piaget's terminology, existing categories will have to be accommodated to the complex Christian revelation of God, including the Christian experience of God in worship and prayer. Yet this process of accommodation is subsequent to the realization that it is necessary – and this pressure is primarily christological. It is therefore important to note that, from the standpoint of historical theology, the dogmatic formulation of the Trinity only becomes a genuine possibility once agreement had been reached on the community of faith's understanding of the identity of Jesus Christ.

13. This means that systematic theology cannot begin by assuming any doctrine of the Trinity. The concept of the Trinity is not itself included in the fundamental revelation of faith – for example, in the Bible – but is the outcome

of an extended process of faithful yet critical reflection on that revelation. The doctrine of the Trinity is the church's last word about God, the apex of its theological trajectory, the conclusion of its long pilgrimage of theological reflection. Schleiermacher was right to insist that the Trinity was *der Schluß-stein der christlichen Lehre*, precisely because the empirical method he adopted ultimately led to this goal, even though that goal was not explicit at the beginning of his theological voyage (*Glaubenslehre*, §170). The doctrine of the Trinity – still less some conceptually developed form of that doctrine – simply cannot be allowed to be the foundation of dogmatic reflections, precisely because it is their outcome. The recent spate of ambitious theological speculation grounded in nuanced readings of the concept of *perichoresis* and so forth is ultimately based on the highly questionable assumption that the conclusion of theological arguments can somehow become their foundation.

14. The historical development of Christian doctrine therefore points to (and rests upon) something deeper than the contingencies of historical disputations. Historically, the actuality of the Christian proclamation of Jesus Christ led first to the exploration of his identity and manner of conceptualization; and then to the elaboration of the notion of God necessitated by his life, death, and resurrection. The late development of the doctrine of the Trinity cannot be taken to mean that this was an improper development, or as suggesting that Christianity is fundamentally binitarian (contra Maurice Wiles). The late development of the doctrine reflects the fact that it is the final stage in the trajectory of theological reflection that has been sketched in this paper, and is ultimately dependent on previous stages in that process. The historical unfolding of the Christian mystery is not arbitrary, but reflects the intrinsic nature of that mystery. The dogma of the Trinity is as much a statement about the dogmatic location and significance of Jesus Christ as it is about the God of Israel.

The contribution of the mainline Reformation must be noted at this point. Although the magisterial reformers – Martin Luther, Huldrych Zwingli, and John Calvin – were critical of many aspects of the received tradition of the church, they did *not* direct criticism against any of these core elements we have identified in the fundamental trajectory of theological analysis. All agreed on the actuality of the church, conceding that the medieval church, while in need of reformation at various points in its life and thought, was nevertheless a *Christian* church. Christology was not a matter of significant debate at the time of the Reformation, either between the magisterial reformers themselves, or between the reformers and their Catholic opponents. Likewise with the Trinity. (Yet it may be noted that all three – the actuality of the church, christology, and the Trinity – were the subject of divisions and debate within the minority radical wing of the Reformation.)

15. At first sight, this might suggest a theological equivalent to Ernst Haeckel's discredited "theory of recapitulation" (1866), according to which

ontogeny recapitulates phylogeny. On this view, the development of the embryos of a given species recapitulates the evolutionary history of that species. Yet I am not endorsing either Haeckel's theory or its spurious theological application. The key point is that *the historical development of Christian doctrine mirrors its internal structures*. As each layer is removed, the next becomes accessible. Precisely because doctrinal development is a corporate matter, involving the consensus of the community of faith rather than the private judgment of an individual, the process is gradual and cumulative, resting on the acceptance of previous stages in the analysis of the church's proclamation.

It has long been known that there are important parallels between the historical development of Christian doctrine and the ordering of a systematic account of its leading themes. This was pointed out by James Orr in his 1897 Elliot lectures at Western Theological Seminary, Allegheny, Pennsylvania. (See James Orr, *The Progress of Dogma*. London: Hodder & Stoughton, 1901.) As Orr points out:

> Has it ever struck you, then – you will not find it noticed in the ordinary books, but I am sure your attention cannot be drawn to it without your perceiving that there must be more underlying it than meets the eye – what a singular *parallel* there is between the historical course of dogma, on the one hand, and the scientific order of the textbooks on systematic theology on the other? The history of dogma, as you speedily discover, is simply the system of theology spread out through the centuries ... The temporal and logical order correspond. The articulation of the system in your textbooks is the very articulation of the system in its development in history.

16. Thus the first iteration – that is to say, the following through of the trajectory of reflection, mirrored in the development of Christian doctrine, for the first time. One element of this iteration can be set out like this:

Actuality of church → theory of the church

In other words, reflection within the church on its identity and tasks leads to a theory of the church – that is to say, we move from a descriptive account of the church's identity and action to a more prescriptive account. However, although the Donatist controversy forced at least a degree of conceptual clarification at this point, the early church does not appear to have regarded ecclesiology as being of critical importance. Reflection within the church focused primarily, not on the identity of the church itself, but on the nature of its proclamation and witness – that is to say, on the figure of Jesus himself. Ecclesiology was regarded as subordinate to Christology.

The real theological reflection thus focuses on the identity of Jesus Christ, and the consequences of this for the Christian understanding of God. This can be represented very briefly as follows, although this grossly simplifies the situation (for example, Christian anthropology also flows out of Christology).

Actuality of church → Christology → Trinity

Again, note that the Trinity is the outcome, not the presupposition, of this process. Note also that the "actuality of the church" includes the various levels of revelation, such as texts, actions, and artifacts.

17. But now that this process is complete, the second iteration can begin. Whereas the first stage of the iterative process began by recognizing merely the actuality of the church, there can be no legitimate objection to the construction of a trinitarian ecclesiology by the "reflecting back" of the outcome of the process of theological reflection to one of its earlier stages. Similarly, while it might be argued that there is an implicit trinitarian structure to the actuality of Christian worship, an iterative approach to the theological task allows this to be viewed and structured in an explicitly trinitarian manner, thus allowing new depths of insight and an enhanced appreciation of the dynamics of praise.

The essential point is to recognize this process of iteration for what it actually is. The doctrine of the Trinity is an initial theological conclusion – a temporary resting place which, once reached, can be used as the basis for a deeper level of engagement with aspects of Christian thought and practice. To take an obvious example: after the first iteration, a trinitarian theology of revelation can be developed, which is both faithful to the phenomenology of how God is known, while possessing a firm theological foundation that secures its dogmatic identity and purpose. The Trinity, to reiterate, is not a starting point, but a conclusion – but once that conclusion has been accepted, it may be reflected back, functioning either as the basis of additional ideas, or as an interpretive framework through which existing ideas or practices may be seen more clearly and understood more deeply.

18. Closure may be said to have taken place when successive iteration yields no further significant advances. At this point, a point of equilibrium has been reached, and no further advance is possible. In designating this point "closure," I do not mean that everything has been resolved, that all loose ends have been tied up, and that a full and comprehensive grasp has been secured on every aspect of the Christian gospel. The nature of reality imposes certain limitations on what can be known and how it can be represented. Rather, we can be said to have secured "closure" in the sense that we have arrived at a theological resting place which is not of our own making, but which is secured by the realities we are seeking to explore.

19. This brief theoretical sketch of an iterative approach to theological methodology indicates its close correspondence to the actuality of doctrinal development within the church, as well as illuminating aspects of contemporary

theological debates. The parallels with the shape of Schleiermacher's *Glaubenslehre* will be obvious, reflecting the fact that both our approaches represent an empirically based, essentially inferential approach to the tasks of systematic theology. But where I differ from Schleiermacher is that he *ends* with the doctrine of the Trinity, whereas I *pause for breath*, before returning to repeat the whole exercise, but with an enhanced capacity for understanding and appreciation. In the case of Barth, there are clear and significant differences, most notably in his presumption of the doctrine of the Trinity as a concomitant of the actuality of revelation. However, after a single theological iteration, I am able to join him in offering a trinitarian approach to the actuality of revelation. But where Barth seems to treat revelation in somewhat abstract, unhistorical terms, my approach allows me to begin from the historical actuality of revelation, before returning to offer a theoretical justification and elaboration of the idea.

20. So how is this process to be visualized? Two obvious analogies come to mind. First, a linear model of iterative loops, as follows (again, grossly simplified):

Iteration 1
Actuality of church → Christology → Trinity

The intellectual outcomes of this first iteration are now transferred as *working assumptions* to the beginning of the second iteration, which traverses the same ground again – but this time, yielding a trinitarian theology of revelation, an incarnational account of human existence, and so forth. These outcomes are then transferred as working assumptions to the third iteration, and so forth. This could be modeled on nested loops in computer programming, perhaps with conditional branching, which terminates when closure appears to have taken place.

The second visual image is that of a spiral – perhaps a spiral staircase. Each completion of the iterative cycle moves us back to the beginning – but also up a level. This way of visualizing the process allows us to emphasize the idea of the elevation of understanding, which is a central theme of the iterative approach to theology that I envisage. Theology does not merely circle its objects of reflection: it aims to gain an enhanced appreciation and grasp of its object as it engages and reflects. Closure may be said to take place when circling the spiral does not lead to elevation – in other words, when the theological trajectory appears to have reached a plateau.

21. Finally, we must return to the Pauline injunction in the New Testament, which exhorts us to "put everything to the test, and hold on to what is good" (1 Thessalonians 5.21) – a notion that is expressed in the Reformation principle *ecclesia semper reformanda*. On this view, "reformation" does not

designate a once-for-all event which can now be considered to be complete, but a continuous process of theological vigilance and attentiveness, which scrutinizes every aspect of Christian life and thought, and inquires as to how its authenticity might be explored and confirmed. Theology, if it is to be Christian, can never be content with the wooden repetition of dogmatic formulae of the past; it constantly reexamines them, to ensure that they are faithful representations of the gospel, adequate both to the conceptualities of Christianity and to the situations in which they are to be used.

In light of this point, we must be careful to avoid both the modernist error of premature closure and the postmodern error of a refusal to attempt (or expect) any degree of closure. To speak of theological closure is not to preclude constant reexamination, but to report on the communal consensus concerning where that process of exploration has arrived. Rowan Williams is good on this:

> The history of doctrine has the paradoxical character of a repeated effort of definition designed to counter the ill effects of definition itself – rather like the way in which a good poet will struggle to find a fixed form of words that will decisively avoid narrowing and lifeless fixtures or closures of meaning.

(Rowan Williams, "Newman's *Arians* and the Question of Method in Doctrinal History." In *Newman after a Hundred Years*, edited by Ian Ker and Alan Hill, 265–85. Oxford: Oxford University Press, 1990, quote at 285.)

Applying these insights to the iterative approach to systematic theology set out in this working paper, it will be obvious that one conclusion stands out – the need for *reiteration*. In other words, the theologian must go through the cycles of iteration from time to time, partly for self-reassurance concerning the reliability and authenticity of the ideas derived in this manner, and partly as a matter of public accountability to the community of faith (1 Thessalonians 5:21). Mistakes have been made and will continue to be made; the need for a corrective mechanism is obvious. And part of that corrective mechanism is a willingness to begin the cycle of theological reflection all over again, not merely in response to external challenges to dogmas such as the Trinity, but also as a matter of candor and fidelity. Theological vigilance is thus critical to ecclesiastical integrity.

CHAPTER 10

The Church as the Starting Point for a Scientific Dogmatics

Where do we begin to tell a story? At what point do we jump into a hermeneutical circle? How can we begin *anywhere*, when all our starting points themselves seem to presuppose certain beliefs, which suggest we ought to have started somewhere else? The theological grass always seems greener on the other side of the methodological fence. Yet when we place ourselves at such alternative starting points we find ourselves facing the same dilemma: once more, we are forced to assume and trust, where we had hoped to demonstrate and prove. While some historians have suggested that the history of western philosophy is primarily the quest for an unshakeable foundation of ideas, it is not unreasonable to propose that the identification of a starting point for critical reflection is of equal importance.

Yet one cannot simply acknowledge the difficulties in determining or defining a theological launch pad, and then pass on to other matters. Whether we like it or not, we have to start *somewhere*. The indefinite postponement of the entire theological enterprise until unanimity on this matter has been achieved is totally unrealistic. The theological ship does not remain in harbor until agreement is reached on this matter, in that the voyage is already under way, and that harbor is now far behind. Recognizing this fact, a scientific theology proposes that we begin with what we observe, and then proceed, by a process involving abduction, iteration, construction, and *le bon sens* (Pierre Duhem), to build the best account of reality that we can manage. For in the end, the starting point is only of critical importance if the theological expeditionary venture is made once, and only once. Yet an iterative approach allows constant revisiting, continual reexamination, and above all, constant *questioning* as the exploration continues.

As I have stressed, a scientific dogmatics adopts an essentially iterative, empirical approach to theology, which determines that its starting point is that which is *observable*, and thus requires to be explained, represented, and appropriated. Its starting point does not determine its ending point, in that the iterative method of a scientific dogmatics ensures that derived insights can be incorporated into the process of theological analysis and elaboration in successive iterations. Yet we must begin somewhere, and in some way.

Starting from the Visible Reality of the Church

The starting point for a scientific dogmatics is the actuality of the church *as an observable reality* – not a *theory* of the church, but the observable fact that a church exists as a social, spatial entity, and that Christians inhabit its physical, social, and spiritual structures. Calvin makes this point with characteristic precision: believers exist within the church prior to any theoretical reflection as to why it is there or what it is:[1]

> I shall begin then, with the church, into the bosom of which God is pleased to gather his children, not only so that they may be nourished by her assistance and ministry while they are infants and children, but also so that they may be guided by her motherly care until they mature and reach the goal of faith. "For what God has joined together, no one shall divide" (Mark 10:9). For those to whom God is Father, the church shall also be their mother.

It is not possible, on the basis of an empirical methodology, to begin with or from an ecclesiology which seeks to define the doctrine of the church in terms of the Trinity;[2] we may, however, eventually find our way there. The Trinity marks an important resting place on our long intellectual pilgrimage of faith, but it cannot be its beginning, nor its point of departure. It is only by revisiting our beginnings in the light of our endings that we can hope to begin ascending the spiral of theological reflection that leads to an enhanced appreciation of the conceptual beauty and intellectual coherence of faith. We start with the brute fact of the existence of the church as a social entity. We do not end there; but we cannot presuppose our endings as we begin.

---

[1] John Calvin, *Institutes*, IV.i.9–10.

[2] For an approach which takes the Trinity as its starting point, see the helpful discussion of Miroslav Volf, *After Our Likeness: The Church as the Image of the Trinity*. Grand Rapids, MI: Eerdmans, 1998, especially 127–8, 191–220. I find myself methodologically unable to share this approach, at least without having to go through several iterations of the theological procedures I shall describe in this and the preceding chapter.

Asserting that a scientific dogmatics begins with the actuality of the church does *not* mean that a scientific dogmatics begins with an explicit ecclesiology.[3] To do so is to begin with a theoretical preconception of what a church is or ought to be, rather than with the phenomenological actuality of what a church appears to be, as an experienced, social reality.[4] In arguing that theological reflection begins with the church, I am speaking about the observable social reality embodied in human history. "The Body of Christ takes up physical space here on earth" (Dietrich Bonhoeffer).[5] The construction of an ecclesiology – which I take to be critical yet constructive reflection on how that ecclesial reality understands itself, or how it is to be understood by others – follows encountering the church as a social entity. For reasons that will become clearer as our discussion proceeds, the *actuality* of the church takes theological priority over any specific *theory* of the church. Yet the empirical approach to the acquisition of human knowledge that is of such central importance to the theological methodology of the "scientific theology" project demands that we begin with what may be observed, and then proceed to interpretation. Encounter precedes, even though it cannot entirely be disentangled from, interpretation.

An empirical theological method begins from the empirical actuality of the church – something that can be experienced. It is the visible reality of the church that leads us to ask the fundamental questions that propel us on a theological trajectory. Karl Barth was clear on this point, and he needs to be heard here:[6]

> In the Apostles' Creed, it is not an invisible structure which is meant, but a very visible gathering [*eine sehr sichtbare Zusammenkunft*] which has its origins with the twelve Apostles. The first congregation was a visible group, which aroused a visible, public uproar. If the church does not possess this visibility, then it is not the church.

More recently, this theme has been developed by Stanley Hauerwas, and we shall return to consider his insights later in this essay.

---

[3] It may, of course, be pointed out that such reflections can hardly be avoided: Eberhart Jüngel, "Credere in Ecclesiam: Eine ökumenische Besinnung." *Zeitschrift für Theologie und Kirche* 99 (2002): 177–95. But this does not negate this fundamental point about where such reflections begin.

[4] An excellent example of an ecclesiology constructed around a single theoretical principle is that of Karl Barth. See Nicholas M. Healy, "The Logic of Karl Barth's Ecclesiology: Analysis, Assessment and Proposed Modification." *Modern Theology* 10 (1994): 253–70. For a comparison of Barth and Robert Jenson at this point, see Ian A. McFarland, "The Body of Christ: Rethinking a Classic Ecclesiological Model." *International Journal of Systematic Theology* 7 (2005): 225–45.

[5] Dietrich Bonhoeffer, *Discipleship*. Minneapolis: Fortress, 2001, 225.

[6] Karl Barth, *Dogmatik im Grundriß: Vorlesungen gehalten im Sommersemester 1946 an der Universität Bonn*. Zurich: Evangelischer Verlag, 1947, 167–8.

But first, we must consider what, on the face of it, might seem to be a formidable objection to this approach. In what sense can any *empirical* theological method engage with, still less begin from, the church? Is not the proper domain of application of such a method nature itself? How can a theology which is characterized primarily by an engagement with what may be observed conceivably begin with the church?

The force of this point must be conceded immediately. As a simple matter of historical fact, empirical approaches to theology have tended to follow intellectual trajectories very similar to those associated with the Boyle Lectures, which we considered earlier in this collection of essays. For the empiricists of the early eighteenth century, it was axiomatic that the proper subject of an empirical method was the natural world. In exploring such approaches earlier in this volume, we noted several fundamental problems that it faced – most significantly, the serious problem that nature is not a self-interpreting entity or agent, but is epistemologically malleable, possessed of a generous conceptual plasticity. Historically, the idea of a self-interpreting natural theology is a dead end. Nature requires interpretation – and for that reason, requires an interpreter. Such an interpretation is provided by the Christian tradition, embodied institutionally in the church. The church, however, was regarded as a social entity, not a natural entity – and hence as lying outside the scope of the empirical method.

So how (if at all?), it must then be asked, can an empirical method engage with a social entity such as the church? Perhaps empiricism can cope with the idea of the built, physical structures that we call "churches" – but surely not the social realities of communities, beliefs, and practices which constitute churches in a broader, and theologically more astute, sense?[7] It is a fair point. It is very difficult to see how the empirical method of John Locke, for example, could be found to be theologically productive at this juncture. Yet the answer is to be found in the way in which, partly in response to Locke's shortcomings, our understandings of what constitutes "experience" have developed over the years. We shall turn to consider this point immediately.

Can Theology be Empirical? John Locke versus John Dewey

In what sense can Christian theology be empirical? One of the most influential answers was set out by John Locke in the late seventeenth century. It was

---

[7] There are some important reflections on such points in the writings of Chicago Divinity School theologian Bernard Meland (1871–1993). See Nancy Frankenberry, "Meland's Empirical Realism and the Appeal to Lived Experience." *American Journal of Theology and Philosophy* 5 (1984): 117–29; Tyron Inbody, *The Constructive Theology of Bernard Meland: Postliberal Empirical Realism.* New York: Oxford University Press, 1995.

destined to play a decisive role in shaping the English natural theology tradition, based on the idea of the neutral, objective observer contemplating a detached natural world. The fundamental principles of Locke's empiricist philosophy are set out in *An Essay Concerning Human Understanding* (1690), which represents the culmination of twenty years of reflection on the origins and limits of human knowledge. According to Locke, human knowledge is always to be understood fundamentally as the relation between ideas. Much of the *Essay* is devoted to an extended, highly influential argument that all of our ideas, whether simple or complex, are ultimately derived from experience.[8]

Perhaps the most significant consequence of this empiricist approach is that human knowledge must be recognized to be severely limited, both in terms of its scope and its certainty. Nevertheless, Locke held that we have no grounds for complaint about the limitations of our knowledge; the important thing was to recognize these limits, and learn to work and act within them. Locke's religious views are consistent with this empirical approach. Christianity is shown to be "reasonable" within the parameters of this empirical approach to knowledge.[9]

A fundamental theme which dominates early English empiricism is that of the validity of ideas.[10] In what manner, and to what extent, can our ideas be shown to be valid? What discriminatory apparatus may be used to allow us to make judgments concerning the reliability of assertions and opinions? Locke, as one might expect, champions evidence-based argument. We must, he insists, do our utmost to conform our ideas to what we experience. Although Locke's discussion of the evidential basis of knowledge is not entirely satisfactory – for example, he appears to confuse *minimally satisfactory* evidence with *ideal* evidence[11] – there is no disguising his passion for allowing what we experience of the world to determine what we believe to be true of the world. *"Our*

---

[8] See, for example, Michael Ayers, *Locke: Epistemology and Ontology*. London: Routledge, 1991. On Locke's religious influence, see Alan P. F. Sell, *John Locke and the Eighteenth-Century Divines*. Cardiff: University of Wales Press, 1997.

[9] For important interactions with Locke's somewhat truncated and attenuated understanding of faith, see Kim Ian Parker, "John Locke and the Enlightenment Meta-narrative: A Biblical Corrective to a Reasoned World." *Scottish Journal of Theology* 49 (1996): 57–73; Stephen N. Williams, "John Locke on the Status of Faith." *Scottish Journal of Theology* 40 (1987): 591–606.

[10] Carlo E. Huber, "Der englische Empirismus als Bewusstseinsphilosophie: Seine Eigenart und das Problem der Geltung von Bewusstseinsinhalten in ihm." *Gregorianum* 58 (1977): 641–73. For comments on how the concept of an "idea" is understood by English empiricism of this era, see Jonathan Bennett, *Locke, Berkeley, Hume: Central Themes*. Oxford: Oxford University Press, 1977, 21–58.

[11] Nicholas Wolterstorff, *John Locke and the Ethics of Belief*. Cambridge: Cambridge University Press, 1996, 70–1.

Knowledge, therefore, is *real*, only so far as there is a conformity between our *Ideas* and the Reality of Things."[12] Having defeated any notion that knowledge arises from innate ideas, Locke appeals to experience as the ultimate arbiter of truth:[13]

> Let us then suppose the Mind to be, as we say, white Paper, void of all Characters, without any *Ideas*; How comes it to be furnished? Whence comes it by that vast store, which the busy and boundless Fancy of Man has painted on it, with an almost endless Variety? Whence has it all the materials of Reason and Knowledge? To this I answer, in one word, From *Experience*.

Locke offers an account of how the human mind analyzes experience, reconstituting it to give the rich assortment of simple and complex ideas which furnish the human intellectual world. It is an account that is not without its difficulties, perhaps most significantly the core belief that "the mind knows not things immediately, but only by intervention of the ideas it has of them."[14] So how does Locke go about doing theology? It is a matter of no small importance to him, not least because it illuminates the problematic relationship of "faith" and "knowledge." Our concern, however, focuses particularly on how he believes that knowledge of God can be attained empirically, if only to help clarify the problems that any empirical method will encounter if applied to the realm of theology. Locke held, as a matter of ontological certainty, that the mind could only be directly aware of its own contents. Ideas are mental representations of entities.[15] So how does the human mind arrive at the idea of God, and identify what the characteristics of such a God might be? Having insisted that "God has given us no innate *Ideas* of himself," how does this idea come about in the human mind? And how might this idea be distinguished from fictional or imaginary ideas? "Where is the head that has no *Chimeras* in it?"[16] How, then, might such an imaginary chimera be distinguished from God, using Locke's methodology?

It is to Locke's credit that he engages with this question in some detail, even if the answer he provides leaves his readers tantalizingly unpersuaded. Locke lays down the following principle as axiomatic: "We have the Knowledge of

---

[12] John Locke, *An Essay Concerning Human Understanding*, edited by P. H. Nidditch. Oxford: Clarendon Press, 1975, IV.iv.2; 563.28–30.

[13] Ibid, II.i.2; 104.15–20.

[14] Ibid, IV.iv.3; 563.27–8.

[15] Ibid, IV.xxi.4. This does not mean, of course, that *all* ideas are to be thought of as representations. Locke himself, for example, clearly insists that "archetypes" (complex ideas of non-substantial entities, such as the idea of a triangle) are not necessarily representations of the external world: see *Essay* IV.iv.5.

[16] Ibid, IV.x.1; 619.4.

our own Existence by Intuition; of the *Existence of God* by Demonstration; and of other Things by Perception."[17] In view of the importance of this brief statement, we may explore it further before focusing on Locke's approach to God.

Perception is, for Locke, "the first step and degree towards Knowledge, and the Inlet of all the Materials of it."[18] It is the means by which the human mind reflects upon the complexities of sensory experience, and begins to disentangle and reassemble its components. A full account of Locke's epistemology would deal with how such ideas as color, shape, taste, and movement are constructed. Locke offers a sophisticated explanation of how the human mind is able to reduce complex sensations to simple elements, and to construct new, complex ideas from these elements.[19]

It is quite clear that Locke does not regard "God" as a simple idea, but as the outcome of a process of reflection on the relationship of a series of ideas, accumulated by the human mind in the course of its encounter with the world. Having accumulated ideas, the question now arises of how the human mind correlates them by a process of juxtaposition and comparison.[20] Locke identifies two such methods of correlation: intuition (by which the relationship between two ideas is immediately apparent: a triangle is not a square) and demonstration (in which the mind has recourse to intermediate ideas to establish the relationship between them). The relationship between these "degrees of knowledge" can be summarized as follows:[21]

> Sometimes the Mind perceives the Agreement or Disagreement of two *Ideas* immediately by themselves, without the intervention of any other: And this, I think, we may call *intuitive Knowledge*.

Yet where demonstrative knowledge is concerned, Locke holds that a series of intervening or intermediate ideas must be constructed, in order to establish a bridge or connection between those ideas that are known, and those that are to be inferred from them. This means that ideas arrived at in this manner have a lesser degree of probability than those derived from intuition. "This Knowledge by intervening Proofs, though it be certain, yet the evidence of it is *not* altogether *so clear* and bright, nor the assent so ready, as in *intuitive* Knowledge."[22]

---

[17] Ibid, IX.i.2; 618.17–19.

[18] Ibid, II.ix.15; 149.3–4.

[19] Ibid, II.ii.1–30.

[20] Ibid, IV.ii.1–8.

[21] Ibid, IV.ii.1; 530.28 – 531.2.

[22] Ibid, IV.ii.4; 532.26–8. For comment on the varying degrees of certainty of such types of knowledge, see Wolterstorff, *John Locke and the Ethics of Belief*, 56–8.

A recognition of the limits of human knowledge is therefore fundamental to Locke's empirical approach to valid human knowledge. Since knowledge arises from ideas, it follows:[23]

1 That we can have knowledge only to the extent that we have ideas.
2 That we cannot have knowledge beyond our perception of the agreement or disagreement of those ideas.

After weighing up the implications of these statements, Locke concludes that "the extent of our Knowledge comes not only short of the reality of Things, but even of the extent of our own *Ideas*."[24]

Locke therefore regards the idea of God as not arising directly from the human mind's analysis (or "decomposition") of its sensory perceptions, but by reflecting on the ideas that arise from such a process of analysis. Let us return to Locke's basic assertion: "We have the Knowledge of *our own Existence* by Intuition; of the *Existence of God* by Demonstration; and of other Things by Perception."[25] So how does this lead to a knowledge of God's existence, and, more specifically, an understanding of God's nature?

The first point is resolved as follows. Since we know intuitively that we exist as thinking beings, and since nothing can be made to exist except by something else that exists in itself, while exceeding anything that it has created, it follows that there must exist, from all eternity, an all-powerful being, which is usually called "God." Setting this out more fully, we may begin by noting Locke's emphasis on the human capacity to think – something that cannot be accounted for on the basis of the material elements from which humanity is constituted.[26] The human capacity to think requires explanation.[27]

> To shew therefore that we are capable of *knowing*, i.e., *being certain that there is a GOD*, and how we may come by this certainty, I think that we need go no further than our selves, and that undoubted knowledge we have of our own Existence.

This knowledge of our own existence thus generates an additional idea – that of God as the "source and original" of power. Since matter is inert, the human capacity to think cannot be explained by asserting the eternity of unthinking matter. It is necessary to propose the existence of a thinking, creative Being

---

[23] Locke, *Essay*, IV.iii.1–2; 538.25 – 539.2.
[24] Ibid, IV.iii.6; 539.31–3.
[25] Ibid, IX.i.2; 618.17–19.
[26] It may be noted here that Locke frequently asserted that atheism (as defended by Thomas Hobbes) amounted to the supposition that matter is itself eternal.
[27] Ibid, IX.x.1; 619.20–3.

from all eternity. "This discovery of the necessary Existence of an eternal Mind does sufficiently lead us into the Knowledge of God."[28]

It is immediately evident that Locke's arguments for the existence of God follow the traditional lines of the cosmological argument. The best explanation of what may be observed is a rational, eternal, creator God:[29]

> From the Consideration of our selves, and what we infallibly find in our own Constitutions, our Reason leads us to the Knowledge of this certain and evident Truth, that *there is an eternal, most powerful, and most knowing Being*; which whether any one will please to call *God*, it matters not. The thing is evident, and from this *Idea* duly considered, will easily be deduced all those other Attributes which we ought to ascribe to this eternal Being.

Yet this does not mean that this God is an idea directly derived from experience; it is a complex idea, arrived at through a process of reflection on what existing ideas imply. We have no direct experience of God, in the way in which we experience "redness" or "an apple." Experience itself does not generate the idea of God, which is the outcome of reflection on what is perceived.

Turning to the nature of God, we find that Locke adopts a strategy of extrapolation from the known. God is characterized by the projection to infinity of those human attributes and qualities that are to be affirmed:[30]

> If we examine the idea of the incomprehensible supreme Being, we shall find, that we come by it the same way; and that the complex *Ideas* we have both of God, and separate Spirits, are made up of the simple *Ideas* we receive from *Reflection*; v.g., having from what we experiment in our selves, got the *Ideas* of Existence and Duration; of Knowledge and Power; of Pleasure and Happiness; and of several other Qualities and Powers, which it is better to have, than to be without; when we would frame an *Idea* the most suitable we can to the supreme Being, we enlarge every one of these with our *Idea* of Infinity; and so putting them together, make our complex *Idea of God*.

We see here the contours of a classic approach to natural theology, which inspired and undergirded two centuries of English explorations of the idea. God is not known directly; the existence and attributes of God are to be inferred from active human reflection on what is observed in the external world. The notion of God is thus actively constructed as an explanation of what the observer sees.

---

28 Ibid, IX.x.12; 615.7–8.
29 Ibid, IX.x.6; 621.4–10.
30 Ibid, II.xxiii.33; 314.25–35.

Locke's approach is of great historical interest. Yet it will be clear that Locke's concept of experience makes it difficult to deal with social realities such as the state or church. Locke himself had views on both these social realities, as is clear from his *Letters on Toleration*.[31] Yet neither can really be said to come within the scope of his philosophical method.

With this point in mind, we may turn to consider John Dewey. Dewey's early writings are characterized by a distaste for philosophies of experience which are atomistic, abstract, or reductionist. Although he is particularly critical of the atomizing tendencies of British empiricism – such as Locke – he is equally critical of the Hegelian project's abortive attempt to arrive at the concrete individual through the abstract universal. In his early article "The New Psychology" (1884), Dewey argued that the irreducible complexity of human experience was perhaps best preserved and transmitted by art, rather than philosophy or science, precisely because of the scientific tendency to dissect it, breaking it down into its component parts, rather than conserve its integrity. Instead of "preserving the mystery" or "saving the phenomena" – to note two particularly luminous theological and philosophical themes – such approaches merely reduced the particular to the abstractions of logic:[32]

That rich and colored experience, never the same in two nations, in two individuals, in two moments of the same life – whose thoughts, desires, fears and hopes have furnished the material for the ever-developing literature of the ages, for a Homer and a Chaucer, a Sophocles and a Shakespeare, for the unwritten comedies and tragedies of daily life – was neatly and carefully dissected, its parts labeled and stowed away in their pigeon-holes, the inventory taken, and the whole stamped with the stamp of *un fait accompli*.

As Dewey's project developed, we see an increasing emphasis on the need to broaden the concept of "experience," beyond the mere categories of cognitive understanding, to embrace the categories of culture as much as of nature.

Dewey's most significant analysis of the empirical method is his *Experience and Nature*, based on lectures delivered in 1925. For Dewey, experience represents the starting point of authentic philosophical reflection. We begin from experience, and as a result of the process of reflection on that experience, are enabled to return to that experience, and appreciate it with new depth and insight. Dewey makes this point as follows. He begins by noting the basics of

---

[31] See, for example, Mario Montuori, *John Locke on Toleration and the Unity of God*. Amsterdam: J. C. Gieben, 1983; Richard Vernon, *The Career of Toleration: John Locke, Jonas Proast, and After.* Montreal/London: McGill-Queen's University Press, 1997.

[32] John Dewey, "The New Psychology." *Andover Review* 2 (1884): 278–89.

any empirical method: "the subject matter of primary experience sets the problems and furnishes the first data of the reflection which constructs the secondary objects." These secondary objects "*explain* the primary objects, they enable us to grasp them with *understanding*, instead of just having sense-contact with them."[33]

This understanding enables a new depth of engagement with the natural world. In view of the importance of Dewey's analysis at this point, we should hear him at length, as he sets out the foundation of his enhanced encounter with experience:[34]

> [The secondary objects] define or lay out a path by which return to experienced things is of such a sort that the meaning, the significant content, of what is experienced gains an enriched and expanded force because of the path or method by which it was reached. Directly, in immediate contact it may be just what it was before – hard, colored, odorous, etc. But when the secondary objects, the refined objects, are employed as a method or road for coming at them, these qualities cease to be isolated details; they get the meaning contained in a whole system of related objects; they are rendered continuous with the rest of nature and take on the import of the things they are now seen to be continuous with.

Dewey's point is that an atomistic, abstract account of the world can be avoided; instead, the empirical method can lead to a holistic account of reality, in which theory acts as a guide to its interpretation and appreciation.

An authentic empirical method is therefore grounded in experience, but allows us to revisit that experience with a new insight, intensity, and sense of wonder. Dewey thus proposes a "first-rate test of the value of any philosophy" as follows: "does it end in conclusions which, when they are referred back to ordinary life-experiences and their predicaments, render them more significant, more luminous to us, and make our dealings with them more fruitful?"[35] An inadequate understanding of experience "is a source of oppression to the heart and paralysis to imagination."[36] Dewey thus stresses that the word "experience" is complex, embracing subject and object, act and material.[37] Dewey critiques previous approaches to experience, noting that these tended to emphasize, and occasionally be reduced to, the process of "experiencing," excluding *what* was actually being experienced.[38]

---

[33] John Dewey, *Experience and Nature*, 2nd edn. New York: Dover, 1958, 4–5.
[34] Ibid, 5.
[35] Ibid, 7.
[36] Ibid, 11.
[37] Ibid, 8.
[38] Ibid, 16–17.

Dewey thus extends the notion of what may be investigated empirically far beyond the somewhat narrow confines of the British empirical tradition, especially as it is found in Locke. The category of "experience" is extended, to the point where the word "culture" seems a more appropriate designation. Experience is just too complex, too variegated, too dense, to be comprehended on the basis of an inadequate conception of the empirical method. Faced with this difficulty, there is an inevitable tendency to truncate experience, to make it more amenable to analysis:[39]

> In reality, the account given concerns only a selected portion of the actual experience, namely that part which defines the act of experiencing, to the deliberate omission, *for the purpose of the inquiry in hand*, of *what is experienced*.

Too often, Dewey suggests, a preconceived or predetermined notion of what properly constitutes "experience'" is allowed to determine the outcome of the empirical method. Yet for Dewey, the notion of "experience" cannot be limited and degraded in this manner. It involves drawing "an arbitrary line between nature and experience";[40] it involves prejudging and predetermining what may be "experienced" in a manner which supposes that we must reflect on the world before we experience that world.

Dewey's approach immediately overcomes much of the Lockean aporia, opening the way to an empirical engagement with a far more generously defined realm of experience, embracing nature and culture – intellectual domains that had often been bifurcated, not in order to *clarify*, but in order to *separate*. That process is continued by John Searle, who insists upon the reality of social realities, both as entities that shape our world and as entities that may be investigated by the empirical method. In his important essay *The Construction of Social Reality*, Searle stresses that social realities cannot be dismissed as "constructions" without a basis in reality in the observable world. While being perfectly prepared to concede that the "fundamental features of that world are as described by physics, chemistry and the other natural sciences," Searle insists that we should accept the existence of phenomena within that world which are *not* physical or chemical, belonging rather to the realm of *social* reality:[41]

> How can there be an objective world of money, property, marriage, governments, elections, football matches, cocktail parties and law-courts in a world that consists

---

[39] Ibid, 17–18; emphasis in original.
[40] Ibid, 21.
[41] John R. Searle, *The Construction of Social Reality*. London: Allen Lane, 1995, 1. See further his earlier work, *The Rediscovery of the Mind*. Cambridge, MA: MIT Press, 1992.

entirely of physical particles in fields of force, and in which some of these particles are organized into systems that are conscious biological beasts, such as ourselves?

Searle's point is that physics concerns itself with one particular stratum of the real world; it does not – indeed, it cannot – exclude there being other levels which demand different approaches and levels of explanation.

The use of "social constructions" in the natural and social sciences, contrary to some postmodern interpretations, is not to be understood as an arbitrary determination or the pure invention of ideas on the basis of the free choice of the individual thinker or a community of discourse. The development of such social constructs as "race" or "intelligence" is empirically based, and represents a legitimate and warranted means of gaining a tighter grasp on the reality being studied. It is to be seen as a principled exercise in attempting to understand the world as best as possible, and to develop for this purpose whatever tools or conceptualities are best suited to the tasks of the individual natural science in question, and the level of reality it engages. Indeed, as I argue consistently throughout A Scientific Theology, a realist approach to the world is not called into question through the recognition of socially constructed aspects of the explanations offered by the natural sciences.[42] Searle rightly stresses that a legitimate and necessary distinction is to be made between "brute facts" and "social facts" – but both categories are still *real*.

The church may therefore be regarded as a "social fact" – an aspect of the world which is accessible to a properly conceived empiricist methodology, and which can therefore function as the starting point for a scientific dogmatics. But why choose to start there?

The Church as an Empirical Social Reality

A scientific dogmatics, here understood as the constructive application of the method developed in the three volumes of A Scientific Theology, takes as its starting point the observation that there exists a complex, variegated entity within the world called "the church," which has certain observable character-istics that demand explanation and representation. The empirical reality (or, perhaps better, realities) that self-designates as "church" includes, as part of its observable characteristics, certain habits, beliefs, and practices which reflect and embody an understanding of its distinctive identity and purpose.[43] It is the

---

[42] See A Scientific Theology 2: Reality, xiii–xv.

[43] John Milbank's notion of theology as "explicating Christian practice" should be noted here: see John Milbank, " 'Postmodern Critical Augustinianism': A Short *Summa*

task of systematic theology to bring this entire complex of practices – verbal and non-verbal, imaginative, ethical, devotional, and reflective – which embody the church's identity to the level of conscious articulation, and explore the inner logic that holds together its beliefs and practices, habits and acts. Ecclesiology is fundamentally self-reflection within the Christian community upon that community's origins, identity, and mission.

At first sight, this might seem to reduce theology to descriptive sociology. It is an understandable, though quite fallacious, judgment. I have no intention of reducing ecclesiology to sociology, an error that I regard as being comparable to reducing theology to anthropology. However, this does *not* mean that we can overlook the fact that the church is a social reality, any more than we can ignore the fact that the human beings who theologize do so using human conceptualities and means of reflection that are, at least in part, open to anthropological analysis. We do not cease to be human beings when doing theology, after all. And nor does the church cease to be a social reality, whatever else it may be.

Throughout the three volumes of *A Scientific Theology*, I made regular reference to "the Christian tradition," developing the general line of argument found in Alasdair MacIntyre about the critical role of traditions in mediating frameworks of rationality. Yet critical readers will have noted that this notion of the Christian tradition was articulated in rather generalized terms, which failed to take account of the fact that this tradition is not some abstract set of ideas, vaguely floating around like pollen in a gentle, directionless, intellectual breeze, but is institutionally embodied in the church.

This does not necessarily imply an institutional ecclesiology, such as that set out with such vigor at the First Vatican Council, which contrasts so sharply with the ecclesiological minimalism of so much modern Protestantism. It simply notes the inescapable, empirical observation that Christian theology cannot ignore – that Christian ideas are mediated within the flux of history by the Christian church. Indeed, on certain Protestant readings of the central ecclesiological issues, to mediate authentically Christian ideas, such as the promises of God, in word and sacrament, is to be a Christian church.

Consider this question: how is Christianity encountered in the world? Through reading the Bible? But the Bible is the creation of the church, intended to preserve both the foundational narratives of the Christian faith and their correct interpretation. It cannot be regarded as a text that fell from heaven. Nor can the critical role of the Christian community in interpreting that text be

---

in Forty-Two Responses to Unasked Questions." *Modern Theology* 7 (1991): 225–37. There are important parallels here with both Alasdair MacIntyre and Charles Taylor – see, for example, Charles Taylor, *Sources of the Self: The Making of the Modern Identity*. Cambridge, MA: Harvard University Press, 1989, 204.

marginalized. Through preaching? Through Christian literature? Through Christian witness? The list might go on, but the point remains the same – that Christianity is encountered in history through the church, whether directly or indirectly. The manifestation of the Christian God in history both constitutes the community of faith and is in turn proclaimed by that community. As John Webster points out:[44]

> This manifestation does not simply take the form of an announcement. As the manifestation of God's purpose for his creatures, it is limitlessly potent and creative; it generates an assembly, a social space (we might even say a polity and a culture). In that space, the converting power of the gospel becomes visible in creaturely relations and actions. That visible form is not a straightforward natural quantity, but is possessed of a special visibility, created by Christ and Spirit and so perceptible only at their behest. Yet there is a form of creaturely assembly to which the gospel necessarily gives rise, and that form is the communion of saints.

The most systematic attempt to subvert any role for the church in finding God was the natural theology tradition, on which we have reflected extensively elsewhere in this volume. That tradition is ultimately incapable of disclosing God without presupposing God, either through cultural memories inherited from the church or a set of assumptions borrowed from the Christian community of faith. Where nature demands to be interpreted by its observers, the church proclaims its right to interpret itself and to be recognized as a valid standpoint from which reality – including nature – may be encountered, explained, and represented.

The church is thus the observatory; nature is what is observed through the prisms and lenses of that specific observatory – and is thus to be seen, from this specific, tradition-mediated perspective, as God's creation, and hence as a pointer to the Christian God. Without the trinitarian hermeneutical apparatus that is distinctive to the Christian faith,[45] nature cannot legitimately lead us – or be assisted to lead us – to the "God and Father of our Lord Jesus Christ" (2 Corinthians 1:3; 1 Peter 1:3). The conclusion of an appeal to nature for knowledge of God is already embedded in the structures of the argument that finds that God in the natural world.

---

[44] John B. Webster, "On Evangelical Ecclesiology." *Ecclesiology* 1 (2004): 9–35, quote at 10.

[45] One of the best accounts of this aspect of the doctrine of creation is found in Robert Jenson. See Colin S. Gunton, "Creation and Mediation in the Theology of Robert W. Jenson: An Encounter and a Convergence." In *Trinity, Time, and Church: A Response to the Theology of Robert Jenson*, edited by Colin Gunton, 80–93. Grand Rapids, MI: Eerdmans, 2000.

The central question of the *identity* of the church must be answered through engaging with the *phenomenon* of the church, as a living social reality. The church cannot be reduced to any of its many levels – such as its ideas, actions, or values. It is a complex, multilayered social reality, each stratum of which plays a role in shaping its identity and function. Which of those strata is foremost in its public self-presentation or its internal self-definition at any given point is often determined by historical contingencies, rather than anything bearing any obvious semblance to theological consistency.[46] The task of any theology is to identify the *phenomena*, prior to their interpretation and any form of theological interpretation which amounts to prescriptive normalization.

On engaging with the social reality of the church, it becomes clear that it designates a stratified entity, with its identity and function coded at different levels. None of these levels can be identified with ease as taking epistemological or theological priority; they are all part of an interconnected web of identity. Although we can distinguish these levels for the sake of clarity, as a means of aiding conceptual analysis, it must be stressed that they cannot be isolated in this manner in the living world. They are interconnected, bonded together in a complex and dynamic manner which means that one must always be discussed in terms of others. The word "church" thus denotes an interactive system, not an aggregate of individual elements. In what follows, we shall explore some of these levels, and comment briefly on their significance.

(1) Perhaps the most obvious of levels is that of the church as a physical structure – a building. Whatever the term "church" ultimately designates, it clearly must embrace these tactile footprints in the sand of human culture. Yet it rapidly becomes clear that the structure of the building reveals something of its purpose. Perhaps most obviously, the building is a place of assembly – the occasional physical habitation of the people of God. The structure of the building has much to say about the beliefs and values of that community. Many of the great churches of the Middle Ages were cross-shaped, so that their architecture expressed the central place of the cross of Christ in the life of the community of faith. Certain styles of church architecture – particularly Gothic and Baroque – represented attempts to use the structure of church buildings to reinforce certain central Christian beliefs, or to aid in the vital process of visualization and actualization. For example, Gothic cathedrals generated a sense of spaciousness through the creative use of height and light, thus generating and sustaining a

---

[46] The history of early Christian communities is especially luminous in this respect, as an initial concern for personal and corporate holiness gave way to a pressing concern for doctrinal purity. For some valuable reflections on what it meant to be a "Christian church" in this formative period, see Rowan Williams, *Why Study the Past? The Quest for the Historical Church*. London: Darton, Longman, & Todd, 2005, 32–59.

sense of the presence of God and heaven on earth.[47] Stained glass windows were used to assist with the visualization of central gospel narratives, and inscriptions to reinforce the community's understanding of its purpose in meeting together, and the place of the church in the greater order of things.

(2) Following on from this, the church may be thought of as a social structure – a network of relationships, often described in terms of its officers (such as bishops) and authority structures (councils, synods, and so forth).[48] These can be argued to be intrinsic to the gospel, not imposed upon it from without.[49] The identity of these structures is often closely linked with specific functions, most notably the preservation of the identity of the church. As Irenaeus of Lyons emphasized in the second century, such institutional elements were an essential means of securing the faithful transmission and embodiment of the ideas and values of the Christian communities.[50] It is important to note that while they were critical of many aspects of existing ecclesiastical institutions, which they regarded as having been corrupted through dubious historical precedents, the Protestant reformers of the sixteenth century were fully aware of the importance of institutions in this process of transmission, and developed modifications of existing structures which they believed were more consonant with scripture.[51]

(3) Perhaps more fundamentally, the church is a community, a group of people, with a distinct shared identity which transcends the identity of its

---

[47] See the essay of Christoph Markschies, *Gibt es eine "Theologie der gotischen Kathedrale"? nochmals: Suger von Saint-Denis und Sankt Dionys vom Areopag*. Heidelberg: Universitätsverlag C. Winter, 1995.

[48] There are some important reflections on the theological importance of such structures in *Lumen Gentium*. For an excellent analysis, see Herwi Rikhof, *The Concept of Church: A Methodological Inquiry into the Use of Metaphors in Ecclesiology*. London: Sheed & Ward, 1981.

[49] See especially the arguments of John B. Webster, "The Self-Organizing Power of the Gospel of Christ: Episcopacy and Community Formation." In *Community Formation in the Early Church and the Church Today*, edited by R. Longenecker, 179–93. Peabody, MA: Hendriksen, 2002.

[50] Kenneth E. Kirk, ed., *The Apostolic Ministry: Essays on the History and the Doctrine of Episcopacy*. London: Hodder & Stoughton, 1946; Gregory Baum and Andrew M. Greeley, *The Church as Institution*. London: Burns & Oates, 1974.

[51] See John M. Tonkin, *The Church and the Secular Order in Reformation Thought*. New York: Columbia University Press, 1971; Gillian R. Evans, *Problems of Authority in the Reformation Debates*. Cambridge: Cambridge University Press, 1992. The specific forms of institutions are considered in works such as Pieter Coertzen, "Presbyterial Church Government: Ius Divinum, Ius Ecclesiasticum, or Ius Humanum?" In *Calvin, Erbe und Auftrag: Festschrift für Wilhelm Neuser zu seinem 65. Geburtstag*, edited by W. van 't Spijker, 329–42. Kampen: Kok, 1991.

individual members, without negating it.[52] The community gathers together to recall, celebrate, and affirm its shared faith through the public and private reading of scripture, and the liturgical commemoration of both the foundational events of its faith, and their perceived significance. Of particular importance is the manner in which Christian communities came to be differentiated from Jewish communities, which involves perceptions on both sides of this growing divide concerning the distinctive identities of the two communities.[53] While this aspect of the church's identity is amenable, in part, to sociological analysis, this does not for one moment mean that it can be "explained" on this basis. This level of the church's identity is open to being explored using sociological categories – but there are serious limitations to how far that process can be taken. Nor does it mean, as some writers in the postliberal school seem to believe, that we can treat the church simply as a sociolinguistic community, with a distinctive language which can be analyzed in isolation from other levels of its identity.

(4) The church is distinguished by its ideas and the narratives which embody them. The role of Creeds should be noted here, both as a means of defining membership of Christian communities, as much as articulating and communicating their ideas.[54] The retelling of the narrative of faith in the eucharistic celebration should also be noted here, as should the strongly narrative structure of many biblical passages.

(5) The Christian community is distinguished by its decision to orientate its life and action around scripture. While Christianity is not a textual religion in the manner that Islam is, the central role of the Christian Bible in corporate worship, preaching, personal devotion, and individual study must be recognized. The deliberate, purposeful decision to submit to the authority of this text – whether directly, or through the mediated authority of the community – is a unique feature of the Christian church.

(6) The community of faith is distinguished by its practices – perhaps most notably, through the recollection of the foundational events of faith in the

---

[52] For the important idea that the church is fundamentally a "polity," see Robert W. Jenson, *Systematic Theology*, 2 vols. New York: Oxford University Press, 1997–9, Vol. 2, 189–210. This approach is explored by David S. Yeago, "The Church as Polity? The Lutheran Context of Robert W. Jenson's Ecclesiology." In *Trinity, Time, and Church: A Response to the Theology of Robert Jenson*, edited by Colin Gunton, 201–37. Grand Rapids, MI: Eerdmans, 2000.
[53] N. T. Wright, *The New Testament and the People of God*. Minneapolis: Fortress, 1992, 447–52.
[54] On which see J. N. D. Kelly, *Early Christian Creeds*, 3rd edn. New York: Longman, 1981.

proclamation and celebration of the death and resurrection of Christ.[55] Others can be added – baptism, marriage, funerals – each of which reflects certain quite distinctive ideas and values of the church. As Hauerwas has rightly pointed out throughout his career, the sacraments are of crucial importance to the public manifestation of the gospel. "The story of Jesus is not simply one that is told; it must be enacted."[56] Alasdair MacIntyre's notion of "social practices" is also of considerable importance here,[57] not least because of its integration within his tradition-based approach to rationality and ethics as a whole. While it would be easy to make such practices the foundation of a means of teaching theology,[58] they are inadequate in themselves to serve as the foundation of a systematic theology, precisely because they represent only part of a greater whole.

(7) The community of faith *witnesses* to what it is. This point has been emphasized by Stanley Hauerwas throughout his career.[59] The church is a community, a *polis*, a distinctive people shaped by the narrative of God, and capable of bearing and enacting this story – an enactment which takes place sacramentally and morally.[60] The church is the "faithful manifestation" of this embodiment of God's narrative in the world; as a result, "the church does not have a social ethic; the church is a social ethic."[61] In its enactment of this story, the church can be said to witness – in many ways, and at many levels – to this divine narrative.[62] To put this point pithily: *ontology determines manifestation.*

---

[55] For an elaboration of this point, see Kathryn Tanner, "Theological Reflection and Christian Practices." In *Practicing Theology: Beliefs and Practices in Christian Life*, edited by Miroslav Volf and Dorothy C. Bass, 228–42. Grand Rapids, MI: Eerdmans, 2002.

[56] Stanley Hauerwas, *The Peaceable Kingdom: A Primer in Christian Ethics*. Notre Dame, IN: University of Notre Dame Press, 1983, 107.

[57] For the notion, see Alasdair MacIntyre, *After Virtue*. London: Duckworth, 1985, 187–8.

[58] See, for example, Reinhard Hütter, *Suffering Divine Things: Theology as Church Practice*. Grand Rapids, MI: Eerdmans, 2000. See also Miroslav Volf, "Theology for a Way of Life." In *Practicing Theology: Beliefs and Practices in Christian Life*, edited by Miroslav Volf and Dorothy C. Bass, 245–63. Grand Rapids, MI: Eerdmans, 2002.

[59] It is a dominant theme in his recent Gifford Lectures. See Stanley Hauerwas, *With the Grain of the Universe: The Church's Witness and Natural Theology*. London: SCM Press, 2002.

[60] For Hauerwas on this point, see Arne Rasmusson, *The Church as Polis: From Political Theology to Theological Politics as Exemplified by Jürgen Moltmann and Stanley Hauerwas*. Lund: Lund University Press, 1994, especially 190–351.

[61] Hauerwas, *The Peaceable Kingdom*, 99.

[62] Stanley Hauerwas, *A Community of Character*. Notre Dame, IN: University of Notre Dame Press, 1981, 105.

The command to witness is not based on the assumption that we are in possession of a universal truth which others must also "implicitly" possess or have sinfully rejected. If such a truth existed, we would not be called upon to be witnesses, but philosophers. Rather, the command to be a witness is based upon the presupposition that we only come to the truth through the process of being confronted by the truth.

Other levels of ecclesial identity could easily be added – for example, in relation to the use of liturgy,[63] and distinctive Christian symbols, such as the cross.[64] My concern in this essay, however, is not to bring together a collection of such levels of church existence, as if I were a happy collector of *Lepidoptera*, scouring the Oxfordshire countryside for new specimens to augment an already tediously large accumulation. What is rather more important is the greater truth that underlies the multi-layered social reality that we call "the church." The point is that *this is where theology begins – by encountering this social entity, either directly or in its socially, textually, or verbally extended forms.*

Stanley Hauerwas on Seeing the Church

As hinted earlier, one of the most significant recent stimuli to reflection on the importance of the church to Christian theology and ethics is found in the writings of Stanley Hauerwas.[65] One of the most significant themes within Hauerwas' theological project is his explicit recognition that treating Christianity simply as a set of ideas leads to a serious distortion of its character.[66] Rather, it is to be seen as a distinctive way of life, made possible by the gracious action of the Holy Spirit, which orients its adherents to the Father through Jesus Christ. Even as early as 1971, Hauerwas had realized the importance of acting within a world which was accessible to the senses – a world that could be seen. In an important critique of "situation ethics," Hauerwas appropriated Iris Murdoch's observation that we can act only in a world that we can see.[67] Beginning from this point – the empirical

---

[63] Geoffrey Wainwright, *Doxology: The Praise of God in Worship, Doctrine and Life*. New York: Oxford University Press, 1980.

[64] On which see the substantial body of work produced by Erich Dinkler, gathered together as Erich Dinkler, *Signum Crucis: Aufsätze zum Neuen Testament und zur christlichen Archäologie*. Tübingen: Mohr, 1967.

[65] For some useful reflections, see Robert W. Jenson, "The Hauerwas Project." *Modern Theology* 8 (1992): 285–95.

[66] There is a particularly good discussion of this in Stanley Hauerwas, *Sanctify Them in the Truth: Holiness Exemplified*. Edinburgh: T&T Clark, 1998.

[67] Iris Murdoch, "Vision and Choice in Morality." In *Christian Ethics and Contemporary Philosophy*, edited by Ian T. Ramsey, 195–218. London: SCM Press, 1966.

foundations of which will be obvious – Hauerwas argues that we need a framework or lens through which we may "see" the world of human behavior.[68] This, he insists, is provided by sustained, detailed, extended reflection on the Christian narrative:[69]

> The primary task of Christian ethics involves an attempt to help us see. For we can only act within the world we can see, and we can only see the world rightly by being trained to see. We do not come to see just by looking, but by disciplined skills developed through initiation into a narrative.

A scientific theology demands that we see the world in a certain way, as a certain thing. Or to put this more pointedly, "the church serves the world by giving the world the means to see itself truthfully."[70]

This naturally raises the question of how we learn to see it in such a way. How is this habit acquired? And how is it validated? For Hauerwas, the answer lies in being initiated into a narrative – that of the Christian tradition, which is embodied, embedded, and transmitted by the church. Rowan Williams expresses much the same idea when he speaks of a process by which "the particularities of experience are brought slowly into interconnection with the communally confessed truth of God's nature and activity."[71] It is here that any Christian theology worthy of that name must begin, and from here that it must gain its ideational bearings. Ecclesiology therefore follows on from the observable existence of the church, including its witness to its identity and function. An already existing church begins to give thought to its identity, role, and function on the basis of its many levels of existence.[72] The church becomes what it already is, by actualizing in its thought and action what it has been called and structured to achieve and to be.

We need to set aside, once and for all, any idea that ecclesiology (critical and constructive reflection on the nature of being a church) precedes the ministry

---

[68] See Stanley Hauerwas, *Vision and Virtue: Essays in Christian Ethical Reflection.* Notre Dame, IN: Fides Publishers, 1974. Hauerwas notes in particular the importance of Julius Kovesi, *Moral Notions.* London: Routledge & Kegan Paul, 1967.

[69] Stanley Hauerwas, "The Demands of a Truthful Story: Ethics and the Pastoral Task." *Chicago Studies* 21 (1982): 59–71, quote at 65–6.

[70] Hauerwas, *The Peaceable Kingdom*, 101–2.

[71] Rowan Williams, "Teaching the Truth." In *Living Tradition: Affirming Catholicism in the Anglican Church,* edited by Jeffrey John, 29–43. London: Darton, Longman, & Todd, 1991, quote at 41.

[72] For a useful review of some of the contemporary concerns, see Bernd Jochen Hilberath, "Forschungsbericht: Schwerpunkte und Tendenzen in der Ekklesiologie." *Theologische Quartalschrift* 181 (2001): 238–46.

and mission of that church. The life of the church is already under way, like a ship at sea, before it begins the task of reflecting on its identity. From the standpoint of already undertaking that ministry and mission, the church pauses to reflect, inquiring how this might be done better, and how it might be done more authentically.

A scientific dogmatics therefore begins with the actuality of the church as a worshipping, witnessing, socially embodied tradition. Theology arises through the church reflecting on its witness, inferring what is contained and transmitted within its many levels of existence. This does not raise any particularly significant difficulties for an empirical theological method, and is entirely consistent with its emphases and distinctive concerns. Insights resulting from a late point in this analytical trajectory can be fed back into earlier points through the iterative procedure described in the previous working paper. The derivation of a trinitarian or christological ecclesiology is entirely legitimate; this does not, however, take place in the initial theological iteration, but at a later stage in the ongoing process of constructive theological reflection.

Hauerwas argues that the church enables us to see things as they really are – to develop the discipline of seeing things for what they really are, through a process of faithful and critical reflection on the embodied Christian narrative, which is in turn grounded in the fact that Christians *inhabit* this tradition. Christians are at one and the same time shaped by this tradition's intellectual, moral, and spiritual contours, and, on the other, resourced by precisely those contours to reexamine, reappraise, and where necessary reconstruct the tradition in an attempt to be faithful to what it is called to be. *Ecclesia reformata, ecclesia semper reformanda!*

Transignification and Transvaluation: The Church and New Ways of Seeing Things

So what new way of "seeing" does this tradition allow? In bringing this working paper to a close some important points may be made. Each requires development and defense. Yet each is an essential element of the process of intellectual reflection and recalibration that we call "Christian theology."

I   The Exploration of Faith

First, the church is responsible for the identification and examination of its own distinct identity and agenda. To do theology is, at the very least, to have a living knowledge of a living faith, not simply as ideas, but as ideas that transform, transfigure, and transvalue. The identification of the core ideas and values of the Christian tradition is the result of the *inhabitation* of that tradition, both in terms of *finding out* and *finding why*. Theology concerns the transfer of intellectual resources from skimming the surface to plumbing the depths of faith. The critical yet constructive exploration of the contours of faith is the starting point of the theological task.

Yet it is not an end in itself. The study of the Christian tradition can easily degenerate into making Christianity a hobby. One studies Christian ideas and the customs of churches out of interest, where others might collect stamps of the British Empire under Queen Victoria, or rural Wessex folk customs at the time of Thomas Hardy. When the study of Christian ideas becomes an end in itself, their entire purpose has been compromised. For what is important is not what they are in themselves, but what they seek to *express*, and what they seek to make possible. George Herbert made this point powerfully in his poem "The Elixir":[73]

> A man that looks on glass,
> On it may stay his eye,
> Or, if he pleaseth, through it pass,
> And then the heav'n espy.

Herbert proposes that we consider a window as an analogy for Christian doctrine. It is an image that is as familiar to us today as it was in Herbert's time. A window can be considered as a work of art in itself, especially if it is decorated with colored panes of glass, or painted illustrations. We can easily focus our attention on it, appreciating the intricacy of its construction, or noticing dust and grime that need to be cleaned away. Yet the window has served its purpose properly only when we look *through* it and see what lies beyond – perhaps one of the exquisite gardens that ornamented the great houses of the early seventeenth century, or a beautiful landscape leading to the mountains in the far distance. If we merely look *at* the window, we miss what lies beyond. Christian theology is only partly about the study of ideas; it is more fundamentally about *what those ideas make possible*.

2 The Identification of the Christian God

As part of its clarification of the identity-giving "deposit of faith," the church receives a particular vision of God, which, though not inconsistent with human reason, nonetheless transcends it. The name of God and the reality of God are

---

[73] For some helpful reflections on Herbert's theology, sadly making little reference to this theologically profound poem, see Elizabeth Clarke, *Theory and Theology in George Herbert's Poetry: "Divinitie and Poesy Met."* Oxford: Clarendon Press, 1997.

not unknown, but are given – not given in the realm of common human experience, but in those acts of divine self-disclosure and self-impartation that the church has learned to call "revelation."[74] The Christological focus and foundation of such a knowledge of God, which is a determinative feature of the Christian tradition, both intellectual and doxological, leads to a trajectory of theological elaboration which is, in the first place, ultimately Chalcedonian, and in the second, trinitarian.[75] These are to be seen as "islands of doctrinal stability" which this process of exploration and clarification identifies and brings to conscious articulation, even though their fundamental themes were implicit from the outset. The order of theological reflection and analysis, put in its simplest possible form, is:

Actuality of church → Christology → Trinity

3   The Transignification of the World

The embodied tradition that we call "the church" makes possible a new way of seeing the world. We *see* things as something – and we come to see the world in a new way on account of faith. "I believe in Christianity as I believe that the Sun has risen – not only because I see it, but because by it, I see everything else."[76] The whole enterprise of natural theology begins within the community of faith, dependent from the outset upon the critical legitimating insights of that faith. Christian theology aims to tell the truth about what it sees – and it sees the world in a specific way: as God's creation, capable of disclosing, within the limits of its capacities, something of the nature and character of its creator. The world takes on a new significance. It has been *transignified.*

---

[74] For important analysis and reflection, see Robert W. Jenson, *The Triune Identity: God According to the Gospel.* Philadelphia: Fortress, 1982, 1–55; Christopher R. Seitz, "Handing over the Name: Christian Reflection on the Divine Name YHWH." In *Trinity, Time, and Church: A Response to the Theology of Robert Jenson,* edited by Colin Gunton, 23–41. Grand Rapids, MI: Eerdmans, 2000.

[75] See especially the superb collection of essays dealing with these themes in Stephen T. Davis, Daniel Kendall, and Gerald O'Collins, eds., *The Trinity: An Interdisciplinary Symposium on the Trinity.* Oxford: Oxford University Press, 2002; Stephen T. Davis, Daniel Kendall, and Gerald O'Collins, eds., *The Incarnation: An Interdisciplinary Symposium on the Incarnation of the Son of God.* Oxford: Oxford University Press, 2004.

[76] C. S. Lewis, "Is Theology Poetry?," in *Essay Collection and Other Short Pieces,* 10–21. London: Harper Collins, 2000, 21.

In his poem "The Elixir," George Herbert used the image of the philosopher's stone to help his readers appreciate the new approach to reality that God brought to human life:[77]

> This is the famous stone
> That turneth all to gold:
> For that which God does touch and own
> Cannot for less be told.

One of the great quests of the Middle Ages was to find a magic formula or tool that would allow base metal to be turned into precious gold. The "philosopher's stone" possessed the ability to transmute lesser things into something precious, and was ardently sought throughout this restless age. Other sources spoke of an "elixir" – a liquid derived from this mysterious stone, which possessed the power to bring about physical and spiritual regeneration.

In using this powerful imagery throughout this poem, Herbert points to the power of the Christian vision of God to transform the way we see things. The world is transmuted from a base metal to something that God "doth touch and own," which cannot be "told" – an old English way of expressing the idea of "reckoned" or "valued" – for anything less.

4   The Transvaluation of Human Existence

The Christian tradition also makes it possible and makes it necessary to see humanity in a new light. Human identity and activity are transvalued. Human acts are not to be seen as self-elicited in order to gain access to the kingdom, but as divinely elicited, as an act of thanksgiving and praise for what God has already done. Admission to the kingdom is not by conformity to its ethical norms, but by transformation through its grace-filled and grace-bestowing narrative of forgiveness, acceptance, and renewal. Once more, George Herbert writes lyrically of this process of transvaluation that results:

> A servant with this clause
> Makes drudgery divine:
> Who sweeps a room as for Thy laws,
> Makes that and th'action fine.

The point that Herbert makes so powerfully is that our idea of what is needed to earn favor with God and maintain the ensuing relationship is assimilated to secular cultural norms; the gospel demands transvaluation of such notions.

---

[77] The importance of alchemy as a source of such symbolism is best appreciated through studies such as Vladimír Karpenko, "Alchemy as *Donum Dei.*" *International Journal for Philosophy of Chemistry* 4 (1998): 63–80.

5   Seeing One's Own Tradition: Ecclesiology

One of the questions that the Christian tradition forces upon us is ultimately reflexive in nature: what understanding of the *bearer* of the Christian tradition does that tradition itself demand? To revert to George Herbert's analogy: what does the church see when the Christian tradition becomes a mirror in which it sees its own face, rather than a window through which it sees the world beyond its bounds? Ecclesiology is a proper part of the theological task of the church, even if it is not its primary focus. Indeed, an inappropriate concern with ecclesiology is tantamount to theological narcissism, a form of morbid introspection with the church's own identity rather than with engagement with the world beyond the bounds of the church. The history of doctrine has much to teach us here, in that ecclesiology only became of major importance once other, more significant questions had been addressed.[78]

Conclusion

This brief essay on the starting point for a scientific dogmatics runs somewhat counter to many contemporary trends in theology – yet it is an approach that I believe to be entirely legitimate in the light of the nature of theological method that I defend in my "scientific theology" project. When linked with the notion of theological iteration, it offers an approach to theology which is firmly grounded in the earthly realities that we inhabit, while entirely capable of ascending upwards in a hermeneutical arc to embrace heights of theological reflection. It now remains to apply this approach, consistently and thoroughly, and see where it takes us on that great pilgrimage of intellectual exploration that we call "theology."

---

[78] Even then, it may be recalled that the Donatist controversy was actually local, reflecting specific sociological questions in Roman North Africa, even if Augustine's theological status ensured they became of wider significance.

Bibliography

Aarsleff, Hans. *From Locke to Saussure: Essays on the Study of Language and Intellectual History.* Minneapolis: University of Minnesota Press, 1982.

Albert, David Z. *Quantum Mechanics and Experience.* Cambridge, MA: Harvard University Press, 1992.

Albert, David Z., and Barry Loewer. "Tails of Schrödinger's Cat." In *Perspectives on Quantum Reality*, edited by R. Clifton, 81–92. Dordrecht: Kluwer, 1996.

Alford, John A. "Jesus the Jouster: The Christ-Knight and Medieval Theories of Atonement in Piers Plowman and the 'Round Table' Sermons." *Yearbook of Langland Studies* 10 (1996): 129–43.

Allott, Robin. "Evolution and Culture: The Missing Link." In *The Darwinian Heritage and Sociobiology*, edited by J. M. G. van der Dennen, D. Smillie, and D. R. Wilson, 67–81. Westport, CT: Praeger, 1999.

Alston, William P. *Perceiving God: The Epistemology of Religious Experience.* Ithaca, NY: Cornell University Press, 1991.

Anderson, Ray S. "Barth and a New Direction for Natural Theology." In *Theology Beyond Christendom: Essays on the Centenary of the Birth of Karl Barth*, edited by John Thompson, 241–66. Allison Park, PA: Pickwick Publications, 1986.

Archer, Margaret, Andrew Collier, and Douglas V. Porpora, eds. *Transcendence: Critical Realism and God.* London: Routledge, 2004.

Arenas, Luis. "Matemáticas, método y *mathesis universalis* en las Regulae de Descartes." *Revista de Filosofía* 8 (1996): 37–61.

Ashley, Kathleen M. "The Guiler Beguiled: Christ and Satan as Theological Tricksters in Medieval Religious Literature." *Criticism* 24 (1982): 126–37.

Assmann, Jan. *Ma'at: Gerechtigkeit und Unsterblichkeit im alten Ägypten.* Munich: C. H. Beck, 2001.

Assmann, Jan, Bernd Janowski, and Michael Welker, eds. *Gerechtigkeit: Richten und Retten in der abendländischen Tradition und ihren altorientalischen Ursprüngen*. Munich: Fink, 1998.

Atkins, Peter. "The Limitless Power of Science." In *Nature's Imagination: The Frontiers of Scientific Vision*, edited by John Cornwell, 122–32. Oxford: Oxford University Press, 1995.

Avital, E., and E. Jablonka. "Social Learning and the Evolution of Behavior." *Animal Behavior* 48 (1994): 1195–9.

Ayers, Michael. *Locke: Epistemology and Ontology*. London: Routledge, 1991.

Baldwin, James M. *Darwin and the Humanities*. Baltimore: Review Publishing, 1909.

Ball, John A. "Memes as Replicators." *Ethology and Sociology* 5 (1984): 145–61.

Barnaby, Wendy. "Evolution of Social Behaviour Patterns in Primates and Man." *Interdisciplinary Science Reviews* 23 (1998): 95–8.

Barth, Karl. *Die christliche Theologie im Entwurf*. Munich: Kaiser Verlag, 1927.

—— *Die kirchliche Dogmatik*. 30 vols, *Studienausgabe*. Zurich: Theologischer Verlag, 1988–99.

—— *Die protestantische Theologie im 19. Jahrhundert: Ihre Vorgeschichte und ihre Geschichte*. 2nd edn. Zurich: Evangelischer Verlag, 1952.

—— *Dogmatik im Grundriß: Vorlesungen gehalten im Sommersemester 1946 an der Universität Bonn*. Zurich: Evangelischer Verlag, 1947.

Battles, Ford Lewis. "God was Accommodating Himself to Human Capacity." *Interpretation* 31 (1977): 19–38.

Bauckham, Richard. *God Crucified: Monotheism and Christology in the New Testament*. Grand Rapids, MI: Eerdmans, 1998.

Beam, Craig Allen. "Gadamer and MacIntyre: Tradition as a Resource of Rationality." *Kinesis* 25 (1998): 15–35.

Beckmann, Klaus M. *Der Begriff der Häresie bei Schleiermacher*. Munich: Kaiser Verlag, 1959.

Bedau, Mark A. "Weak Emergence." In *Philosophical Perspectives: Mind, Causation, and World*, edited by James Tomberlin, 375–99. Oxford: Blackwell, 1997.

Beiser, Frederick C. *The Sovereignty of Reason: The Defense of Rationality in the Early English Enlightenment*. Princeton, NJ: Princeton University Press, 1996.

Benin, Stephen D. *The Footprints of God: Divine Accommodation in Jewish and Christian Thought*. Albany: State University of New York Press, 1993.

Bennett, Jonathan. *Locke, Berkeley, Hume: Central Themes*. Oxford: Oxford University Press, 1977.

Bennett, M. R., and P. M. S. Hacker. *Philosophical Foundations of Neuroscience*. Oxford: Blackwell, 2003.

Berry, R. J. *Neo-Darwinism*. London: Edward Arnold, 1982.

Bhaskar, Roy. *A Realist Theory of Science*. 2nd edn. London: Verso, 1997.

Bienert, Wolfgang A. "Zur Logos-Christologie des Athanasius von Alexandrien in *contra gentes* und *de incarnatione*." In *Papers Presented to the Tenth International Conference on Patristic Studies*, edited by E. A. Livingstone, 402–19. Louvain: Peeters, 1989.

Blackmore, Susan J. *The Meme Machine*. Oxford: Oxford University Press, 1999.

Bloch, Maurice. *How We Think They Think: Anthropological Approaches to Cognition, Memory, and Literacy.* Boulder: Westview, 1998.

—— "A Well-Disposed Social Anthropologist's Problem with Memes." In *Darwinizing Culture: The Status of Memetics as a Science,* edited by Robert Aunger, 189–23. Oxford: Oxford University Press, 2000.

Blomme, Robert. *La Doctrine du péché dans les écoles théologiques de la première moitié du XIIe siècle.* Louvain: Editions J. Duculot, 1958.

Boesch, Christophe. "The Emergence of Cultures Among Wild Chimpanzees." In *Evolution of Social Behaviour Patterns in Primates and Man,* edited by W. G. Runciman, J. Maynard Smith, and R. I. M. Dunbar, 251–68. Oxford: Oxford University Press, 1996.

—— "Three Approaches for Assessing Chimpanzee Culture." In *Reaching into Thought: The Minds of the Great Apes,* edited by A. E. Russon, K. A. Bard, and S. T. Parker, 404–29. New York: Cambridge University Press, 1996.

Bonhoeffer, Dietrich. *Discipleship.* Minneapolis: Fortress, 2001.

Bowler, Peter J. *The Non-Darwinian Revolution: Reinterpreting a Historical Myth.* Baltimore: Johns Hopkins University Press, 1988.

Boyd, Robert D., and Peter J. Richerson. *Culture and the Evolutionary Process.* Chicago: University of Chicago Press, 1985.

—— "Why Culture is Common, but Cultural Evolution is Rare." In *Evolution of Social Behaviour Patterns in Primates and Man,* edited by W. G. Runciman, J. Maynard Smith, and R. I. M. Dunbar, 77–93. Oxford: Oxford University Press, 1996.

—— "Why Does Culture Increase Human Adaptability?" *Ethology and Sociobiology* 16 (1996): 125–43.

—— "Memes: Universal Acid or a Better Mousetrap?" In *Darwinizing Culture: The Status of Memetics as a Science,* edited by Robert Aunger, 143–62. Oxford: Oxford University Press, 2000.

Brown, Hunter. "Alvin Plantinga and Natural Theology." *International Journal for Philosophy of Religion* 30 (1991): 1–19.

Bruce, Steve. *God Is Dead: Secularization in the West.* Oxford: Blackwell, 2002.

Buchdahl, Gerd. "History of Science and Criteria of Choice." In *Minnesota Studies in the Philosophy of Science,* edited by Roger H. Steuwer, 204–30. Minneapolis: University of Minnesota Press, 1970.

Buckley, Michael J. *At the Origins of Modern Atheism.* New Haven, CT: Yale University Press, 1987.

Bultmann, Rudolf. "Is Exegesis Without Presuppositions Possible?" In *The Hermeneutics Reader: Texts of the German Tradition from the Enlightenment to the Present,* edited by Kurt Mueller-Vollmer, 241–8. Oxford: Blackwell, 1986.

Bunge, Mario. "Ten Modes of Individualism – None of Which Works – and Their Alternatives." *Philosophy of the Social Sciences* 30 (2000): 384–406.

Burgio, Alberto, and Antonio A. Santucci, eds. *Gramsci e la rivoluzione passiva.* Rome: Editori Riuniti, 1999.

Burns, J. Patout. "Economy of Salvation: Two Patristic Traditions." *Theological Studies* 37 (1976): 598–619.

Campbell, Donald T. "Blind Variation and Selective Retention in Creative Thought as in Other Knowledge Processes." *Psychological Review* 67 (1960): 380–400.

—— "A General 'Selection Theory' as Implemented in Biological Evolution and in Social Belief-Transmission-With-Modification In Science." *Biology and Philosophy* 3 (1988): 413–63.

Carafiol, Peter. *Transcendent Reason: James Marsh and the Forms of Romantic Thought.* Tallahassee: University Presses of Florida, 1982.

Carnap, Rudolf. *Der logische Aufbau der Welt.* Hamburg: Felix Meiner Verlag, 1998.

Carnell, Corbin Scott. *Bright Shadow of Reality: Spiritual Longing in C. S. Lewis.* Grand Rapids, MI: Eerdmans, 1999.

Carpendale, Jeremy I. M., and Ulrich Miller. "Social Interaction and the Development of Rationality and Morality: An Introduction." In *Social Interaction and the Development of Knowledge,* edited by J. I. M. Carpendale and U. Miller, 1–18. Mahwah, NJ: Lawrence Erlbaum Associates, 2004.

Carrithers, Michael. *Why Humans Have Cultures: Explaining Anthropology and Social Diversity.* Oxford: Oxford University Press, 1996.

Cartwright, Nancy. *How the Laws of Physics Lie.* Oxford: Clarendon Press, 1983.

Cavalli-Sforza, L. L. "Cultural Evolution." *American Zoologist* 26 (1986): 845–55.

Cavalli-Sforza, L. L., and M. W. Feldman. *Cultural Transmission and Evolution: A Quantitative Approach.* Princeton, NJ: Princeton University Press, 1981.

Chadwick, Owen. *From Bossuet to Newman: The Idea of Doctrinal Development.* Cambridge: Cambridge University Press, 1957.

Chaitin, Gregory J. *Information-Theoretic Incompleteness.* Singapore: World Scientific, 1992.

Chapman, Michael. *Constructive Evolution: Origins and Development of Piaget's Thought.* Cambridge: Cambridge University Press, 1988.

Chomsky, Noam. *Knowledge of Language: Its Nature, Origin, and Use.* New York: Praeger, 1986.

Clarke, Elizabeth. *Theory and Theology in George Herbert's Poetry: "Divinitie and Poesy Met."* Oxford: Clarendon Press, 1997.

Clayton, Philip. *Mind and Emergence: From Quantum to Consciousness.* Oxford: Oxford University Press, 2004.

Clemoes, Peter. "King and Creation at the Crucifixion: The Contribution of Native Tradition to *The Dream of the Rood.*" In *Heroes and Heroines in Medieval English Literature,* edited by Leo Carruthers, 31–43. Cambridge: Brewer, 1994.

Cloak, F. T. "Is a Cultural Ethology Possible?" *Human Ecology* 3 (1975): 161–81.

Coertzen, P. "Presbyterial Church Government: Ius Divinum, Ius Ecclesiasticum, or Ius Humanum?" In *Calvin, Erbe und Auftrag: Festschrift für Wilhelm Neuser zu seinem 65. Geburtstag,* edited by W. van 't Spijker, 329–42. Kampen: Kok, 1991.

Coleman, Piers. "Many-Body Physics: Unfinished Revolution." *Annales de l'Institut Henri Poincaré* 4 (2003): 1–22.

Colyer, Elmer M. *How to Read T. F. Torrance: Understanding his Trinitarian and Scientific Theology.* Downers Grove, IL: Intervarsity Press, 2001.

—— *The Promise of Trinitarian Theology: Theologians in Dialogue with T. F. Torrance.* Lanham, MD: Rowman & Littlefield, 2001.

—— "Alister E. McGrath, A Scientific Theology, Volume 1 – Nature." *Pro Ecclesia* 12 (2003): 226–31.

Colyer, Elmer M. "Alister E. McGrath, A Scientific Theology, Volume 2 – Reality." *Pro Ecclesia* 12 (2003): 492–7.

—— "Alister E. McGrath, A Scientific Theology, Volume 3 – Theory." *Pro Ecclesia* 13 (2004): 233–40.

Congar, Yves. "La 'réception' comme réalité ecclésiologique." *Revue des sciences philosophiques et théologiques* 56 (1972): 369–403.

Conradi, Peter J. *The Saint and the Artist: A Study of the Fiction of Iris Murdoch*. 3rd edn. London: Harper Collins, 2001.

Conry, Yvette. *L'Introduction du Darwinisme en France au XIXe siècle*. Paris: Vrin, 1974.

Conte, Rosaria. "Memes Through (Social) Minds." In *Darwinizing Culture: The Status of Memetics as a Science*, edited by Robert Aunger, 83–119. Oxford: Oxford University Press, 2000.

Costigan, Richard F. "Bossuet and the Consensus of the Church." *Theological Studies* 56 (1995): 652–72.

Coveney, Peter, and Roger Highfield. *Frontiers of Complexity: The Search for Order in a Chaotic World*. New York: Fawcett Columbine, 1996.

Crook, Zeba Antonin. "The Synoptic Parables of the Mustard and the Leaven: A Test-Case for the Two-Document, Two-Gospel, and Farrer-Goulder Hypotheses." *Journal for the Study of the New Testament* 78 (2000): 23–48.

Crossan, John Dominic. "Seed Parables of Jesus." *Journal of Biblical Literature* 92 (1973): 244–66.

Darwin, Charles. *The Origin of Species*. Harmondsworth: Penguin, 1968.

Davidson, Luke. "Fragilities of Scientism: Richard Dawkins and the Paranoid Idealization of Science." *Science as Culture* 9 (2000): 167–99.

Davies, Paul. *The Cosmic Blueprint: New Discoveries in Nature's Creative Ability to Order the Universe*. New York: Simon & Schuster, 1988.

Davis, Stephen T., Daniel Kendall, and Gerald O'Collins, eds. *The Trinity: An Interdisciplinary Symposium on the Trinity*. Oxford: Oxford University Press, 2002.

—— eds. *The Incarnation: An Interdisciplinary Symposium on the Incarnation of the Son of God*. Oxford: Oxford University Press, 2004.

Dawkins, Richard. "Replicator Selection and the Extended Phenotype." *Zeitschrift für Tierpsychologie* 47 (1978): 61–76.

—— *The Extended Phenotype: The Gene as the Unit of Selection*. Oxford: Freeman, 1981.

—— "Universal Darwinism." In *Evolution from Molecules to Men*, edited by D. S. Bendall, 403–25. Cambridge: Cambridge University Press, 1983.

—— *The Blind Watchmaker: Why the Evidence of Evolution Reveals a Universe without Design*. London: Longman, 1986.

—— *The Selfish Gene*. 2nd edn. Oxford: Oxford University Press, 1989.

—— *River out of Eden: A Darwinian View of Life*. London: Phoenix, 1995.

—— *Unweaving the Rainbow: Science, Delusion and the Appetite for Wonder*. London: Penguin, 1998.

—— *A Devil's Chaplain*. London: Weidenfeld & Nicolson, 2003.

de Clerk, D. M. "Droits du démon et nécessité de la Rédemption: les écoles de Abélard et de Pierre Lombard." *Recherches de théologie ancienne et médiévale* 14 (1947): 32–64.

Dennen, J. van der, David Smillie, and Daniel R. Wilson, eds. *The Darwinian Heritage and Sociobiology*. Westport, CT: Praeger, 1999.

Depew, David J., and Bruce H. Weber. *Darwinism Evolving: Systems Dynamics and the Genealogy of Natural Selection*. Cambridge, MA: MIT Press, 1996.

Desmond, Adrian J. *The Politics of Evolution: Morphology, Medicine, and Reform in Radical London, Science and Its Conceptual Foundations*. Chicago: University of Chicago Press, 1989.

Deuser, Hermann. "Kritische Notizen zur theologischen Wissenschaftstheorie." *Evangelische Theologie* 36 (1976): 216–25.

Dewey, John. "The New Psychology." *Andover Review* 2 (1884): 278–89.

—— *Experience and Nature*. 2nd edn. New York: Dover, 1958.

Dillon, M. C. *Merleau-Ponty's Ontology*. Bloomington: Indiana University Press, 1988.

Dimas, Panagiotis. "True Belief in the Meno." *Oxford Studies in Ancient Philosophy* 14 (1996): 1–32.

Dinkler, Erich. *Signum crucis: Aufsätze zum Neuen Testament und zur christlichen Archäologie*. Tübingen: Mohr, 1967.

Dulles, Avery. "Faith and Revelation." In *Systematic Theology: Roman Catholic Perspectives*, edited by Francis Schlüssler Fiorenza and John P. Galvin, 89–128. Minneapolis: Augsburg Fortress, 1992.

Dupré, John. *The Disorder of Things: Metaphysical Foundations of the Disunity of Science*. Cambridge, MA: Harvard University Press, 1993.

Durham, William H. *Coevolution: Genes, Culture, and Human Diversity*. Stanford, CA: Stanford University Press, 1991.

Eco, Umberto. *The Limits of Interpretation*. Bloomington: Indiana University Press, 1990.

—— *The Search for the Perfect Language*. Oxford: Blackwell, 1995.

Erlemann, Kurt. *Das Bild Gottes in den synoptischen Gleichnissen*. Stuttgart: Kohlhammer, 1988.

Evans, Gillian R. *Problems of Authority in the Reformation Debates*. Cambridge: Cambridge University Press, 1992.

Fallenstein, Matthias. *Religion als philosophisches Problem: Studien zur Grundlegung der Frage nach der Wahrheit der Religion im religionsphilosophischen Denken von Heinrich Scholz, Europäische Hochschulschriften. Reihe 23, Theologie*. Frankfurt am Main: Lang, 1981.

—— *Religion als philosophisches Problem: Studien zur Grundlegung der Frage nach der Wahrheit der Religion im religionsphilosophischen Denken von Heinrich Scholz*. Frankfurt am Main: Peter Lang, 1981.

Feyerabend, Paul K. "Professor Hartmann's Philosophy of Nature." *Ratio* 5 (1963): 91–106.

Fine, Gail. *Plato on Knowledge and Forms: Selected Essays*. Oxford: Oxford University Press, 2003.

Fisch, Harold. "The Scientist as Priest: A Note on Robert Boyle's Natural Theology." *Isis* 44 (1953): 252–65.

Fitzmyer, Joseph. "Historical Criticism: Its Role in Biblical Interpretation and Church Life." *Theological Studies* 50 (1989): 249–52.

Flieger, Verlyn. *Splintered Light: Logos and Language in Tolkien's World.* Revd. edn. Kent, OH: Kent State University Press, 2002.

Foucault, Michel. *The Order of Things: An Archaeology of the Human Sciences.* New York: Random House, 1970.

Fraassen, Bas van. "The Pragmatics of Explanation." *American Philosophical Quarterly* 14 (1977): 143–50.

Frankenberry, Nancy. "Meland's Empirical Realism and the Appeal to Lived Experience." *American Journal of Theology and Philosophy* 5 (1984): 117–29.

Fretheim, Terence E. *The Suffering of God: An Old Testament Perspective.* Philadelphia: Fortress, 1984.

Galef, Bennett G. "Social Enhancement of Food Preferences in Norway Rats: A Brief Review." In *Social Learning in Animals: The Roots of Culture,* edited by C. Heyes and B. Galef, 49–64. New York: Academic Press, 1996.

Gardeil, A. *Le Donné révélé et la théologie.* 2nd. edn. Paris: Editions du Cerf, 1932.

Gärtner, Bertil. *The Areopagus Speech and Natural Revelation.* Uppsala: Almqvist & Wirksells, 1955.

Geertz, Clifford. "Common Sense as a Cultural System." In *Local Knowledge: Further Essays in Interpretative Anthropology,* edited by Clifford Geertz, 73–93. New York: Basic Books, 1983.

Geisser, Hans. *Glaubenseinheit und Lehrentwicklung bei Johann Adam Möhler.* Göttingen: Vandenhoeck & Ruprecht, 1971.

Georgianna, Linda. *The Economy of Salvation in "The Canterbury Tales."* Lewiston, NY: Edwin Mellen Press, 1990.

Gestrich, Christof. *Neuzeitliches Denken und die Spaltung der dialektischen Theologie: Zur Frage der natürlichen Theologie.* Tübingen: Mohr, 1977.

Glick, Thomas F. *The Comparative Reception of Darwinism.* Austin: University of Texas Press, 1972.

Gnuse, Robert K. *The Dream Theophany of Samuel: Its Structure in Relation to Ancient Near Eastern Dreams and Its Theological Significance.* Lanham, MD: University Press of America, 1984.

Gore, Charles. *The Incarnation of the Son of God.* London: John Murray, 1922.

Gould, Stephen Jay. *Wonderful Life: The Burgess Shale and the Nature of History.* New York: Norton, 1989.

—— *Life's Grandeur: The Spread of Excellence from Plato to Darwin.* London: Jonathan Cape, 1996.

—— *The Structure of Evolutionary Theory.* Cambridge, MA: Belknap, 2002.

Gould, Stephen Jay, and Richard C. Lewontin. "The Spandrels of San Marco and the Panglossian Paradigm: A Critique of the Adaptationist Programme." *Proceedings of the Royal Society of London* B 205 (1979): 581–98.

Graham, T. A. "Constraints and Spandrels in Gould's *Structure of Evolutionary Theory.*" *Biology and Philosophy* 19 (2004): 29–43.

Gramsci, Antonio. *Gli intellettuali e l'organizzazione della cultura.* 6th edn. Milan: Giulio Einaudi Editore, 1955.

Gray, H. H. "Renaissance Humanism: The Pursuit of Eloquence." In *Renaissance Essays*, edited by P. O. Kristeller and P. P. Wiener, 199–216. New York: Harper & Row, 1966.

Grube, Dirk-Martin. *Unbegründbarkeit Gottes? Tillichs und Barths Erkenntnistheorien im Horizont der gegenwärtigen Philosophie*. Marburg: Elwert Verlag, 1998.

Grumett, David. "Church, World and Christ in Teilhard de Chardin." *Ecclesiology* 1 (2004): 87–103.

Gunton, Colin S. "Creation and Mediation in the Theology of Robert W. Jenson: An Encounter and a Convergence." In *Trinity, Time, and Church: A Response to the Theology of Robert Jenson*, edited by Colin Gunton, 80–93. Grand Rapids, MI: Eerdmans, 2000.

Hallpike, Christopher R. *The Principles of Social Evolution*. Oxford: Clarendon Press, 1986.

Hammer, Felix. *Genugtuung und Heil: Absicht, Sinn und Grenzen der Erlösungslehre Anselms von Canterbury*. Vienna: Herder, 1967.

Hanson, N. R. *Patterns of Discovery: An Inquiry into the Conceptual Foundations of Science*. Cambridge: Cambridge University Press, 1961.

Harman, Gilbert. "The Inference to the Best Explanation." *Philosophical Review* 74 (1965): 88–95.

Harris, David. *From Class Struggle to the Politics of Pleasure: The Effects of Gramscianism on Cultural Studies*. London: Routledge, 1992.

Harris, Marvin. *Cultural Materialism: The Struggle for a Science of Culture*. New York: Random House, 1979.

Hart, David Bentley. *The Beauty of the Infinite: The Aesthetics of Christian Truth*. Grand Rapids, MI: Eerdmans, 2003.

Hartmann, Nicolai. *Zum Problem der Realitätsgegebenheit*. Berlin: Pan-Verlagsgesellschaft, 1931.

—— *Zur Grundlegung der Ontologie*. 3rd edn. Meisenheim am Glan: Anton Hain, 1948.

Hauerwas, Stanley. *Vision and Virtue: Essays in Christian Ethical Reflection*. Notre Dame, IN: Fides Publishers, 1974.

—— *A Community of Character*. Notre Dame, IN: University of Notre Dame Press, 1981.

—— "The Demands of a Truthful Story: Ethics and the Pastoral Task." *Chicago Studies* 21 (1982): 59–71.

—— *The Peaceable Kingdom: A Primer in Christian Ethics*. Notre Dame, IN: University of Notre Dame Press, 1983.

—— *Sanctify Them in the Truth: Holiness Exemplified*. Edinburgh: T&T Clark, 1998.

—— *With the Grain of the Universe: The Church's Witness and Natural Theology*. London: SCM Press, 2002.

Haught, John F. *The Promise of Nature*. New York: Paulist Press, 1993.

—— *God after Darwin: A Theology of Evolution*. Boulder: Westview Press, 2000.

—— "The Boyle Lecture 2003: Darwin, Design, and the Promise of Nature." *Science and Christian Belief* 17 (2005): 5–20.

Healy, Nicholas M. "The Logic of Karl Barth's Ecclesiology: Analysis, Assessment and Proposed Modification." *Modern Theology* 10 (1994): 253–70.

Heisenberg, Werner. "Über den anschaulichen Inhalt der quantentheoretischen Kinematik und Mechanik." *Zeitschrift für Physik* 43 (1927): 172–98.

Herdt, Jennifer A. "Alasdair MacIntyre's 'Rationality of Traditions' and Tradition-Transcendental Standards of Justification." *Journal of Religion* 78 (1998): 524–46.

Hermes, Hans. "Heinrich Scholz. Die Persönlichkeit und seine Werk als Logiker." In *Heinrich Scholz: Drei Vorträge*, 25–45. Münster: Aschendorff, 1958.

Hesse, M. B. *The Structure of Scientific Inference*. New York: Macmillan, 1974.

Heyes, Cecilia M., and Bennett G. Galef. *Social Learning in Animals: The Roots of Culture*. New York: Academic Press, 1996.

Hilberath, Bernd Jochen. "Forschungsbericht: Schwerpunkte und Tendenzen in der Ekklesiologie." *Theologische Quartalschrift* 181 (2001): 238–46.

Hill, Kim, and A. Magdalena Hurtado. *Aché Life History: The Ecology and Demography of a Foraging People*. New York: Aldine de Gruyter, 1996.

Hodgson, Geoffrey M. "Darwinism in Economics: From Analogy to Ontology." *Journal of Evolutionary Economics* 12 (2002): 259–81.

Hoitenga, Dewey J. *Faith and Reason from Plato to Plantinga: An Introduction to Reformed Epistemology*. Albany: State University of New York Press, 1991.

Holderness, Graham. "The Sign of the Cross: Culture and Belief in *The Dream of the Rood*." *Literature and Theology* 11 (1997): 347–71.

Holland, J., K. Holyoak, R. Nisbett, and P. Thagard. *Induction: Process of Inference, Learning and Discovery*. Cambridge, MA: MIT Press, 1986.

Holland, John H. *Emergence: From Chaos to Order*. Oxford: Oxford University Press, 2000.

Hooker, Morna D. "Chalcedon and the New Testament." In *The Making and Remaking of Christian Doctrine*, edited by Sarah Coakley and David A. Pailin, 73–93. Oxford: Clarendon Press, 1993.

Howell, Kenneth J. *God's Two Books: Copernican Cosmology and Biblical Interpretation in Early Modern Science*. Notre Dame, IN: University of Notre Dame Press, 2002.

Hull, David L. "The Naked Meme." In *Learning, Development and Culture: Essays in Evolutionary Epistemology*, edited by H. C. Plotkin, 273–327. New York: Wiley, 1982.

—— "Darwinism as a Historical Entity: A Historiographic Proposal." In *The Darwinian Heritage*, edited by David Kohn, 773–812. Princeton, NJ: Princeton University Press, 1985.

—— "God of the Galapagos." *Nature* 352 (1991): 485–6.

—— "Taking Memetics Seriously: Memetics Will Be What We Make It." In *Darwinizing Culture: The Status of Memetics as a Science*, edited by Robert Aunger, 43–67. Oxford: Oxford University Press, 2000.

Hultgren, Arland J. *The Parables of Jesus: A Commentary*. Grand Rapids, MI: Eerdmans, 2000.

Hüntelmann, R. *Möglich ist nur das Wirkliche: Nicolai Hartmanns Modalontologie des realen Seins*. Dettelbach: Verlag J. H. Röll, 2000.

Hurtado, Larry W. *Lord Jesus Christ: Devotion to Jesus in Earliest Christianity*. Grand Rapids, MI: Eerdmans, 2003.

Huyssteen, J. Wentzel van. *Essays in Postfoundationalist Theology*. Grand Rapids, MI: Eerdmans, 1997.

—— *The Shaping of Rationality: Toward Interdisciplinarity in Theology and Science*. Grand Rapids, MI: Eerdmans, 1999.

Inbody, Tyron. *The Constructive Theology of Bernard Meland: Postliberal Empirical Realism*. New York: Oxford University Press, 1995.

Isenberg, I., and R. D. Dyson. "The Analysis of Fluorescence Decay by a Method of Moments." *Biophysical Journal* 9 (1969): 1337–50.

—— "Analysis of Exponential Curves by a Method of Moments, with Special Attention to Sedimentation Equilibrium and Fluorescence Decay." *Biochemistry* 10 (1971): 3233–41.

Jaitner, Arne. Zwischen Metaphysik und Empirie: zum Verhältnis von Transzendental- philosophie und Psychoanalyse bei Max Scheler, Theodor W. Adorno und Odo Marquard. Würzburg: Konigshausen & Neumann, 1999.

Jaki, Stanley L. *The Origin of Science and the Science of its Origin*. Edinburgh: Scottish Academic Press, 1978.

Jenson, Robert W. *The Triune Identity: God According to the Gospel*. Philadelphia: Fortress, 1982.

—— "The Hauerwas Project." *Modern Theology* 8 (1992): 285–95.

—— *Systematic Theology*. 2 vols. New York: Oxford University Press, 1997–9.

Jepsen, Alfred. "*sdq* und *sdqh* im Alten Testament." In *Gottes Wort und Gottes Land*, edited by H. G. Reventloh, 78–89. Göttingen: Vandenhoeck & Ruprecht, 1965.

Johansson, Ingvar. *Ontological Investigations*. London: Routledge, 1989.

—— "Hartmann's Nonreductive Materialism, Superimposition, and Supervenience." *Axiomathes* 12 (2001): 195–215.

Johnson, George. *Fire in the Mind: Science, Faith and the Search for Order*. New York: Alfred A. Knopf, 1995.

Johnson, Roger A. *The Origins of Demythologizing: Philosophy and Historiography in the Theology of Rudolf Bultmann*. Leiden: Brill, 1974.

Jüngel, Eberhart. "Credere in ecclesiam: Eine ökumenische Besinnung." *Zeitschrift für Theologie und Kirche* 99 (2002): 177–95.

Kaczor, Christopher. "Thomas Aquinas on the Development of Doctrine." *Theological Studies* 62 (2001): 283–302.

Kähler, Martin. *Die Wissenschaft der christlichen Lehre*. Leipzig: Deichert, 1893.

Karpenko, Vladimír. "Alchemy as *Donum Dei*." *International Journal for Philosophy of Chemistry* 4 (1998): 63–80.

Kauffman, Stuart A. *Investigations*. Oxford: Oxford University Press, 2000.

Keating, James F. "The Natural Sciences as an *Ancilla Theologiae Nova*: Alister E. McGrath's *A Scientific Theology*." *The Thomist* 69 (2005): 127–52.

Kelly, Alfred. *The Descent of Darwin: The Popularization of Darwinism in Germany, 1860–1914*. Chapel Hill: North Carolina University Press, 1981.

Kelly, J. N. D. *Early Christian Creeds*. 3rd edn. New York: Longman, 1981.

Ker, Ian T. "Newman's Theory: Development or Continuing Revelation?" In *Newman and Gladstone*, 145–60. Dublin: Veritas Publications, 1978.

Kestenbaum, Victor. *The Grace and Severity of the Ideal: John Dewey and the Transcendent.* Chicago: University of Chicago Press, 2002.

Keynes, Randal. *Annie's Box: Charles Darwin, his Daughter and Human Evolution.* London: Fourth Estate, 2001.

Kilby, Karen. *Karl Rahner: Theology and Philosophy.* London: Routledge, 2004.

Kitchener, Richard F. "Piaget's Social Epistemology." In *Social Interaction and the Development of Knowledge*, edited by J. I. M. Carpendale and U. Miller, 45–66. Mahwah, NJ: Lawrence Erlbaum Associates, 2004.

Klee, Robert. "Micro-Determinism and Concepts of Emergence." *Philosophy of Science* 51 (1984): 44–63.

Kleiner, Scott A. "Problem Solving and Discovery in the Growth of Darwin's Theories of Evolution." *Synthese* 62 (1981): 119–62.

—— "The Logic of Discovery and Darwin's Pre-Malthusian Researches." *Biology and Philosophy* 3 (1988): 293–315.

Kluge, E. H. W. "Frege, Leibniz and the Notion of an Ideal Language." *Studia Leibnitiana* 12 (1980): 140–54.

Köpf, Ulrich, ed. *Historisch-kritische Geschichtsbetrachtung. Ferdinand Christian Baur und seine Schüler.* Sigmaringen: Verlag Thorbecke, 1994.

Kovesi, Julius. *Moral Notions.* London: Routledge & Kegan Paul, 1967.

Kretzmann, Norman. *The Metaphysics of Creation: Aquinas's Natural Theology in Summa contra gentiles II.* Oxford: Clarendon Press, 1999.

Kuper, Adam. *Culture: The Anthropologists' Account.* Cambridge, MA: Harvard University Press, 1999.

—— "If Memes are the Answer, What is the Question?" In *Darwinizing Culture: The Status of Memetics as a Science*, edited by Robert Aunger, 175–88. Oxford: Oxford University Press, 2000.

Laland, Kevin N., and Gillian R. Brown. *Sense and Nonsense: Evolutionary Perspectives on Human Behaviour.* Oxford: Oxford University Press, 2002.

Lash, Nicholas. *Change in Focus: A Study of Doctrinal Change and Continuity.* London: Sheed & Ward, 1973.

Lefrançois, Guy R. *Theories of Human Learning.* 3rd edn. Pacific Grove, CA: Brooks/ Cole Publishers, 1995.

Lenski, Richard E. "Phenotypic and Genomic Evolution During a 20,000-Generation Experiment with the Bacterium Escherichia coli." *Plant Breeding Reviews* 24 (2004): 225–65.

Lenski, Richard E., and Michael Travisano. "Dynamics of Adaptation and Diversification: A 10,000-Generation Experiment with Bacterial Populations." *Proceedings of the National Academy of Sciences, USA* 91 (1994): 6808–14.

Lewis, C. S. *Rehabilitations and Other Essays.* Oxford: Oxford University Press, 1939.

—— "The Weight of Glory." In *Screwtape Proposes a Toast*, 94–110. London: Collins, 1965.

—— *Christian Reflections.* Grand Rapids, MI: Eerdmans, 1967.

—— *Miracles: A Preliminary Study.* New York: Macmillan, 1978.

—— "Is Theology Poetry?" In *C. S. Lewis: Essay Collection*, 1–21. London: Collins, 2000.

Lightman, Bernard V. *The Origins of Agnosticism: Victorian Unbelief and the Limits of Knowledge*. Baltimore: Johns Hopkins University Press, 1987.

Lindberg, David C., and Ronald L. Numbers. *God and Nature: Historical Essays on the Encounter between Christianity and Science*. Berkeley: University of California Press, 1986.

Lipton, Peter. *Inference to the Best Explanation*. London: Routledge, 2004.

Lloyd, G. E. R. *Polarity and Analogy: Two Types of Argumentation in Early Greek Thought*. Cambridge: Cambridge University Press, 1966.

Lloyd, Seth. "Ultimate Physical Limits to Computation." *Nature* 406 (2002): 1047–54.

Lockwood, Michael. *Mind, Brain and the Quantum*. Oxford: Blackwell, 1989.

Luisi, Pier Puigi. "Emergence in Chemistry: Chemistry as the Embodiment of Emergence." *Foundations of Chemistry* 4 (2002): 183–200.

Lumsden, Charles J., and Edward O. Wilson. *Genes, Mind and Culture: The Coevolutionary Process*. Cambridge, MA: Harvard University Press, 1981.

—— *Promethean Fire: Reflections on the Origin of the Mind*. Cambridge, MA: Harvard University Press, 1983.

Lynch, Aaron. *Thought Contagion: How Belief Spreads Through Society*. New York: Basic Books, 1996.

McCormack, Bruce L. *Karl Barth's Critically Realistic Dialectical Theology: Its Genesis and Development, 1909–1936*. Oxford: Clarendon Press, 1997.

McCray, Alexa T. "An Upper-Level Ontology for the Biomedical Domain." *Comparative and Functional Genomics* 4 (2003): 80–4.

McFarland, Ian A. "The Body of Christ: Rethinking a Classic Ecclesiological Model." *International Journal of Systematic Theology* 7 (2005): 225–45.

McGrath, Alister E. "Rectitude: The Moral Foundations of Anselm of Canterbury's Soteriology." *Downside Review* 99 (1981): 204–13.

—— "Divine Justice and Divine Equity in the Controversy between Augustine and Julian of Eclanum." *Downside Review* 101 (1983): 312–19.

—— "Karl Barth als Aufklärer? Der Zusammenhang seiner Lehre vom Werke Christi mit der Erwählungslehre." *Kerygma und Dogma* 81 (1984): 383–94.

—— *Thomas F. Torrance: An Intellectual Biography*. Edinburgh: T&T Clark, 1999.

—— *The Intellectual Origins of the European Reformation*. 2nd edn. Oxford: Blackwell, 2003.

—— *Iustitia Dei: A History of the Christian Doctrine of Justification*. 3rd edn. Cambridge: Cambridge University Press, 2005.

MacIntosh, J. J. "Robert Boyle's Epistemology: The Interaction between Scientific and Religious Knowledge." *International Studies in the Philosophy of Science* 6 (1992): 91–121.

MacIntyre, Alasdair. *After Virtue*. London: Duckworth, 1985.

Macken, John. *The Autonomy Theme in the Church Dogmatics of Karl Barth and His Critics*. Cambridge: Cambridge University Press, 1990.

MacKenzie, Iain M. *God's Order and Natural Law: The Works of the Laudian Divines*. Aldershot: Ashgate, 2002.

McKenzie, Ross H. "Foundations of the Dialogue between the Physical Sciences and Theology." *Perspectives on Science and Christian Faith* 56 (2004): 242–54.

McLaughlin, Brian P. "The Rise and Fall of British Emergentism." In *Emergence or Reduction? Essays on the Prospects of Non-Reductive Physicalism*, edited by A. Beckermann, H. Flohr, and J. Kim, 49–93. Berlin: de Gruyter, 1992.

Mahlmann, T. "Was ist Religion in der Religionsphilosophie von Heinrich Scholz?" In *Religion im Denken unserer Zeit*, edited by W. Härle and E. Wölfel, 1–33. Marburg: N. G. Elwert, 1986.

Makin, Gideon. *The Metaphysics of Meaning: Russell and Frege on Sense and Denotation.* London: Routledge, 2000.

Markschies, Christoph. *Gibt es eine "Theologie der gotischen Kathedrale"? nochmals: Suger von Saint-Denis und Sankt Dionys vom Areopag.* Heidelberg: Universitätsverlag C. Winter, 1995.

Maschner, Herbert D. G. *Darwinian Archaeologies.* New York: Plenum, 1996.

Maurer, Wilhem. "Das Prinzip der Organischen in der evangelischen Kirchengeschichtsschreibung des 19. Jahrhunderts." *Kerygma und Dogma* 8 (1962): 256–92.

Mayr, Ernst. *Toward a New Philosophy of Biology: Observations of an Evolutionist.* Cambridge, MA: Belknap, 1988.

—— *What Evolution Is.* New York: Basic Books, 2001.

Mesoudi, Alex, Andrew Whiten, and Kevin N. Laland. "Is Cultural Evolution Darwinian? Evidence Reviewed from the Perspective of *The Origin of Species*." *Evolution* 58 (2004): 1–11.

Meynell, Hugo. "Newman on Revelation and Doctrinal Development."

Midgley, Mary. *Science as Salvation: A Modern Myth and its Meaning.* London: Routledge, 1992.

—— *Science and Poetry.* London: Routledge, 2001.

—— *Evolution as a Religion: Strange Hopes and Stranger Fears.* 2nd edn. London: Routledge, 2002.

Milbank, John. " 'Postmodern Critical Augustinianism': A Short *Summa* in Forty-Two Responses to Unasked Questions." *Modern Theology* 7 (1991): 225–37.

Mithen, Steven J. *The Prehistory of the Mind: The Cognitive Origins of Art, Religion, and Science.* New York: Thames & Hudson, 1999.

Moberly, R. W. L. "To Hear the Master's Voice: Revelation and Spiritual Discernment in the Call of Samuel." *Scottish Journal of Theology* 48 (1995): 443–68.

Moffat, James. "Tertullian and Aristotle." *Journal of Theological Studies* 17 (1916): 170–1.

Molendijk, Arie L. *Aus dem Dunklen ins Helle: Wissenschaft und Theologie im Denken von Heinrich Scholz: mit unveröffentlichten Thesenreihen von Heinrich Scholz und Karl Barth.* Amsterdam: Rodopi, 1991.

—— "Ein heidnische Wissenschaftsbegriff. Der Streit zwischen Heinrich Scholz und Karl Barth um die Wissenschaftlichkeit der Theologie." *Evangelische Theologie* 52 (1992): 527–45.

Molnar, Paul D. "Some Dogmatic Implications of Barth's Understanding of Ebionite and Docetic Christology." *International Journal of Systematic Theology* 2 (2000): 151–74.

Moltmann, Jürgen. *Gott in der Schöpfung: ökologische Schöpfungslehre.* Munich: Kaiser Verlag, 1985.

—— *Der Geist des Lebens: eine ganzheitliche Pneumatologie.* Munich: Kaiser Verlag, 1991.

Montuori, Mario. *John Locke on Toleration and the Unity of God.* Amsterdam: J. C. Gieben, 1983.

Moore, James R. *The Post-Darwinian Controversies: A Study of the Protestant Struggle to Come to Terms with Darwin in Great Britain and America, 1870–1900.* Cambridge: Cambridge University Press, 1979.

—— "Theodicy and Society: The Crisis of the Intelligentsia." In *Victorian Faith in Crisis: Essays in Continuity and Change in Nineteenth-Century Religious Belief,* edited by Richard J. Helmstadter and Bernard Lightman, 153–86. Basingstoke: Macmillan, 1990.

Morowitz, Harold J. *The Emergence of Everything: How the World Became Complex.* Oxford: Oxford University Press, 2002.

Morris, Simon Conway. *The Crucible of Creation: The Burgess Shale and the Rise of Animals.* Oxford: Oxford University Press, 1998.

—— *Life's Solution: Inevitable Humans in a Lonely Universe.* Cambridge: Cambridge University Press, 2003.

Müller, Carl Werner. *Gleiches zu Gleichem: ein Prinzip frühgriechischen Denkens.* Wiesbaden: Harrassowitz, 1965.

Murdoch, Iris. "Vision and Choice in Morality." In *Christian Ethics and Contemporary Philosophy,* edited by Ian T. Ramsey, 195–218. London: SCM Press, 1966.

—— *The Sovereignty of Good.* London: Macmillan, 1970.

—— *Metaphysics as a Guide to Morals.* London: Penguin, 1992.

Murphy, Howard R. "The Ethical Revolt against Christian Orthodoxy in Early Victorian England." *American Historical Review* 60 (1955): 800–17.

Murphy, Nancey C. *Beyond Liberalism and Fundamentalism: How Modern and Postmodern Philosophy Set the Theological Agenda.* Valley Forge, PA: Trinity Press International, 1996.

Myers, Benjamin. "Alister McGrath's *Scientific Theology.*" *Reformed Theological Review* 64 (2005): 15–34.

Nagel, Thomas. *The View from Nowhere.* New York: Oxford University Press, 1986.

Nagy, Gregory. *The Best of the Achaeans: Concepts of the Hero in Archaic Greek Poetry.* Revd. edn. Baltimore: Johns Hopkins University Press, 1999.

Neugebauer, Otto. *Astronomy and History: Selected Essays.* New York: Springer-Verlag, 1983.

Nevo, Eviatar. *Mosaic Evolution of Subterranean Mammals: Regression, Progression, and Global Convergence.* Oxford: Oxford University Press, 1999.

Newman, Murray. "The Prophetic Call of Samuel." In *Israel's Prophetic Heritage: Essays in Honor of James Muilenburg,* edited by B. W. Anderson and W. J. Harrelson, 86–97. London: SCM Press, 1962.

Nichols, Aidan. *From Newman to Congar: The Idea of Doctrinal Development from the Victorians to the Second Vatican Council.* Edinburgh: T&T Clark, 1990.

Niebuhr, Richard R. "Schleiermacher on Language and Feeling." *Theology Today* 17 (1960): 150–67.

Odom, H. H. "The Estrangement of Celestial Mechanics and Religion." *Journal of the History of Ideas* 27 (1966): 533–58.

Oppenheim, Peter, and Hilary Putnam. "The Unity of Science as a Working Hypothesis." In *Minnesota Studies in the Philosophy of Science*, edited by Herbert Feigl. Minneapolis: University of Minnesota Press, 1958.

Oppenheimer, J. Robert. *Science and the Common Understanding*. Oxford: Oxford University Press, 1954.

Orr, James. *The Progress of Dogma*. London: Hodder & Stoughton, 1901.

Pannenberg, Wolfhart. "The Appropriation of the Philosophical Concept of God as a Dogmatic Problem of Early Christian Theology." In *Basic Questions in Theology*, 119–83. London: SCM Press, 1971.

—— *Wissenschaftstheorie und Theologie*. Frankfurt am Main: Suhrkamp Verlag, 1977.

—— "God and Nature." In *Toward a Theology of Nature: Essays on Science and Faith*, 50–71. Louisville, KY: Westminster/John Knox Press, 1993.

Parker, Kim Ian. "John Locke and the Enlightenment Metanarrative: A Biblical Corrective to a Reasoned World." *Scottish Journal of Theology* 49 (1996): 57–73.

Peacocke, Arthur. "Complexity, Emergence, and Divine Creativity." In *From Complexity to Life: On the Emergence of Life and Meaning*, edited by Niels Henrik Gregersen, 187–205. Oxford: Oxford University Press, 2003.

Peckhaus, Volker. "Hilbert, Zermelo und die Institutionalisierung der mathematischen Logik in Deutschland." *Berichte zur Wissenschaftsgeschichte* 15 (1992): 27–38.

—— *Logik, Mathesis universalis und allgemeine Wissenschaft: Leibniz und die Wiederentdeckung der formalen Logik im 19. Jahrhundert*. Berlin: Akademie Verlag, 1997.

Penrose, Roger. *The Road to Reality: A Complete Guide to the Laws of the Universe*. London: Jonathan Cape, 2004.

Pfleiderer, Georg. *Theologie als Wirklichkeitswissenschaft: Studien zum Religionsbegriff bei Georg Wobbermin, Rudolf Otto, Heinrich Scholz und Max Scheler, Beiträge zur historischen Theologie; 82*. Tübingen: J. C. B. Mohr (Paul Siebeck), 1992.

Piaget, Jean. *Le Langage et la pensée chez l'enfant*. Neuchâtel: Delachaux and Niestle, 1923.

—— *La Naissance de l'intelligence chez l'enfant*. Neuchâtel: Delachaux & Niestle, 1936.

Piaget, Jean. *La Construction du réel chez l'enfant*. Neuchâtel: Delachaux & Niestle, 1937.

—— "Problems of Equilibration." In *Topics in Cognitive Development 1*, edited by M. H. Appel and L. S. Goldberg, 3–14. New York: Plenum, 1977.

Piattelli-Palmarini, Massimo. "Ever Since Language and Learning: Afterthoughts on the Piaget–Chomsky Debate." *Cognition* 50 (1994): 315–46.

Placher, William C. *Narratives of a Vulnerable God: Christ, Theology, and Scripture*. Louisville, KY: Westminster/John Knox Press, 1994.

Plantinga, Alvin. "Reason and Belief in God." In *Faith and Rationality*, edited by Alvin Plantinga and Nicholas Wolterstorff, 16–93. Notre Dame, IN: University of Notre Dame Press, 1983.

Pocklington, Richard, and Michael L. Best. "Cultural Evolution and Units of Selection in Replicating Text." *Journal of Theoretical Biology* 188 (1997): 79–87.

Polkinghorne, John. *The Way the World Is*. London: SPCK, 1983.

—— *Science and Creation: The Search for Understanding*. London: SPCK, 1988.

Porter, Jean. "Tradition in the Recent Work of Alasdair MacIntyre." In *Alasdair MacIntyre*, edited by Mark C. Murphy, 38–69. Cambridge: Cambridge University Press, 2003.

Poulshock, Joseph. "Universal Darwinism and the Potential of Memetics." *Quarterly Review of Biology* 77 (2002): 174–5.

Prenter, Regin. "Das Problem der natürlichen Theologie bei Karl Barth." *Theologische Literaturzeitung* 77 (1952): 607–11.

Prinz, Friedrich. "Die Kirche und die pagane Kulturtradition. Formen der Abwehr, Adaption und Anverwandlung." *Historische Zeitschrift* 276 (2002): 281–303.

Putnam, Hilary. *Mind, Language, and Reality*. Cambridge: Cambridge University Press, 1975.

Rahner, Karl. "Chalkedon – Ende oder Anfang?" In *Das Konzil von Chalkedon: Geschichte und Gegenwart*, edited by Alois Grillmeier and Heinrich Bacht, 3–49. Würzburg: Echter-Verlag, 1951–4.

Rasmusson, Arne. *The Church as Polis: From Political Theology to Theological Politics as Exemplified by Jürgen Moltmann and Stanley Hauerwas*. Lund: Lund University Press, 1994.

Reames, Kent. "Metaphysics, History, and Moral Philosophy: The Centrality of the 1990 Aquinas Lecture to MacIntyre's Argument for Thomism." *The Thomist* 62 (1998): 419–43.

Rendtorff, Rolf. " 'Covenant' as a Structuring Concept in Genesis and Exodus." *Journal of Biblical Literature* 108 (1989): 385–93.

Reventloh, Henning Graf. *The Authority of the Bible and the Rise of the Modern World*. London: SCM Press, 1984.

Rief, Josef. *Der Ordobegriff des jungen Augustinus*. Paderborn: Schoningh, 1962.

Rikhof, Herwi. *The Concept of Church: A Methodological Inquiry into the Use of Metaphors in Ecclesiology*. London: Sheed & Ward, 1981.

Roberts, Jon H. *Darwinism and the Divine in America: Protestant Intellectuals and Organic Evolution, 1859–1900*. Madison: University of Wisconsin Press, 1988.

Rogers, A. R. "Does Biology Constrain Culture?" *American Anthropologist* 90 (1989): 819–31.

Rosch, Eleanor, and Barbara B. Lloyd. *Cognition and Categorization*. New York: Laurence Erlbaum Associates, 1978.

Rousselot, Pierre. "Petit théorie du développement du dogme." *Recherches de science religieuse* 53 (1965): 355–90.

Rowell, Geoffrey. *Hell and the Victorians: A Study of the Nineteenth-Century Theological Controversies concerning Eternal Punishment and the Future Life*. Oxford: Clarendon Press, 1974.

Rubin, Ronald. "Descartes' Validation of Clear and Distinct Apprehension." *Philosophical Review* 86 (1977): 197–208.

Runciman, W. G. "Greek Hoplites, Warrior Culture, and Indirect Bias." *Journal of the Royal Anthropological Society* 4 (1998): 731–51.

Runciman, W. G. "The Diffusion of Christianity in the Third Century AD as a Case-Study in the Theory of Cultural Selection." *European Journal of Sociology* 45 (2004): 3–21.

Ruse, Michael. "Darwin's Debt to Philosophy: An Examination of the Influence of the Philosophical Ideas of John F. Herschel and William Whewell on the Development of Charles Darwin's Theory of Evolution." *Studies in the History and Philosophy of Science* 66 (1975): 159–81.

—— *Darwin and Design: Does Evolution Have a Purpose?* Cambridge, MA: Harvard University Press, 2003.

Russett, Cynthia Eagle. *Darwin in America: The Intellectual Response, 1865–1912.* San Francisco: W. H. Freeman, 1976.

Salmon, Wesley C. "Religion and Science: A New Look at Hume's *Dialogues*." *Philosophical Studies* 33 (1978): 143–76.

Samuel, Otto. "Der ontologische Gottesbeweis bei Karl Barth, Immanuel Kant und Anselm von Canterbury." *Theologische Blätter* 14 (1935): 141–53.

Sanderson, Stephen K. *Social Evolutionism: A Critical History.* Oxford: Blackwell, 1992.

Sauer-Thompson, Gary, and Joseph Wayne Smith. *The Unreasonable Silence of the World: Universal Reason and the Wreck of the Enlightenment Project.* Aldershot: Ashgate, 1997.

Sauter, Gerhard. "Die Begründung theologischer Aussagen – wissenschaftstheoretisch gesehen." *Zeitschrift für evangelische Ethik* 15 (1971): 299–308.

—— "Der Wissenschaftsbegriff der Theologie." *Evangelische Theologie* 35 (1975): 283–309.

Scheler, Max. *Der Formalismus in der Ethik und die materiale Wertethik: neuer Versuch der Grundlegung eines ethischen Personalismus.* 4th edn. Bern: Francke, 1954.

Schilling, Kurt. "Zur Frage der sogenannten 'Grundlagenforschung.' Bemerkungen zu der Abhandlung von Heinrich Scholz: Was ist Philosophie?" *Zeitschrift für die gesamte Naturwissenschaft* 7 (1941): 44–8.

Schmid, Rudi. "History of Viral Hepatitis: A Tale of Dogmas and Misinterpretations." *Journal of Gastroenterology and Hepatology.*

Schoeps, Hans Joachim. *Theologie und Geschichte des Judenchristentums.* Tübingen: J. C. B. Mohr, 1949.

—— "Ebionite Christianity." *Journal of Theological Studies* 4 (1953): 219–24.

Scholz, Heinrich. *Das Wesen des deutschen Geistes.* Berlin: Grote'sche Verlagsbuchhandlung, 1917.

—— *Religionsphilosophie.* Berlin: Reuther & Reichard, 1921.

—— "Wie ist eine evangelische Theologie als Wissenschaft möglich?" *Zwischen den Zeiten* 9 (1931): 8–51.

—— "Warum ich mich zu Karl Barth bekenne. Ein Beitrag zu einer Studie über Treue gegen Linientreue." In *Antwort: Karl Barth zum siebigsten Geburtstag,* edited by Ernst Wolf, 865–9. Zollikon: Evangelischer Verlag, 1956.

—— "Was ist Philosophie? Der erste und der letzte Schritt aud dem Wege zu ihrer Selbstbestimmung." In *Mathesis Universalis: Abhandlungen zur Philosophie als strenger Wissenschaft,* edited by Hans Hermes, 341–87. Darmstadt: Wissenschaftliche Buchgesellschaft, 1961.

Schreiner, Susan Elizabeth. *The Theater of His Glory: Nature and the Natural Order in the Thought of John Calvin.* Durham, NC: Labyrinth Press, 1991.

Searle, John R. *The Rediscovery of the Mind.* Cambridge: MIT Press, 1992.

—— "Rationality and Realism: What is at Stake?" *Daedalus* 122 (1993): 55–83.

—— *The Construction of Social Reality.* New York: Free Press, 1995.

Seitz, Christopher R. "Handing over the Name: Christian Reflection on the Divine Name YHWH." In *Trinity, Time, and Church: A Response to the Theology of Robert Jenson,* edited by Colin Gunton, 23–41. Grand Rapids, MI: Eerdmans, 2000.

Sell, Alan P. F. *John Locke and the Eighteenth-Century Divines.* Cardiff: University of Wales Press, 1997.

Sereno, M. I. "Four Analogies between Biological and Cultural/Linguistic Evolution." *Journal of Theoretical Biology* 151 (1991): 467–507.

Service, Elman R. *Primitive Social Organization: An Evolutionary Perspective.* 2nd edn. New York: Random House, 1971.

—— *Origins of the State and Civilization: The Process of Cultural Evolution.* New York: W. W. Norton, 1975.

Shanahan, Timothy. "Methodological and Contextual Factors in the Dawkins/Gould Dispute over Evolutionary Progress." *Studies in History and Philosophy of Science* 31 (2001): 127–51.

Shennan, Stephen. *Genes, Memes and Human History: Darwinian Archaeology and Cultural Evolution.* London: Thames & Hudson, 2002.

Shipway, Brad. "The Theological Application of Bhaskar's Stratified Reality: The Scientific Theology of A. E. McGrath." *Journal of Critical Realism* 3 (2004): 191–203.

Shore, Bradd. *Culture in Mind: Cognition, Culture, and the Problem of Meaning.* Oxford: Oxford University Press, 1998.

Sider, Robert D. *Ancient Rhetoric and the Art of Tertullian.* Oxford: Oxford University Press, 1971.

—— "Credo quia absurdum?" *Classical World* 73 (1978): 417–19.

Simon, Josef. "Zum wissenschafts-philosophischen Ort der Theologie." *Zeitschrift für Theologie und Kirche* 77 (1980): 435–52.

Smith, Eric A., and Bruce Winterhalder. *Evolutionary Ecology and Human Behavior.* New York: Aldine de Gruyter, 1992.

Smith, Temple, and Harold Morowitz. "Between Physics and History." *Journal of Molecular Evolution* 18 (1982): 265–82.

Söhngen, Gottlieb. "Rectitudo bei Anselm von Canterbury als Oberbegriff von Wahrheit und Gerechtigkeit." In *Sola Ratione,* edited by H. Kohlenberger, 71–7. Stuttgart: Friedrich Frommann Verlag, 1970.

Solmsen, F. "Nature as Craftsman in Greek Thought." *Journal of the History of Ideas* 24 (1963): 473–96.

Sperber, Dan. "Anthropology and Psychology: Towards an Epidemiology of Representations." *Man* 20 (1985): 73–89.

—— *Explaining Culture: A Naturalistic Approach.* Oxford: Blackwell, 1996.

—— "An Objection to the Memetic Approach to Culture." In *Darwinizing Culture: The Status of Memetics as a Science,* edited by Robert Aunger, 163–73. Oxford: Oxford University Press, 2000.

Spini, Debora. *Diritti di Dio, diritti dei popoli: Pierre Jurieu e il problema della sovranità, 1681–1691, Studi storici.* Turin: Claudiana, 1997.

Steinberg, Diane. "Method and the Structure of Knowledge in Spinoza." *Pacific Philosophical Quarterly* 79 (1998): 152–69.

Stevenson, Lionel. "The Key Poem of the Victorian Age." In *Essays in American and English Literature Presented to Bruce Robert Mcelderry Jr.,* edited by Max F. Schulz, 260–89. Athens: Ohio University Press, 1967.

Steward, Julian H. *Theory of Culture Change: The Methodology of Multilinear Evolution.* Urbana: University of Illinois Press, 1963.

Stock, Eberhard. *Die Konzeption einer Metaphysik im Denken von Heinrich Scholz, Theologische Bibliothek Töpelmann; Bd. 44.* Berlin: Walter de Gruyter, 1987.

Strinati, Dominic. *An Introduction to Theories of Popular Culture.* London: Routledge, 1995.

Struman, Renate. "De la perpétuité de la foi dans la controverse Bossuet-Julien (1686–1691)." *Revue d'histoire ecclésiastique* 37 (1941): 145–89.

Stuhlmacher, Peter. *Gerechtigkeit Gottes bei Paulus.* Göttingen: Vandenhoeck & Ruprecht, 1965.

Swinburne, Richard. *The Resurrection of God Incarnate.* Oxford: Clarendon Press, 2003.

Symons, Donald. "On the Use and Misuse of Darwinism in the Study of Human Behavior." In *The Adapted Mind,* edited by J. H. Barkow, L. Cosmides, and J. Tooby, 137–59. Oxford: Oxford University Press, 1992.

Tanner, Kathryn. "Theological Reflection and Christian Practices." In *Practicing Theology: Beliefs and Practices in Christian Life,* edited by Miroslav Volf and Dorothy C. Bass, 228–42. Grand Rapids, MI: Eerdmans, 2002.

Taylor, Charles. *Sources of the Self: The Making of the Modern Identity.* Cambridge, MA: Harvard University Press, 1989.

Thiel, John E. *Senses of Tradition: Continuity and Development in Catholic Faith.* Oxford: Oxford University Press, 2000.

Thompson, Daniel P. "Schillebeeckx and the Development of Doctrine." *Theological Studies* 62 (2001): 303–21.

Thompson, Evan. *Colour Vision: A Study in Cognitive Science and the Philosophy of Perception.* London: Routledge, 1995.

Thonnard, F. J. "Justice de Dieu et justice humaine selon Saint Augustin." *Augustinus* 12 (1967): 387–402.

Todes, Daniel P. *Darwin without Malthus: The Struggle for Existence in Russian Evolutionary Thought.* Oxford: Oxford University Press, 1989.

Tolkien, J. R. R. "Beowulf: The Monster and the Critics." In *The Monster and the Critics and Other Essays,* 5–48. London: Harper Collins, 1997.

Tomasello, Michael. "Do Apes Ape?" In *Social Learning in Animals: The Roots of Culture,* edited by C. Heyes and B. Galef, 319–46. New York: Academic Press, 1996.

Tonkin, John M. *The Church and the Secular Order in Reformation Thought.* New York: Columbia University Press, 1971.

Tooby, John, and Leda Cosmides. "The Psychological Foundations of Culture." In *The Adapted Mind*, edited by J. H. Barkow, L. Cosmides, and J. Tooby, 19–136. Oxford: Oxford University Press, 1992.

Torrance, Thomas F. "The Problem of Natural Theology in the Thought of Karl Barth." *Religious Studies* 6 (1970): 121–35.

—— *The Ground and Grammar of Theology*. Charlottesville: University of Virginia Press, 1980.

—— *The Incarnation: Ecumenical Studies in the Nicene-Constantinopolitan Creed* AD *381*. Edinburgh: Handsel Press, 1981.

—— *Preaching Christ Today: The Gospel and Scientific Thinking*. Grand Rapids, MI: Eerdmans, 1994.

Trapè, Agostino. *Sant'Agostino: introduzione alla dottrina della grazia*. 2 vols. Rome: Citta Nuova, 1990.

Travisano, Michael, J. A. Mongold, A. F. Bennett, and Richard E. Lenski. "Experimental Tests of the Roles of Adaptation, Chance, and History in Evolution." *Science* 267 (1995): 87–90.

Turner, Frank M. *Contesting Cultural Authority: Essays in Victorian Intellectual Life*. Cambridge: Cambridge University Press, 1993.

Tweyman, Stanley. "Truth, No Doubt: Descartes' Proof that the Clear and Distinct Must Be True." *Southern Journal of Philosophy* 19 (1981): 237–58.

Van Valen, Leigh M. "How Far Does Contingency Rule?" *Evolutionary Theory* 10 (1991): 47–52.

Vanhoozer, Kevin J. *The Drama of Doctrine: A Canonical-Linguistic Approach to Christian Theology*. Louisville, KY: Westminster John Knox Press, 2005.

Vernon, Richard. *The Career of Toleration: John Locke, Jonas Proast, and After*. Montreal/London: McGill-Queen's University Press, 1997.

Volf, Miroslav. *After our Likeness: The Church as the Image of the Trinity*. Grand Rapids, MI: Eerdmans, 1998.

—— "Theology for a Way of Life." In *Practicing Theology: Beliefs and Practices in Christian Life*, edited by Miroslav Volf and Dorothy C. Bass, 245–63. Grand Rapids, MI: Eerdmans, 2002.

von Balthasar, Hans Urs. *Herrlichkeit: Eine theologische Ästhetik*. 3rd edn. Einsiedeln: Johannes Verlag, 1988.

von Guten, A. F. "In principio erat verbum: une évolution de Saint Thomas en théologie trinitaire." In *Ordo sapientiae et amoris: image et message de Saint Thomas d'Aquin*, edited by Carolos-Josaphat Pinto de Oliveira, 119–41. Fribourg: Editions Universitaires, 1993.

Wagner, Hans. "Die Schichtentheoreme bei Platon, Aristoteles und Plotin." *Studium Generale* 9 (1957): 283–91.

Wainwright, Geoffrey. *Doxology: The Praise of God in Worship, Doctrine and Life*. New York: Oxford University Press, 1980.

Webster, John B. "The Self-Organizing Power of the Gospel of Christ: Episcopacy and Community Formation." In *Community Formation in the Early Church and the Church Today*, edited by R. Longenecker, 173–93. Peabody, MA: Hendriksen, 2002.

—— "On Evangelical Ecclesiology." *Ecclesiology* 1 (2004): 9–35.

Weikart, Richard. *Socialist Darwinism: Evolution in German Socialist Thought from Marx to Bernstein.* San Francisco: International Scholars Publications, 1999.

Weiss, Roberto. *The Renaissance Discovery of Classical Antiquity.* Oxford: Blackwell, 1988.

Weiss, Roslyn. *Virtue in the Cave: Moral Inquiry in Plato's Meno.* New York: Oxford University Press, 2001.

Wells, R. S. "The Life and Growth of Language: Metaphors in Biology and Linguistics." In *Biological Metaphor and Cladistic Classification*, edited by H. H. Hoenigswald and L. F. Wiener, 39–80. Philadelphia: University of Pennsylvania Press, 1987.

Wendt, Hans Heinrich. *System der christlichen Lehre.* Göttingen: Vandenhoeck & Ruprecht, 1907.

Werkmeister, W. H. *Nicolai Hartmann's New Ontology.* Tallahassee: Florida State University Press, 1990.

Westerholm, Stephen. *Perspectives Old and New on Paul: The "Lutheran" Paul and His Critics.* Grand Rapids, MI: Eerdmans, 2004.

Westfall, Richard S. "The Scientific Revolution of the Seventeenth Century: A New World View." In *The Concept of Nature*, edited by John Torrance, 63–93. Oxford: Oxford University Press, 1992.

Wheeler, Michael. *Ruskin's God.* Cambridge: Cambridge University Press, 1999.

White, Leslie A. *The Science of Culture: A Study of Man and Civilization.* New York: Farrar, Straus, 1949.

―― *The Evolution of Culture: The Development of Civilization to the Fall of Rome.* New York: McGraw-Hill, 1959.

Wieacker, Franz. *Römische Rechtsgeschichte: Quellenkunde, Rechtsbildung, Jurisprudenz und Rechtsliteratur.* Munich: C. H. Beck, 1988.

Williams, George C. "Mother Nature Is a Wicked Old Witch!" In *Evolutionary Ethics*, edited by Matthew H. Nitecki and Doris V. Nitecki, 217–31. Albany: State University of New York Press, 1995.

Williams, George C., and Randolph Nesse. "The Dawn of Darwinian Medicine." *Quarterly Review of Biology* 66 (1991): 1–22.

Williams, Rowan. *Arius: Heresy and Tradition.* London: Darton, Longman, & Todd, 1987.

―― "Does it Make Sense to Speak of Pre-Nicene Orthodoxy?" In *The Making of Orthodoxy*, edited by Rowan Williams, 1–23. Cambridge: Cambridge University Press, 1989.

―― "Newman's *Arians* and the Question of Method in Doctrinal History." In *Newman after a Hundred Years*, edited by Ian Ker and Alan Hill, 265–85. Oxford: Oxford University Press, 1990.

―― "Teaching the Truth." In *Living Tradition: Affirming Catholicism in the Anglican Church*, edited by Jeffrey John, 29–43. London: Darton, Longman, & Todd, 1991.

―― "Doctrinal Criticism: Some Questions." In *The Making and Remaking of Christian Doctrine*, edited by Sarah Coakley and David A. Pailin, 239–64. Oxford: Clarendon Press, 1993.

―― *Why Study the Past? The Quest for the Historical Church.* London: Darton, Longman, & Todd, 2005.

Williams, Stephen N. "John Locke on the Status of Faith." *Scottish Journal of Theology* 40 (1987): 591–606.

Williams, Walter G. "Jeremiah's Vision of the Almond Rod." In *A Stubborn Faith: Papers on Old Testament and Related Subjects Presented to William Andrew Irwin*, edited by Edward C. Hobbs, 90–9. Dallas: Southern Methodist University Press, 1956.

Wilson, Edward O. *Sociobiology: The New Synthesis*. Cambridge, MA: Harvard University Press, 1975.

Witt, Ronald G. *In the Footsteps of the Ancients: The Origins of Humanism from Lovato to Bruni*. Leiden: Brill, 2000.

Wojcik, Jan W. *Robert Boyle and the Limits of Reason*. Cambridge: Cambridge University Press, 1997.

Wolff, Robert Lee. *Gains and Losses: Novels of Faith and Doubt in Victorian England*. London: John Murray, 1977.

Wolterstorff, Nicholas. *John Locke and the Ethics of Belief*. Cambridge: Cambridge University Press, 1996.

Woolf, Rosemary. "Doctrinal Influences on *The Dream of the Rood*." *Medium Aevum* 27 (1958): 137–53.

Worrall, John. "Fresnel, Poisson and the White Spot: The Role of Successful Predictions in the Acceptance of Scientific Theories." In *The Uses of Experiment: Studies in the Natural Sciences*, edited by David Gooding, Trevor Pinch, and Simon Schaffer, 135–57. Cambridge: Cambridge University Press, 1989.

Worthing, Mark W. *Foundations and Functions of Theology as Universal Science: Theological Method and Apologetic Praxis in Wolfhart Pannenberg and Karl Rahner*. Frankfurt am Main: Peter Lang, 1996.

Wright, David F. "Accommodation and Barbarity in John Calvin's Old Testament Commentaries." In *Understanding Poets and Prophets*, edited by A. Graeme Auld, 413–27. Sheffield: JSOT Press, 1993.

Wucherer-Huldenfeld, Augustinus Karl. "Sein und Wesen des Schönes." In *Theologie und Ästhetik*, edited by G. Pöltner and H. Vetter, 20–34. Vienna: Herder, 1985.

Yeago, David S. "The Church as Polity? The Lutheran Context of Robert W. Jenson's Ecclesiology." In *Trinity, Time, and Church: A Response to the Theology of Robert Jenson*, edited by Colin Gunton, 201–37. Grand Rapids, MI: Eerdmans, 2000.

Yeo, Richard R. "William Whewell's Philosophy of Knowledge and its Reception." In *William Whewell: A Composite Portrait*, edited by Menachem Fisch and Simon Schaffer, 175–99. Oxford: Clarendon Press, 1991.

Young, Robert. "Malthus and the Evolutionists: The Common Context of Biological and Social Theory." *Past and Present* 43 (1969): 109–45.

Ypma, Tjalling J. "Historical Development of the Newton-Raphson Method." *SIAM Review* 37 (1995): 531–51.

Ziman, John. *Reliable Knowledge: An Exploration of the Grounds for Belief in Science*. Cambridge: Cambridge University Press, 1978.

Index

accommodation
  as psychological notion 171–2,
    180–2, 197
  as theological notion 169
Addison, Joseph xxiii, 54
aesthetics and the natural order 49–53
Alston, William 67
analogical argumentation, limits of 44–5,
  147–9
Ancilla theologiae xviii, 4
Anderson, Philip W. 104–5
Anselm of Canterbury 189–92
Aquinas, Thomas 16, 40, 68
Arianism 198
Arnold, Matthew 56, 143
assimilation and development of
  doctrine 169–82, 197–8
  and accommodation 180–2
  and Ebionitism 173–6, 198
  and Pelagianism 176–8
Augustine of Hippo 163, 177–8, 188–9

Barth, Karl 1, 16, 65, 71–2, 113–15,
  169, 194, 202
Baur, Ferdinand Christian 122
Bedau, Mark 102
Bentley, Richard 67
Bhaskar, Roy xxv, 2, 12
Blackmore, Susan 149, 151
Blake, William 51
Bloch, Maurice 143
Bonaventure 60

Bonhoeffer, Dietrich 206
Bossuet, Jacques-Bénigne 122
Boyle Lectures 73–5, 83
Boyle, Robert 73–4
Broad, C. D. 103
Browne, Sir Thomas 72
Buckley, Michael 81
Bunge, Mario 148
Butler, Joseph 125

Calvin, John 51, 169, 205
Campbell, Donald T. 130, 144–5
Carnap, Rudolf 99
Cavalli-Sforza, Luigi 131–2
Chaitin, Gregory J. 102
Chomsky, Noam 172–3
church
  distinction between actuality and
    theory of 195–6, 200–1,
    205–6
  as starting point for a scientific
    dogmatics 204–29
  stratification of concept 219–23
  as visible or observable entity
    206–7, 223–5
Cicero, Marcus Tullius 137, 176–7
Clark, Samuel 74
Cloak, F. T. 130, 145
closure, and an iterative theological
  method 182, 194–203
contingency, as factor in evolution
  155–68